Maps and History

Maps and History

Constructing Images of the Past

Jeremy Black

Yale University Press
New Haven and London

Set in Bembo by Best-set Typesetter Ltd, Hong Kong
Printed in the United States

Library of Congress Cataloging-in-Publication Data

Black, Jeremy.
   Maps and history/Jeremy Black.
   Includes bibliographical references and index.
   ISBN 0-300-06976-6
   1. Historiography.   2. History—Methodology.   3. Historical
geography—Maps. I. Title.
D13.854   1997
907.2—dc20   96-41293
                                       CIP

A catalogue record for this book is available from the British Library.

10 9 8 7 6 5 4 3 2 1

For Pippa
Because she asked for a second book

Contents

Acknowledgments

I am very grateful to a large number of individuals and institutions for their help with this project. First and foremost are the libraries that collect, store and make available historical atlases, and their staff whom without exception I have found helpful and a pleasure to deal with. I have worked most in the Map Library of the British Library, but would also like to record my gratitude to the librarians of the Royal Geographical Society, the National Library of Scotland and the libraries of the Universities of British Columbia, Cambridge, Colorado (Boulder), Durham, Newcastle, Oxford, Texas, Western Ontario and York (Ontario), to Ball State, Denver and Texas Christian Universities and to South Australia House in London.

The research was assisted by a J.B. Harley Research Fellowship in the History of Cartography, a Christopherson Fellowship and a Mid-Career award both from the University of Durham, and a grant from the Nuffield Foundation. The crucial assistance of each of these awards is gratefully acknowledged. In order to understand the problems of historical mapmaking I sought to discuss them with as many practitioners as possible: with scholars, editors, cartographers and publishers. I am grateful to a large number who took the time to talk to me, including M. Barke, Michael Blakemore, R.J. Buswell, Thomas Cussans, Martin Gilbert, Mark Greenslade, Simon Hall, Terry Hardaker, John Haywood, R.H. Hewsen, Eric Homberger, Andrew Lawson, Colin McEvedy, Malcolm McKinnon, Paul Magocsi, Bob Moore, Don Parkes, Anne Piternick, Andrew Porter, Francis Robinson, Richard Ruggles, Herbert Sandford, Geoffrey Scammel, Joseph Schwartzberg, Graham Speake, Richard Talbert, Barry Winkleman and Liz Wyse. Many others generously took the time to reply to my letters.

Earlier drafts of sections of the book were read by John Andrews, Sarah Bendall, Frank Carter, Brian Catchpole, Catherine Delano-Smith, Johannes Dörflinger, Paul Dukes, Felipe Fernandez-Armesto, Colin Flint, James Forsyth, Peter Furtado, Mark Galeotti, Walter Goffart, László Gróf, Paul Harvey, Roger Kain, George Lukowski, David Moon, Robert Peberdy, John Plowright, David Potter, Martyn Rady, Bill Roberts, Brendan Simms, David Sturdy, Peter Waldron, Armin Wolf, and Daniel Woolf. I am also grateful for the comments of four anonymous readers on either the synopsis or the text.

I am most grateful to Robert Baldock for his encouragement and to Wendy Duery for her secretarial assistance. I have only been able to write this book thanks to Sarah's love and attention and it is dedicated to another very special person, our daughter Pippa, one of the two 'maps' of our lives.

Preface

Maps and History, a study of the mapping and mappability of the past, offers an approach to the understanding of history, both the past and the way in which it is studied and presented. Most historians have given very little consideration to historical mapping. Historical atlases, i.e. atlases (generally books in which half or more of the space consists of maps) composed of historical maps, tend to be taken for granted, treated like basic reference books, akin to chronologies, dictionaries and encyclopaedias. Yet, like such works, they can be fruitfully analysed. The visual images they offer are influential in creating and sustaining notions of historical situations, and are particularly appropriate as a theme for inquiry given the recent stress on nations as imagined political communities, on the role of images as a means of creating perceptions of power and, more generally, on iconographic aspects of political and cultural authority.

Geography was and is more than a background or backdrop to historical events and processes. The nature of our understanding of space and of spatial relationships is of consequence, and historical atlases provide a means for assessing how these have changed over time. Considering the past use of historical atlases also provides an opportunity to discuss their present and future potential – important as the content of these works has changed considerably since the Second World War. In addition, it is necessary to offer a cartographic perspective, to discuss what can be mapped effectively, what information is best presented in map form and how it should be treated. Important in their own right, historical atlases thus also offer ways of understanding and presenting the past.

I

Developments to 1800

In recent decades the understanding of maps and mapping, of cartography and the history of cartography, has altered and widened to include traditions of representation that do not accord with the customary Western definitions. This is related to a critique of what has been presented as a triumphalist conception of the map and the development of mapmaking, a critique associated in particular with the late Brian Harley.[1] An understanding of the past at least partially in cartographic terms is not and was not restricted to Western societies. Instead, in a number of independent contexts there was interest in spatial relations because of the nature of religious foundation myths, although there is a distinction between understanding spatial relationships and understanding cartography. In New Caledonia, for example, society was organized into spatially differentiated clans with reference to mythical ancestors. A sense of spatial relationship and control was based on dwelling foundation mounds and the routes between them, and the geography of the region included the mythological place in which man originated and the entrance to the subterranean country of the dead. There was clearly a well-developed sense of mental mapping, and it is possible today to map such relationships.[2] In Australia aboriginal maps depict ancestral stories and traditional relations with the environment.[3] Such maps existed not only in the mind – unmanifested mental maps – but also in sand paintings and carvings – manifested mental maps. That such maps were not reproduced in manuscript or print in no way decreases their accuracy, although printing does make the creation of a readily repeatable visual image far easier. The relationship between the picture story in cartoon-strip style that moves in place as well as time and cartographic origins in certain societies, for example Ancient Egypt, Aztec Mexico and among the North American Native Americans, is potentially very interesting and would repay investigation.

It is no part of the agenda of this book to suggest or imply that manuscript or printed representations are superior to mental maps or that oral culture is deficient as a means for constructing, describing and analysing spatial relationships. The printed world of maps is scarcely autonomous. Yet, in studying the mappability of the past by reference to historical atlases it is inevitably the case that attention is concentrated on the culture of print. It is certainly outside the scope of this work to consider how spatial notions and understandings of the past have changed within oral cultures.

Developments in China

The history and pre-history of the historical atlas are commonly understood in Western terms. The first known historical atlas is generally given as the *Parergon* of Abraham Örtel (Ortelius), published in Antwerp in 1579, initially as part of his general atlas, but from 1624 as a separate work. Yet it is also possible to draw attention to independent developments in China. The first map in China dates from about 2100 BC and appeared on the outside of a *ding* (ancient cooking vessel), and a map of a graveyard produced between 323–15 BC was uncovered in a tomb in 1977. Maps in China certainly became more common under the Western (or 'Former') Han dynasty (206 BC–AD 9), although very few have survived from before the twelfth century. Among the maps that have disappeared is the *Yü Küng Ti Yü Thu* (Map of the territory of the Yugong) of Phei Hsiu/Pei Xiu (AD 224–71), the founder of scientific cartography in China. Appointed Minister of Works in 267, Phei Hsiu was an active mapmaker. He shared the Chinese fascination with legendary and historic times and sought to map the Tribute of Yü in order to clarify the geography of ancient times, to compensate for the destruction and loss of Qin maps and to improve on what he regarded as the inadequate maps of the Later Han. Phei Hsiu presented his eighteen-sheet map to the Emperor, who kept it in the secret archives. The preface claimed:

> referring back to antiquity, I have examined, according to the *Yugong* [an ancient work of geography], the mountains and lakes, the courses of the rivers, the plateaus and plains, the slopes and marshes, the limits of the nine ancient provinces and the sixteen modern ones, taking account of commanderies and fiefs, prefectures and cities, and not forgetting the names of places where the ancient kingdoms concluded treaties or held meetings; and lastly, inserting the roads, paths and navigable waters.

The sources of information available to Phei and his final achievement may have been in large part works of the imagination, but his was an attempt to fix the past in cartographic terms.[4]

From the twelfth century, maps were frequently used in various types of publication such as administrative works and histories. The oldest printed Chinese historical atlas is a twelfth-century Song work, the *Lidai Dili Zhi Zhang Tu* (Easy to use maps of geography through the dynasties) attributed to Shui Anli. This was a collection of 44 maps of dynastic territories from legendary times to the Song dynasty, originally produced in a woodblock edition, a reproduction of which, edited by Tan Qixiang, was published in Shanghai in 1989. We know almost nothing about Shui Anli, but a Southern Song dynasty writer says he was from Shu, that he was summoned to court, but died before he arrived there. Some editions give the compiler as Su Shi, a noted Song official and poet, whereas some bear no name. The blocks were produced in Shu, a minor state in what is now Sichuan province. A Qing edition, which seems to be directly descended from the Song editions, has the date 1099 at the end of the colophon, so it is possible that this was the date of presentation, but it is impossible to be certain.[5]

This work, apparently the oldest printed historical atlas, is fascinating because it reveals that from the outset the selection of maps and presentation of material in historical atlases involved issues of politics and propaganda. The atlas encouraged a sense of irredentism by showing, through graphic illustration, what had been Chinese and what had been taken away, and thus *feeding* dreams of what might be again. Naomi Standen has drawn attention to this work in her thesis on the Chinese frontier and argues that one of the most striking aspects of the atlas is the constancy with which the Great Wall is shown, and its depiction even for legendary times when, whether or not walls were already being built, there was certainly no single 'Great Wall'.[6] Standen has suggested that given that the border lines are shown with relative accuracy in regard to the Wall, the Wall must be there primarily as an orientation feature, but she also argues that representations of the Wall as a constant feature would have had the effect of reinforcing Chinese ideas about the 'natural' extent of China. In the period of the later Northern and early Southern Song, when this atlas was produced, there was a great deal of concern about the northern frontier of China and where it should lie. The frontier had not lain in the place desired by the Chinese for over a century. The non-Chinese Kitan Liao dynasty had acquired a small but important region south of the Wall in 936, and this had been confirmed by the Treaty of Shanyuan (1005). The situation deteriorated from the Chinese point of view when the non-Chinese Jurchen Jin expanded into the northern third of Song territory in 1126. The contents of the *Lidai Dili Zhi Zhang Tu* atlas are related to Standen's thesis that post-Shanyuan (1005) regimes encouraged an ethnocentric reaction against the non-Chinese as part of their legitimating and state-strengthening process. Showing what had been conquered and controlled, the depiction of past glories in spatial terms thus offered a powerful programmatic visual message. A similar message was conveyed by a thirteenth-century map of former capitals.[7]

If Song concern with territorial integrity can be related to pressure from the north, it also reflected both an ability to think in historical terms and a turning towards a spatial rather than a cosmological definition of what China meant. It would however be misleading to suggest that an ability to think in historical terms necessarily led to historical mapping. The ability of Chinese regimes to think in such terms was already well established before the Song. Histories had been submitted for imperial approval, and written at least partially under imperial auspices since Sima Qian's *Shiji* (Records of the grand historian) produced during the Han; and this excludes the much older mythologized 'histories' of the golden age. During the Tang (618–907) much thought was given to historical writing, and the evolving formal system of producing history reached its mature form. Although not fully practised during the Tang itself, mostly due to military upheavals,[8] the Tang system of historical compilation was adopted by all subsequent dynasties, and was actually followed to a greater rather than a lesser extent. This was also a period of mapping – an edict of 780 ordered that 'maps with explanations' be submitted every three years – but not apparently of historical cartography.

By contemporary world standards, although the art of drawing topographical maps to scale, as practised in the Later Han period (AD 25–220), had probably been lost, medieval China had a strong interest in mapping, and there was much information available that could be mapped. The government was assiduous in collecting reports by envoys. Dynastic histories contained geographical sections which described the territories controlled by China; these sections have preserved numerous maps, often transcribed from other sources. From the twelfth century, if not earlier, numerous *fangzhi*, gazetteers of various parts of China, were compiled, normally with maps of the district, prefecture or province described.[9] The practice was originally used by court-appointed officials to familiarize themselves with the history, economy, flora and fauna, and important families of the area they had been sent to govern. These local gazetteers also gave travel distances and often included maps of some of the cities or the entire district. Later gazetteers incorporated the information of earlier ones, thereby offering an historical dimension.

Yet, despite the changes in Chinese mapping, there is no sign of development in Chinese historical atlases. In part, this reflected a rather limited interest in the outside world and a very limited knowledge of its history. There was nothing to compare with the role of the Bible and the Classics in European society. These works provided very extensive texts that were spatially specific in what they discussed and that generally depicted events in what were distant, foreign countries for most Europeans. In addition, after their major episode of Indian Ocean exploration in the fifteenth century, the Chinese did not benefit from the massive expansion in cartographic information that the Europeans gained in their explorations from the fifteenth century on.

After Shui Anli the next significant figures in the history of Chinese historical atlases were Hong Liangji (1746–1809), Li Zhaoluo (1769–1841) and Yang Shoujing (1839–1915). A scholar, inspector of education and active writer, Hong produced atlases devoted to particular periods of Chinese history: the Sixteen Kingdoms, the Three Kingdoms and the Eastern Chin. He did not, however, consider the history of foreign states.[10] A contemporary, Zhang Xuecheng (1738–1801), wanted to develop gazetteers so that they became total histories of regions, including sets of maps, but his impact on the production of gazetteers was limited. Zhang Qi (1765–1833) published a work on the geography of the Late Chou period in 1815, and Li Zhaoluo published in 1832 and 1838 atlases designed to accompany his dictionaries of place names. There was interest in mapping past geographies, for example the changing course of the Yellow River, because they were regarded as a necessary aspect of the understanding and thus appreciation of ancient wisdom as reflected in the writings of sages. Yang Shoujing, director of the school at Wuchang from 1902 until 1908 and a leading bibliophile, compiled the *Li-tai Yü-ti Yen-ko Hsien-yao T'u* (1906–11), an historical atlas of China dynasty by dynasty, a work of traditional conception and scope.[11]

Thus, despite the fact that it was a map-using culture, the compilation of the first historical atlas in the world in third-century-AD China, and the interest of the *Lidai Dili Zhi Zhang Tu* atlas, China was not central to the development of historical atlases. Elsewhere, in the pre-modern Islamic world there were major advances in developing the mathematical and astronomical bases of celestial and geographical cartography, but theory was not matched by practice.[12] South Asian map production was also limited.[13] It was Europe that was to be central to the subsequent development of historical atlases.

The Pre-History of the European Historical Atlas

The 'pre-history' of the historical atlas in Europe was a long one, for the characteristic works of that genre were preceded by others that are less easy to define, notably individual maps depicting the Holy Land at the time of Christ, or the Classical world, such as the map of ancient Greece produced by the Venetian cartographer

Ferdinando Bertelli in 1564.[14] Such maps probably would not have been regarded as historical in the same way as they are today. Without exactly being contemporary, their contents made up so large a part of people's intellectual baggage as to give them a distinctly contemporay tincture.

The Bible was a significant inspiration for mapping. There was interest in the location of places mentioned in it and also the wish to construct a geography that could encompass Eden. Early Church Fathers, including Eusebius in the early fourth and Jerome in the late fourth and early fifth centuries, possibly drew maps to further their investigation of biblical toponomy. A now lost map of the Holy Land possibly by Eusebius may have been the first to show the divisions of the Twelve Tribes of Israel.[15] The copy of Jerome's works that includes maps is far later, a twelfth-century manuscript that comes from Tournai[16] and may have been made there. The maps are closely related to the Cotton, Hereford and other world maps from contemporary England and neighbouring areas. There is nothing to suggest a strong connection with Jerome and it is much more likely that the copyist simply added the maps from some other source, thinking that they would be an appropriate accompaniment to the text. The medieval tradition of wall decorations and manuscript illumination provided opportunities for scriptural mapping. The great *mappae mundi* (world maps) of the thirteenth and early fourteenth century produced in the English tradition – Ebstorf, Vercelli, Hereford, Duchy of Cornwall – conveyed historical and other information in a geographical framework, whereas chronicles used a chronological framework. The route of the Exodus, for example, was shown on the Hereford world map. More specifically, the *mappae mundi* can be seen as analogous to medieval narrative pictures that present events that occurred at different moments in the same scene.[17]

In addition to such Christian productions there were also Jewish maps. It has been suggested that a map may have accompanied the Book of Jubilees written in the second century BC, and it is possible that there was a cartographic tradition in Hebrew biblical commentary.[18] Maps of the Holy Land survive in manuscripts dating from the thirteenth to the fifteenth century. They stemmed from originals probably drawn by Rashi (Rabbi Solomon ben Isaac). The Jewish tradition of mapmaking influenced its Christian counterpart. The commentaries of Nicolas of Lyra, *Postillae litteralis super totam Bibliam*, written between 1323 and 1332, drew on Rashi and included a number of maps that were subsequently influential.[19]

The mapping of biblical themes had a new impetus and took a new form in the sixteenth century as a result of the Reformation and the spread of printing. Such maps were particularly characteristic of Reformation bibles, so that 'the history of maps in Bibles is part of the history of the Reformation'.[20] The Protestants sought to spread knowledge of the Bible, making its printing a major priority, and maps were the obvious way to communicate biblical geography and thus to establish and illustrate its truth. In his *Lectures*, Luther revealed his wish to have 'a good geography and more correct map of the Land of Promise'.[21] Maps were published as illustrations to biblical commentaries and explanations from the 1520s, the first being a version of Lucas Cranach's map of the Exodus in the 1525 edition of the Old Testament published by Christopher Froschauer. The first map to be printed in England appeared in 1535 and illustrated the Exodus.[22] Later in the century bibles printed in Europe included maps of such subjects as Eden and the division of Canaan among the twelve tribes of Israel. Biblical maps were updated to incorporate developments in astronomy and cartography, but as Paradise and the Garden of Eden were believed in they were also located in many maps. The first printed Jewish map of the Holy Land appeared in 1560.[23]

The Bible was not the only text to receive cartographic treatment. The Benedictine monk Thomas Elmham (d. *c.* 1428), in his *Historia monasterii sancti Augustini Cantuariensis* (History of St Augustine's monastery, Canterbury), on which he finished work in 1414, used a plan of the Isle of Thanet to illustrate the legend of Dompneva's hind in which the monastery of St Augustine received lands delineated by the route of a running hind.[24] Such an illustration was unusual, however, and very few medieval narratives included a map. An awareness of historical cartography depended on a clear sense of the past as separate. This entailed a realization both of the limited, because contingent, value of earlier maps and of the fact that the past was distinct, required mapping and could be mapped. Thus, in the fifteenth century Ptolemaic maps were at first treated as authoritative, though in 1427 they were supplemented by Claudius Clavus's map of northern Europe; and the Ptolemaic account was only gradually replaced by new works, a process that was accelerated by printing and European exploration. This left Ptolemaic and other Classical maps as separate, historical works, as their subsequent publication history indicated. The 1513 Strasbourg edition of Ptolemy's *Geography* was the first to separate modern from ancient maps and in 1578 Mercator issued the Ptolemaic maps alone, without any modern supplements; thus they could stand as an unrevised atlas of the Classical world.[25]

Early Modern Mapping

The situation in Europe changed radically in the sixteenth and seventeenth centuries. Maps were first printed in Europe in the 1470s. They could therefore be more speedily produced and widely distributed. As a result, most mapmakers had more, and more recent, maps to refer to when they were producing their own. Printing facilitated the exchange of information, the processes of copying and revision that were so important for mapmaking. Printing also led to an emphasis on the commercial aspect of mapmaking and a public world of maps, and thus to a new dynamic for the production of maps and the propagation of mapping.

In contrast, the use of maps in, for example, the Ottoman empire was far more restricted. The panegyric Ottoman royal histories produced by the official court historians contained some illustrations from the 1530s and several of these were maps, but the works were in manuscript and their wider impact was limited. In addition, the Turks came to be influenced by European printed views and maps,[26] for an aspect of printing was that it aided the dissemination of cartographic images, models and techniques to foreign states and cultures.

Maps came to play a greater role in Europe in a number of fields, for example judicial disputes. By the end of the sixteenth century, estate maps were well established, whether supplementing or replacing written surveys. These maps were then used in court cases.[27] Changing notions of history were also important, particularly the emergence of a quasi-modern secular historical awareness, deriving from both the Renaissance's sense of a typology and progression of historical eras (Classical-medieval-modern) and the related Protestant sense of Early Church-

Medieval Church–Reformed Church. This underlay or motivated a desire to represent the past in an 'objective' cartographic manner.

Maps were increasingly published as part of texts. In large measure this change was due to the impact of humanism and, specifically, the emphasis that was placed on literal rather than allegorical interpretations of scripture and the Classics and also on the accuracy and clarity of the text.[28] Historical maps were an aspect of the new textualism of the Renaissance. Most of the maps did not directly reflect the new cartographic knowledge produced by the beginning of the age of European exploration. Exploration shifted attention from the Mediterranean to the Oceanic,[29] and the Spanish empire introduced the idea of *Relaciones geográficas* into the New World at an early stage of colonization, partly with the aim of elucidating the political boundaries or tribute-reach of pre-conquest states, but the nature of historical knowledge and interest was such that the contents of historical atlases did not develop in the same way.

Nevertheless, historical atlases reflected the increasing interest in and understanding of cartography. They can also be seen as an aspect of the development of thematic mapping which has been presented as a refinement from the mid-seventeenth century.[30] Some writers were clearly interested in creating maps. There was a relationship between antiquarian studies and maps, certainly in England and Italy in the fifteenth and sixteenth centuries. The Kentish antiquary and mapmaker William Lambarde (1536–1601) not only published the first English county history, the *Perambulation of Kent* (London, 1576), but also drew a map of the Anglo-Saxon kingdoms: the first had been produced by Matthew Paris in the mid-thirteenth century, while the Anglo-Saxon scholar and cartographer Lawrence Nowell's thirteen-section mid-sixteenth-century map of England and Wales gave place names in Old English and used Old English letter forms. The maps in the works of historians such as John Norden (1548–c. 1625) and William Camden (1551–1623) can be considered as precursors to atlases, but it is important to note that these authors did not initially think they were writing history.[31] A series of Dutch historical maps showing Zeeland at successive dates from the seventh to the late thirteenth century, stemming apparently from Egmont Abbey, was originally thought to derive from actual medieval maps but is now recognized as being historical reconstruction. The series may have been produced as a form of regional historical atlas. The maps were copied on several occasions in the sixteenth and seventeenth centuries.[32]

There was an increasing tendency for historical writers and, more important, historical readers, especially in the seventeenth century, to want to relate time to place. Earlier there had been many remarks to the effect that geography was an important ancillary to history – a kind of second eye – but these were essentially rhetorical before about 1580, and possibly later. The relationship between space and time is complex, but there are signs of important shifts in interest and perception in the seventeenth century. There were close relations between history and geography in handbooks of history in the seventeenth and early eighteenth centuries. There were dozens of such works, ranging from potboilers such as Peter Heylyn's *Microcosmus, or a Little Description of the Great World. A Treatise Historicall, Geographicall, Politicall, Theologicall* (Oxford, 1621) to major popular encyclopaedias such as Louis Moreri's *Le grand dictionnaire historique* (Lyons, 1674; 19th edn, Paris, 1743–9) the basis of *The Great Historical, Geographical and Poetical Dictionary* (London. 1640).

The concept and use of maps spread. Travel literature did not begin in this period, and there had of course been in the medieval period pilgrim guides and representations of the sites travellers visited. However, thereafter, especially in the seventeenth century, there was increased travel to places of interest by a broader segment of the social elite – an elite now far more familiar with its own history than its medieval or sixteenth-century ancestors had been. Thus, the wish to have guidebooks gained fresh impetus. In the seventeenth and early eighteenth centuries it is possible to detect a sense of history and of place converging in travel diaries such as those of Celia Fiennes or John Percival, which refer repeatedly to particular places as being established historic sites. The higher degree of historical literacy produced a need for books that formally connected geography with the past. Book readers sought a history informed by precise cartography and a cartography that was in turn historically accurate – by contrast, for example, to the many early-modern illustrative woodcuts that used generic images of 'a city' to represent Paris, Nuremberg, Venice, etc., at any date.

Two aspects of change in this period are harder to assess. First, a consciousness of the past that increasingly placed a stress on place rather than, or in addition to, chronology can be detected and possibly related to a growing sense of separate sovereign political bodies and of national patriotism. Power helped to frame political awareness and to form political consciousness.

Second, there was a change in the notion of time and thus of its impact. Some Renaissance theorists of time, notably those who accepted the arguments of Copernicus on terrestrial motion, explained it as simply a product of the spatial rotation of the earth, a dimension that was accordingly without particular relevance. Different scientific accounts of time came to be offered. John Locke in his *Essay concerning Human Understanding* (London, 1690) constructed time as a psychological experience of duration with no necessary connection to spatial movement. The significance of time, the separation between past and present, came to be more strongly asserted and more readily understood and, in creating the past as a subject, made its depiction as different more of an issue. Historical maps, maps drawn to depict past events, were conscious historical statements dependent on a sense of the past as a separate sphere, one that was of relevance and could be interrogated, but which remained separate.

The notion of sight also altered. Scientific developments undertaken by the Dutch in the seventeenth century, especially in optics, caused them to stress *sight* as the sense through which God reveals his creation most clearly to mankind. This admiration for the sense of sight led painters to attempt to 'describe' the world as they viewed it. Dutch cartography has been linked to Dutch painting as both attempted the 'description' of physical reality.[33] Thus greater value came to be placed on geographical 'realism' in cartography rather than on the older stylized maps which did not depend on accurate topographical description. Vermeer presented Clio with an historic map of the United Provinces on the wall.

Maps came to play a greater role in the culture of print in the seventeenth century. The numbers of historical and geographical works from this period that are now missing their maps, or have had later ones pasted in instead of known originals, suggest that even then it was popular to rip or cut maps out and collect them separately, although as many books were bound on purchase it is possible that maps were not inserted because they might get damaged. John Speed's *A Prospect of the Most Famous Parts of the World* (London, 1627) included 'A Briefe Description of the Civil

Wares and Battails fought in England, Wales, and Ireland', illustrated by a double-page black-and-white map of 'The Invasions of England and Ireland with all their civil wars since the Conquest', a map first published *c.* 1601. This map arguably had faults, not least in its depiction of events greatly separated in time, as simultaneous, a traditional device, characteristic of *mappae mundi*, which, in this case, led to a work that was crowded and without apparent form or analysis. It is not surprising that the pictures of fleets arriving were impressionistic, but the map was arresting, illustrative and definitely added visual interest to the book. Speed's county maps also included historical information, for example sites of battles. Some narrative histories included maps. The translation of Thucydides by Thomas Hobbes, first published in 1629, contained maps which were clearly conceived to help illustrate the text; rather than as simple adornment. The conjuncture of time and space in art and/or maps, especially maps of the Bible, had for long been one in which the significance of chronology and the separation of past and present were limited. The breakdown of this separation transformed the sense of the past and thus historical cartography.

Ortelius

The first historical atlas arose as a result of the mapmaking of one of the leading cartographers of the sixteenth century, Abraham Ortelius (1527–98). Born in Antwerp, Ortelius was well-travelled in France, Italy and Germany. He turned to cartography in the early 1560s and created a map-book, the *Theatrum Orbis Terrarum* (Theatre of the World), which was published in Antwerp in 1570. This work became very popular and about 40 editions had appeared by 1612. Ortelius was able to purchase a new house in Antwerp in 1581.

Ortelius was also interested in Classical geography. He published a map, *Romani imperii imago* in 1571 and in 1578 the *Synonymia geographica sive populorum, regionum, insularum, urbium . . . appellationes et nomia*, a major repertorium of geographical names that provided an alphabetical list of place-names mentioned by Classical authors with, against each, the names employed at other periods. The following year, Ortelius began to draw historical maps for the *Theatrum*. These maps of the Classical world – the *Parergon* – were his own work, unlike the copies of other maps that he used for the contemporary world in the *Theatrum*. Between 1579 and 1598 he drew 38 maps for the *Parergon* and this section of the *Theatrum* grew from 12 plates in the 1584 Latin edition to 26 in 1591, 32 in that of 1595 and 38 in 1603. After Ortelius's death more plates were added. The accompanying text was also by Ortelius. The *Parergon* was translated into French, Italian, German and English, the English edition of the *Theatrum*, containing 43 plates in the *Parergon* section, appearing in 1606. The final version of the *Parergon* was published as a separate book in Antwerp in 1624 by Balthasar Moretus, though the 1595 *Parergon* also appeared as a separate edition in Antwerp that year. Ortelius had the Roman 'Peutinger' map engraved and published in 1598, probably the first printed facsimile of a Classical map; it was subsequently included in several editions of the *Parergon*. Thus, the *Parergon* was a very successful work, and its impact was spread by translation and new editions.

The *Parergon* began with 'Sacred Geography': the Bible took precedence over the world of the Classics. The journeys of the Patriarchs and of St Paul readily lent themselves to cartographic depiction as did those of Alexander the Great and Aeneas. The Classical world was presented in great detail, although the *Parergon*'s maps

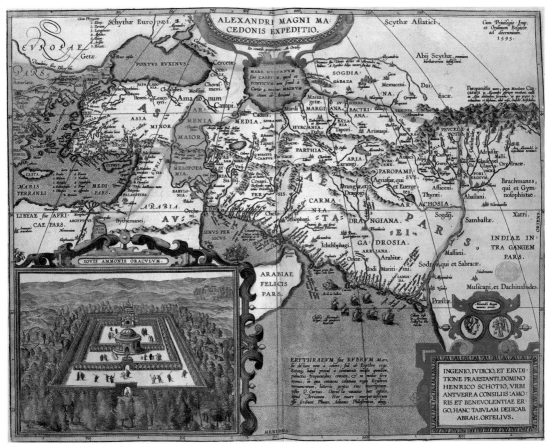

1. The East, imagined and real: a section of the map of Asia from the Aegean to the Indus from the first Western historical atlas, Abraham Ortelius's *Parergon*, initially part of his *Theatrum Orbis Terrarum* (Antwerp, first published 1570, this edition 1555). This map illustrates Alexander the Great's expedition and conquests. For sixteenth-century Europeans the Classical world was their source as well as a measure of the achievements of their civilization. Alexander's fleet is depicted with sixteenth-century boats.

centred on Rome rather than Greece. The emphasis on Italy detracted from due attention being given to the Near and Middle East, and there was no sense of chronological progress in the organization of the maps. The map of the campaigns of Alexander was followed by that of the travels of Ulysses. In addition, Ortelius was affected by current concerns. The Low Countries, in his map of them in the Roman period, consists of the seventeen provinces belonging to the Habsburgs, creating a sense of territorial coherence that was misplaced for the earlier age. Sixteenth-century boats were depicted in the picture of Alexander the Great's fleet that accompanied the map of Asia from the Aegean to the Indus, showing Alexander's conquests. Aside from maps and text, Ortelius also included a number of views including two fantasy views: 'Tempe' and 'Daphne'.[34]

The *Parergon* represented the significant shift from the single-sheet historical map to the atlas. The idea of maps systematically produced to a common purpose was very much a 'modern' project, in the sense of a fusion of utility and the consequences of the technology of printing, including predictability and quantity. In addition, the idea of an atlas had a symbolic authority which transcended that of the individual maps.

Seventeenth-Century Historical Mapping

The *Parergon* was followed by other historical atlases sharing a common subject: the world of the Bible and the Classics. Knowledge of this world was seen by pedagogues and princes alike as a vital aspect of genteel education[35] and there was a growing awareness that a cartographic perspective was important to this process. This led to the printing of Classical maps, but also to an increased demand for historical atlases. There was some variety in the works produced. In 1650 the English Royalist, Thomas Fuller (1608–61), had published his atlas of the Holy Land, *A Pisgah-Sight of Palestine and the confines thereof, with the history of the Old and New Testament acted thereon*. He placed Mt Pisgah, from which Moses had viewed the Promised Land, north of the Dead Sea. Each map was preceded by a description. The book was a success.

One of the more important historical atlases was that by Philippus Cluverius, the *Introductio in universam geographiam, tam veterem quam novam*, published in Leyden in 1629 (later editions included those published in Amsterdam in 1697 and 1711). Cluverius's maps depicted towns, mountains, roads and provincial boundaries, but lacked dates. Maps of the Low Countries in Classical times or Spain Old and New thus offered no sense of chronological specificity, or of progression, bar a stark contrast of unspecified old and new. Joannes Janssonius's *Accuratissima orbis antiqui delineatio; sive geographia vetus, sacra et profana* (Amsterdam, 1652), to which a text was added by Georg Horn or Hornius, Professor of History at Leiden, was an important work that was translated into English and French in the eighteenth century. The *Nucleus geographiae antiquae et novae* (Jena, 1676) by the Halle professor Christoph Keller or Cellarius (1638–1707) was reprinted under different titles. He was also responsible for a major text in Classical geography, the *Notitia orbis antiqui* (Leipzig, 1701–6). Cellarius made considerable progress in the accurate depiction of Classical geography.

The genre of historical atlases also developed. The maps in Ortelius's atlas had lacked any thematic or chronological order, but the latter was supplied in Philippe de La Ruë's *La Terre Sainte en six cartes géographiques* (Paris, 1651). In this atlas the maps of the Holy Land were presented in chronological order, from early Canaan to modern times. Nevertheless, most atlases did not follow this example. It is clear that in the seventeenth century scant value was attached to a chronological, sequential series of maps. In part, this was probably because the circumstances depicted in different maps were seen as having only a limited interrelationship and, instead, as having a direct relationship with modern readers. Furthermore, these readers could be presumed to supply the chronological placing of the maps if such was required.

Like many other important atlases in the seventeenth century, La Ruë's work was published in Paris. Other important works published there included the *Parallela geographiae veteris et novae* (1647–9) by Philippe Briet (1601–68), a Jesuit academic who had already in 1641 published a map of Palestine including an inset of the Exodus. Briet's comparison of ancient and modern geography reflected the role of the Classics as a point of reference and source of information. The comparison of ancient and modern was to be an important theme in historical geography until the early twentieth century.

There was a strong interest in mapping the past in French circles, partly because this was of direct relevance to Bourbon attempts to use historical claims to justify

French expansionism, and partly because of a more long-term interest in French history that reflected the increase in national consciousness among the elite. The latter interest led to a development of French historical geography in the form of Nicolas Sanson's geographical commentaries on Caesar's Gallic wars and Bergier's reconstruction of Roman routes.[36] Sanson's maps included *Galliae antiquae* (Paris, 1642) and *Gallia vetus ex C. Iulii Caesaris commentariis descripta* (Paris, 1649), though he also produced maps of other areas in the Classical period, for example Britain and Spain. They were published again in Paris in 1750: throughout the history of the historical atlas the primacy of commercial considerations has been most clearly displayed in the eagerness to re-use material. It was less expensive to use ready-made blocks than to pay for new designs. The expenses involved in map production were such that the investment usually had to be recouped over a long timescale.

In the seventeenth century there was also an extension of the cartographic range to the post-Roman period, including a map of France under Clovis engraved by Bercy in about 1680 that appeared in two editions.[37] It depicted woods, rivers, towns, mountains, tribes and some boundaries presented in dotted lines. Pierre Duval's *Cartes et tables, pour la géographie ancienne, pour la chronologie, et pour les itinéraires, et voyages modernes* (Paris, 1665) was not restricted to the established Classical repertoire of journeys, and was one of the atlases that presented maps in chronological order. In addition, the atlas included three maps covering the expansion of the Roman empire. Duval's atlas was, however, an example of historical cartography that lacked the scholarly goal and knowledge of the ancient geography mapped by, for example, Sanson, Delisle and D'Anville. Comparisons of ancient and modern geography were more weighty than drawing maps as companions to the ancient poets and historians. In the seventeenth century there was, therefore, an important increase in the quantity of historical mapping. Furthermore, the sense of the past as having a distinct spatiality increased. For example, in an atlas of 1652 J. Mejer paired medieval and modern town plans of Schleswig-Holstein.

The Mapping of the Early Modern World

Improvements in the mapping of the contemporary world were important in creating the basis for more accurate historical maps: the improvements might not affect the historical information that could be depicted, but they made a major difference by ensuring that the cartographic background was more accurate. This was particularly important as maps depicted physical features, especially mountains and rivers, as well as towns, roads, battles and frontiers. There had been considerable stylization in the depiction of physical features, for example islands and coastlines, in medieval and early Renaissance maps, as the mapmakers were primarily concerned with recording their existence rather than their accurate shape. In their *Portolani* and *Isolarii* the Italians simply presented coastlines in a schematic form. In part this was a matter of contemporary conceptual standards,[38] but the nature of the information available to mapmakers was also important. The trend in fifteenth- to seventeenth-century maps was away from pictorial (specific) representation and towards symbols (generalized) in all but outlines, but there was emphasis on the need for precision in the portrayal of the crucial physical outlines: coastlines and rivers.

European cartographic knowledge of other continents increased greatly in the sixteenth and seventeenth centuries but nonetheless remained limited. Coastal regions were generally the only well-mapped areas. European knowledge of the interior of other continents was limited and these interiors were thus poorly mapped by them. This situation also reflected the navigational rationale of many maps. For example, the Venetian Vincenzo Coronelli's *Route maritime de Brest à Siam et de Siam à Brest* (Brest, 1687) was essentially a map of coastal regions. Etienne de Flacourt's map of Madagascar (1666) was accurate largely for the south-east of the island, where the French had established Fort Dauphin in 1642. In d'Anville's *Carte de l'Inde* of 1752 most of east-central India was labelled 'Grand espace de pays dont on n'a point de connoissance particulière'. Desnos's map *L'Asie* (Paris, 1789) included all of Asia, although the mapping of Tibet was very vague; but then the twelfth-century 'Jerome' map of Asia had been likewise.

Even coastal regions were not always well mapped. In Robert's map of the *Archipel des Indes Orientales* (1750), a caption 'Le fond de ce Golphe n'est pas bien connu' appears for the coastline of the Teluk Tomini in the Celebes (Sulawesi). The *Carte plate qui comprend l'Isle de Ceylon* (1775) includes the captions 'Isles Laquedives dont le détail n'est pas exactement connu' and 'on ne connoit, ni le nombre, ni la grandeur, ni la situation respective des Isles Maldives'. The Australian coast was not fully charted until the Flinders and Baudin expeditions of the 1800s.

Nevertheless, more of the world was mapped by Europeans and this directly benefited historical scholarship and atlases, most appropriately with the *Atlas nouveau et curieux des plus célèbres itinéraires . . . 1246 . . . 1696* (Leyden, 1714) by a Leyden book-seller and publisher, Pierre van der Aa (1659–1733). Each of the 139 black and white maps appeared on a separate sheet and the explorers were organized by region of the world, with those who ranged widely presented first and most impressively on a global scale. Better geographical descriptions made it easier to understand or seem to understand historical fragments. Gibbon's assessment of the history of North Asia, a vast region of great importance to him because of its role as a source of 'barbarian' attacks, owed much to information acquired on an expedition that Peter the Great had sent to Siberia under von Strahlenberg, who had also compiled a map of 'Great Tartary'.[39]

Within Europe there were major improvements in mapping in the seventeenth and eighteenth centuries. They took three forms. First, cadastral maps – maps made for taxation or administrative purposes – which resulted in increased familiarity with cartography. In much of Europe, early large-scale maps were cadastral. They often involved the mapping of estates which led to greater accuracy in identifying estate boundaries. Cadastral mapping was employed extensively by the Swedes, both in Sweden and in their German conquests in the seventeenth century. Such mapping was seen as a necessary complement to land registers and thus as the basis of reformed land taxes. The Swedish Pomeranian Survey Commission of 1692–1709 was designed to provide the basis for a new tax system. Detailed land surveys of Piedmont and Savoy, establishing the ownership and value of land, were completed in 1711 and 1738 respectively, while cadastral mapping of Lombardy was carried out in the late 1710s with the backing of the Emperor Charles VI.[40]

The second major development was the growing importance of large-scale military surveys, though chronologically military mapping had long preceded cadastral. The Austrians, who ruled Sicily between 1720 and 1735, used army engineers to prepare the first detailed map of the island. The French military engineers of the

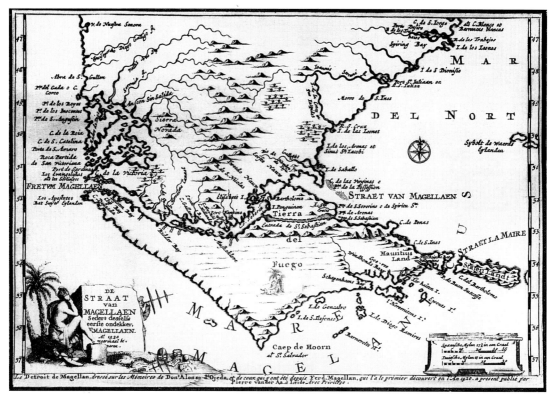

The map contains the following visible labels:

Y. de Nuestra Senora · Gallego · R. de Diego · C. de S. Iorge · à C. Blanco et Barranos Blancas · Porta De la los Reis · Spiring Bay · R. de los Trabajos · I. de los Leones

M A R

Abra de S. Gallen · Serrania R · Porto S. Iulian en en S. Iulian · I. de S. Dionisio

R. del Cada o C. Corco · Morro de S. Ines

Pt. de los Reyes · D E L   N O R T

Pt. de los Inocentes · R. S. Cruz · I. de las Leones

Pt. de S. Augustin · Sierra Nevada

C. de la Roie · I. de los Arenas et Sinus St. Iacobi

C. de S. Catelina

Porto de S. Amaro · Syböt de waerld Eylanden

Roca Partida

de San Victoriana · R. de Saballo

Port de Sardinas

Los Evangelistas als los Sortinges · C. de las Virginas o Pte. de la Possession

FRETVM MAGELLANI · de la Victoria

Elisabeth I. · Bartholome · STRAET VAN MAGELLAEN · S

Los Apostolos Dat Sus al Eylanden · I. Penguinon · Pte. de SS. Severino e da Spiritu St.

Tierra · Pte. de Arenas · Pte. de SS. Sebastian

Entrada de St. Sebastian · C. de Penas

del · C. de S. Ines

Fuego · Mauritius Land · STRAET LA MAIRE

Schoenhams · Gea Staien Landt

Caep de Hoorn · C. del Bartholome · Pte. de Buen Successo

at St. Salvador · I. de Goncalvo · I. Nassauitsen I.s

I. de S. Ilefonso · I.le Diego Ramires

M A C E L · Barneveits I.s

DE STRAAT van MAGELLAEN Sedert desselfs eerste ondekker, E. MAGELLAEN. Ao 1520 gevonden etc.

Le Detroit de Magellan, dressé sur les Mémoires de Don'Alonso d'Ojeda, et de ceux qui y ont été depuis Ferd. Magellan, qui l'a le premier découvert en l'An 1520. a present publié par Pierre van der Aa à Leide, Avec Privilège.

2.   The World Understood. As European knowledge of the world increased, so interest grew in past exploration. A map of Magellan's discovery in 1520 of a route round South America from *Atlas nouveau et curieux des plus célèbres itinéraires* by Pierre van der Aa (Leyden, 1714).

period, such as Pierre Bourcet, tackled the problems of mapping mountains, creating a clearer idea of what the alpine region looked like. Following the suppression of the 1745 rebellion there was a military survey of Scotland which served as the basis for more accurate maps. A major military survey of Bohemia was begun in the 1760s and completed under Joseph II. Lower Austria was surveyed from 1773 and an enormous survey of Hungary completed in 1786. Frederick II had Silesia mapped.[41]

The third major development was the improved measurement of longitude. Until the eighteenth century there were no clocks accurate enough to give a ship's meridional position, and longitudinal mapping faced problems. Many islands were placed too far to the west or the east; combined with the failure of captains to know where their ships were, this caused shipwrecks, for example on the Scilly Isles. Vincenzo Coronelli's *Route maritime de Brest à Siam et de Siam à Brest* was based on the Jesuit mission sent to Siam (Thailand) by Louis XIV in 1685. It carried a note saying that the map employed two sorts of longitudinal markings, those generally agreed and those based on information from the Jesuits. Major differences were revealed by a comparative French map of 1739, *Carte de l'Océan Oriéntale ou Mers des Indes dressée au dépost des cartes plans et journaux de la marine comparée avec la carte hollandoise de Ptietergoos et la carte angloise de Thornton.*[42]

In response to an Act of Parliament of 1714 offering a reward for the discovery of a method of determining longitude at sea, John Harrison devised a chronometer that erred by only eighteen miles in measurement of the distance of a return journey to Jamaica in 1761–2. Progress on land was swifter. Triangulation had been used to construct maps since the sixteenth century, but its use was becaming more common. In 1679–83 the French Académie had worked out the longitudinal position in France. A geodetic survey of France was carried out. In 1708–17 the Jesuit Jean-Baptiste Régis supervised the first maps of the Chinese empire to be based on astronomical observation and triangulation.[43]

An improved ability to calculate longitude, combined with the use of triangulation surveying, affected mapping, obliging and permitting the drawing of new maps. Old maps appeared redundant. Hermann Moll noted in the *Atlas geographus* (1711–17) that

> the curious, by casting their eye on the English map of France, lately done and corrected according to the observations of the Royal Academy of Sciences at Paris, may see how much too far Sanson has extended their coasts in the Mediterranean, the Bay of Biscay, and the British Channel.[44]

The establishment of accurate values for longitude led to improvements in historical atlases, improvements that benefited writers such as Edward Gibbon. Thus the historical atlases produced by Cellarius, Delisle and d'Anville were better than their seventeenth-century predecessors, work for example by Cluverius. It became possible to locate most places accurately, and the development of accurate and standard means of measuring distances made it easier for mapmakers to understand, assess and reconcile the work of their predecessors.[45] Aside from specific improvements in mapping techniques and concepts, which by the late seventeenth century were pretty well developed, maps were increasingly created for general reference beyond the *ad hoc* circumstances, military, cadastral or otherwise, of their inception. Maps also became more predictable as mapping conventions developed. Even at the end of the seventeenth century, there was no standard alignment of maps, but in the following century the convention of placing North at the top was established. Improvements in cartography led to increasing awareness of cartographic distinctiveness and change and criticism of the efforts of predecessors, as in *The Construction of Maps and Globes* (London, 1717), which has been attributed to John Green.[46]

As in subsequent periods, however, changes in information availability or depiction not only created commercial opportunities, but also produced pressures. The costs of mapping and the financial, legal and production issues that major new projects entailed – for example obtaining the necessary investment, sales and cash-flow, legal disputes about ownership, copyright, payments and profits, and the need to secure a consistently high standard of workmanship from engravers – drew cartography into a complex commercial world.

Greater Carto-Literacy

The habit of referring to maps increased in the eighteenth century; they were the cartographic equivalent of the interest in statistical information that affected those concerned with 'political arithmetic'. Maps had been used in the recording of European frontiers since at least the fifteenth century and were increasingly used from the sixteenth onwards as their potential became more widely appreciated. A map was used for the negotiations that led to the Anglo-French Treaty of Ardres of 1546. The Tordesillas line separating Portuguese and Spanish spheres of control was a common feature of sixteenth-century maps of the Atlantic. As maps were more and more widely used, they increasingly gave form to political territoriality and resulting interests and concerns. In 1712, during the negotiations over ending the War of the Spanish Succession, Torcy, the French foreign minister, urged his British counterpart to look at a map in order to see the strategic threat posed by the Alpine demands of Victor Amadeus II of Savoy-Piedmont.[47] The French foreign office created a geographic section in 1772 and in 1780 it acquired the collection of about 10,000 maps of the famous geographer d'Anville. One measure of the growing importance of maps was sensitivity about allowing copies to be made.[48]

A map that formed part of an Anglo-Dutch treaty of 1718 delineated the frontier between the United Provinces and the Austrian Netherlands. This owed much to the publication in 1711 of the Fricx map of the Low Countries, the first relatively large-scale military map of Europe. The frontier was fixed literally on a map, signed and sealed by plenipotentiaries as an annex to that treaty. This practice became established by the end of the century.

Maps were increasingly referred to in crises and in time of war by diplomats and politicians. In 1718 the engraver and mathematician Reeve Williams published his defence of British foreign policy, *A Letter from a Merchant to a Member of Parliament, Relating to the Danger Great Britain Is in of Losing her Trade, by the Great Increase of the Naval Power of Spain with a Chart of the Mediterranean Sea Annexed*; 9000 copies of the pamphlet were printed. The inclusion of a map added to its interest. The *Worcester Post-Man* reported that

> a notable book was delivered to the Members of Parliament, with a chart annex'd of the Mediterranean Sea, whereby it demonstrately appears of what importance it is to the trade of Great Britain, that Sicily and Sardinia shall be in the hands of a faithful ally, and if possible not one formidable by sea. That these two islands lie like two nets spread to intercept not only the Italian but Turkey and Levant trade.[49]

In 1758 Lord George Sackville had written to the Earl of Holdernesse, British Secretary of State, about military operations in Germany, 'You will see Cappenburgh in the map.' Sir James Harris, British envoy to The Hague, recorded of the Cabinet meeting he attended in London on 23 May 1787, as the Dutch crisis neared its height, that the Duke of Richmond, Master General of the Ordnance, 'talked of military operations – called for a map of Germany – traced the marches from Cassel and Hanover, to Holland, and also from Givet to Maestricht [*sic*]'. Thus the possibilities of French and British-subsidized German intervention were outlined to the Cabinet by the use of a map. The following day Harris saw William Pitt the Younger. He recorded that Pitt 'sent for a map of Holland; made me show him the situation of the Provinces'. George III used a map to follow the Prussian invasion of France in 1792. In 1800 George Canning wrote to his successor as Under-Secretary of State in the Foreign Office, 'What do you think of the Italian news? and what consolation does Pitt point out after looking over the map in the corner of his room by the door?'[50]

The greater use of maps, or increased carto-literacy, fed the appetite for the production of more historical maps. There was a growing emphasis on what was seen as accuracy, on representation in the two-dimensional map of features that were both correctly proportioned and in the correct relative location. For both contemporary and historical maps this affected a major subject, the depiction of frontiers. A firmer grasp of the nature of a linear frontier developed, one that was possibly associated with improved mapping and a more definite perception of the nature of political sovereignty, although the notion of such frontiers long predated the improvements in mapping in the seventeenth and eighteenth centuries. For example, Charlemagne's division of his dominions among his three sons in 806 drew on a number of territorial criteria, including the linear. The second clause read:

> To our beloved son Pippin: Italy, which is also called Langobardia; and Bavaria as Tassilo held it, except for the two *villae* called Ingolstadt and Lauterhofen which we once bestowed in benefice on Tassilo and which belong to the district called the Nordgau; and that part of Aleman'nia which lies on the southern bank of the river Danube and the boundary of which runs from the source of the Danube to where the districts of the Klettgau and the Hegau meet on the river Rhine at the place called Enge [near Schaffhausen] and thence along the river Rhine, upstream, to the Alps – whatever lies within these bounds and extends southwards or eastwards, together with the duchy of Chur and the district of the Thurgau.[51]

Nevertheless, poorly defined boundaries on the ground, and thus territorial divisions that were difficult to represent clearly on maps, had been an integral feature of the medieval period. They were a consequence of its 'mind-set', with an approach to territory in legal/feudal rather than spatial terms. The societies of the period lived with a pronounced degree of tension over frontier zones, areas of overlapping jurisdiction and divided sovereignty.[52]

A more spatially territorial approach to frontiers developed in the seventeenth and eighteenth centuries, although this process remained incomplete at the time of the French Revolution. Rivers were used to delimit frontiers in the Peace of Nijmegen in 1678 and a similar policy was followed in the Peace of Ryswick in 1697. A stronger interest in precision inspired advances in mapping, which in turn gave the spatial aspects and pretensions of territoriality a new cartographic precision, though the general problems of cartography remained – the scale of the line on the map, delineation and emphasis through colour and style.

Increased precision in the mapping of frontiers was as important as the related consolidation of territorial sovereignty and increasing state monopolization of organized violence. All were different facets of the consolidation and spread of governmental authority and the erosion of the distinctive features of border zones, and all encouraged the use of frontier lines on maps, both contemporary, and – because the 'differentness' of the past was only partially grasped – historical. The implementation of firm frontiers was bound up with the existence of more assertive states and growing state bureaucracies, which sought to know where exactly they could impose their demands for resources and where they needed to create their first line of defence. Fortifications and garrisons provided an opportunity for large-scale mapping of border regions and mountain passes.

Mapping the Classical World

If locating the present came to be of greater importance to politicians and estate-owners and of interest to readers, the same was also true of the past. Maps came to play an integral role in the presentation of the past, indeed to be a way in which the past could be presented. In addition, knowledge of the world of the Bible and the Classics remained a vital aspect of genteel education and cartography was increasingly seen as an aid to knowledge. Maps of the biblical world were presented in this light and some important works were produced, including *Paläestina ex monumentis veteribus illustrata* (Utrecht, 1714) by the Utrecht professor of Oriental languages and religious history, Adrian Reland, and the *Heilige Geographie of aardryckskundige Beschryving van alle de Landen, enz in de H.S. Voorkommende* (Utrecht, 1758) by Albert Bachien, a military chaplain.[53]

A pedagogic emphasis characterized the historical atlases of the Classical world. The preface to *Geographia Classica. The Geography of the Ancients, So Far Describ'd As It Is Contained in the Greek and Latin Classicks. In Twenty-Nine Maps of the Old World, and its Several Kingdoms and Provinces: Wherein the Chief Places Mentioned in Homer, Virgil, Ovid, Lucan, Eutropius, Cornelius Nepos, Justin, Quintus Curtius, Sallust, Livy, Caesar, Plutarch, Xenophon, Herodotus, and Many Other Ancient Authors Are Described. To Which Is Added, a Map of the Places Mentioned in the Old and New Testaments. A Collection Long Wanted, and Now Published for the Use of Schools* (London, 1712) declared:

> if a Master was to describe to his Scholar, from his Virgil, the Navigation of Aeneas . . . [it] can only be made intelligible . . . in a Map . . . [It] will make the Reading their Authors less tedious and more profitable to them, since they will not only with more Distinction apprehend the Matters their Authors treat of, but with reasonable Exactness judge of the Actions described by them, when . . . they have a tolerable Notion of the Countries through which their Armies are said to pass.[54]

The emphasis in the preface on the low price of the work reflected the extent to which the pedagogic purpose of this atlas, like many other later historical atlases, led it to have a different commercial rationale to that of non-educational works.

The *Atlas historique* (Amsterdam, 1705) of Henri Abraham Châtelain (though also attributed to Zacharias Châtelain), dedicated to John 1st Duke of Marlborough, referred in its preface both to the public desire for knowledge and to the inseparable nature of geography and history, adding 'La Carte est un secours que l'on fournit par les yeux à l'imagination' ('The map is a help provided to the imagination through the eyes'). The atlas contained much text and many genealogical charts and one of its maps, entitled 'Plan de l'Histoire Universelle', wrongly included Persia and Poland in the Roman empire. However, the atlas was not restricted to the ancient world. There were maps of the Spanish empire, France and the Low Countries, the last locating battles from the sixteenth century on. This was the first atlas with the title *Atlas historique*.

There were both more atlases of the Classical period and more general historical atlases in the eighteenth century than ever before. The *Geographia Classica* obviously met a demand, for it reached an eighth edition in 1747. The Classical scholar Samuel Patrick (1684–1748) edited Cellarius's *Nucleus Geographiae Antiquae et Novae* (Jena, 1676) as *Geographia Antiqua* (London, 1731) and this Classical atlas enjoyed a long life, with eight London reprints by 1812. However, it was not without serious error: the map of Britain had the Antonine wall too far south. The 1789 edition of *Geographia Antiqua* was described as 'designed for the Use of Schools, and of Gentlemen who make the Ancient Writers their Delight or Study'.

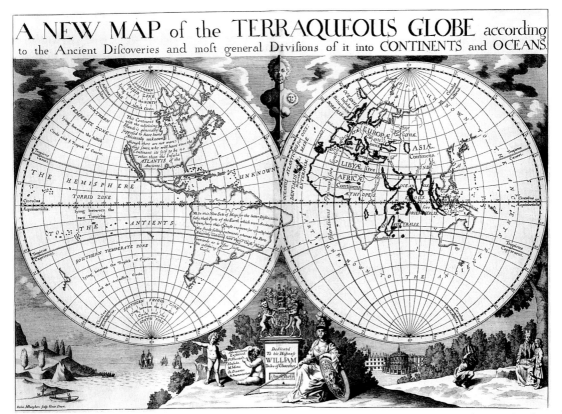

3. Comparisons of ancient and contemporary were common in early-modern European culture. In his *New Set of Maps Both of Antient and Present Geography* (Oxford, 1700), Edward Wells revealed contemporary knowledge as being far more extensive. An entire hemisphere was 'unknown to the Antients' unless North America was their Atlantis. Even so, the Ancients could not map it, whereas the Moderns could. California was believed to be an island.

Similarly, the works of Edward Wells (1667–1727), an Oxford academic who was very interested in geography, went through several editions. His *Treatise of Antient and Present Geography, Together with a Sett of Maps in Folio*, first published in Oxford in 1701, appeared in a fifth edition in 1738; his *Historical Geography of the New Testament . . . Adorned with Maps* (London, 1708) in a third in 1718. Wells's *New Set of Maps Both of Antient and Present Geography* (Oxford, 1700), dedicated to Princess Anne's son, the Duke of Gloucester, had pedagogic purposes as the full title made clear: '*the most remarkable differences of antient and present geography may be quickly discerned by a bare inspection or comparing of correspondent maps; which seems to be the most natural and easy method to teach young students.*' Thus, in the first map, one of the world, 'those parts of the Earth which were anciently known, have their coasts engraven (as usually) with the shade falling outwards whereas the parts anciently unknown have their coasts shaded inwards'. Like most mappers of the Holy Land, Wells had never visited it.[55]

The Dutch cartographer Hermann Moll, who settled in London at the end of the seventeenth century, published a large number of maps of the contemporary world and two important works that ranged more widely. The *Atlas geographus . . . Ancient and Modern* appeared in five volumes in 1711–17. *Thirty-Two New and Accurate Maps of the Geography of the Ancients* was published in Latin and English versions in 1721 and later editions followed in 1721, 1732 and 1739.

The impact of individual works was increased by translation. *A Compleat Body of Ancient Geography, Both Sacred and Profane; Exhibiting the Various Empires, Kingdoms, Principalities, and Commonwealths, throughout the Known World, in Fifty-Two Maps, Selected from the Best Authors* (The Hague, 1741) was the translation of the Latin work by Joannes Janssonius and Georg Hornius. It covered the history of the world from its origins to the fall of the Roman empire and noted the extent to which cartography offered the possibility of enlarging human understanding: 'the whole Terrestrial Globe, however unmeasurable and inexplicable it may seem to be, is now by the art and dexterity of geographers clearly and distinctly represented within the narrow bounds of a small map.'[56] The work was also published in French at The Hague in the same year as *Description exacte de l'univers, ou l'ancienne géographie sacrée et profane*.

A number of important works appeared on the continent, including the *Descriptio orbis antiqui in XLIV tabulis exhibita* (Nuremberg, 1724) by Johann David Köhler (1684–1755), professor at Altdorf and from 1735 the first Professor of History at Göttingen, and Christoph Weigel. They provided detailed maps of the ancient world. In 1757 *Twelve Maps of Ancient Geography Drawn by the Sieur d'Anville*, originally published by Jean Baptiste Bourguignon d'Anville (1697–1782) in Paris in 1738–40 as part of a multi-volume study of ancient history, appeared as a single work in London. The title-page referred to the value of such a work for understanding modern Classical scholarship: 'Being useful and necessary for the readers of the several editions of Mr. Rollin's *Ancient History*, and all other writers on that subject.' D'Anville followed a scholarly approach in his mapping of the past, which was reflected in his *Dissertation sur l'étendue de l'ancienne Jérusalem et de son Temple, et sur les mesures hebraïques de longueur* (Paris, 1747), *Traité des mesures itinéraires anciennes et modernes* (Paris, 1769) and *Géographie ancienne abrégée* (Paris, 1782). D'Anville's work led to the appearance in Nuremberg, a major centre of cartographic publication, of the *Atlas antiquus Danvillianus* (1784) and the *Atlas antiquus Danvillianus minor* (1798). The English edition of his work was still being reprinted in the early nineteenth century.

The increasing number of titles was demonstrated by the case of Britain. In London *Geographia antiqua delineata*, designed for 'the use of schools', was published in 1775, and a *Complete Body of Ancient Geography* in 1795. The former, engraved by the prominent London map engraver Thomas Jefferys, emphasized the need for maps to explain the Classics, but, like so many other works, offered no sources for its 31 maps. These atlases were followed in 1797 by an *Atlas Classica*, which included a map of the boundaries and sites of battles of Saxon England. *Bowles's Geographia Classica*, 'principally designed for the use of schools', was published in London in about 1790 by Bowles and Carver, the map and print warehouse in St Paul's Churchyard. Its 32 maps were largely based on those of Moll, though the map of 'Ancient Asia' after the Flood, which illustrated the initial habitations of Noah's descendants, was based on a map by the antiquarian William Stukeley.

Antiquarian research led to the production of a number of individual maps. Stukeley, who greatly developed British field archaeology, produced *Ingratiam itinerantium curiosorum Antonini Aug. itinerarium per Britanniam* (London, 1723) and *An Account of Richard of Cirencester . . . with his Antient Map of Roman Brittain . . . the Itinerary thereof* (London, 1757). The latter was unwittingly based on the forgeries of Charles Bertram (1723–65), a London-born English teacher in the school for naval cadets in Copenhagen, whose work was accepted as a major source on the Roman geography of Britain until the late nineteenth century, and was published as one of the *Six English Chronicles* (1872) in Bohn's 'Antiquarian Library'. Bertram's other works included a Danish translation of *On the Great Advantages of a Godly Life* (1760).

John Horsley (1685–1732), a Northumbrian archaeologist, Presbyterian minister and teacher, was fortunate in not being the victim of such trickery. He produced a map of Roman Britain, showing roads, tribes, towns and mountains, as part of his *Britannia Romana* (1732), and it was reproduced by d'Anville in 1775. William Roy (1726–90), who played a major role in the mapping of Britain, also carried out archaeological research on the Roman period that led him to produce a number of maps, including one of north Britain in the Roman period.[57] The active and wideranging writer, John Andrews, followed with his map *Roman Britain Collected from Ptolemy Antonines Itinerary* (1797), and a year later another map appeared, *Roman Britain according to Antonius, Ptolemy and the Discoveries of Modern Times* by the antiquarian cleric Thomas Reynolds.

Guillaume Delisle (1675–1726), a leading French mapmaker, produced a number of important maps of Classical themes based on his scholarly knowledge of the period, including *Theatrum Historicum ad Annum Christi 400* (Paris, 1705) and *Orbis Romani descriptio seu divisio per themata post Heraclii tempora* (Paris, 1711). The first was the sole map to appear in what was intended to be a historical atlas of Europe and western Asia in seven maps. Increasingly, Europe, particularly western Europe was being mapped in some detail for the Classical period. Thus, the roads, towns, rivers and mountains of western Iberia in the Roman era were mapped in the *Mapa de la Lusitania antiqua, con su correspondencia moderna* (Madrid, 1789). Maps complemented illustrations. Thanks to both, the Classical world was grasped in increasingly graphic ways.

The Post-Classical World

Though ancient geography and its mapping remained prestigious scientific pursuits, there were also more moves to map the post-Classical world, not least because of the growing interest in medieval geography and history. This represented an important lessening of the imaginative grip of the Ancient world. Cellarius wished to give his *Notitia Orbis Antiqui* (Leipzig, 1701–6) a continuation into the Middle Ages, a period that he played a role in naming. A set of maps was accordingly drawn and engraved by the Nuremberg cartographer J.B. Homann, but there was no text when Cellarius died in 1707. Homann's plates were not published until 1776 when they were included as part of the *Appendix triplex notitiae orbis antiqui Christophori Cellarii* (Leipzig). His treatments of the medieval period, such as maps of Germania and Belgia, were unsuccessful. Köhler began a continuation of his Classical atlas but, finding it too great a project, instead began a *Kurtze und gründliche Anleitung zu der alten und mittleren Geographie nebst XII. Land Chärtgen (Compendium geographiae antiquae et mediae)* (Nuremberg, 1730–65). This 'Brief and Thorough Introduction to Ancient and Medieval Geography' comprised 39 small maps, of which twelve covered the medieval period, though in no particular order.

Johann Matthias Hase or Haas (1684–1742), Professor of Mathematics at Wittenberg, was a better cartographer, who also made several important innovations. In 1728 he set out his plan for a historical atlas and in 1743, the year after his death, his *Historia universalis politica, Part 3, Tabulae geographicae . . . de summis imperiis* (Nuremberg) appeared. Hase was interested in the theme of empires and continued it until the modern European empires. Thus, there was coverage of ancient empires, including those of Egypt, Assyria, Persia under Darius, Alexander the Great, Parthia and Rome, the last in three maps; as well as of the rise of Islamic power and the empire of Charlemagne and several maps on the history of the Holy Roman (medieval German) Empire from the reign of Otto I in the tenth century to the death of Charles VI in 1740. The emphasis on Islamic empires was novel, as was the mapping of Byzantium under Justinian. Hase's maps also spanned the Eurasian world: far from being restricted to the Classical world, the atlas also included the Mongols, for example. A collection of Hase's historical maps of the Holy Roman Empire was published as *Mappae VII geographicae pro illustrandis totidem periodis historiae Germaniae* (Nuremberg, 1750) and this can be seen as the first atlas of German history. The collection of Hase's historical maps, the *Atlas historicus comprehendens imperia maxima seu monarchias orbis antiqui historice, chronologice et geographice repraesentatas*, published in Nuremberg in 1750, was reprinted as late as 1813–14.[58]

At about the same time, the *Atlas complet des révolutions que le globe de la terre a éprouvées depuis le commencement du monde jusqu'à présent* was drafted in Paris. This work, of which the common attribution to Gilles Robert de Vaugondy has recently been rejected,[59] consisted of 66 maps. Based on the same outline plan, they provided a history of territorial control organized by chronological sequence rather than by geographical area or theme. The series was also right up to date, going from the dispersal of Noah's children to the 1737 acquisition of Lorraine by the father-in-law of Louis XV of France. Each double-folio map showed Eurasia from Britain to Korea, and each map was followed by text. Despite the coverage of the eighteenth century, the chronological emphasis was not modern: 31 of the maps were devoted to the medieval period.[60]

A similar plan was adopted by Lunceau de Boisgermain in his *Atlas historique, ou cartes des parties principales du globe terrestre, assujetties aux révolutions séculaires qu'il a éprouvées pour servir à l'histoire des temps qui ont suivi la Création* (Paris, 1760–1). This was projected as a twenty-map work, though Boisgermain only produced three. This work was followed by *Les Révolutions de l'univers offrant les divisions politiques des différentes régions* (Paris, 1763): all the maps in it had a common base designed by Michel Picaud that stretched over two folios and covered England to Japan. Both this and the work by Boisgermain contained very little after 1500, while the *Complete Body of Ancient Geography by Monsr. D'Anville* (London, 1795) contained only one map depicting western Europe 'in an intermediate state, between Ancient and Modern Geography'.

Les Révolutions de l'univers contained 30 maps and covered history from the dispersal of Noah's children to the 'réunion' of Lorraine to France. The atlas was related to the draft *Atlas complet des révolutions*. The pseudonymous author 'Dupré' has been identified as Philippe de Prétot, although Walter Goffart has cast doubt on this.[61] The atlas presented geography as the servant of history: 'La Géographie est principalement utile pour la lecture et l'étude de l'Histoire.' The scope of the atlas was Eurocentric in that, although the maps included Asia, the intention was to cover history as understood by Europeans: 'toute la partie de l'ancien continent qui a été le théâtre des révolutions que l'Histoire ancienne et moderne nous présent'. The preface to the atlas was also interesting because it commented on two earlier efforts.

The largely abortive historical atlas by Delisle was criticized because the maps were only intended to cover up to 90°E, thus excluding the Orient. Hase's work was criticized because the maps were in quarto and therefore too small, because they did not extend to cover the Orient and because there was no common base map. Seeking to take the whole of human history as its subject – from biblical origins to the modern day – the atlas put an emphasis on continual change that contrasted greatly with the more static nature of traditional atlases of biblical and Classical history.

Köhler's successor at Göttingen, Johann Christoff Gatterer, produced maps and an historical atlas to assist his students in the 1770s. He devoted particular attention to the medieval period, and was especially interested in the Asiatic powers that invaded Europe. Gatterer was far from Eurocentric and ignored modern history, producing no maps on the period after 1517.[62] This accorded with the emphasis in German teaching at this period. More generally, scholars tended to avoid the recent past. Thomas Pelham wrote to his father in 1776 of 'a kind of modern history which historians have not yet come down to' and the following year Professor Pestel told Philip Yorke that he wished to teach him what was 'not to be found in any book that he knows of, which was to give a sort of system of policy and of the present Balance of Europe, drawn from the facts that have happened since the period mentioned [1648], a study which he says is entirely new, and not followed in our universities'.[63]

Historical mapping was not only carried on at the global, or at least Eurasian, scale. A map of England in the post-Roman period, dedicated to the Duke of Gloucester, was published by Christopher Browne in 1700 (later states of it were issued in 1735, 1760 and 1770). The map showed the 'ancient and present government being divided as in the Saxon-Heptarchy also into dioceses, judges-circuits and counties' as well as the sites of major battles. A series of eight maps of Paris, all on the same scale and in chronological order, showing its development from Roman *Lutetia* until the seventeenth century, was published in Nicolas de La Mare's *Traité de la police . . . on y a joint une description historique et topographique de Paris et huit plans gravés* (Paris, 1705). These maps have also been attributed to Nicolas de Fer. The most ambitious regional historical atlas in the period was by Menso Alting (1636–1713), Burgomaster of Groningen. In 1697 and 1701 he published a fourteen-map, two-part historical atlas of the United Provinces from the first century BC until after the major North Sea floods of the thirteenth century.[64] This gave a sense of continuity to a polity that in fact was a sixteenth-century creation. Maps of the United Provinces prior to that did not correspond to any political reality.

Matthäus Seutter's *Historia Circuli Bavarici* (Augsburg, 1745) employed a number key for its map of Bavaria in order to depict what had happened in its history. A more politically pointed map appeared eleven years later when Britain and France went to war: *A Map of the Antient Dominions of the Kings of England in France* (London, 1756). This only depicted boundaries, but that was all that was required to make the point that the British monarchy, which still claimed the throne of France, had once found the Channel no hindrance to its ambitions. A black and white map of *Norvegia Antiqua* by G. Schönning was published in Copenhagen in 1779. It depicted places, rivers and provincial boundaries, but made no reference to the date of what was being depicted and offered no suggestions of change through time. A similar problem affected Robert's undated map of 'Germanie Ancienne', covering the area from

Belgrade to the Low Countries. This depicted rivers, hills and boundaries, but there was no guide to chronology and the map simultaneously presented political situations widely different in time without acknowledging the fact.

The first historical atlas of France, the *Atlas historique et géographique de la France ancienne et moderne* by the Paduan mapmaker Giovanni Antonio Rizzi-Zannoni (1736–1814), was published in Paris in 1764; a quarto version followed the octavo original in 1765. There was no other such atlas for another half century. The atlas covered French history in 60 maps, providing the best coverage of the history of any eighteenth-century country: Hase, in contrast, had devoted only seven maps to Germany. The expansion of France was presented in a positive light, and Rizzi-Zannoni covered recent events. Thus the map of contemporary France bore the title, 'La France Renaissante sous le Règne heureux de Louis XV le Bien-Aimé' (France reborn under the happy reign of Louis XV, the Well-Beloved). This did not prevent Rizzi-Zannoni from defrauding the government.[65] A single-sheet map of France during the reign of Henri IV (1589–1610), published in Paris in 1787, used colour to depict Henri's patrimonial domain and also foreign enclaves within France, and provided a fair amount of detail on the warfare of the period.

In 1797 John Andrews produced a work that, as with so many eighteenth- and nineteenth-century historical atlases, failed to live up to its title, *Historical Atlas of England; Physical, Political, Astronomical, Civil and Ecclesiastical, Biographical, Naval, Parliamentary, and Geographical; Ancient and Modern; from the Deluge to the Present Time.* The Introduction stated that 'Those unacquainted with Geography can never form a proper judgment of the facts recorded in history, as they must strike the mind in a confused manner, without order and without connection.' Historical atlases were necessary to 'give a clear view of all those places which are most distinguished in a history of this country'. Yet only four of the thirteen plates were historical; the rest dealt with physical and ecclesiastical topics. There were maps of the Ancient Britons, Roman Britain, Saxon Britain and Britain at the time of the Danelaw, but nothing later.

Though limited, Andrews's atlas was very different from the maps of Speed. Decorative details had been reduced: historical atlases had changed. They were affected by the same processes that affected non-historical counterparts: the desire to appear scientific, to separate the map from its decoration.[66] The increased use of colour also affected different types of mapping. Johannes Hubner (1668–1731), rector of the Johanneum in Hamburg, is said to have originated the idea that the lands ruled by the same monarch or republic should be painted in the same colour. The purpose was didactic-historical, rather than didactic-geographical. Since the maps were intended to illustrate history, by clarifying the territories of particular princely dynasties, toponymy and, to an extent, topography were neglected. Quite often lesser towns and villages on, for example, the maps of the leading German carto-graphic producer – Homann of Nuremberg – are identified only by the first letter of their name so as not to clutter the map and obscure the name of the larger territorial unit. By contrast, eighteenth-century French and English maps tended to colour only the borders of territories and not the territories themselves.

The Mapping of Frontiers

With his maps of the expansion both of France and of the French royal domain,

Rizzi-Zannoni clearly embraced the frontier line. He did so without any difficulty, partly because of the scale he was employing and partly because of increasing confidence in the drawing of lines on maps. As so often, historical mapping reflected contemporary mapping. The idea of natural frontiers – readily grasped geographical entities, principally mountains and rivers – became an established aspect of geographical description and political discussion, though the selection of such frontiers was not free from serious problems. Rivers were not yet generally canalized, as so many were to be in the nineteenth century. Their courses shifted, islands were created and disappeared, and river courses could be affected by drainage works. Rivers were, however, extensively used as the basis for frontiers. At the end of the Russo-Swedish war of 1741–43 Russia, by the Treaty of Åbo, secured a triangular slice of south-east Finland, based on a new river line. The Swedo-Finnish boundary at the head of the Bothnian Gulf remained on the line of the Kemijoki until 1809 when the Russians pushed it west to the Tornionioki. River lines including the Dvina, Niemen, Bug and Vistula were used in the three partitions of Poland in 1772, 1793 and 1795.

Defining mountainous frontiers could be difficult, not least because it was unclear how they should be defined. Disputes were a major theme in Franco-Savoyard negotiations after the Peace of Utrecht of 1713. The Convention of Paris of 1718 left several issues outstanding. Negotiations in the late 1750s culminating in the Treaty of Turin of 1760 marked a step forward. Eight maps, defining the watershed, played an integral role in the treaty, having the same weight as its text. Nevertheless, until the mid-nineteenth century it was very difficult to map mountainous areas. Serious problems were encountered in getting people on the mountains and there were also difficulties with topographic mapping. There was also no consistency in the depiction of topographic information.[67]

The French Revolution

The French Revolutionary and Napoleonic period lent renewed energy to mapping the contemporary world and thus provided a better base for historical mapping. The Revolution replaced jurisdictional-territorial criteria when radically redrawing frontiers within and outside France. For a society that created a new calendar and a new unit of measurement (the metre), such a spatial reinterpretation was not a surprising conception. The new political order could incorporate former frontiers as *ancien régime* polities took on a new existence – Genoa becoming the Ligurian Republic, Tuscany the Kingdom of Etruria – but even when this was the case there were modifications, while elsewhere there were major changes, especially in Germany and northern Italy. This lent renewed interest to the process of territorial change, undermining the sense of territorial continuity. New frontiers were mapped, while Napoleon's invasion of Egypt and Palestine led to the first accurate map of the region, the French army carrying out the surveying. The Napoleonic regime and its wars provided major stimuli for the detailed mapping of Europe to serve political, financial and military purposes, and to satisfy the quest for information that the regime displayed.[68] The wars also stimulated mapping by France's enemies, not least in Britain by the Board of Ordnance as concern developed about a possible French invasion.[69] In addition, mapping projects begun before the Revolution were brought to completion. A survey of Holstein, Lübeck and Hamburg, begun for administrative and taxation purposes in 1763, was published in 68 sheets between 1789 and 1806.[70]

For most Europeans, 'internal' frontiers had been as significant as their international counterparts, and they had often been difficult to distinguish, both on the ground and on maps. They had crucial judicial and financial functions. This was especially marked in western Europe, with its denser and more historical fabric of jurisdictional authorities, and the accompanying vitality of local privilege. The two types of frontiers were difficult to distinguish on seventeenth-century maps. This mental world was not to change appreciably until the impetus and focus that the French Revolution gave to nationalism altered the European political consciousness and gave renewed interest to historical mapping.

2

The Nineteenth Century

In the preface to his *Popular Atlas of Comparative Geography* (London, 1870), William Hughes wrote that the 'alliance' of history and geography 'forms the basis of the study known as "Comparative Geography," a main object of which is the exhibition of the successive changes in the distribution of states, with their attendant alterations of frontier, which are presented by a particular region of the globe, viewed at succeeding periods of time'. These changes were the major theme of nineteenth-century historical atlases. They reflected the values of the age with its emphasis on territorial power and coherent statehood. Yet, as in other periods, there was considerable variety in the types of historical atlases that were produced.

The Traditional Agenda

The Classical World

The traditional cartographic agenda remained important in the early nineteenth century. The Classical world was central not only to education but also to much else. The roles of ancient Greece and Rome in political and moral thought and as cultural beacons ensured, for example, that many of the new developments of the century sought Classical references. Thus, ancient Greek and Roman models played a role in the constitutionalism and imperialism of the period.

The Classical world continued to play a major role in historical atlases. The *Atlas de tableaux et de cartes gravé par P.F. Tardieu pour le cours complet de cosmographie, de géographie, de chronologie et d'histoire ancienne et moderne par Edme Mentelle* (2nd edn, Paris, 1804) began with a map of the world that was not specifically historical, and then offered a plate devoted to 'the world known by the ancients', a common theme, another to the Assyrian empire, which was given excessively extensive frontiers including all of Anatolia and Persia as well as Bactria, a fourth on ancient Greece, a fifth providing plans of Athens, Sparta and Syracuse, a sixth on Italia Antiqua, a seventh on Gaul, and then a shift to modern Europe with no maps covering the intervening period. The following year, however, Robert Wilkinson in his *Atlas classica* (London, 1805) added Saxon England and Charlemagne's empire to the Classical world and in the 1808 edition a map of 'The Kingdom of Jerusalem with its Environs at the time of the Crusades' appeared. The preface declared the hope that the atlas would 'be found to be a pleasing and useful addition to the library of the Divine, the Scholar, and the private Gentleman'. It was certainly seen as a successful model: another edition appeared in 1842. James Playfair, Principal of the United College, St Andrews, produced an atlas of Classical maps in 1808 to accompany his *System of Geography Ancient and Modern* (Edinburgh, 1810–14). The same maps were also used in his *New General Atlas Revised and Modern* (Edinburgh, 1822).

Works such as *Smith's Classical Atlas* (London, 1809), Christian Gottlieb Reichard's *Orbis terrarum veteribus cognitus* (1818–31), Samuel Butler's *Atlas of Ancient Geography* (London, 1822), the *New Classical and Historical Atlas* (Edinburgh, 1829), *Jones' Classical Atlas* (London, 1830), William Murphy's *Comprehensive Atlas* (Edinburgh, 1832), Aaron Arrowsmith's *Atlas of Ancient Geography* (London, 1842), *Mitchell's Ancient Atlas* (Philadelphia, 1844), James Tate Head's *First Classical Maps* (London, 1845) and *Philips' School Classical Atlas* (Liverpool, 1855) illustrate the fascination with the ancients. However, William Hughes, an active mapmaker and Professor of Geography in the College for Civil Engineers, referred in his *Illuminated Atlas of Scripture Geography* (London, 1840) to the problem with much of the mapping of the ancient world:

> The absence of a strictly chronological arrangement in the delineation of boundaries and localities has been felt as an important defect in the maps generally prepared for the illustration of ancient geography: ancient and modern, classical and scriptural, appellations have been mixed together, without regard to the period of history to which they relate in such a manner as to leave on the mind of the student no distinct impression of the actual condition of a country at any one period. Yet this synchronism of geography . . . constitutes, when presented to view, the most important guide in tracing the progress of a nation's civilisation, since without it we are unable to form an estimate of its condition either internally or with reference to other countries. It is a particular object of the present Atlas to preserve this, by successively delineating the Holy Land . . .[1]

Hughes's criticism was a fair one and many of the Classical atlases offered little more than maps of, for example, ancient Gaul that showed rivers, places and (dateless) boundaries, but without any suggestion of chronological development. Their principal purpose was to display the location of places prominent in Classical works, often with direct comparisons with modern names. This was explicit in such works as Aaron Arrowsmith's *Orbis Terrarum Veteribus Noti Descriptio. A Comparative Atlas of Ancient and Modern Geography* (London, 1828). As with a number of Classical atlases, the pedagogic purpose of this work was directly linked to a particular institution. Its title page declared that it was 'for the use of Eton School' and it was indeed dedicated to the headmaster. Arrowsmith also produced *An Atlas of Ancient Geography; For the Use of King's College School* (London, 1842).

The *Harrow Atlas of Classical Geography* was published in 1857, one of the publishers being Crossley and Clarke, the school bookseller. There was also a junior version. The atlas drew attention to the problems of the available sources. The second map, devoted to the 'world as known to the Ancients. The East', carried with it a warning: 'Scythia was inhabited by various nomad nations, whose names cannot be placed in a map with any accuracy. Many of the names of these nations given by ancient authors are fabulous. The ancients were not aware that the Sea of Aral was distinct from the Caspian.' There was a note on map 20, that of Egypt: 'A long list of names is given by Ptolemy and Pliny of places south of Syene and of the Great Cataract: they are not inserted here, as it appears impossible to show to what modern positions they correspond.'

James Tate Head, Headmaster of Richmond Grammar School, emphasized educational purposes in his *First Classical Maps* (London, 1845). The preface explained the principles underlying the maps and the way in which lettering in particular was used:

> It is the particular object of the following maps prominently to exhibit those places, and those only, which possess a leading interest in the ancient history of Greece and Rome and their principal connections and dependencies: and, by rendering very conspicuous the great outlines and natural features of each country, to invite the eye and the attention to its more important localities. With this view, (after a free erasure of other names,) the towns and rivers, etc. of primary importance have been marked by dark capital letters: open capitals are used to designate the countries themselves and their larger districts. Other places of consequence or interest from various causes, as for instance the birth of distinguished men, have been given in italics, greater or less, as the case seemed to require.

Head criticized the absence of such a selection and ordering in other atlases:

> It is very certain, that the young Classical scholar is seriously discouraged from consulting his maps, by the difficulty with which (even if latitude and longitude be supplied) he detects the position of any required place; crowded as the surface is with names of apparently equal importance, though possessing no interest whatever to him either naturally or historically.

Head made the Mediterranean more conspicuous 'by a deeper and broader line of coasts' and even took advantage of the central fold 'for pointing out the division of the Roman Empire into its Eastern and Western portions, – a division not merely geographical, nor of fanciful value, when we take into account the essential difference of character between the one class of nations and the other – of the two portions'.

The Reverend George Butler's *Public Schools Atlas of Ancient Geography* (London, 1877) was specifically designed to help those reading Classical authors. He explained the particular value of his work for pupils trying to follow campaigns:

> In studying the history of any great campaign, such as Caesar's Gallic Wars, a very good general knowledge of the geography of the country can be obtained by any boy who will take the trouble to work out the details of the campaign with his Ancient Atlas before him, and the corresponding map in the Modern Atlas at hand for purposes of reference. If the habit of tracing on a map the movements of armies be once acquired, historical details will readily fix themselves on the memory. Without the assistance of the eye the memory will very soon throw off the burden of details which have never been really comprehended and studied intelligently.

The growth of research into the Classical world, not least archaeological investigations, ensured that considerable advances were made in the interpretation of the period. An increase in the amount of information available was accompanied by a greater ability, and to some extent willingness, to judge it and to differentiate the material, creating a categorization in terms of 'reliable' and 'less certain'. For example, Charles Newton of the British Museum prepared a fold-out map of *British and Roman Yorkshire* that was published by the Archaeological Institute of Great Britain and Ireland in 1847. This distinguished between 'ascertained Roman roads', 'ancient roads of which the general direction has been ascertained, but which have not been accurately traced throughout', and supposed lines of ancient roads. Similarly, 'ascertained' Roman stations were distinguished from doubtful ones. This provided both a challenge and an opportunity for the mapmakers. In 1867 Alexander Keith Johnston produced a new edition of his *School Atlas of Classical Geography* (Edinburgh, 1867). The extended title referred to it as 'embodying the results of the most recent investigations' and the preface claimed that 'Recent researches and investigations have so widely extended and modified our knowledge of Classical Geography, as to demand the construction of an entirely new series of maps'. Part of the new work was possible thanks to the help of William Ewart Gladstone, Chancellor of the Exchequer 1852–55 and 1859–66, leader of the Liberal party from 1867, and future Prime Minister. Gladstone was a noted Classical scholar and author of three books on Homer. One was the source of Johnston's 'Map of the Outer Geography of the Odyssey', and the book was also used for two of the maps of Greece, but Gladstone was no mere passive source. As the preface noted, he had 'enhanced the favour by revising the proof-sheets of the plates and text, as adapted for this Atlas'. Scholarship was also reflected in the map of Roman Britain in Charles Pearson's *Historical Maps of England* (London, 1869), where the author offered the observation: 'Compared with most existing maps, mine of Roman Britain will appear very bare of names; as I have not felt warranted in giving a local habitation to tribes whose limits I was unable to determine.'[2] Pearson had been Professor of Modern History at King's College, London.

In William Murphy's *Comprehensive Classical Atlas* (Edinburgh, 1832), dedicated to the rectors and masters of the High School and New Academy of Edinburgh, the preface acknowledged the role of James Rennell in 'advancing the knowledge of Ancient Geography'. Rennell (1742–1830) worked as many years as Surveyor-General of the East India Company's possessions in Bengal before turning to the geography of Herodotus, leading eventually to his *Treatise on the Comparative Geography of Western Asia* (London, 1831). Rennell became the leading British geographer in the decade after Sir Joseph Banks's death in 1820, and was as interested in Classical geography, publishing for example on Babylon, Troy and the march of the Ten Thousand, as in the study of winds and currents. However the 'advancement' of knowledge was affected by the habit of seeing the past in the light of the present. Thus, for example, the Hellenistic world was identified with the world of modern Europe in the age of its colonial empires.[3]

Some atlases still appeared in which the sole maps devoted to history treated the Classical world. This was true for example of J. Andriveau-Goujon's *Atlas classique et universel de géographie ancienne et moderne* (Paris, 1856). Maps of the Classical world dominated other atlases, sometimes as a result of the continued role of the Classics in education. This was true of five of the six historical maps in the *Atlas géographique et historique à l'usage de la classe de quatrième* (2nd edn, Paris, 1878) by F. Oger,

Professor of History and Geography at the Collège Saint-Barbe. The other map, placed first, was an historical map of France showing its provinces and departments.

The Berlin scholar Heinrich Kiepert (1818–99) was responsible for a number of works including the *Topographisch-historischer Atlas von Hellas und den hellenischen Colonien* (Berlin, 1841–46), the *Historisch-geographischer Atlas der alten Welt* (Weimar, 1848) and *Acht Karten zur alten Geschichte* (Berlin, 1859). The 1870s saw important advances in British mapping of the Ancient world. This was largely due to the distinguished Classical and biblical scholar William Smith (1813–93), who was responsible for two works published in 1874. The first, *Dr. William Smith's Ancient Atlas. An Atlas of Ancient Geography* (London, 1874), provided extensive notes on the sources for each map which even extended to pointing out the limitations of the sources. For example, that on 'Hispania' observed:

> It is extremely difficult to construct an accurate and tolerably complete map of ancient Spain, for the topographical statements of Strabo and Mela are generally confined to the coast districts; Pliny gives statistical surveys and in part alphabetical lists of towns rather than topographically arranged materials. Ptolemy's map, on the other hand, is evidently full of great errors, so that those places which are based on its authority alone must always be very uncertain. We are, therefore, here more than elsewhere dependent upon the Itineraries, the ruins, and the inscriptions . . . forged inscriptions . . . the recent maps of modern Spain are not altogether to be depended upon . . . they frequently differ from one another.[4]

An Atlas of Ancient Geography, Biblical and Classical, to Illustrate the Dictionary of the Bible and the Classical Dictionaries appeared the same year. This major work, with 43 maps, was edited by Smith and George Grove.[5] Grove was Secretary of the Palestine Exploration Fund and author of the articles on biblical topography in Smith's *Dictionary of the Bible*. The Classical maps were drawn by Charles Müller, their biblical counterparts by Trelawny Saunders. Another edition followed in 1875. Smith's preface to the 1874 edition emphasized the novelty of the work and stressed the importance of providing precise locations and geographical information:

> This Atlas, the preparation and execution of which have occupied eighteen years, is the first attempt, either in this country or on the continent, to give a complete set of maps of the Ancient World on a scale corresponding in size to the best Atlases of modern geography. The large size of the present maps allows space for exhibiting the natural features of each country, and for adding, wherever it was possible, the modern names underneath the ancient ones. This combination of ancient and modern names, which is a distinctive feature in the present Atlas, is of the greatest assistance in understanding ancient geography, and ascertaining the exact sites. A comparison of maps of the modern world with those of antiquity, even if both are executed on the same scale, is always troublesome and often useless, since ancient geography, in many cases, has to take notice of insignificant modern villages and ruins, which are of no importance in the present day, and are consequently not marked in the ordinary maps.

Smith offered an instructive contrast of the new work with its most illustrious predecessor, one that not only indicated his own intentions, but also helped to establish a typology of approaches in historical cartography:

The only large Atlas hitherto published, comprising the whole domain of ancient geography is Spruner's 'Atlas Antiquus,' in thirty-one maps, improved by Menke (Gotha, 1865). But this Atlas is constructed on an entirely different plan from the present one, besides being on a smaller scale. Only a limited portion of it is devoted to the geographical representation of particular countries: by far the larger part contains maps exhibiting historical surveys at particular periods, and small supplementary charts of certain epochs of ancient history. The number of such historical maps might be increased indefinitely, without adding in any way to the scientific value of an Atlas. For on the one hand the historical changes in the distribution of countries are so simple that no special maps are needed to understand them; and, on the other hand, it happens only rarely that the geographical data concerning the political relations of certain historical periods have been handed down to us in sufficient completeness to enable us to give a correct picture of them in a map. Such maps, therefore, always contain much that depends upon the mere conjectures of their authors, and, consequently, are often more misleading than trustworthy as guides. In the present Atlas each country is delineated in a separate map on a large scale; but we have also given in addition a sufficient number of Historical Maps on a smaller scale . . .

Smith also directed attention to the sources used: 'The cartographical part of the Classical Atlas is based, first, upon Strabo, the text of which has been much improved in the edition . . . by Müller . . . secondly upon the improved edition of the Geographi Minores . . . by the same editor' and so on. Müller's work on Ptolemy was also cited as a source in avoiding the errors of earlier works. The map of India was prepared by Henry Yule, the much-travelled editor of Marco Polo's writings. George Butler's introduction to his *Public Schools Atlas of Ancient Geography* referred to the numerous recent works that reference had been made to: Forbiger's *Handbuch der alten Geographie* (Leipzig, 1848), Spruner's historical atlas, Kiepert's *Hellas* and *Atlas Antiquus*, John Cramer's map of Italy (Cramer published his *Description of Ancient Italy* in 1826), William Smith's *Dictionary of Greek and Roman Geography* (London, 1854) and his *Student's Manual of Ancient Geography* (London, 1861) and H.F. Tozer's *Geography of Greece* (London, 1873).

Research-based maps of the Classical world continued to appear in the closing decades of the century. They reflected the development of archaeology and also the rising numbers in the academic profession. Important works included the series *Forma urbis Romae*, maps of Rome and ancient Italy, that appeared in 1893–1901.

Mapping the Bible

By the second half of the century biblical atlases had benefited greatly from archaeological research in Palestine and their topography was increasingly precise. Major works included Richard Palmer's *The Bible Atlas or Sacred Geography Delineated in a Complete Series of Scriptural Maps* (London, 1823), Samuel Arrowsmith's *Bible Atlas* (London, 1835), Heinrich Kiepert's *Bibelatlas nach den neuesten und besten Hilfsquellen gezeichnet* (Berlin, 1847), Richard Riess's *Die Länder der Heiligen Schrift. Historisch-geographischer Bibelatlas* (Freiburg, 1864), Theodor Menke's *Bibelatlas in acht Blättern* (Gotha, 1868) and Hermann Guthe's *Bibel Atlas in 21 Haupt-und 30 Nebenkarten* (Leipzig, 1911).[6] Such works enjoyed considerable sales and influence, an achievement assisted by translations. Palmer's atlas, for example, appeared in a German edition and Kiepert's was published in London as *The New Biblical Atlas and Scripture Gazetteer* (1852).

Historical atlases of the Bible were found in the Protestant more than the Catholic, let alone the Orthodox, world. The Anglo-German relationship was related to the increasing emphasis on the study of the Bible in a way that challenged the literal inspiration of scripture and the influence of German Protestant biblical scholarship in Britain. David Friedrich Strauss contradicted the historicity of super-natural elements in the gospels in his *Das Leben Jesu* (Tübingen, 1835–36), a work translated by the English novelist George Eliot as *The Life of Jesus, Critically Examined by Dr. David Strauss* (London, 1846). There was a clear cartographic dimension to the enterprise of directing scholarship to establishing and demonstrating the truth of scripture, and yet also a ready market among readers who lacked any interest in scholarly controversy. The introduction to *Wyld's Scripture Atlas* (London, no date), by the geographer James Wyld (1790–1836),claimed:

> The Reader of the Bible may here trace the wanderings of the early patriarchs of the Hebrew race, mark the traditional sites of their encampments and dwelling-places, or the hallowed spots in which their remains reposed in death, and note the reputed scenes of the numerous battles and other thrilling events which impart so much of human interest to the inspired records. It is believed that even in the present age of critical (and often of sceptical) inquiry, these qualities will be found to possess sufficient attraction for the simply devotional readers of the Bible, to justify the publishers in the reissue of a work which thus identifies locally every place mentioned in the Sacred Narrative, and exhibits with topographical precision at least the supposed scenes of the most deeply-impressive events in the history of mankind.

The pedagogic role of the Bible was also reflected in historical maps, such as Creighton's *New Historical Map of Palestine* (London, 1831), a fold-out sheet without text depicting the boundaries of the twelve tribes, the Exodus, cities and forts, and the thirteen maps in the *Wall Maps of Scripture History* published by the Edinburgh map-publishers W. and A.K. Johnston in the 1860s.

The variety of biblical atlases, their complex typology, was obviously present in the nineteenth century. Old works could be reprinted with little or no reference to scholarly advances. Thus in 1835 the Society for Promoting Christian Knowledge published a new edition of Edward Wells's *Historical Geography of the New Testament . . . Adorned with Maps* of 1708; the work had been reprinted, with his Old Testament volume, in 1801, and again in 1809. Yet there was also, particularly in the second half of the century, a strong wish to incorporate recent biblical scholarship and, therefore, an emphasis on the most recent discoveries and discussions. William Hughes emphasized the value of increased information in the introduction to his *Illuminated Atlas of Scripture Geography* (London, 1840). The researches of Edward Robinson, Professor of Biblical Literature at New York Union Theological Seminary, influenced the work of Kiepert. Archaeological and topographical studies in the field added to the available information immeasurably.

Archaeological information greatly increased as a result of the work of Captain, later Field Marshal, Kitchener and Captain Conder of the Royal Engineers, who were sent in 1871 by the Palestine Exploration Fund of London to make a survey and to collect information relevant to the Bible. They mapped the Holy Land west of the Jordan and also recorded the names and described the visible remains of several thousand sites; many were successfully identified with biblical sites.[7] In 1881 the Palestine Exploration Fund published a *Map of Western Palestine* in 26 sheets.

William Smith's preface to the *Atlas of Ancient Geography, Biblical and Classical* (London, 1874) stressed again the value of detailed information – the crucial combination of scale and precision – and the degree to which recent research had transformed the situation:

> Biblical Atlases certainly exist, but they are so small in size, or so imperfect in execution, or so often framed for the support of private theories, that no examination of the topography can be obtained from them adequate to the present demands of Biblical study, which, in the case of the Holy Land, often depends for its results on the power of comparing very minute points. And, in addition to this, it is only within a recent date that any really accurate information as to the geography of the Holy Land or the Peninsula of Sinai . . . has been obtainable. Less than ten years ago . . . no systematic attempt had been made to survey the country and make a map on the same scale of size or minuteness as other regions. The distance, the difficulties, even the very sacred and familiar character of the spots seemed to stand in the way. The impulse given to the study by the *Biblical Researches* of Dr. Robinson, and by the *Sinai and Palestine* of Dean Stanley, led the way first to the ordnance survey of Jerusalem, and next to the establishment of the Palestine Exploration Fund . . . and of the Sinai Exploration Society, whose survey is completed . . .
>
> In the construction of the Assyrian maps and elsewhere, use has been made, for the first time, of the Turco-Persian survey, as well as of the labours of Layard and Rawlinson . . . The map of Babylon and the surrounding district has been revised by Captain Felix Jones, the able officer who made the survey of the Tigris and Euphrates Valley.

The atlas lived up to its preface. The maps were detailed and there were notes on each. The survey referred to, however, was not the end of nineteenth-century research in Palestine. Topographical mapping was followed by increased archaeological activity. In 1890 Flinders Petrie applied to the Tell el-Hesi site his theory of the stratified formation of an ancient city mound, the first time this had been done in biblical archaeology.[8]

The interaction of advances in knowledge with the precise and controversial nature of biblical scholarship encouraged the production of weighty works that presented themselves in the context of a developing scholarly process, reflecting in prefaces and notes on the maps with reference to the limitations of the evidence. This can be seen clearly in a major work that represented the culmination of nineteenth-century scholarship in this field and, like several other such works, appeared early in the following century: a natural consequence of the time taken to produce such atlases. The preface to the *Atlas of the Historical Geography of the Holy Land* (London, 1915), by George Adam Smith, Principal of the University of Aberdeen, declared:

> The contents of an adequate Historical Atlas of any land must comprise at least the following five: –
> 1. Some representation of the world to which the land belongs. This should include the general features of that world, physical and political, and in particular should

exhibit the kingdoms and empires between which the land was placed and by which its history and culture have been most deeply influenced, along with the delineation of the main lines of its traffic with these.

2.   The general features of the physical and economic geography of the land itself, as well as the detailed representation on a large scale of its various provinces – including natural features, towns and villages, with their names at various periods, and the lines of communication between them.

3.   A succession of maps of the political geography of the land, exhibiting its divisions, frontiers, and historical sites at various periods.

4.   Some illustration of the conceptions of the land and of the world to which it belongs, prevalent at former periods of its history.

5.   A series of 'Notes to the Maps', including a list of the ancient, or contemporary, and the modern, authorities for each; and, in the case of most of the historical maps, statements of the principal events in the periods to which they refer, with some explanations or arguments for the frontiers, lines of traffic, and historical sites which are delineated upon them.

These were not only fine sentiments. Smith, who employed modern critical techniques and was familiar with Hebrew and Arabic sources, repeatedly introduced a proper note of caution. He was an Old Testament specialist who was aware of developments in geography and archaeology. Thus, in the preface, he gave his view on frontiers, the principal subject depicted in historical atlases of the period:

Political frontiers cannot be determined except approximately, especially where there were no distinct natural lines of demarcation. In such circumstances they oscillated from reign to reign, and even probably from year to year, as in the case of the border between Northern Israel and Judah, or in the cases of the suburban territories of the Decapolis and other free cities of Syria. It would be an even more precarious task to attempt to draw the exact frontiers of the Tribes of Israel. On the other hand, it is extremely probable that so strong a natural frontier in Moab as the valley of the Arnon was almost constantly a political frontier as well; and the historical evidence is in agreement with this conclusion.

The notes on individual maps underlined Smith's caution and drew attention to the availability and accuracy of information. For map 31, 'Palestine before the coming of Israel. 1500 to 1250 BC', Smith wrote:

The difficulty of the geographical data of this period is due not to their meagreness, but to the fact that the races then appearing in Palestine were numerous and in constant movement; and that the names for them were not used in the Old Testament nor elsewhere in any exact sense.

For map 33, 'Palestine in the time of Saul', Smith emphasized the problems with boundaries: 'The frontiers indicated on the map are, of course, only approximate. This is true in particular of the Israelite extension over Galilee, the East of Jordan, and southwards into the Negeb.'[9] Smith's atlas was used by the British army and T.E. Lawrence during the First World War.

Le Sage and Nineteenth-century French Publications

Despite these emphases, historical atlases that were not primarily Classical/biblical also started to appear in greater numbers in the first half of the century. The *Atlas historique, généalogique, chronologique et géographique* (Paris, 1802–4) of Le Sage (Marie-Joseph-Emmanuel-Auguste Dieudonné de Las Cases, Marquis de la Caussade, 1766–1842) was the most important in the early decades of the century: its circulation was immense, and the preface of the 1829 Paris edition described the work as the *vade mecum* of merchants, scholars and men of the world. Le Sage was the pseudonym of an émigré marquis and former naval lieutenant lacking any real qualifications for acting as a mapmaker or historian. Settled in London, Las Cases became a teacher of history, astronomy, geography and mathematics, and an active producer of maps. His atlas, published in monthly parts in 1799–1800, initially appeared in English as the *Genealogical, Chronological, Historical and Geographical Atlas* (London, 1801). The list of subscribers was headed by George III and most of the royal family and included numerous aristocrats, 32 clerics, and 32 academies and schools taking a total of 61 copies. Las Cases returned to Paris in 1802 where his amateur status did not prevent him from earning a fortune. The 1802 Paris edition was officially adopted by the Ministry of the Interior for use in French schools and by the Foreign Ministry for the use of legations. After that, as the 1814 Paris edition noted, five editions appeared in Paris and an unofficial French edition in Florence in 1807, as well as editions at Philadelphia and St Petersburg and German and Italian translations. Another English edition appeared in 1813. The American edition, first published in Philadelphia in 1820, included maps of the New World.

Though very popular, the atlas had its limitations. Las Cases made much use of 'genealogical and chronological maps': genealogical tables and time-charts; the 'geographical' maps were clearly secondary. He presented all his maps as similar devices to disseminate knowledge by fixing location. The plan of the work printed in the 1801 edition stated:

> If it were possible, in studying history, to see the personage of which it is spoken, constantly in its chronological place, without having recourse to chronology, and always surrounded by its ancestors and descendants, without being constrained to study genealogy . . . it is certain it would then be engraved on the memory, attended by all the advantages that would assist the recollection, and rectify the judgment; for while the ear listened to the history of any one, the eye would see at the same time the precise epocha of their existence, their contemporaries, parentage, relations, etc.

A system of this sort would undoubtedly reduce the study of history to that of geographical maps, and the abstract efforts of memory to merely the mechanical exercise of the eyes, but Las Cases, it was declared, had succeeded. Pupils, it was claimed, find

> relative spaces impossible to confuse. In short, they have learnt upon the historical map, the distance of time, as they learn that of places upon the geographical, and have followed on one, the change of events and successions, as on the other the turnings of roads and windings of provinces, and they will determine with as much ease and precision, the situation of Elizabeth in respect to William the Conqueror, or George the Third, as they would that of London to Edinburgh or Portsmouth.

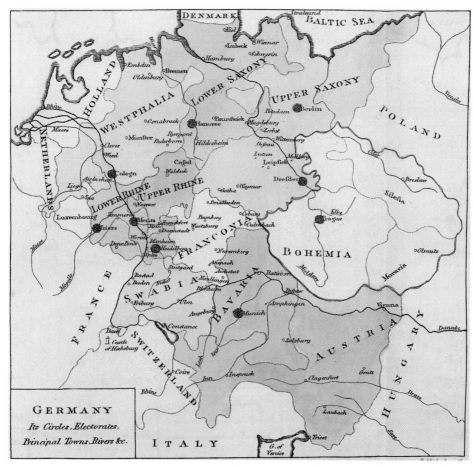

4. Map of Germany from the English edition of Las Cases's *Atlas historique, généalogique, chronologique et géographique* (Paris, 1802–4). A poor map that contained inaccuracies. The emphasis on the imperial circles was misleading; and this legalistic approach ensured that Prussia was not shown as a separate state and its acquisitions of Silesia and part of Poland were not recorded.

The use of the word atlas to describe a book that tried to locate and describe by the use of tables rather than maps was not peculiar to Las Cases. In 1826 Adrien Balbi published his *Atlas éthnographique du globe ou classification des peuples anciens et modernes d'après leurs langues* (Paris), a work that similarly used tables instead of maps for its classification.

Rather than chronologically sequential maps, Las Cases was guided by the country-by-country practice of geographical atlases. His favourite device was the gaudily coloured line, used to show campaigns, for example those of Alexander, the Ten Thousand, Hannibal, Gustavus Adolphus, Charles XII, Charles Edward Stuart (Bonnie Prince Charlie), Napoleon and Suvorov. Las Cases keenly praised his own maps. That of French history was 'quite new in its composition . . . it shows by a difference of colour, the original domain of the crown, and points out the order and nature of the several reunions by which the kingdom has been composed, under what king, and by what colour'. Gains by violence were coloured red, by inheritance green, and by marriage, treaty or purchase yellow. The overall effect, however, was very crude.

The map of Germany also employed a colour code to differentiate Austria, Bavaria, Saxony and Prussia: 'cyphers above each province indicate the order in which those provinces were acquired.' Again, the effect was poor. The physical background was essentially ignored and the execution was poor. The map of the Roman empire offered no date. That of the British Isles 'exhibiting all the battle places, landings, civil wars etc' was a confused map that showed the campaigns of Charles I, Charles II and Bonnie Prince Charlie, the first looking especially messy. Again, no physical background was provided.

Las Cases's references to problems he faced with his sources indicate his limitations and prejudices. For the map of Africa he wrote:

> There are scarcely any two nations, or indeed any two geographers, who agree in the division of Africa, the inland parts being entirely unknown, and the coasts very imperfectly explored . . . a burning climate, desolate wastes, moving sands, inhabitants either barbarous or brutish, ferocious animals, venomous reptiles, all conspire to exhibit Africa as the refuse of the world, and the malediction of nature.

For the map of the 'Barbarian' invasions of the Roman empire, in which the routes were colour-coded, Las Cases wrote:

> Several authors, both ancient and modern . . . offer much upon the origin, name, and history of these different nations, but they seldom agree in their opinions, and an attempt to reconcile them would be but loss of time . . . While endeavouring to trace the origin of these fugitive tribes, we seem still pursuing them through their impenetrable woods and difficult morasses, where as we advance, the traces of their footsteps disappear. The attempt to class them scrupulously is vain, and equally so to fix with exactitude the point of their departure. How, indeed, can it be otherwise? Their origin is lost in the night of time; their name must have been often confounded with that of their conquerors or their allies.

His map of the barbarian invasions of the Roman empire was in fact especially weak.[10]

New editions of Las Cases brought changes. The preface to the 1829 edition emphasized the value of the work as spanning the divide between Classical and modern times, a theme that was intellectually and commercially far more relevant in the nineteenth than in the preceding century. The preface also underlined the value of the simultaneity of visual image:

> Il perce l'obscurité des temps fabuleux, et traverse, sans s'égarer, les ténèbres qui séparent la civilisation ancienne de la civilisation moderne. Le même coup d'oeil embrasse la formation et la perte des dynasties, le berceau, les progrès et le déclin des nations.

The new edition offered more maps of Germany, including ones of the Confederation of the Rhine, Germany in 1812 and Germany in 1815, the last showing the 1813 campaign against Napoleon. A political map of Europe in 1826, in which Britain was referred to as 'the dictator of the seas', was produced to provide a comparison with the situation in 1812.

A number of other important French historical atlases appeared in this period, but none had the impact of Las Cases. The *Atlas de la géographie universelle ancienne et*

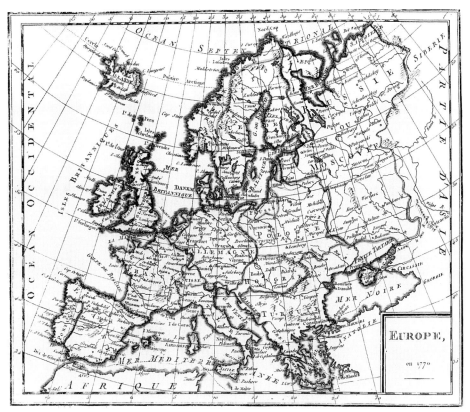

5. 'Europe in 1770' from the *Atlas de la géographie universelle ancienne et modern* (Paris, 1816) by Edmé Mentelle and Conrad Malte-Brun. This provided the base for a cartographic presentation of recent history, for it could be contrasted with maps of the situation in 1803 and 1816. Poland was still an important state and Russia lacked a Black Sea coastline. The map is anachronistic in its depiction of Italy.

moderne (Paris, 1816), by Edmé Mentelle and Conrad Malte-Brun, continued the practice of jumping from the Classical to the modern world, in this case maps of Europe in 1770, 1803 and 1816, and of ignoring the intervening period. A.H. Brué's *Atlas universel de géographie physique, politique et historique, ancienne et moderne* (Paris, 1822) had few maps in the historical section and all were devoted to the ancient world: the dispersion of peoples until the time of Moses, the world known to the ancients, the empire of Alexander the Great, ancient Egypt, Greece, Italy, Asia Minor and Gaul and the Roman empire under Constantine. The second edition, published in 1838, added maps of the world known to the Hebrews, an interesting variant on the world known to the ancients, which meant the Greeks and the Romans; ancient Spain, Britain and Germany; and a map of Europe at the time of Charlemagne, a vital point of reference for French commentators, but there was nothing between that map and that of Europe in 1789. A note on the latter plate commented:

> Sur ce tableau des divisions politiques de l'Europe en 1789, nous indiquons les liens qui se rattachent à l'histoire depuis la fin du 9me siècle jusqu'en 1789. Ne voulant pas multiplier, dans notre Atlas, les cartes historiques, nous avons surchargé de noms

quelques parties de cette carte, ainsi que la carte présentant le démembrement de l'Empire de Charlemagne afin que le lecteur puisse suivre facilement les divisions politiques intermédiaires entre les époques représentées par les deux cartes.

The gap was still unfilled in the 1869 and 1875 editions, the second of which was extensively revised by Levasseur in order to take note of research on the ancient world, not least the information presented in the atlases by Spruner-Menke and Kiepert, and the work of the Commission des Gaules.

The *Atlas universel de géographie ancienne et moderne* (Paris, 1829) was a work with official credentials. Dedicated to Charles X, it was produced by P. Lapié, 'Premier Géographe du Roi' and head of the topographical section of the Ministry of War, and A.E. Lapié, professor at the military academy of Saint-Cyr. The introduction emphasized the importance of geography and the atlas devoted considerable attention to the Classical world before making what was to be the common omission after the map of Charlemagne's Europe: after a plate devoted to Europe in 800, the following maps tackled 1500 and 1789. The atlas also adopted the customary teleological prejudice against the medieval world. The discoveries of the fifteenth century, such as printing, were presented with the reflection 'L'Europe secoura insensiblement le joug de la barbarie, de la superstition et du fanatisme'.[11]

The same year, also in Paris, Maxime-Auguste Denaix began the publication of his *Atlas physique, politique et historique de l'Europe*. He rejected the technique Kruse adopted of including maps at regular time intervals and instead concentrated on the periods of greatest change in Europe's political divisions. Denaix emphasized the role of environmental considerations. His twelfth map, 'Divisions Anciennes et Modernes de l'Europe comparées entre elles et déterminées par les circonstances physiques les plus remarquables', employed a hydrographic analysis to map Europe on the basis of its river basins, and then related political divisions to this analysis. Denaix also published an *Atlas physique, politique et historique de la France* in 1836–37. Antoine-Philippe Houzé published his *Atlas universel historique et géographique* in 1837–38. Houzé's atlas began with a map of Eden, Ur, Babel and Ararat, followed by another showing the division of the earth among the three sons of Noah. It also, however, provided numerous detailed maps of France, as well as a large number of maps devoted to the history of other parts of Europe: for example, ten for Britain, twelve for Germany and eight for Spain. Asian history, in contrast, received only three maps.

The growth in the market for historical atlases was reflected by the fact that in some years more than one was published in Paris. Thus in 1840 there appeared Auguste-Henri Dufour and Th. Duvotenay's *La Terre. Atlas historique et universel de géographie* and E. Soulier and J. Andriveau-Goujon's *Atlas élémentaire simplifié de géographie ancienne et moderne*. The former included sixteen historical maps, thirteen of the Classical world and one each of fifth-century Europe, the Mongol empire and the empire of Charlemagne. This was a somewhat conventional choice, but the introduction emphasized the need for novelty: 'abandonnant la vieille routine de reproduire sans cesse les nouvelles cartes d'après les anciennes, ce qui perpétue les erreurs'.[12] The Soulier and Andriveau-Goujoun work included a map, 'Migrations des Peuples', that showed all peoples as diffused from the Caucasus, Mongolia or Ethiopia: 'these three races confirm the Mosaic text'; a map that thereby satisfied nineteenth-century interest in ethnic origins in biblical terms. Aside from the

6. An early attempt at cartographic environmentalism. A map of ancient and modern divisions of Europe related to river basins from *Atlas physique, politique et historique de l'Europe* (Paris, 1829) by Maxime-Auguste Denaix. The map made little sense of modern Britain, Russia and Spain.

barbarian invasions, post-Classical Europe was depicted in 800, at the time of the Crusades, in 1556, 1789 and 1812 and France in 481, 507, 888, 987, 1152, 1422, 1483, 1648 and 1715. In contrast, the edition of Charles V. Monin's *Atlas classique de la géographie, ancienne, du Moyen age, et Moderne* (Paris) published for the 1847–48 school year included no maps covering Europe for the period between the tenth century and 1813. Yet there were fourteen standard maps of the Classical world, all of them centred on the Mediterranean, whereas the maps of the modern world included Africa and the New World.

Kruse and Nineteenth-century German Publications

Christian Kruse (1753–1827) was a schoolmaster, then tutor to the sons of the Duke of Oldenburg, and then Professor of History at Leipzig. His *Atlas und Tabellen zur Übersicht der Geschichte aller europäischen Länder und Staaten* (Leipzig, 1802–18), produced with his son Friedrich, omitted antiquity and, using the same base map of Europe and the Near East, produced sequential maps covering each century from 400 to 1700, and then 1788, 1811 and 1816. Kruse's maps focused on territorial control, presenting blocks of territory separated by clear frontiers – a misleading view

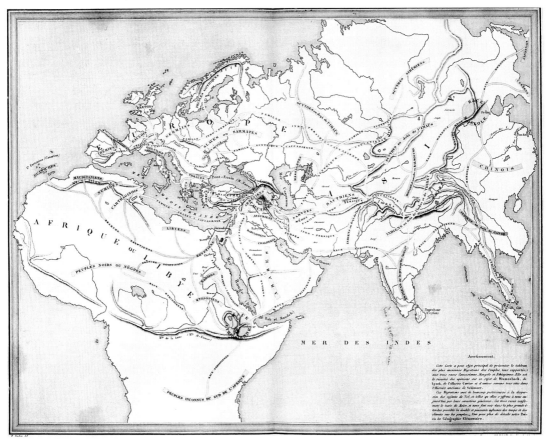

7. Migration was of great interest in the nineteenth century. As a study of roots and movements, this map from the *Atlas élémentaire simplifié de géographie ancienne et moderne* by E. Soulier and J. Andriveau-Goujon (Paris, 1840) was accompanied by a note that acknowledged sources and drew attention to the role of climate in ethnographic history. The migrations were not dated: the past was presented as a single image.

of the medieval and (though to a lesser extent) early-modern period. The physical background, especially the depiction of mountain ranges, had deficiencies. Nevertheless, however much it is necessary to be cautious about adopting a 'progressive', teleological and judgmental attitude, Kruse's atlas was more impressive than that of Las Cases with its diagrammatic images and cruder maps, part of the progressive development of a particular tradition. The publication of maps at regular chronological intervals was an important innovation, as was the exclusion of most of Asia and of antiquity.

Kruse's atlas was successful, the fifth edition appearing in 1834. It was also translated into French and published in Paris in 1836 as the *Atlas historique des états européens*. The preface by the translator, Philippe Lebas, criticized Las Cases's atlas for its concentration on genealogy and the lack both of sufficient historical detail and adequate maps. Lebas emphasized the impartiality of Kruse's atlas and stated that it had not been composed to 'satisfy any national vanity'.

A number of other important historical atlases appeared in Germany in the 1820s and 1830s, a period in which a large number of such works appeared in Europe, and in which there was growing interest in geography and modern history as subjects for academic and intellectual consideration.[13] Friedrich Wilhelm Benicken's *Historischer Schulatlas oder Übersicht der allgemeinen Weltgeschichte* (Weimar, 1820) devoted only four of its fourteen maps to the Classical world. Another four covered the medieval period, including the reign of Charles V, and the last six were devoted to more recent history. Benicken's atlas was followed by a library version that differed from the school book, his *Historischer Hand-Atlas zur Versinnlichung der allgemeinen Geschichte aller Völker und Staaten* (Weimar, 1824). His atlases were at the technological cutting edge – drawn on stone by Anton Falger and lithographed – but they were commercial failures: unwieldy, printed on grey paper and unattractive to use, although there was also an edition printed on good paper. In addition, the maps were not large enough to provide adequate intelligibility for the detail. Julius Löwenberg also tackled the post-Classical world in his *Historisch-Geographischer Atlas zu den allgemeinen Geschichtswerken von C. V. Rotteck, Pölitz und Becker in 40 colorirten Karten* (Freiburg, 1839) and the *Historischer Taschenatlas des Preuszischen Staats, bestehend aus 16 Histor. Geographischen Karten, mit erläuterndem Texte* (Berlin, 1840). His 1839 atlas began with the world at the time of Cyrus and then the Roman empire under Augustus, before providing a series of maps of Europe, the Near East and North Africa, followed by a number of detailed maps. The atlas included a map of the 'War of Liberation' against France of 1813–15 with an inset plan of the battle of Leipzig. The atlas was Eurocentric, although Löwenberg added maps for the empires of Genghis Khan and Tamerlane and for the New World in the 1842 edition. There was considerable detail and use of colour in John Valerius Kutscheit's *Volständiger Historisch-Geographischer Atlas des deutschen Landes und Volkes* (Berlin, 1842): the maps were organized by medieval dioceses. Two years later he produced a specialized atlas of the medieval period, a sign of increasing differentiation in historical atlases. The fifteen maps of Kutscheit's *Handatlas der Geographie des Mittelalters* (Berlin, 1844) gave due weight to eastern Europe, and its maps of Germany and northern Italy provided considerable detail on territorial control.

Spruner

The situation was thus already changing when in Gotha in 1846 there appeared the *Historisch-geographischer Hand-Atlas zur Geschichte der Staaten Europa's von Anfang des Mittelalters bis auf die neueste Zeit* by Karl von Spruner (1803–92), a Bavarian army officer. Spruner, described in 1902 by R.L. Poole as 'the founder of the modern historical atlas',[14] produced an atlas depicting the development of Europe primarily from the perspective of the growth and interaction of its states. If he was the 'founder', it was in method and rigour, emphasis on maps and insistence on sound sources. Spruner had little time for Las Cases's work.

    Theodor Menke (1819–92) was responsible for a heavily revised third edition of Spruner's work, again published by the Gotha house of Justus Perthes. The *Spruner-Menke Hand-Atlas für die Geschichte des Mittelalters und die neueren Zeit* (Gotha, 1880) was particularly influential. Maps of European history were treated together and before those of individual states, so that there was no consolidated chronological sequence of maps. The atlas included linguistic maps and townplans, but social and economic topics were neglected. The maps were detailed, sometimes greatly so. For

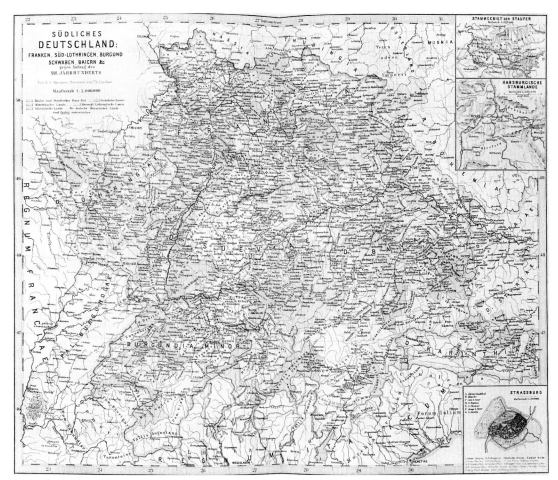

8. 'Southern Germany in the Thirteenth Century' from the *Spruner-Menke Hand-Atlas für die Geschichte des Mittelalters und die neueren Zeit* (Gotha, 1880). A great medieval past was depicted. The map spread to Lyon and Venice. The town-plan of Strassburg was a reminder of the long-German identity of Strasbourg. Detailed territorial maps of the medieval Empire were, and still are, a characteristic feature of German historical atlases.

example, a full two pages were devoted to north Italy 1137–1302, a map that showed the different fiefs. Germany was mapped in great detail, capturing the multiplicity of territories. For the thirteenth century, Germany was split into north and south, the map of the former including the Low Countries, that of the latter Lorraine and Switzerland. This was an accurate reflection of the Holy Roman Empire of the period, but also arguably a reflection of a late nineteenth-century attitude that did not emphasize the territorial circumscription of Germany.

As with Spruner's original work, military themes were stressed. Thus the plate on Germany at the beginning of the nineteenth century included battle or campaign maps for Ulm, Austerlitz, Auerstadt, Jena, Eylau, Friedland, Eggmühl, Essling and Wagram. Two alone were devoted to the battle of Leipzig. In contrast, Belle Alliance (Waterloo) was covered in only one map, which stressed the Prussian role, and a map of a similar size was devoted to the Franco-Prussian engagement at Ligny two days earlier. The plate of Germany in the age of Frederick the Great included maps of eighteen battles and one siege, while that of Germany 1648–1742 included maps of the Prussian victory at Fehrbellin and of the Palatinate in order to illustrate the French invasions of 1674 and 1689–70. The mapping of battles concentrated heavily on those in which German rulers had been involved, and, in addition, there was a big map of the war zone of 1870–71. However, other battles, including Antioch, Bannockburn, Varna, Pavia and Mohacs, were depicted. The battle plans were weakened by their general failure to show movement. The amount of space devoted to the Byzantine empire was a positive aspect of the atlas. The *Spruner-Menke Atlas Antiquus* had already been published in Gotha in 1865.

G. Droysens's *Allgemeiner historischer Handatlas* (Bielefeld and Leipzig, 1886) drew heavily on the Spruner-Menke atlas. Droysens's was a world historical atlas that was heavily dominated by German themes. Most striking were the precise and highly coloured double-page maps of German history. They were an excellent demonstration of what the historical atlas could offer in terms of aesthetic appeal, interest and information. Fine lines and the plentiful use of colour permitted the clear presentation of complex territorial situations. This was a conquest of the complexity of the past by the clarity of modern cartography, comparable to the way in which the contemporary non-European world was being tackled by nineteenth-century European mapping.

Droysens's atlas included no maps on economic history and the territorial maps did not include economic material, but space was devoted to military topics. There were plans of the siege of Magdeburg (1631) and the battle of Leipzig (1813) and two pages were given over to battle plans of the German Wars of Unification from 1864 to 1871, including a detailed plan of Sedan, and a whole page for the Franco-German war zone.

The influence of Spruner's works in the nineteenth century was important, and was acknowledged, for example, by British historical atlases. John Sherren Brewer, Professor of English History and Literature at King's College, London, in the introduction to his *Elementary Atlas of History and Geography* (London, 1854), claimed that Spruner had 'most ably executed' the cartographic dimension of history. *The Historic Geographical Atlas of the Middle and Modern Ages . . . Based on the Historisch-Geographischer Hand-Atlas of Dr Spruner* (London) was published in 1853 and William Hughes's *A Popular Atlas of Comparative Geography: Comprehending a Chronological Series of Maps of Europe and Other Lands . . . Based upon the Historisch-Geographischer Hand-Atlas of Dr Spruner* (London) in 1870. In his preface, Hughes wrote:

> the work of Dr Spruner, upon which the present Atlas is based, is one of the most esteemed authorities on the subject of comparative Geography. The elaborate research, and minute precision of detail, which characterise the 'Historisch-Geographischer Hand-Atlas', have deservedly made it a standard of reference in our own country. These qualities, however, though admirable when regarded from a German point of view, or with reference to the study of ecclesiastical history, are (not unnaturally) carried to an extent which, to the general reader of history, involves needless complication of detail.

The authorized English edition of Spruner had been published by the German-born London publisher Nicholas Trübner in 1861. It was designed to thwart an unauthorized edition and was published at 'the unprecedently moderate price' of 15 shillings

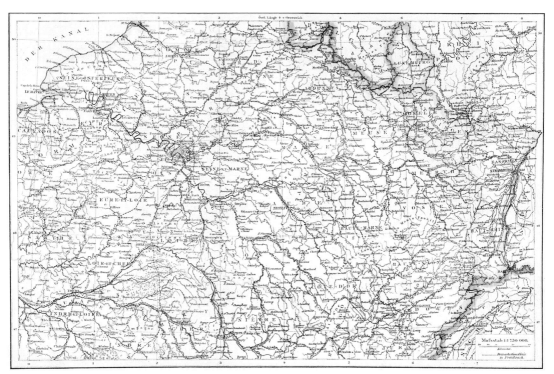

9. 'The Franco-German War Zone' from G. Droysens's *Allgemeiner historischer Handatlas* (Bielefeld and Leipzig. 1886). Prussian greatness and German unity had been won at the expense of France in 1870–71. The map helped both to chart the course of the campaigns and to remind the reader that they had been conducted in France, not Germany. This implied contrast to the Napoleonic Wars was possibly a comment on Prussian leadership.

(75 pence) in order to make 'it accessible to the large and increasing class of historical students and to general readers of the most moderate means'. The preface presented maps 'as a ready means of inculcating historical facts', while the appeal of history, at once full of narrative interest and exemplary, was referred to when the atlas was described as 'appealing to the eye' and exhibiting 'vividly the consequences of diplomatic negotiation, the violent changes of war, and the gradual progress of colonization and civilization', the two clearly seen as equivalents. An American edition was published in New York the same year by B. Westermann and Co. In 1866 Trübner also published an English edition of Menke's *Orbis antiqui descriptio*. Spruner's map of Saxon England was, however, criticized by Charles Pearson, in his *Historical Maps of England* (London, 1869), for adding 'a few arbitrary conjectures' to its source.

Battles and the Military

Spruner's atlases reflected an army training and career, a military emphasis that was characteristic of historical atlases in the late nineteenth century, although it scarcely began there. The cartographic treatment of military history was divided between the mapping of long-past campaigns, such as those of Hannibal and Caesar, and the depiction of wars that were so recent that it is unclear how far the term 'historical' is helpful. Thus in 1760 Heinrich Count von Bünau had published his *Essai d'un atlas historique, geographique, topographique et militaire, contenant en XVII cartes militaires tous les mouvemens, marches, campemens, positions et batailles, et tout ce qui s'est passé d'interessant dans la campagne de 1757 entre l'armée françoise et celle des alliés*. In the nineteenth century historical atlases were also produced to cover recent wars. Thus the Peninsular War gave rise to *Atlas Militaire. Mémoires sur les opérations militaires des Français en Galice, en Portugal, et dans la Vallée du Tage en 1809* (Paris, no date) and to James Wyld's *Maps and Plans, Showing the Principal Movements, Battles and Sieges, in which the British Army Was Engaged during the War from 1808 to 1814 in the Spanish Peninsula* (London, 1840). Based on the surveys by Thomas Mitchell, this was a detailed work dedicated 'to the British Army as a tribute humbly offered to its meritorious services and its high character'. In the keys the French were referred to as 'the Enemy'. The atlas itself was a source of conflict: Mitchell and his publisher, the cartographer Wyld, quarrelled over money and acknowledgments.[15] William Siborne's successful *History of the War in France and Belgium in 1815* (London, 1844) appeared with a folio atlas that offered an effective combination of contoured battlefields and army positions indicated by colour. In addition, battles were clarified by the use of a number of maps for individual battles, for example three for Waterloo. Dufour and Duvotenay's *Atlas de l'histoire du consulat et de l'empire* (Paris, 1859) contained very detailed maps of battle sites. An *Atlas histórico y topográfico de la Guerra de Africa en 1859 y 1860* was published in Madrid in 1861.

The centennial of American independence and the recent spur to interest in military cartography provided by the American Civil War, the course of which had been recorded by newspaper maps,[16] led to the production of the first American atlas of military history. This was compiled by Henry B. Carrington, an academic at Wabash College, and was based on the maps in his lengthy *Battles of the American Revolution . . . with Topographical Illustration* (1876). In 1881 Carrington published the maps in *Battle Maps and Charts of the American Revolution*.[17]

The crucial role of the military in nineteenth-century cartography extended to the creators and subjects of historical atlases. For example, the *Atlas physique, politique et historique de l'Europe* (Paris, 1829) by Maxime-Auguste Denaix was published by a graduate of the École Polytechnique who had gone into the army before moving to the Dépôt Général de la Guerre, was engraved by Richard Wahl who had been trained at the Dépôt Général, and was published under the sponsorship of the Vicomte de Caux, the Minister of War. The atlas devoted considerable space to depicting the territorial shifts of 1792–1815, the crucial consequence of the warfare of the period, and to marking the sites of battles. By the time of the 1836 edition, which was published with the approval of Caux's successor as Minister of War, Denaix was head of the administration at the Dépôt. Benicken, author of the *Historischer Schulatlas* and *Hand-Atlas*, was a retired Prussian captain. He also published an edition of Polybius on war as well as his own *Die Elemente der Militär-Geographie von Europa* (Weimar, 1821). The Freiherr von Kausler, author of the *Atlas des plus memorables batailles, combats et sieges* (Dessau, 1847), was a major-general in the Württemberg army. Louis Etienne Dussieux was professor of history at the military academy at Saint-Cyr. He produced historical atlases in the 1840s that he emphasized were not compilations; originality was clearly seen as important for intellectual and commercial reasons.

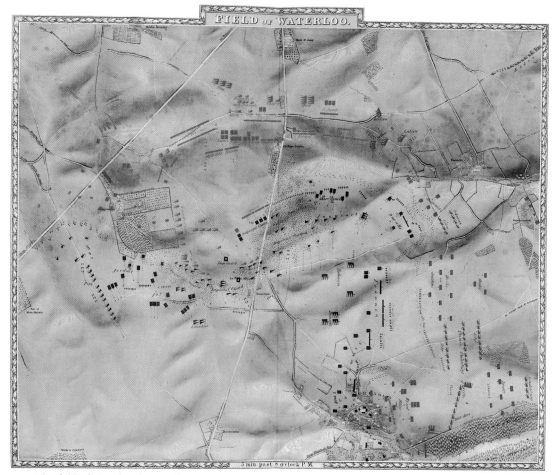

10. The field of Waterloo from William Siborne, *History of the War in France and Belgium in 1815* (London, 1844). An effective combination of contoured battlefields and army positions indicated by colour. This map of the last stage of the battle showed the Prussians (in green) advancing on the French. Captain Siborne had earlier produced a model of the battlefield, based upon a personal survey, that was publicly exhibited.

However, even atlases that lacked military sponsorship devoted considerable space to warfare. J.J. Hellert's *Nouvel atlas physique, politique et historique de l'empire ottoman* (Paris, 1843) had a historical section solely devoted to eight full-page battle plans and five sieges. There were no maps of the development of the empire, a topic that might have been treated. The maps of the contemporary situation reflected another aspect of the relationship with the military as they were based on those at the topographical depot at the Russian War Ministry. *A New Classical and Historical Atlas*, which was published in Edinburgh in 1849, included maps to illustrate the Trojan War, Alexander the Great's campaigns, the siege of Syracuse, the March of the Ten Thousand, Hannibal's campaigns, and the battles of Salamis, Plataeae, Issus and Arbela.

New Technology

The nineteenth was the century in which the historical atlas was established firmly on the European scene. This development reflected a number of factors, which can be summarized as push and pull, supply and demand. Reliable maps became easier to provide and to publish. Most of the world had been mapped, and the political boundaries in Europe, and increasingly in the European political world as a whole, were now precise. The printing of colour became easier, and thus more information could be presented. As more historical atlases were produced, so a growing fund of information for further works was created.

Technological changes were of great consequence. Mechanized papermaking became commercially viable in the 1800s, leading to the steam-powered production of plentiful quantities of inexpensive paper, and the steam-powered printing press developed in the same period. Although there were no significant developments in typesetting until the 1880s, these changes created a much larger potential audience for the cartographer and ensured that cartography had to adapt to the challenge. Numerous maps had to be produced, their specifications had to be appropriate and it was necessary to ensure that a new readership was interested in maps and carto-literate.

Aside from the changes resulting from the mass production of printed material, there were also specific changes in map production which resulted in a greater process of specialization that encouraged and reflected the creation of specialized map publishers such as W. and A.K. Johnston (1826) and John Bartholomew and Son (1820s) in Edinburgh, George Philip and Son (1834) in London and Justus Perthes (1785) in Gotha.[18] Map-colouring ceased to be a manual process and was instead transformed by the onset of common colour printing.

Lithography made a major impact in the 1820s and was partly responsible for an increase in the quantity and range of maps produced, not least the development of thematic mapping. Lithography was able to produce inexpensive maps for teaching. Historical atlases produced by lithography in the 1820s included Antoine Schneider's *Nouvel atlas pour servir à l'histoire des Iles Ioniennes* (Paris, 1823) and the *Atlas der alten Welt in XVI illuminirten Charten* (Düsseldorf, 1829). There was a transitional period in mid-century. For example, the *Atlas des campagnes de l'empereur Napoleon en Allemagne et en France* (Paris, 1844), prepared under the direction of Lieutenant-General Jean-Jacques Pelet, head of the Dépôt, consisted of eleven folded maps in a slipcase. Eight were engraved and three lithographed. British and American publishers were slow to take up lithography: George Philip introduced it in 1846, W. and A.K. Johnston in about 1865 and John Bartholomew and Son in 1880. Lithography itself was developing: metal plates were substituted for stone, and lithography came to include the transfer technique and eventually photolithography.[19] In lithographic transfers the design from an engraved plate was transferred to a litho stone, on which alterations could be made (such as insertion of historical information, redrawing of boundaries, etc.) without affecting the original plate. Thus the same plate could be used as the basis for a whole series of maps printed from litho stones, with variant features – for example, for different historical periods – imposed on each. Alterations might be made on the stones between different printings of the map; and maps might still be printed direct from the original plate. The plate itself might be altered, and these alterations would appear on any litho transfer made subsequently. From the late 1850s plates were being engraved which seem never to have been printed from directly – they were used solely as a source of lithographic transfers. The advantage was a much finer line and neater lettering than could easily be achieved by drawing on the litho stone.

The impact of new technology was seen in works such as William Hughes's *The Illuminated Atlas of Scripture Geography* (London, 1840), a work that benefited from the early use of colour printing. The maps were by Charles Wright and used colour woodblock and letterpress. Hughes prided himself on his 'Patent Illuminated Maps': 'by a novel method of printing, the various divisions of the countries are covered with distinct colours, so that the boundaries are clearly perceived at the first view.' Using gum arabic, Hughes depicted the mountains in white rather than the usual black, 'distinctly and prominently relieved by the coloured ground', and thus ensured that they did not clash with the names printed on the map which were in black.[20]

Historical atlases benefited from the general advances in cartographic production. For example, the Edinburgh map-publisher John Bartholomew first introduced what was termed 'contour layer colouring' in a commercial series of maps. They were put on show at the Paris Exhibition of 1878.[21] Colour came to play a more prominent role in mapping, and was seen as both a commercial opportunity and challenge. Multi-colour printing from more than one plate had become possible with the advent of engraving, although it was never common. Colour became more important in the nineteenth century when it was used to define appeal. Thus in 1830 the London publisher Jones and Co. produced *Jones' Classical Atlas, on an Entirely New Plan; The Ancient and Modern Names of Places Being Given on the Same Map, but Printed, for the Sake of Perspicuity, in Different Coloured Ink*. A lithographed edition was published in 1853. A major reason for the success of the most popular German school historical atlas, *F.W. Putzger's Historischer Schul-Atlas*, first published in Bielefeld and Leipzig in 1877, was its relatively low price: 1.5 marks. This was in part due to the fact that the colours were printed, rather than coloured by hand, a more expensive process.[22]

Colour-conventions also developed. For example, the use of pink or red to denote the British empire began in the first half of the century. Henry Teesdale's *New British Atlas* (1831), which showed only areas of India under British control, was one of the first recorded examples of the use of red to show British possessions. The 1841 edition of this atlas was the first to use the red convention for all British colonies. The colour was probably chosen for its striking effect. It did not come into general usage, however, until after 1850 with the development of chromo-lithography (colour printing) and thematic mapping, and was popularized by school wall maps and atlases. Foreign atlases, nevertheless, continued to use other colours for the British empire. Clausolles and Abadie's *Atlas historique et géographique de la France* (Paris, 1846) used colour to distinguish between royal domains and fiefs that were in effect independent. Dufour and Amari used black for relief and modern place names and red for Arab names in their *Carte comparée de la Sicile moderne avec la Sicile au XIIᵉ siècle d'après Édrisi et d'autres géographes arabes* (1859). The map vividly made the point that Sicily had an Arab past and also presented the Arab geographers in a readily comprehensible fashion.

3

Nationalism and Eurocentrism in Nineteenth-century Historical Atlases

Nationalism

The establishment of mass schooling organized on a national basis increased the demand for national history, and the growth of academic history and geography at university level and in public consciousness[1] further created a pedagogic demand for atlases. The pedagogic value of historical maps was emphasized in works such as *The Public Schools Historical Atlas* (London, 1885) by C. Colbeck, Assistant-Master at Harrow School. Published by a major publisher – Longman – this work went into a third edition in 1891 and many of the maps were used by S.R. Gardiner in his *School Atlas of English History* (London, 1899).

Publishers responded to the demand and the number of historical atlases greatly increased. Thus in France Victor Duruy's *Atlas de géographie historique universelle* (Paris, 1841) was followed by Louis Dussieux's *Géographie historique de la France ou histoire de la formation du territoire français* (Paris, 1843) and his other atlas of history, the *Atlas général de géographie physique, politique, historique* (Paris, 1849), C.F. Delamarche's *Atlas de géographie historique du Moyen Âge* (Paris, 1844), Drioux and Leroy's *Atlas universel et classique de géographie ancienne, romaine, du Moyen Âge et moderne* (Paris, 1878) and P. Foncin's *Géographie historique* (Paris, 1888), a book that provided lessons on the history and territorial formation of countries, each accompanied by a map. The 1836 edition of Denaix's *Atlas physique, politique et historique* formed, as the title-page noted, 'les Xe XIe et XIIe livraisons du nouveau cours de géographie générale'. The 1855 edition was published with the approval of the Minister of Public Instruction.

Drioux and Leroy's *Atlas d'histoire et de géographie* (Paris, 1867) appeared in different versions related to the requirements of particular school years. One tackled ancient and medieval history, although the maps had their deficiencies. That of the Near East, which shared plate one with a map of Palestine, was designed to show the principal places mentioned in the Bible. It was confusing, since it showed, with no overlaps and no hint that they were not simultaneous, Persia, Media, Assyria and Mesopotamia, the latter two divided by the Tigris and with Nineveh on the boundary. The map for Europe 814–1453 was supposed to cover the partition of Charlemagne's empire, the Arab conquests and the Crusades. Another volume

11. 'Europe 814–1453' from Drioux and Leroy's *Atlas d'histoire et de géographie* (Paris, 1867), a crude school atlas that covered large periods of time with one map. The insets reflected the interests of French readers.

covered national history. The foreword made clear the degree to which French atlases that sought the pedagogic market had to conform to official requirements:

> Dans cet Atlas destiné à des enfants . . . nous avons pris à tâche de nous conformer aux instructions de Son Excellence le Ministre de l'Instruction publique, à l'esprit aussi bien qu'à la lettre du *Plan d'études,* conciliant toujours la portée de l'enseignement avec l'âge des élèves: *cartes historiques,* pour les grands traits de l'histoire nationale.[2]

The maps emphasized French territorial extent, not least under Charlemagne and Napoleon, and a map of the 'départements réunis' under Napoleon III made it clear that he was a worthy ruler of France.

After France lost the war with Germany in 1870–71 and Napoleon III fell, a different message was conveyed. Lamothe's *Carte des agrandissements successifs de la France sous la monarchie, la république et l'empire* (Paris, 1873) was headed 'La France des Bourbons. Telle qu'ils l'ont reçue. Telle qu'ils l'ont faite.' The map showed the *départements* gained at successive stages of French history and those lost under Napoleon III and, in case the message was not sufficiently clear, added 'En Résumé, La France a reçu: 85 départements et demi plus l'Algérie, des Bourbons, la moitié d'un département de la 1re République, 3 départements de Napoléon III. D'Autre part, par le fait de Napoléon III, puis de la République, la France a perdu 3 départements et demi, les plus riches de son territoire.' Geographical awareness was seen as a crucial aspect of nationalism; geography and history were both given major roles in patriotic civic education.[3]

Historical atlases can be seen as part of a continuum that included works on historical geography, especially political geography, that contained maps. For example, there were eighteen maps to the 143-page text in François-Émile de Bonnechose's *Géographie historique et politique de la France, comprenant les réunions successives des provinces, et les principales divisions politiques . . . avant 1789, comparées avec les divisions actuelles* (Paris, 1847, 2nd edn, 1877).

The title of Rudolph von Wedell's historical atlas emphasized its pedagogic purpose: *Historisch-geographischer Hand-Atlas in sechs und dreissig Karten . . . Zum Gebrauche für höhere Bürger-Schulen, Gymnasiën und Militair-Bildungs-Anstalten . . .* (Berlin, 1843–49). Wedell, a captain in the Prussian infantry, included battle plans and maps of specific interest to German readers such as that of the Teutonic Order in Prussia, but also offered considerable detail on other topics, including, on one page, nine maps of Spain from the Roman period until 1500. The first edition of what was to be and is still the leading German school historical atlas, *F.W. Putzger's Historischer Schul-Atlas zur alten, mittleren und neuen Geschichte* (Bielefeld and Leipzig) was published in 1877. The Saxon secondary school teacher Friedrich Wilhelm Putzger (1849–1913) and the publishers Velhagen and Klasing launched a work that reached its 25th edition in 1901.[4]

The educational market was price-sensitive and historical atlases directed at students made a point of their low price. Thus the preface to Alexander Keith Johnston's *Half-Crown Atlas of British History* (Edinburgh, 1871) stated: 'Teachers and students alike, have long felt the want of a connected series of maps, prepared expressly to illustrate the leading events of history, adapted for schools, and published at a price so moderate as to be brought within the reach of all learners.'[5] In addition, with growing literacy and wealth, the general book-reading public increased. Readers were avid for information. There was a great interest in statistics, and increased mapping was a part of this process. The rapidity of growth ensured that people wanted and needed new maps of towns and railways. Railway timetables often contained maps. Official statistical cartography developed in some countries, such as Prussia, but consumerism was more important. Readers were more used to seeing maps, not least in bibles, newspapers and magazines, and on stamps and consumer products, especially tins. Children saw maps displayed at schools, often as a visual centre in classrooms, a splash of colour and a suggestion of new horizons in spaces otherwise drained of imaginative potency. Like their newspaper-reading parents, children learned to read maps. Maps played a crucial role in imperializing states, explaining through depiction new links and ambitions.

Historical atlases, and indeed wall maps, played a role in this process, though the impact of the strong currents of nationalism cannot be assessed precisely. The growth of nation states and national empires were both cause and consequence of *mentalités* that were more focused on the nation, and this extended to the past, for past greatness and pretensions were crucial components of national myths, and the continuity of present and past was stressed. The development of nation states could be displayed through historical atlases, and national school systems played a major role in the propagation of such works.

German historical atlases were especially important in this development. With a large and literate population, a strong sense of national identity that earlier disunity now served to accentuate, a good cartographic tradition and active publishers, Germany produced a number of major historical atlases. For a nationalist age history provided a vital account setting present goals and problems in a historical context. Thus Droysens's 1886 atlas included a map showing how seventeenth-century France had extended its power in Alsace, a vital prelude to the German *revanche* in the Franco-Prussian war of 1870–71. The historical atlas gave a cartographic dimension to the lesson that the Austrian-led empire had been unable to defend Germany while its Prussian successor was more victorious and more German. Similarly in this period, the leading German secondary school atlas, *Putzger's Historischer Schul-Atlas* (Bielefeld and Leipzig, for example 1903 edition) devoted two pages to maps of Prussia's Danish, Austrian and French wars in the period 1864–71. Unification was thus a crucial part of German history, part of the direction in which it was going, a development that was naturally presented to the reader as he or she read through the book. German history dominated Carl Wolff's *Historischer Atlas* (Berlin, 1877), an atlas of European history with nineteen plates, because, aside from the six maps specifically on Germany, the country was central to the seven maps of much of central Europe (including France and northern Italy). Wolff made extensive use of colour in order to distinguish territories, for example in the map of central Europe in 1250 which distinguished numerous French, German and Italian principalities.

The extent to which works based on historical atlases published in other countries differed from the original was one aspect of nationalist cartography. Thus, in his *Popular Atlas of Comparative Geography* (London, 1870), William Hughes offered a British dimension on the Spruner atlas on which his work was based:

> Both in the maps themselves, and the brief commentary by which they are accompanied, the editor of the present volume has sought to treat the subject from a more strictly English point of view, and with reference to the general rather than the more special wants of the student of mediaeval and modern history at large . . . It has also been the editor's aim to illustrate the growth of British power in the East and West, and to show with precision the present limits of her widely-extended colonial empire.[6]

Aside from specific points, the historical atlases of the period, with their political emphasis and their mapping in terms of internally undifferentiated blocs of territory separated by clear linear frontiers, were conducive to an approach to the past that focused on undivided sovereignty and the development of the state. The major exception was arguably the mapping of German states, such as Württemberg and Saxony, in the Putzger atlas, for here was displayed the extraordinary territorial intermixture of jurisdictions. This was also seen in the detailed historical atlas of Saxony, *Erläuterungen des Atlas zur Geschichte der Sächsischen Länder* (Grimma, 1853). Its 22 maps revealed a precision in the mapping of territorial boundaries that was to characterize German historical cartography.

Complex maps such as that of Albertine Saxony in 1652 in the *Atlas zur Geschichte der Sächsischen Länder* counterbalanced too great an emphasis on neat linear frontiers separating large blocks of territory, but it was not easy to depict the overlapping nature of jurisdictions and power in the Holy Roman Empire effectively, and as a consequence the maps underlined the distinct territorial nature of authority, which

12. 'Central Europe in 1250' from Carl Wolff's *Historischer Atlas* (Berlin, 1877). Colour was used to depict the large number of territories in the Holy Roman Empire. This precise territorialization was a characteristic of German historical cartography and one that was made necessary by the desire to record the existence and boundaries of the numerous states of the empire.

was such a central theme of nineteenth-century historical atlases. A cartography that had few means to depict shared sovereignty thus accorded with a *mentalité* and pedagogic system that had little time for it. Territorial control was the principal theme in a work dedicated to Charles X of France by the Géographe du Roi, Adrien-Hubert Brué, the *Atlas géographique, historique, politique et administratif de la France composé de 24 cartes, sur lesquelles sont tracées, titrées et enluminées les limites, divisions ecclésiastiques, civiles, militaires, judiciaires et administratives de la France, aux principales époques de son histoire, avant et depuis l'établissement de la monarchie dans les Gaules jusqu'au règne de François I* (Paris, 1828). The introduction claimed that historical geography was a neglected topic and that history and geography complemented each other:

La géographie doit être une compagne fidèle de l'histoire; elle en rend l'étude plus sûre et plus facile. Sans les secours qu'elle lui prête, ses tableaux ressemblent à des peintures d'une belle ordonnance, d'un dessein admirable, si l'on vent, mais qui manquent de lumière; la mémoire erre alors confusément dans un chaos de faits et de dates qui ne se rapportent à rien; au moyen de ces secours, au contraire, tout se fixe avec ordre; l'histoire a décrit un événement: la géographie fait voir en quelque sorte le lieu qui en fut le théâtre; l'un et l'autre s'aidant mutuellement restent ineffaçablement empreints dans l'esprit du lecteur.

By following the successive political-territorial changes of France cartographically, the 'chaos' of its history would be clarified. Unlike Kruse's atlas of Europe, the Brué atlas deliberately did not produce maps to cover chronological sequence with regular intervals but, instead, concentrated on times of change. Rizzi-Zanoni's earlier effort was dismissed as only 'un essai' (a trial) and indeed the Brué was a more impressive work, conveying far more information and doing so clearly. His notes on the maps drew attention to the problem of availability of information, specifically to the lack of relevant material for the medieval as compared to the Classical period. The accompanying text drew attention to problems: for example, how much of northern France was still Roman in 481, whether the Bretons had been conquered by Clovis and how France was divided among Clovis's children. For the last, Rizzi-Zanoni was criticized for falsely claiming that contemporary sources gave precise limits. The last map dealt with France at the end of the reign of Louis XI and the text closed by claiming that the French invasion of Brittany in 1488 had fulfilled the twin goals of destiny and necessity: 'Ainsi fut uni à la couronne ce duché, qui en était séparé depuis près de sept siècles, et qui laissait une porte toujours ouverte à l'invasion des étrangers.' The theme of national unification as more than a matter of territorial control was outlined in the preface to Clausolles and Abadie's *Atlas historique et géographique de la France* (Paris, 1846):

> Les difficultés qui se présentent dans l'étude de notre histoire ne viennent pas absolument du grand nombre d'éléments divers dont s'est composée la nationalité française, mais plutôt de la succession trop souvent interrompue des principes qui ont mis en jeu ces éléments; et des causes qui les ont enfin poussés à l'unité ... on voit comment toutes les parties du territoire ont été ramenées successivement en un même corps, quelle puissance de vie a donné naissance aux formes de gouvernement qui se sont succédées, ce que chaque régime nouveau a conservé des régimes éteints; en un mot, comment s'est formée l'unité du peuple français au sein de tant de races diverses et de provinces opposés l'une à l'autre.

The atlas also emphasized its national character by renouncing the use of names 'd'une latinité barbare' for the maps of the Merovingian period and, instead, only using French names.[7]

   The use of maps of the past in order to make political points was seen in the *Géographie historique de la France. Atlas spécial* by two teachers, J.L. Sanis and Delalleau de Bailliencourt (Paris, no date, *c.* 1854–61), which was published under Napoleon III and was critical of the preceding governments. The text opposite the map of France under Louis XVIII, Charles X, Louis-Philippe and the Second Republic (1815–48) claimed that these regimes had not tried to modify the terms of the Congress of Vienna, terms that it alleged humiliated France.[8] In addition, the atlas offered evidence of France's heroic and successful past. The first section, on France's history, included maps of Charlemagne's empire, the routes of the Crusaders, France under Louis XI, but more maps appeared in the second part covering the campaigns of the Revolutionary and Napoleonic period. Four maps covered the physical basis of the campaign zone and twelve maps followed on the campaigns themselves.

The traumatic nature of the war of 1870–71 affected French geography, history and cartography. Marie-Nicolas Bouillet, Inspecteur-Général de l'Instruction Publique, referred in the preface to the third edition of his *Atlas universel d'histoire et de géographie* (Paris, 1877), the first edition of which had appeared in 1865, to a nearly general change, and linked this to different material in the new edition.[9] Bouillet left the reader in little doubt of the value of strong government. Explaining why he had chosen to map France in the reign of Louis XI, he wrote:

> parce que ce règne marque la fin de l'époque féodale et du moyen âge; le commence- ment de la toute-puissance royale et des temps modernes. C'est la glorieuse transition entre le passé anarchique et l'ordre nouveau qui inaugure la renaissance de la civilisa- tion. Pour bien comprendre cette carte il faut se rappeler ce qu'était la France à l'avénement de Louis XI, afin d'apprécier ce que ce grand homme a fait pour l'unité de la France.[10]

The next map of France was that of Napoleon I. This might appear very much a strong-man view of French history, but the Third Republic that had replaced Napoleon III in 1871 had little sympathy with the medieval period, which was presented as dominated by an anarchic nobility and, in part, by English intervention.

In A.H. Dufour's *Atlas historique de la France* (Paris, 1878) the emphasis was on national extent rather than internal division. As was true of nineteenth-century atlases in general, maps were political not socio-economic. Moments of French weakness were largely avoided. Thus successive maps treated France under Philip Augustus (1180–1223), at the accession of the Valois (1328), under Henry IV (1589– 1610) and under Louis XIV (1661–1715). No attempt was made to map collapses of royal authority during the Hundred Years' War, the French Wars of Religion and the Fronde. The maps were also generous to France territorially. For example, on the map of France under Louis XIV all of Alsace was shown as France, and no attempt was made to indicate the far more complex reality. Similarly, the independ- ence of Lorraine was understated. The maps in *Géographie de la Gaule au VIᵉ siècle* (Paris, 1878), by Auguste-Honoré Longnon (1844–1911), similarly emphasized terri- torial control, presented in terms of homogeneous areas. Longnon was appointed to a chair of the historical geography of France at the Collège de France in 1892.

The full title of the *Atlas Melin historique et géographique* (Moulins-sur-Allier, 1895) clearly indicated its pedagogic nature: 'spécialement établi pour les examens du Baccalauréat et de Saint-Cyr.' The historical section was devoted to France and Europe 1610–1896 and the theme was one of long-term struggle between France and the dominant German power. The first spread, devoted to France and the Austrian Habsburgs in 1610, contained a big map of France and a small one of the Habsburg dominions. The map was accompanied by a misleading text that presented France as defensive and ignored the serious divisions within French policy, especially the views of the *dévots* who sought an anti-Protestant alliance with the Habsburgs: 'Au commencement du XVII siècle, toute la politique européene se résume en ces mots: abaisser la maison d'Autriche. C'est la politique de la France, dont la sécurité est menacée.' The section included a big map for the war of 1870–71.[11] An emphasis on the territorial history of states characterized *The Historical Geography of Europe* (London, 1881) by Edward Augustus Freeman, the Regius Professor of Modern History at Oxford.

Imperialism

An emphasis on territoriality and control over blocs of space was extended to the extra-European world.[12] This was generally presented in terms of 'discoveries' – i.e. European exploration – and the expansion of European colonial power, the latter a preparation for the imperial depiction of the current world in maps such as George Parkin's *The British Empire Map of the World on Mercator's Projection* (Edinburgh, 1893). Thus, for British historical atlases the nineteenth century was an age of colonial gain, not economic growth; usually only one map was devoted to developments in transport links within Britain while industrialization and economic subjects, on the whole, received very limited attention. The atlases often ended with a map of the world showing British possessions and dependencies. Indeed, coverage of post-Napoleonic history generally concentrated on Britain as an imperial power. Alexander Keith Johnston's *Half-Crown Atlas of British History* (Edinburgh, 1871) had four maps covering the post-Napoleonic period: the first of the Indian empire with two smaller maps, one of the Malay Peninsula simply showing British possessions, the other part of China to illustrate the Opium Wars; the second of western Russia to show the Crimean War, with an inset map of Sevastopol and its environs; the third 'Central Europe illustrating Continental Wars 1848–71'; and the last, the world showing British possessions and dependencies and nothing else. Fresh editions appeared in 1892, 1902, 1917 and 1924.

In Alexander Keith Johnston's *Half-Crown Historical Atlas* (Edinburgh, 1891) the last four plates were devoted to a map of Afghanistan to illustrate recent Anglo-Afghan conflicts, with a smaller map of the Afghan-Russian frontier; South Africa to illustrate British wars with the Zulus and Boers in 1879–81, with a smaller map for the Ashanti war of 1873–74; Egypt and Abyssinia 1868–85 to illustrate British interventions, with smaller maps of the Suez Canal and Alexandria and its forts, the latter the scene of a British victory in 1882; and lastly a map of the world showing British possessions and dependencies. The following edition, that of 1902, included three maps to illustrate the Boer War of 1899–1902.

States, regions, natural features and cities outside Europe were identified by European, not native, names, and with equal consistency native boundaries were ignored in favour of the borders of European imperial authority. The British empire was presented as both apogee and conclusion of the historical process, one that began with maps of the twin sources of its culture: the ancient civilizations of the Middle East and Mediterranean, and the Holy Land. Thus, maps offered a teleological view, and a linking of what could be seen as the key elements in world history. This linkage implied a diffusionist model of cultural history in which centres of civilization, most obviously ancient Rome and modern Britain, impacted on the world from their central or prominent position in the projections employed: there was little sense of interaction, not that this could have been readily induced by contemporary cartographic methods, and the principal reverse thrust was that of the barbarian invasions. These were presented as destructive and incoherent: the assault of barbarian peoples in the shape of coloured arrows on the territorial bloc of the Roman empire.

The diffusionist model was presented best in the *Historical Atlas in a Series of Maps of the World, as Known at Different Periods, Constructed upon an Uniform Scale, and Coloured according to the Political Changes of Each Period* (London, 1830), by the

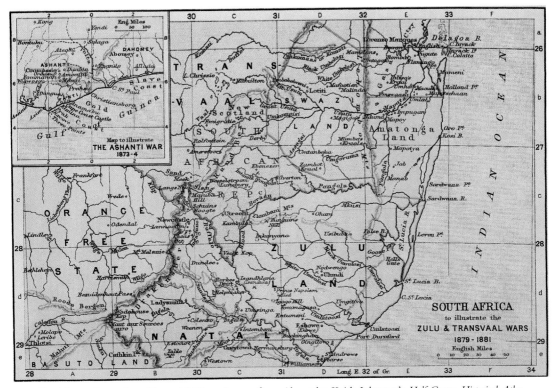

13.   The Map as Recorder of Imperial Wars. A map from Alexander Keith Johnston's *Half-Crown Historical Atlas* (Edinburgh, 1891) which reflected European cartographic assumptions, not least in its use of graticule, scale and in territorial boundaries employed. Battles were not described as victories or defeats; the reader was supposed to know that.

London barrister Edward Quin (1794–1828), though some years earlier a similar concept was used by F.W. Benicken in his *Historischer Schulatlas oder Übersicht der allgemeinen Weltgeschichte* (Weimar, 1820), and also in his large-sized *Historischer Hand-Atlas zur Versinnlichung der allgemeinen Geschichte aller Völker und Staaten* (Weimar, 1824). Educated at Oxford, Quin lacked cartographic experience, but his 21 maps offered a vivid account of global political history presented in chronological order. The atlas was reprinted in 1836, and was also the basis for the *Atlas to Accompany a System of Universal History* by Emma Willard, published that year in Hartford, Connecticut. William Hughes redrew Quin's maps on the hemispherical projection and made some changes in content for another edition in 1846 and another, with a new final map of the world, the *Atlas of Universal History* (London and Glasgow), appeared in 1856 and was reprinted in 1859. The text was also used for the *Universal History from the Creation* (London, 1840).

   Quin's atlas was distinctive for its use of receding clouds, but was also impressive as a global historical atlas that employed a uniform base map. The introduction claimed:

   Its peculiarity consists in exhibiting everything in its real dimensions and just propor-tions, and in adhering to the same scale in all successive delineations. Greece and Persia are seen, for instance, in the relations which they actually bore to each other;

and are not shown, as in many atlases; – the one on a scale of 20 miles to an inch, the other on a scale of 200. And when once laid down, they remain, in each subsequent map, on the same spot, and of the same dimensions.

Colour was used to depict civilization. Beginning with Eden (located in Mesopotamia) and the Deluge, what was 'unknown', by Europeans and the preceding civilizations they acknowledged, was 'enveloped' in darkness – black and grey clouds. Quin explained that 'China and America were as much in existence in the days of Cyrus as they are now, although unknown to the great mass of civilized human beings'. In addition:

> there have always been, in every age of the world, parts of the earth, not unknown to the geographer or the historian, but classed, by their want of civilization, of regular government, and of known and recognized limits, under the general description of *barbarous countries*. Such was Scythia through all antiquity, and such is the interior of Africa at the present moment.
>
> Now, in distinguishing the successive kingdoms of the earth in our maps by appropriate colours, it was obviously impossible to assign any distinguishing tints to tracts like these. The colours we have used being generally meant to point out and distinguish one state or empire from another, and to show their respective limits and extent of dominion, were obviously inapplicable to deserts peopled by tribes having no settled form of government, or political existence, or known territorial limits. These tracts of country, therefore, we have covered alike in all the periods, with a flat olive shading; which the eye of the student will observe on the skirts of all the maps, and which designates throughout the work, those barbarous and uncivilized countries to which we have adverted.

The text in Quin's atlas closely corresponded to the teleology and Eurocentrism of the maps. Thus, for the map of 814–912 readers were informed that 'the paramount importance of the history of Europe, induces us henceforth to commence our narrative with it'. For 1100–1294 progress was associated with the rise of the middle class:

> During our present period, notwithstanding the gross superstition which prevailed, the undefined state of regal power and popular rights, and the many atrocious acts which were perpetrated, Europe was fast emerging from the state of barbarism in which it had been sunk for several centuries. In England, France, Germany and Italy, the Commons or third estate, began to be recognised and respected; industry and commerce were acquiring their due weight and estimation, and through the study of jurisprudence, the rights of persons and of property were better understood.

The following period, 1294–1498, was described in clearly teleological terms: 'The darkness of the middle ages was dispelled and the way cleared for the progress of the Protestant religion by the light of science, literature, and commerce.' The years 1558–1660 proclaimed the superiority of the trade on which Victorian Britain was based: 'nations in general began to regard industry and commerce, rather than mere conquest, as the true sources of wealth and grandeur'. Quin had a low view of Latin America:

Those beautiful countries were at length wrested from a cruel misgovernment and debasing dominion of Spain, but a great majority of their inhabitants had been too long familiar with oppression, and associated with bigotry and ignorance, to be fit to enjoy suddenly the blessings of freedom, and to rank among the settled communities of the civilized world.

It was only in the early nineteenth century that Japan was recognized: 'We have hitherto left Japan unnoticed, because its existence was unimportant to the rest of the world.'[13]

Similar views were expressed in other historical atlases. For the map of Europe at the end of the fourteenth century, Edward Gover, who drew heavily on Spruner, wrote in his *Atlas of Universal Historical Geography* (London, 1854):

the European states were moulded somewhat into their present form, and rapid approaches made towards more liberal and enlightened forms of policy in the regulation of the states, and in maintaining the balance of power. The darkness of the medieval period was now fast dispelling, and the way cleared for the progress of religion, science, literature, and commerce.[14]

Similar attitudes were expressed in twentieth-century works written within a Whiggish, teleological interpretation. Quin's Eurocentric account of relative degrees of civilization was also repeated, and, although the Eurocentrism became less pronounced, the notions of civilization and barbarism, as both distinct and crucial to global history and as best depicted using colour and a different background, were influential in *The World. Its History in Maps* by W.H. McNeill, M.R. Buske and A.W. Roehm (Chicago, 1963). Here the authors argued these notions

can only be borne in upon atlas users if spots of colour are set against vast expanses of neutral tint, representing the portions of the globe where barbarian and savage forms of society prevailed ... comparison from map to map: shows the gradual expansion of agriculture as against hunting and fishing ... the use of solid colours to define the limits of high civilization give visual focus to the maps.[15]

It was scarcely surprising, given attitudes such as Quin's, that many historical atlases ignored the world outside Europe. Thus, Jacques Babinet's *Atlas universel de géographie physique, politique et historique* (Paris, 1862) contained 35 historical maps, but though the bounds of Europe were passed in depicting the Classical world and the Crusades, the atlas was otherwise one of European history. There were no historical maps for the New World in E. Cortambert's *Nouvel atlas de géographie. La géographie ancienne, la géographie du Moyen Âge, cosmographie et la géographie moderne* (Paris, 1868), and the sole historical map for Asia was one of Asia under the Mongols in the thirteenth and fourteenth centuries. That was also the sole Asian map in the same author's *Petit atlas de géographie du Moyen Âge* (Paris, 1868): the Crusades were essentially presented as an episode in European history.

Teleological views affected what was mapped, most obviously with maps of the Classical world. William Murphy's *Comprehensive Classical Atlas* (Edinburgh, 1832) stated, 'Ancient Geography is intimately connected with the study of History, – in tracing the origin of nations, and the progress of discovery with the advances of

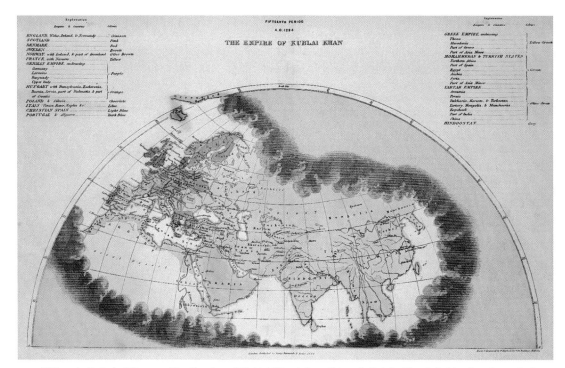

14. 'Fifteenth Period. AD 1294. The Empire of Kublai Khan' from Edward Quin's *Historical Atlas* (London, 1830). The Eurasian world framed in dark clouds. Even as an account of the 'known' world, this was somewhat misleading as knowledge of Central Asia, Arabia and the Sahara was not widely disseminated. The emphasis on Mongol/Tatar power was instructive. English power in Ireland was exaggerated.

mankind in arts, commerce, and civilization.'[16] The map on Africa in the atlas was restricted to North Africa as was invariably the case with atlases of Classical history.

The most dramatic example of a map in the nineteenth century was the large model of the globe built by James Wyld at the time of the Great Exhibition of 1851 in London. 'Wyld's Great Globe' was exhibited in a large circular building in Leicester Square in 1851–62. Gas-lit, it was sixty feet high, about forty feet in diameter and the largest hitherto constructed. Wyld also published, in an edition dedicated to Prince Albert, *Notes to Accompany* his globe. He argued that the globe, which showed on its interior side the physical features of the earth, permitted a better understanding of history. Wyld also exulted in 'the civilizing sway of the English crown . . . an empire more extended than is governed by any other sceptre'. Wyld claimed that traditional approaches to learning minimized the British achievement:

> If we look greedily on our heritage – for to people the world is the destiny of our race – we often fail to recognise what we have already accomplished. A vicious class of school-books, parcelling out the world into antiquated divisions, and representing it principally under its physical aspects affords no adequate idea of political geography, still less of the vast empire of the English race, scattered over the regions of the globe.

The map provided a measure of imperial greatness, doubly so in historical comparison: 'In the height of our exultation, we may look back, and ask what the ancient monarchies were – that portion of the world which Alexander gained, and then sighed because he thought no other world was left to acquire.' Rome provided the central point of reference, as it had done for rulers and writers in European states for centuries: 'Prompted by the historian, we may mark out the speck among the hills, whence Rome sent forth her sons, to make the western world her empire, as our fathers issued in three barks from the Anglian shores of Jutland.' Wyld was in no doubt that the British had brought civilization, that their use of force was beneficial: 'What comparisons suggest themselves between the condition of the Pacific region in the time of Cook and now? What was then held by illiterate savages now constitutes the rising communities of New South Wales ... There are Tahiti and hundreds of islands with Christian churches and schools.' Wyld was also in no doubt of the appeal of military details:

> The Indian hero [by which Wyld meant British not Indian soldiers] will fight his battles over again ... The veteran, fresh from the Atlas of Battles, will ... show how the great Duke [Wellington] prepared and carried out each successive enterprise ... he may illustrate the science of war, the campaigns of Alexander, the march of Hannibal, the labours of Caesar ...

– suitable comparisons with British prowess. The 'naval hero' was also to have the opportunity to make 'known the genius and audacity of Vernon, of Anson, and of Nelson'.[17]

Wyld was no eccentric. He was an active parliamentarian, Master of the Cloth-workers' Company, and a leading promoter of technical education, and had a high reputation as a cartographer. Wyld's *Notes* revealed the extent to which maps provided striking images of power and opportunities to meditate on or exult in the purposes of power. The French anarchist geographer Elisée Reclus proposed that an enormous terrestrial globe be displayed at the Paris Exposition Universelle in 1900.[18]

Wyld's comparison of the Classical and modern world was taken up in David Ansted and C.G. Nicolay's *Atlas of Physical and Historical Geography to Accompany the Manual of Geographical Science* (London, 1858). This included a 'Comparative Chart of Ancient and Modern Geography and Geographical Discovery', which contained, besides three small maps of the world according to Eratosthenes and Strabo, to Herodotus and to Ptolemy, a big map of the modern world with the Persian, Mesopotamian and Roman empires superimposed and also the routes of the leading explorers.

Maps of exploration and the 'known world' reflected and encouraged the related notions of Eurocentrism, diffusion and teleology. Thus the *Atlas of Physical and Historical Geography* (London, 1840) included a map entitled 'Comparative Chart of Ancient and Modern Geography and Geographical Discovery', comparing 'the world as known to the Ancients' and the Persian, Macedonian and Roman empires with the contemporary situation and the British, Russian and American dominions. The direct comparison of ancient Rome and modern Britain was expressed in the preface to Charles Pearson's *Historical Maps of England* (London, 1869) when, in a discussion of the size of the indigenous population, he wrote 'our troops have repeatedly fought in India against greater odds than the Romans ever encountered in the conquest of Britain'.[19]

Despite Eurocentrism, the historical mapping of other continents increased. The Russian geographer J. Klaproth's *Tableaux historiques de l'Asie* (Paris, 1826) extended

from the time of Cyrus to 1825, the 'Epoque de la Prépondérance des Anglais', all
presented on the same base map of Asia. Many of the maps in the atlas provided
relatively little detail on India, and Siberia was largely a blank, but the atlas was a
valuable account of the territorial development of much of Asia. Rudolph von
Wedell's *Historisch-Geographischer Hand-Atlas* (Berlin, 1849) included a map of the
Islamic world until 1000 covering from Spain to India, and another of Asia and
Africa, mostly the former, in the twelfth and thirteenth centuries. However, A.
Houzé's *Atlas universel historique et géographique*, published in Paris in 1849, devoted
only one map to Asia in the period 1227–1849. This had all of Tibet, Sinkiang,
Manchuria and Dzungaria up to Lake Balkhash under China, a situation that was
true for only a portion of the period.

The *Spruner-Menke Hand-Atlas* (Gotha, 1880) did not confuse by putting too
much information on one map. Instead, plate 87 included separate maps for topics
such as the Mongol empire under Genghis Khan, the Mongol states at the time of
Kublai Khan and the empire of Tamerlane. Plate 89, on the Ottoman empire and
its neighbours 1391–1452, devoted as much attention to the Asian as the European
neighbours. Yet the very organization of the atlas was Eurocentric. The first map
was of Europe in the age of Odovacar 476–93. Asia only appeared after Europe and
far more information was offered on the latter, not least because the maps were
relatively large scale. Karl von Spruner, however, also published a special historical
atlas of the non-European world, his *Historisch-geographischer Hand-Atlas zur Geschichte
Asiens, Africa's, America's und Australiens* (Gotha, 1854). This included eighteen sheets
of maps – 10 for Asia, 4 for America, 3 for Africa and 1 for Australia – and its success
led to a second edition in 1855.

The nineteenth-century European view of the world was generally unsympathetic
to other cultures, especially towards the close of the century as European power
spread dramatically. Africa was partitioned and previously impressive states, such as
China and Turkey, seemed increasingly decrepit. British atlases used the Mercator
projection in part because it exaggerated land masses in high latitudes, for example
Canada, and hence the size and importance of the British empire; although it
minimized the size of India. A sense of providential triumphalism was captured in
Edmund McClure's *Historical Church Atlas* (London, 1897). This included colour
maps of the distribution of the world into Anglican dioceses, and the text was full
of a confidence in mission that discouraged any sense of relative values. Thus the
pre-Reformation Church was dismissed in terms of 'the degenerate and the generally
sordid life of the cloister'. McClure recounted the spread of Christianity and was in
no doubt that the growth of European rule greatly contributed:

> the heathen millions of the East are brought ever more and more within touch of a
> power which shall at length win their allegiance, when the vision of Isaiah shall be
> fully realized . . . How has all this come about? The annals of the civilized world for
> the last eighteen centuries will furnish an answer. The history of the spread of the
> Christian faith . . . may be regarded as furnishing a striking evidence of God's ruling
> Providence in the world – an evidence which, while it strengthens our faith, must
> invigorate at the same time our hope of the ultimate and universal triumph of the
> Gospel predicted by prophecy.[20]

Thus divine purpose could be mapped, and maps demonstrated the intentions and

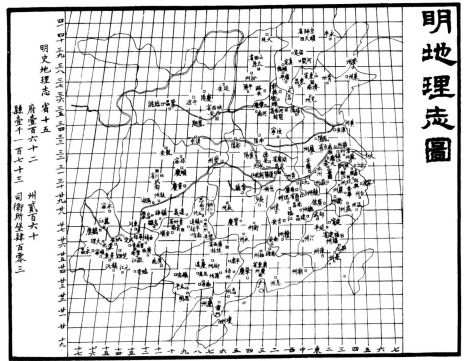

15. The *Historical Atlas of the Chinese Empire* by E.L. Oxenham (2nd edn, London, 1898). Although produced by a British diplomat and published in Britain, this atlas offered an account of Chinese history that was not framed by the European imagination. The emphasis was on the principal cities of successive dynasties, on China, not on foreign invasions or on China in the wider world.

progress of Providence. Such a viewpoint can be seen as not too dissimilar from the cartographic world of earlier civilizations, for example medieval Christendom, but there were differences. Nineteenth-century Europe was a more carto-literate age and the number and range of maps produced were far greater than in any other society hitherto. In addition, there was an effort, albeit not a very pronounced one, to understand other societies in cartographic terms.

The work of E.L. Oxenham was an important instance of the latter. Oxenham, who worked in the British consulate in Sinkiang, published in 1888 an *Historical Atlas of the Chinese Empire from the Earliest Times down to the Close of the Ming Dynasty, Giving in Chinese the Names of the Chief Towns and the Metropolis of Each of the Chief Dynasties of China*. The publication of the work reflected the reach of European power. Though the atlas appeared in Shanghai, the publisher was a European firm, Kelly and Walsh. Oxenham's atlas was especially interesting because he presented China as dynamic rather than decadent. He found value in China's past – 'against Plato and Aristotle place Confucius and Mencius' – and dismissed the

prevailing cant as to the immobility of China. From the times of Yu the Great, a stream of change can be noticed from a number of feudal autonomous states to a single democratic centralised autocracy. The progressive element in Chinese history has been, and is today, the monarchical element. Gradually, and step by step, Emperor after Emperor has whittled away one individual privilege after another. Hereditary

nobility, primogeniture, large estates, parks, religious establishments, and game pre-
serves, have all disappeared and fallen before the resistless pressure of that multitude of China, of which the Son of Heaven is the Representative and the
Incarnation . . . Railways will abolish religious superstition and some cruel customs,
and will purify the lower official ranks; but it is not probable they will change one
atom the fundamental institutions of China.[21]

Oxenham discerned a fundamental continuity in Chinese history, though he exaggerated its capacity to defy change. Nevertheless, although his cartography was
simplistic and the scale of the maps did not permit sufficient detail, his sympathetic
treatment of Chinese history was important. The second edition, published in
London in 1898 by the Royal Geographical Society and the publishers John Murray,
included an English counterpart of each map, printed opposite the Chinese maps of
the first edition. Apart from Oxenham, Chinese history scarcely features in late
nineteenth-century historical atlases, before the arrival of European imperialism in
Asia. Such an emphasis was true of the mapping of the history of most of the world.

Intentions

Historical atlases offered instructive accounts of their intentions, and these, principally contained in prefaces and introductions, are the most important guide to the
attitudes conditioning the compilation of the works. It is mistaken to consider the
maps without a close scrutiny of these texts. Much that they contain is facile,
repetitive, self-evident and bombastic, but there are also revealing guides to intentions, reasons for inclusion or emphasis, and problems encountered. If the self-
referential sections of historical atlases can be self-reverential, they are, nevertheless,
crucial to the assessment of the visual message of the maps.

Edward Gover, in the preface to his *Atlas of Universal Historical Geography* (London, 1854), stated 'that if the *ideal* of an Historical Atlas is to be obtained, it must
be wrought out of the *matériel* which history alone furnishes, and be a reflection of
the sources themselves'. Gover emphasized the problem:

> The Historian may express that which is doubtful by a few strokes of his pen; but the
> Geographer, who has to describe a fact by a line or a single word, is in a different
> position: for the Geography of the Middle Ages, it may be observed, that the *matériel*,
> although abundant, was of a very doubtful and conflicting character . . . to collate and
> compare these various documents, so as to make them available for the purposes of
> geographical representation, involved laborious research of no ordinary character.

This remains the case today.

The previous year Gover had been responsible for *The Historic Geographical Atlas
of the Middle and Modern Ages* (London). This work demonstrated an important aspect
of any study of historical atlases, that of the extent to which the compiler used
familiar or new maps, and the degree to which this throws light on his intentions.
On his title-page, Gover made his debt to Spruner clear, but in his preface he added:

> To render the Atlas more complete for the student of English History, special maps
> of England, Scotland, Ireland, North America, and India have been compiled, as also

one of France, to delineate more fully our political and territorial relations with that country during the eleventh, and three subsequent centuries. And in order to illustrate the period of the Reformation, one of great importance to all the nations of Continental Europe, a Map of Germany is added, showing all the then existing Secular and Ecclesiastical Principalities.

Aside from discussing the sources employed and the problems encountered, the text can highlight the didactic purpose of particular maps. In the authorized English edition of Spruner, published in 1861 by Trübner and Co., the text accompanying map thirteen – Western Europe about the middle of the sixteenth century – included the instruction: 'The great extent of the Continental dominions of the Republic of Venice, no less than that of the Ottoman Empire, reaching far up the Danube, must also be carefully considered.'

The text accompanying the last map in the book, that of the British Isles from 1485 onwards, was triumphalist:

This map serves to connect the history of the British Isles with the period of their greatest progress in the arts of civilization, and which is best evidenced by a reference to any modern map upon which the greatest network of their railways, canals, and turnpike-roads, is accurately laid down. The map of the British Isles of the reign of her most gracious Majesty Queen Victoria, is the best and truest record of the indomitable perseverance and skill of the Anglo-Saxon race.

Thus the atlases of the period were nationalist, imperialist and didactic, with a clear emphasis on territoriality. The preface to the *New School Atlas of Modern History* (London, 1911) by Ramsay Muir, Professor of Modern History at Liverpool University, noted that 'As the Atlas is intended to be used by young people of the greatest colonising nation in history, special attention has been devoted to Indian, American, and Colonial history.' The emphasis was resolutely Eurocentric. The text for plate 48a, 'The British Settlement of Australasia', declared: 'Happy is the nation that has no history. Apart from the Maori wars in New Zealand, the only noteworthy features of the history of Australasia are the dates of the successive settlements, and the chief stages in the exploration of the region, both of which are shown.'[22] Muir was in no doubt of the importance of the national principle and the irrelevance of other bases for state formation. For the map of Europe in 1815 readers were instructed to

Note especially the features of the settlement, which by disregarding national senti-ment produced the principal troubles of the 19th century: (1) The forced union of Sweden and Norway; (2) the similar union of Holland and Belgium; (3) the restora-tion of the old disunion in Italy, and the controlling power exercised by Austria there in the possession of Lombardy and Venetia; the one favourable feature being the expansion of the kingdom of Sardinia by the addition of Liguria and other lands; (4) the revival, in the German Confederation, of a ghost of the old Holy Roman Empire, powerless to achieve anything and useful only as an aid to Austria in checking any movement towards unity or liberty. Germany, however, emerges greatly simplified, and above all with one dominant power, Prussia, capable of becoming a centre of unity.[23]

Similarly, the text for map 25, Europe 1789–1815, in Gover's *Atlas of Universal Historical Geography* (London, 1854) complained of the Congress of Vienna that its 'determinations were guided rather to the advancement of their [the powers present] own individual interests, than for the welfare of the nations whose destinies were in their hands'. Thus most of Poland remained Russian.

The political agenda of the nation state was matched by a cartographic style that stressed undifferentiated blocs of territory, frequently colour-coded, separated by clear linear frontiers. These blocs might also carry details of physical features, but there was only limited concern both with the socio-economic situation and with political identities and activities below the level of the state.

The emphasis on territorial control and the nation state was also related to the expansion in the number of countries producing historical atlases. The earlier agenda of the Classics and the Bible had been international, at least within a North American and European context. Furthermore, books, especially those containing maps, were expensive, readership was limited and the purchasers of expensive works could usually read one of the leading languages of book publication: French, German or Latin. It was therefore possible for a relatively small number of publication centres to satisfy the market for historical atlases.

Conversely, the late nineteenth-century emphasis on state development, the rise of publication in most of the European languages, the more widespread growth of the publishing industry, and the development of national school systems purchasing works in the vernacular encouraged the appearance of historical atlases in more countries. If their agenda was to be primarily that of the development of the state, then works produced in different countries would have varied emphases, and this encouraged the process of expansion.

Historical atlases might duplicate each other's themes, but the national foci ensured that this led to different maps, though foreign editions and translations of individual atlases could extend their influence and limit the extent of diversity. For example *Putzger's Historischer Schul-Atlas* appeared in Austrian (1877), Czech (1896), Polish (1900), Croatian (1902), American (1911; W.R. Shepherd's *Historical Atlas*) and Swiss (1923) editions. F.W. Schubert and W. Schmidt produced an historical atlas for secondary schools in the Austrian part of Austria-Hungary which was published in three parts by the Vienna publishing house Edward Hölzel in 1887–95. Czech translations were published by Hölzel in 1887–98 and the three parts were published by Hölzel as one volume in 1898 with the title *F. Schuberta a V. Schmidta historicko-zeměpisný atlas školní starého, středního a nového věku. Pro české školy střední upravili Dr A. Balcar, Dr J. Vlach a Dr Fr Kameníček* 'F. Schubert's and W. Schmidt's historical-geographical school atlas of ancient, medieval and modern history. Prepared for Czech secondary schools by A. Balcar, J. Vlach and Fr. Kameníček.' The atlas had the conventional maps of the Classical world, but included some good maps of eastern Europe, including one of Bohemia and Moravia in the twelfth century and one of eastern Europe in 1350. The battle plans included the crucial battle of the White Mountain outside Prague in 1620 which re-established Habsburg power in Bohemia for nearly three centuries. As was common with historical atlases in this period, there were no maps tackling economic history, but, instead, numerous maps to show campaign zones or battles.

This work is not intended as a carto-bibliography, but it is important to consider the situation in a few countries in order to avoid an over-concentration on devel-

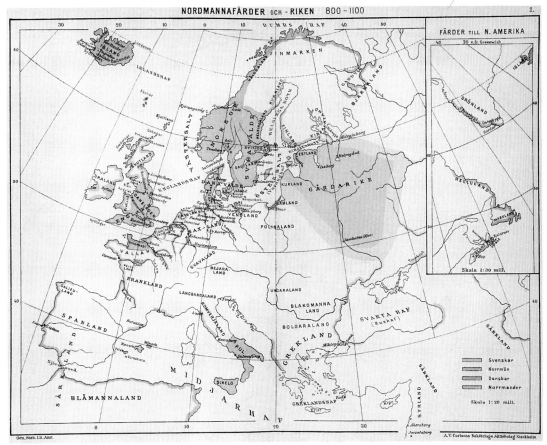

16. 'The Vikings' from Arvid Kempe's *Atlas till Sveriges, Norges och Danmarks Historia* (Stockholm, 1897). A simplistic map that for example provided no indication of chronology. The absence of arrows and dates helped to give the map a static feel. Trade routes were not shown.

opments in Britain, France and Germany, important as they were, and because a national perspective offers a different approach, one that also throws light on developments in Britain, France and Germany. The availability of specialized production and printing facilities was a problem in some countries. The *Atlas historique de Belgique* published by Hanceau in 1872 was printed by Bartholomew. In contrast to the western European works of the period, Arvid Kempe's *Atlas till Sveriges, Norges och Danmarks Historia* (Stockholm, 1897) contained only six maps. They were fairly simplistic and ignored physical geography. The first, devoted to the Vikings 800–1100, exaggerated their territorial impact in North Africa and Europe. The other maps were devoted to Scandinavia and battle plans. Kempe was a secondary school teacher in history and Swedish who also published several topographical works and a school atlas.

Switzerland

The first edition of a *Historisch-Geographischer Atlas der Schweiz*, produced by Vögelin, Meyer von Knonau and Wyss, appeared in 1846–55, followed by a second in 1870.

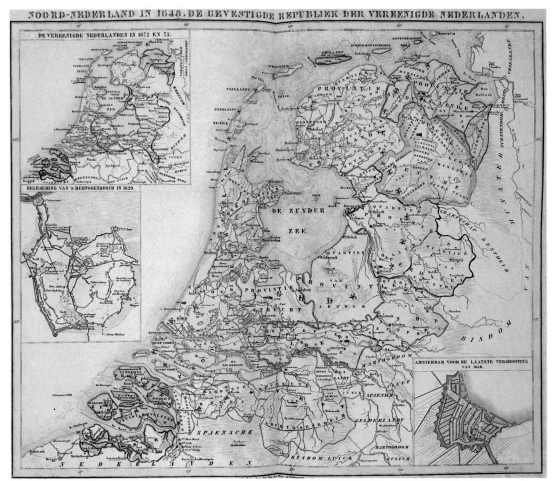

17. 'The United Provinces in 1648' from G. Mees's *Historische Atlas van Noord-Nederland* (Rotterdam, 1865). War was a major theme, not only with the inset plan of the siege of 's-Hertogenbosch in 1629, a Dutch triumph over Spain, but also with the map of the early stages of the Franco-Dutch war of 1672–8 when Louis XIV invaded the Republic.

As was common with atlases of the period, military events were amply depicted. For example, the spread on 1798–1802 included inset maps devoted to the battle sites for the battles of Nidwalden (1798), Zurich (1799) and Rossberg (1806). The atlas devoted half of its space to the medieval period. It included a map of Switzerland under the Romans, but the effect of moving from a European or world scale to that of the country was to lessen the space devoted to the Classical period.

J.S. Gerster published an historical atlas of Switzerland in French and one that indicated by its full title the extensive market such atlases sought: *Atlas historique de la Suisse à l'usage des écoles et des familles* (Neuchâtel, 1875). This contained eighteen maps beginning with the Roman period, and the maps depended on the use of colour. There was also an extensive text. One of the maps was devoted to Switzerland's military history. Much of the atlas mapped Swiss medieval history, and in the notes on the map of Switzerland in 1218–1331 Gerster made clear 'la grande difficulté qu'il y a à démontrer par la cartographie et la couleur, les relations historiques et juridiques des Etats entre eux au moyen âge'. He referred to the problem of the relationship between seigneurs and freemen in the canton of Schwyz.[24]

Gerster's intelligent response to the problem of producing historical atlases, his appreciation that it was far more than a question simply of drawing lines on a map and his determination to communicate that perception, was an attractive contrast to the publicly unreflective nature of much mapmaking. M.-N. Bouillet made a similar point about the difficulties of mapping the medieval period in his *Atlas universel d'histoire et de géographie* (3rd edn, Paris, 1877). He wrote of the map of France at the death of Louis XI: 'Il est à peu près impossible de dresser une carte féodale complète de la France au moyen âge, tant fut grand le morcellement, tant est compliqué le système de vassalité et de suzeraineté des seigneurs vis-à-vis les uns des autres et vis-à-vis du roi.'[25]

The Netherlands

For the Netherlands W.E.J. Huberts produced the *Historisch-Geographische Atlas der Algemeenen Vaderlandsche Geschiedenis* (The Hague, 1855). The 1870 edition consisted of 40 plates. Twelve were devoted to the Classical world, another eighteen to the history of Europe and ten to that of the Netherlands, starting with a plate on the changing coastline of the Zuider Zee, and then with a second on the Netherlands at the end of the thirteenth century. The sieges of Antioch and Jerusalem during the Crusades and the battles of Nieuport and Waterloo were illustrated by small plans.

G. Mees's *Historische Atlas van Noord-Nederland, van de XVIe eeuw tot op Heden* (Rotterdam, 1865) contained, besides its extensive text, sixteen maps that provided considerable detail on politico-territorial developments. The first map, however, presented the northern Netherlands in 1530 when there was no reason to treat it separately from the rest of the Low Countries. Thus the atlas gave Dutch history a misleading coherence and longevity. The introduction discussed errors in the presentation of Dutch history in other atlases. Military history was emphasized. The plate on 1590 included smaller maps on the siege of Antwerp in 1585 and on Maurice of Nassau's lines near Nieuport, that on 1648 included a plan of the siege of 's-Hertogenbosch in 1629, that of 1740–95 included a map of the Prussian invasion in 1787 and that of 1814 a plan of Waterloo. G.J. Dozy's *Historische Atlas der Algemeene Geschiedenis, Afbeeldingen en Kaarten* (Zutphen, no date) began with a map of Jerusalem and the Holy Land, devoted much attention to the Classical world and had low cartographic standards. In the map of Europe in the twelfth century the coastlines of Wales, Norway and the Baltic were wrong.

Poland

Historical atlases also developed in eastern Europe. Differences between countries reflected in part their publishing industries and the size of their reading publics, though politics also played a major role. Concern over the fate of Poland led to interest in its history and this was further encouraged by a relatively large reading public by nineteenth-century eastern European standards. Polish historical cartography began in the eighteenth century with individual maps. The first historical atlases relevant to Poland were produced outside Poland and were intended more for an international readership: they were not written in Polish. The first, Jan Potocki's *Atlas archéologique de la Russie européenne* was published in St Petersburg in 1805. It was followed after the Napoleonic Wars by a series of works published in Polish in what had been Poland. The leading cartographer, Joachim Lelewel, was responsible for a number of works, especially the *Atlas do Historyi i Geografi Starozytney* (Warsaw, 1828). His *Atlas do Dziejów Polskich z Dwunastu Krajobrazów* (Warsaw, 1829) presented Polish history through twelve maps all on the same base. Rather than offering a regular chronological sequence, the maps reflected the major changes of Polish history and covered the situation in 850, 992, 1025, 1139, 1270, 1333, 1375, 1500, 1572, 1586, 1673 and the period of the partitions. The atlas lacked a text but the maps were a potent account of decline.

Other historical atlases were produced by émigrés. For example, Leonard Chodźko was co-author of the *Atlas historique, politique et statistique de la Pologne ancienne et moderne, indiquant ses divers démembrements et partages* (Paris, 1831). In 1846 he published his *Atlas des sept partages de la Pologne et des efforts des polonais pour la regénération de leur patrie en Pologne* (Paris). Jan Marcin Bransener and Piotr Falkenhagen Zaleski produced an *Atlas Containing Ten Maps of Poland Exhibiting the Political Changes that Country has Experienced during the Last Sixty Years from 1772 to the Present Time* (London, 1837).[26] The presentation of Polish history itself was a reminder of the existence of a national identity separate from that of the three powers – Austria, Prussia and Russia – that had partitioned Poland in 1772, 1793 and 1795. The depiction of its historical frontiers was a reminder of past glory and present goals.

Bulgaria

In Bulgaria, in contrast, the process was far slower. Turkish control from 1396 to 1878, the poverty and agrarian nature of the economy, and the lack of a large, affluent, urban Bulgarian reading population limited the development of Bulgarian print culture. The second half of the eighteenth century saw the beginning of a cultural revival, the crucial date being 1762 when Paisij Xilendarski's Slavo-Bulgarian history was completed. However, the first map with a Bulgarian text was not published until 1843, and the map, *Karta na segashnaya Bolgariya, Trakiya, Makedoniya i na prilezhashtite zemi* 'A map of present-day Bulgaria, Thrace, Macedonia and the enclosing lands' by Alexander Hadzirousset, was published in Strasbourg, not Bulgaria. Similarly, the first Bulgarian atlas, compiled by the publisher and bookseller Hristo G. Danov (1828–1911), was printed in Vienna in 1865. Another publisher and bookseller, Dragan Manchov (1824–1908), was responsible for the first Bulgarian historical atlas, *Ucheben istoricheski atlas ot izobrazheniya na pametnici ot izkustvoto i bita na starite i novite narodi* 'School historical atlas of images of monuments of art and folklore by the old and new peoples' (Plovdiv, 1894). This consists of maps (pp. 1–20) and drawings of monuments and works of art (pp. 21–28). Several portraits of Bulgarian and Russian czars are added, the latter testifying to Russia's prominent role in driving out the Turks. Over half the maps refer to Bulgarian territorial changes through the ages. Manchov noted that he used German and Russian historical atlases, but that the Bulgarian maps were his own work, a task he confessed he found very troublesome. This remained the sole Bulgarian historical atlas until wartime territorial claims and government support led to the appearance of a second in 1917.[27]

Hungary

Hungary, in contrast, benefited from a longer period of freedom from the Turks and relative political autonomy, as well as from a comparatively prosperous economy. As with Poland, it is possible to relate the appearance of Hungarian historical atlases to a degree of national self-consciousness, specifically to a process of self-definition within the Habsburg empire. The first Hungarian historical atlas was published in 1751. It was the work of János Tomka-Szászky (1700–62), teacher of history and geography at the grammar school in Pressburg/Pozsony (Bratislava). The *Parvus Atlas Hungariae* contained twenty small maps, engraved by Sebestyen Zeller, also of Bratislava, showing the various geographical areas relevant to Hungarian history: for example, the Urals/Upper Volga region and the Dnieper area, as well as the Carpathian Basin in the time of the Romans, the Huns and the Moravian empire, the Magyar conquest, the county system of Hungary during the Arpad dynasty and the Hungarian section of the *Tabula Itineraria*. Some of the maps were republished two years later in Matyas Bel's *Compendium Hungariae geographicum,* and again in 1781 as *Introductio in geographiam Hungariae antiqui et medii aevi* in a posthumous edition of Tomka-Szászky.

The first large historical map of Hungary, the *Tabula geographica Ungariae veteris ex historia anonymi belae regis notaru,* was by the work of the Jesuit astronomer Miksa Hell (1720–92), made in 1772. He based his map on the information derived from the *Gesta Hungarorum*, written around 1200, after many years of research into the etymology of place names. His map was later published by the historian Daniel Cornides in his *Vindiciae anonymi belae regis notarii* (Buda, 1802).[28]

The nineteenth century lent pedagogic purpose to the publication of historical atlases. The Hungarian cartographer György Jausz (1842–88) published a three-part historical atlas in German in Vienna in 1872–75. The *Historisch-Geographischer Schul-Atlas für Gymnasien, Realschulen und verwandte Lehr-Anstalten* (Vienna and Olmütz, 1872) included a number of maps of Hungary, as well as numerous battle plans. Jausz was headmaster at a girls' high-school in Ödenburg/Sopron in the western part of Hungary, and he produced his atlas for schools in the non-Hungarian part of Austria-Hungary. The Hungarian edition, also by Jausz, was published by the same publishing house, Edward Hölzel, in 1873 under the title *Töténelmi-Földrajzi Iskolai Atlasz* (Historical-Geographical School Atlas).

As in other countries, the development of mass national educational systems ensured that historical cartography was not restricted to atlases. Wall maps also came to play a role. The Hungarian historical congress of 1885 pressed for the production of Hungarian historical wall maps. The Hungarian Geographical Institute, the first Hungarian mapmaking body, was founded in 1890 and in 1891–1907 twenty different wall maps were published.[29]

In 1889 Ágost Helmár compiled a school atlas. The first part, *Iskolai atlasz az ókori történelem tanításához* (School atlas for the teaching of ancient history), containing four maps, was published in Bratislava that year. It was typical that maps of the Classical world should be published first. The following year saw the publication of the remaining three parts to the atlas: devoted to medieval, modern and world history they contained six, six and sixteen maps respectively. The Hungarian government also commissioned an historical atlas for schools. The *Történelmi iskolai atlasz* (School historical atlas), containing 27 maps, was published in three parts in 1897, and some of the foremost Hungarian cartographers and historians of the day were engaged in its production. The individual maps were also put on sale. Another historical atlas, *Atlasz a magyar történelem tanításához* (Atlas for the teaching of Hungarian history), by Karoly Kogutowicz and others, was published in 1913, containing 21 maps. The atlas for world history by the same authors, containing 58 maps, was published the same year.

Russia

The *Atlas Geografickeskii, Istoricheskii i Chronologicheskii Rossiiskago* (Geographical, historical and chronological atlas of the Russian state, compiled on the basis of the history of I.M. Karamzin by I. Akhmatov) (St Petersburg, 1845) contained 71 maps and provided a detailed account of the development of Muscovy. The atlas began with a map of the Near East in the Classical period but rapidly concentrated on the mapping of Russian developments. Map eleven of Europe and Russia *c.* 500 depicted polities in Russia in contrast to the blank spaces commonly shown in western European historical atlases. The barbarian invasions were divided among a number of maps so that chronological specificity replaced misleading simultaneity. This was also the case with Mongol advances, which were depicted in four maps. The last map showed the situation in the late fifteenth century, with Muscovy in control of Novgorod and Pskov and clearly the dominant power in what was to become Russia. The variety of historical cartography and, in particular, the role of pedagogy were also illustrated in the Russian case, for in 1867 Egor Zamyslolvskii edited *Uchebnyi Atlas po Russkoi Istorii* (The student's atlas of Russian history) (St Petersburg). The third edition, published in 1887, contained only sixteen maps and six reproductions of old town-plans. The atlas included maps of Siberia 1581–1886 and of Russian possessions in Central Asia for 1700–1886: their history depended on their being possessed by Russia. The historical maps of Russia included in the Brockhaus and Efron, *Entsiklopedicheskii Slovar* (Encyclopaedic Dictionary) (St Petersburg, 1890–1907) minimized the presence and role of non-Russians. The map showing the growth of the Russian state from the sixteenth century did not mention any non-Russian peoples and misleadingly marked the Chukchis of north-eastern Siberia as having been gained by Russia in the seventeenth century.

The United States

European expansion was also an important theme of American historical atlases in the late nineteenth and early twentieth centuries. Their earlier development had been more limited. The *Atlas* issued with the first and second editions of John Marshall's *Life of George Washington* (Philadelphia, 1st edn, 1804–7, 2nd edn, 1832) consisted of contemporaneous military maps, the American edition of Le Sage/Las Casas first published in 1820 included maps of the New World, but was limited in its scope, and the *Complete Historical, Chronological and Geographical American Atlas* (Philadelphia, 1823) was not really historical.

Five years later, however, appeared Emma Willard's *History of the United States, or Republic of America: Exhibited in Connexion with its Chronology and Progressive Geography by Means of a Series of Maps* (New York, 1828). The title-page further explained the maps, 'The first of which, shows the country as inhabited by various tribes of Indians at the time of its discovery, and the remainder, its state at different subsequent epochs; so arranged, as to associate the principal events of the history and their dates with the places in which they occurred; arranged on the plan of teaching history adopted in Troy Female Seminary.'

Connecticut-born, Emma Hart Willard (1787–1870), a pioneer of education for women, had opened the Middlebury Female Seminary in 1814, Waterford Academy in 1819 and, with more lasting success, the Troy Female Seminary at Troy, New York, in 1821. Willard was the teacher, developed new methods of teaching geography and history and published successful textbooks in both subjects. She fully endorsed what could be described as the orthodoxy of the century for historical cartography, namely the mutual dependence of history and geography for pedagogic reasons. In the preface to her 1828 work she announced that 'the principle derived from the theory of the human mind, and from much practice in teaching (that the true mnemonics of history is to associate the event and its date with the geographical representation of the place where it occurred,) is the foundation of the arrangement' both of the book and of her *Ancient Geography Connected with Chronology, and Preparatory to the Study of Ancient History*, which had been published as a section of *A System of Universal Geography* (1824) by William C. Woodbridge and which consisted of five maps of the Classical world and one of the 'barbarian' invasions. Willard explained her system: 'mnemonics, or artificial memory, consists in assuming something which is an object of sight, separating it into certain divisions, and associating with each, in a certain order, such abstract ideas as we may wish to recollect . . . the event fixes the recollection of the place, no less than the place the event.' She was also sure of the national value of her work: 'The attention of our youth to the interesting events of our history, in connexion with the geography of our country, will probably in the result contribute much to the improvement of our national literature, and consequently to the growth of wholesome national feeling.' Willard's work was successful. The fourth edition of her *History of the United States* appeared in 1831. In 1836 she produced an *Atlas to Accompany a System of Universal History* (Hartford) based on Quin's historical atlas, but not a direct copy. Willard's atlas was shorter and less well-executed than Quin's, a copy but not in any mechanical or precise way.[30]

The Philadelphia publishers E.H. Butler produced in 1844, in their series Mitchell's School Geographies, Samuel Augustus Mitchell's *Ancient Atlas Containing Maps Illustrating Classical and Sacred Geography*. This was a conventional Classical and biblical atlas, beginning with a 'Map of the World as known to the Ancients' and concluding with one of the Barbarian invasions. The latter lacked dates and simultaneously displayed events that had occurred centuries apart: it included the Saracen invasions. The atlas was reprinted in 1870.

J.H. Colton's Historical Atlas was published in New York in 1860. Its full title explained its purpose: *A Practical Class-Book of the History of the World Comprising in a Series of Inductive Lessons, the Origin and Progress of Nations, their History, Chronology, and Ethnology, Combined with their Ancient and Modern Geography. Illustrated by Maps, Ancient and Modern, and Plates Giving Extensive Panoramic Views of Contemporaneous Events, in Every Age and Nation.* The author and mapmaker, F.W. Hunt, had already produced the *Historical Atlas of the American States.* The title-page of his new book sported a maxim, 'Chronology and Geography are the Two Eyes of History', and, far more unusually, a poem:

> From all that *is*, to what has *been*,
> The glance how rich! the range how vast!
> The birth of Time – the rise, the fall
> Of empires, myriads – ages flown;
> Thrones, cities, tongues, arts, records, all
> The things whose echoes are not gone.

Colton's Historical Atlas was restricted in size 'to the limits of a college and school class-book', though, as usual with such works, the publisher also sought to appeal to the general reader. It was 'designed to be equally useful in the parlour and the reading room'. Each plate was linked to a lesson, the last closing with a fine teleological statement of optimism:

> the discoveries of the nineteenth century surpassing all that the human mind ever imagined in any former age . . . The human intellect, enlightened by the experience of every past century, and inspired by the wisdom of every former dispensation, advances now to new triumphs over the physical and mental universe, with a power that is rapidly accumulating.

Joseph Emerson Worcester's *Historical Atlas* (1826; 2nd edn, Boston, 1827; 3rd edn, Boston, 1863) indicated the extent to which an atlas did not have to include maps, for it was a work based on charts. The preface to the *Description and Illustration of Worcester's Historical Atlas, with Questions to Facilitate its Use* (Boston, 1857) noted: 'The design of the Atlas was to facilitate the study of history by the use of a series of Historical Charts, in a manner corresponding, in some measure, to the use of maps in the study of geography.' Visually Worcester's approach offered a different view of power, one that was not frozen in snap-shots as maps were: 'It supposes time to be flowing, in a stream, from the left hand to the right; and represents, at one view, the principal states and empires which have existed in the world, together with their origin, revolutions, decline and fall.'[31]

The *Statistical Atlas of the United States Based on the Results of the Ninth Census* (New York, 1874) included four maps depicting density of population in 1790–1820, 1830–40, 1850 and 1860. These historical demographic maps reflected the interest in statistical manipulation and depiction that the census gave rise to.[32] Fletcher W. Hewes and Henry Gannett, both members of the staff of the Tenth Census, were responsible for *Scribner's Statistical Atlas of the United States, Showing by Graphic Methods their Present Condition and their Political, Social, and Industrial Development* (New York, 1883). The historical section included not only presidential elections, but also maps of distribution of population 1790–1880 in order to illustrate progress of settlement. The maps depicted the position of Indian tribes and railroutes. There was also a map of original land grants during the colonial period.

Lucien H. Smith's *Historical and Chronological Atlas of the United States* (Washington, 1881) consisted of only eight maps, far fewer than the 50 in Alexander Johnston's *History of the United States for Schools* (New York, 1885), the best collection hitherto of American historical maps. Two works by Robert Labberton, *An Historical Atlas* (London, 1885) and a *New Historical Atlas and General History* (London, 1887), were weak. In the prefaces to both he asserted the need for a geographic treatment of history, but his maps were simplistic and offered little geography bar a

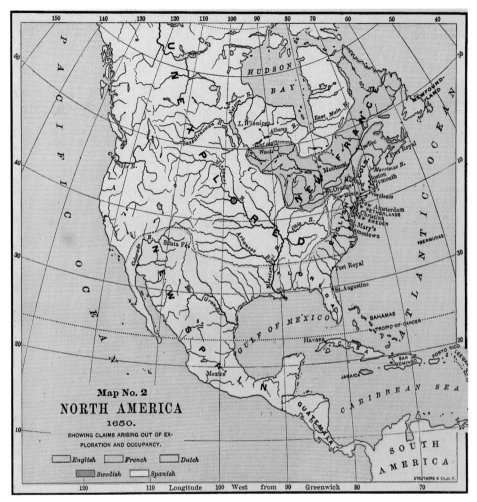

18. 'North America 1650' from Albert Bushnell Hart's *Epoch Maps Illustrating American History* (New York, 1891). The Native American presence was ignored and the impact of the Europeans was greatly exaggerated by focusing on claims rather than the reality of largely coastal settlements.

sense of relative location. The second work devoted fifteen of its 72 maps to American history, but none dealt with the pre-European period. Labberton was an American whose historical consciousness was still very European, as seen, for example, by the large number of maps of the Classical Mediterranean world in his 1885 book. Hewes's *Citizen's Atlas of American Politics, 1789–1888* (New York, 1888) included maps of presidential elections in 1824–84.

A major advance was made by Albert Bushnell Hart, Assistant Professor of History at Harvard. His *Epoch Maps Illustrating American History* was published in New York in 1891, designed to accompany the series of three textbooks, *Epochs of American History*, that he edited in 1891–93. The preface stated with some truth that

> The historical geography of the United States and of the previous colonies has been much neglected; it is therefore difficult to collect material upon which to base historical maps; or to check the results by the published work of other students. This brief series is offered as an attempt to make maps from the records, – from the texts

of grants, charters, and governors' instructions, and from statutes, British, colonial, state, and national. The purpose has been to draw no boundary line for which documentary authority does not exist.

Hart applied this principle to the contentious issues in American history:

> The territorial development of the United States, and the status of territorial slavery, are questions on which no two investigators will precisely agree; the principle adopted has been to make the maps conform to the official treaties and to the laws of the United States, as understood at the time when they were negotiated or enacted.

The atlas began with a map of the physical features of the United States. The next, North America in 1650, showing claims arising out of exploration and occupancy, ignored the Native Americans and exaggerated the power of the Europeans. For example, all of Louisiana, Alabama and Mississippi were allocated to Spain. This exaggeration was also true of the comparable map for 1750, which again ignored the Native Americans. The atlas contained only fourteen maps and had no text. It essentially presented a series of static portrayals of the USA although the map, the 'Status of Slavery in the United States 1775–1865,' was both thematic and long-term.

Scotland

The first historical atlas of Scotland, a work of that title, was published in Edinburgh in 1829 by the bookseller John Lothian. It contained seven maps: two were facsimiles, the other maps were of Scotland under the Romans, under the Picts, during the union of the Picts and Scots and in the fifteenth century, and a map of the Highlands showing clan territories and the wanderings of Charles Edward Stuart.

The high degree of map production in Edinburgh is a reminder of the role of commercial factors in the development and publication of historical atlases. A combination of entrepreneurial ability, production skills, an availability of capital and an absence of governmental direction ensured that Edinburgh became a major publishing centre. Among the historical atlases produced was *The Edinburgh Geographical and Historical Atlas,* first published in monthly numbers in about 1827 by the bookseller David Lizars junior and engraved by his brother William Home Lizars, a noted painter and engraver who was responsible for two later reissues of the atlas.

One of William Home Lizar's apprentices, William Johnston began business on his own account as an engraver in 1825 and the following year founded, in partnership with his brother Alexander Keith, another engraver, the firm of W. and A.K. Johnston. They were responsible for a large number of atlases, some of them historical. These included *The National Atlas of Historical, Commercial and Political Geography* (1843), the atlas to Sir Archibald Alison's *History of Europe* (1848), the *Atlas of Classical Geography* (1853) and the *Half-Crown Atlas of British History* (1871). Both men acquired honours as a result of their work and Alexander Keith Johnston was especially prominent and honoured in geographical circles.

Ethnicity

Alexander Keith Johnston also published *The Physical Atlas* (Edinburgh, 1848), in large part the English version of Heinrich Berghaus's *Physikalischer Atlas* (Gotha, 1845–48).[33] The phytology and zoology section included an ethnographic map of Europe by Gustaf Kombst, a German geographer working in Edinburgh, and another of North America. These maps reflected both increased interest in the mapping of zoological and biological distributions, and a concern with ethnicity that demonstrated the impact of nationalism and a growing intellectual interest in ethnicity in the nineteenth century that built upon such eighteenth-century figures as Montesquieu, with his stress on the importance of geography and climate as determinants in history and Kloots, with his concept of 'natural frontiers'. These notions led to the concept of geopolitics which was developed by Friedrich Ratzel and his disciples, and also to an interest in ethnic distributions. In cartographic terms this was responsible for ethnic maps depicting where the 'nations' of Europe lived and physical maps concentrating on rivers and mountains, anything which could help to define where 'natural' frontiers were to be found.

Although these interests did not necessarily have to affect historical atlases, they did so because they offered new ways of looking at the past and because this was a culture with a strong historical sense, concerned to trace the roots of the contemporary situation and to present it as a natural development. Johnston's *Physical Atlas* argued that 'As there are natural laws for the organization of individual man, so there must be natural laws for the growth and decline of nations.' Ethnicity was seen as crucial:

> The history of mankind exhibits nothing but the development of the different races, varieties, etc. of the human family, partly apart, and for the last three thousand years as mutually influencing each other; so that a progress in the history of mankind is always indicated either by the appearance of a new stock of people on the stage of the world, or by the produce of a crossing of two races.

There was also a clear sense of White superiority: 'Among the nations belonging to the different varieties of the so-called Caucasian species, there is an evident tendency towards improvement, on an increasing scale. This is fully borne out by the history of the last three thousand years.'

Interest in ethnicity combined with the greater use of colour as in Edward Gover's *Historic Geographical Atlas of the Middle and Modern Ages* (London, 1853), the preface of which noted:

> To render the work easy of reference, special attention has been given to tinting and colouring the maps, by which the tribes of particular races, as the Germanic, the Hunnish, the Sclavic, the Mongol, and the Turkish are represented by distinctive colours. This method of colouring will be found of great utility, especially in tracing from map to map the onward or retrogressive course of such tribes, from their former localities to their present possessions, through the various changes and revolutions which have passed over the states, kingdoms, and empires founded by them.

The following year, Gover's *Atlas of Universal Historical Geography* gave as one of its aims the desire to display 'the seats of the most renowned races'. In map fourteen, 'North and East Europe at the beginning of the Fourteenth Century', in the Trübner edition of Spruner published in London in 1861, 'special attention' was 'devoted to the ethnography of the various scattered races of Eastern Europe'.

Ethnicity was both a means of interrogating the past and an important aspect of current tension and confrontation. It was used to define separate communities and peoples. As with maps of state territory there was no sense of a blurring at the margins or of an overlap or mixture, of multi-ethnicity or multiple sovereignty. Ethnographic maps can thus be seen as an aspect of the division of Europe and the world, past and present, into different and opposed units.

This division was given further bite by the continued stress on warfare in historical cartography. This emphasis was true of historical atlases designed for the young as much as for their seniors. Thus the *School Atlas of English History* edited by S.R. Gardiner (London, 1899), and intended to serve as a companion to the *Student's History of England,* included battle plans of Hastings, Bannockburn, Crécy, Poitiers, Agincourt, Edgehill, Marston Moor, Naseby, Dunbar, Steinkirk, Neerwinden, Blenheim, Ramillies, Quebec, Quiberon Bay, the Nile, Copenhagen, Trafalgar and Waterloo. There were also maps to illustrate campaigns and wars: of Henry V's 1415 campaign in France, England during the Wars of the Roses, Germany at the outset of the Thirty Years' War, three maps of England to illustrate the Civil War, and others for the campaigns of 1685 and 1688 in the west of England, 1690 in Ireland, 1691 in western Ireland, Flanders and Brabant to illustrate the campaigns of William III, the Low Countries in 1702 for the War of the Spanish Succession, Britain for the Jacobites in 1745–46, central Europe for the wars of Frederick the Great and again for Napoleon, the Austrian Netherlands in 1792 for the opening stage of the French Revolutionary War, Iberia for the Peninsular War, and Russia for Napoleon's advance on Moscow. There were no maps for economic history but, instead, an unremitting stress on war.

4

Environmentalism and Nationalism

> Our geography is in fact the history of the land.
> Charles Pearson, 1869
>
> History is largely the make of geography.
> Emil Reich, 1903[1]

Environmental Causation

From their beginning, historical maps had generally included physical features, largely rivers and mountains, in order to help locate the places, principally towns, that were mapped, and, though probably to a lesser extent, because such features were what seemed best to fill maps and to add to the regions or countries indicated. Rivers and mountains featured strongly in the sense and awareness of terrain of people before the motor age, and were important features of medieval and early-modern route maps. Such features were not intended as an indication of environmental causation in history; they were illustrative rather than descriptive, let alone prescriptive. This situation changed towards the close of the nineteenth and in the early decades of the twentieth century. Notions of environmental influence in history became more prominent. Some scholars discussed the issue in a fashion that could be described as deterministic, while others preferred a concept of probabilism, but all were united in the view that the physical environment counted. This was not a development restricted to historical atlases. Atlases of the modern world devoted more attention to physical details and that, in turn, made it far easier to provide such information for historical atlases.

There was an awareness that the physical environment was not a constant and this was especially apparent in changing coastlines like those of the Netherlands and south-east England. Such considerations were discussed in scholarly works, such as Charles Pearson's *Historical Maps of England during the First Thirteen Centuries* (London, 1869). However, most historical atlases ignored the issue and treated modern information as a basis for the mapping of the past. Part of the whole concept of environmental causation was, after all, that physical features were longer-lasting than the works of man and much of their influence was traced to this.

Environmental causation was particularly attractive to geographers because it emphasized their importance: they could best explain the present and suggest the future. In addition, environmental causation made geographers better interpreters of the past than historians. It made sense of and underlined the need for historical geography.

Environmental causation was especially valuable for historical cartographers. It made their maps necessary, both as descriptive and as explanatory tools. It became important to replace earlier maps and to map physical features thoroughly. In addition, advances in map production, especially in the printing of colour, made it easier both to include more physical details, most obviously colour-coded contour zones, for example brown for 1000–2000 feet, and to juxtapose such details and those of states and societies. The use of colour increased the density and complexity of information that could be conveyed and thus made the role of the map as an explanatory device easier. This was crucial to the role of historical atlases in this period. Furthermore, greater visual complexity, particularly with the use of colour, increased the aesthetic appeal of maps. Leaving aside the important point that the lesson of the map had to be decoded, there was now more in the average map that had to be assimilated, not least through a process of separating out the components and then integrating them in a comprehensible form. In this lay much of the interest of maps.

It would be mistaken, however, to treat history in isolation. An interest in maps as constitutive, rather than illustrative, of theses characterized a number of disciplines in the period, not least geology.[2] Furthermore, distribution maps played an increasing role in scientific investigation and exposition, whether with the science of mankind or with biological and physical sciences.[3]

There was no single year in which environmental causation came to play a major role in historical cartography. There was no atlas that made an impact comparable to that of Las Cases or was as influential as that by Spruner. In part this reflected the growing size and diversity of the world of historical cartography. In addition, the rise of environmentalism was a process that took time. It looked back to eighteenth-century notions of the role of geography and nineteenth-century interest in nationalism and evolution, concepts that combined to suggest an agenda of political history in which environmentally moulded nation states played a crucial role. There had been a long-term shift towards the concept of 'national interests' at the expense of dynastic interests. The older dynastic approach was based on the notion that a ruler's chief obligation was to protect his dynastic claims to territory wherever it might be; in cartographic terms the challenge was thus how best to present the role of dynasties.

In the eighteenth century the notion that objective national interests existed developed rapidly. In large part, it was a product of the Enlightenment proposition that humans live in a universe governed by natural laws which proclaim, among other things, the existence of 'nations', defined through a mixture of geography, language, culture, physical features, even traits of personality; that the 'interests of nations', essentially, are to be defined in terms of protecting their geographical, cultural and physical (i.e. security) integrity.

Such ideas became more prominent in the nineteenth century as states were increasingly defined in nationalist terms, a process that led to greater interest in ethnic and environmental factors: it was environmental influence that could best explain the differing political trajectories of various ethnic groups, the processes by which they had become nations and states with particular characteristics, interests and cartography. Environmentalism could make these processes appear natural and necessary; it was not an alternative to nationalism. In terms of the relations between nations this situation led to an emphasis on 'natural frontiers', a theme found in the writings of the geopolitical school associated with Germany's leading political scientist, Friedrich Ratzel (1844–1904), and his disciples. Ratzel, who was trained in the natural sciences, presented international relations in the Darwinian terms of a struggle for survival. He saw states as organic and thus ignored divisions within them. The struggle for space was central to Ratzel's *Die Erde und das Leben* (The earth and life) (1902). He emphasized the role of environmental circumstances in affecting the process and progress of struggle between states.[4]

Environmentalism lent new direction to the conventional cartographic emphasis on wars and frontiers. It not only 'fleshed' them out, in particular by providing details of the terrain, but also employed them in a clear explanatory fashion. Accompanying text lent didactic point to many of the maps. In addition, an interest in the consequences of the terrain gave renewed point to the depiction of the interior of countries: they became more than blank spaces with towns and perhaps a few isolated physical features.

Environmental influence and the related greater appreciation of the impact of geography upon history were not alone in creating a different context for historical cartography, raising new issues and providing new information. The effect of 'scientific history', the rise of the historical profession and its development of a scientific ethos and generally more rigorous methods, also gathered pace, ensuring that there was a steadily growing number of fresh interpretations. In time these were to undermine any simple stress on environmentalism.

It is going too far to argue that 'only at the end of the nineteenth century . . . would historical cartography become more objective and scholarly'.[5] Aside from the issue of a teleology of cartography that some will find questionable, more specifically, such an assessment underrates achievements earlier in the century and presents a monolithic interpretation of the situation in this period.

It is clear that historical atlases became more didactic in this period. Didacticism had not been lacking earlier, but the traditional agenda of historical cartography did not call for much. Maps were provided to illustrate the Bible and the Classics, not to explain them. They were narratives produced without maps and intended to be read without them. In so far as maps were required for the Bible and the Classics in the nineteenth century they were so that places mentioned could be located, rather than for explanatory reasons.

This was less the case, however, with the narratives of national history that scholars, other writers and publishers sought to produce, especially so when environmental determinism became prominent. A sense of destiny, Darwinian notions, educational needs and simple curiosity all encouraged a greater emphasis on explanation which could lead to impatience with existing works. In the preface to his *Géographie historique* (Paris, 1888), a work centred on the influence of geography on history designed for use in schools, P. Foncin argued that a fault in historical atlases was that 'sans un livre qui les explique et qu'ils expliquent en même temps, ils sont incompréhensibles' (without a text that explains the maps and that is at the same time explained by them, these are incomprehensible).[6] Every map in the book was accompanied by text.

19. 'Saxon England' from Charles Pearson's *Historical Maps of England* (London, 1869), Extensive woodlands are presented because Pearson argued that they affected the direction of settlement. The coastline of the period is used, but the emphasis on physical features ensures that variations in territorial boundaries and political hierarchies are not captured.

The role of environmental conditions had been mentioned in some historical atlases earlier in the century. In his *Illuminated Atlas of Scripture Geography* (London, 1840), the able William Hughes had regretted the modest role of historical geography:

> Not only does the narrative of past events require in the student a knowledge of the localities which have been the scenes of their occurrence but the influence which physical characteristics have exercised over the formation of the national character – the modes of thought and feeling – the customary associations – the manners and institutions – of the inhabitants of a country, form elements in its condition which must be understood and appreciated before its political and religious history can be read with advantage. The different circumstances under which an inland or a maritime country is placed, and the various influences of the lofty chain of mountains or the wide-spread plain – the parched and arid desert or the fertile valley – the navigable river or the rapid mountain torrent – have exercised a large share in directing the progress of civilisation.[7]

Charles Pearson presented geography as playing a direct role in English history in his *Historical Maps of England* (London, 1869). He argued that the extensive woodlands near the south coast 'explain why England was settled from east and west', and suggested that although 'man triumphs over the elements', this triumph was essentially a matter only of the previous half-century. Pearson also saw geography at work in the great political divisions of the country's history. He saw the mountains as 'the conservative element . . . in our history', and observed that the Roman presence was limited in the upland regions – the south-west, Wales, Galloway and Lancashire – and that 'it was precisely these parts where the nationality was unbroken, that afterwards sustained the struggle against the Saxon'. In the civil war of Stephen's reign (1135–54), 'the Empress Matilda, who represented the not unfrequent combination of a legitimate title and an oppressive government' drew her support from the upland west, Stephen from London 'and the commercial towns of the east'. In the 1260s 'London and the south and east were with the great constitutional leader De Montfort; the north and west sided with the King. In the Wars of the Roses the Yorkist party, which on the whole was that of good government, received partisans from the same district as De Montfort.' Similar comments were made about the Civil War, and then, for the Jacobite uprising in 1745: 'nowhere, except in the Highlands could Prince Charles Edward have raised an army; nowhere but in the north-western counties, still only partially civilized, did he find recruits. Our country is so small, that in Cumberland and Westmoreland at least, the hills are losing their old influence.'[8]

This interpretation neatly linked a conventional view of progress through a limitation of royal authority with a sense that upland areas were socially conservative and politically reactionary. Modern scholarship is more sceptical about De Montfort and the Yorkists, although the geographical basis of support for the two sides in the Civil War receives considerable attention and is often related to socio-economic criteria.

Interest in environmental influences came from geographers as well as historians. Trained mostly in the natural sciences, nineteenth-century geographers assumed a close relationship between humanity and the biophysical environment and sought to probe it in terms of the environmental control that they took for granted. In order to demonstrate this process and to understand the present, geographers looked to the past. This was the case in Canada, for example, where the Laurentian School studied the role of the landscape in affecting human settlement, and in the United States. The history of the latter could be presented in environmental terms. This was true both of America's territorial expansion, which could be made to seem inevitable, and of its internal development, for example the siting of cities[9] and the routes of railroads. Influential works included Albert P. Brigham's *Geographic Influences in American History* (Boston, 1903) and two works by Ellen Churchill Semple, a geographer at the University of Chicago, *American History and its Geographic Conditions* (Boston, 1903) and *Influences of Geographic Environment on the Basis of Ratzel's System of Anthropo-Geography* (New York, 1911). Semple, for example, argued that Africa was inert in part because it lacked any fructifying variety of geographical conditions. Environmentalism was an attractive analytical method for the geographers and historians of successful and expanding states.[10] Furthermore, environmentalism played a crucial role in the organic theory of the state and in the treatment of culture as defined by the integration of nature and society.

Vast and Malleterre

The mono-causal character of environmentalism was to be strongly attacked, especially in France, but in the meantime it had had a great impact on historical atlases. It gave them something new to display, a means of doing so and a more sophisticated pedagogic role. The dependence of history on geography and the role of natural frontiers were themes in H. Vast and G. Malleterre's *Atlas historique. Formation des états européens* (Paris, 1900). The authors both taught at the military academy. The introduction, by General Gustave Léon Niox, who had produced a map of much of Africa in 1894, declared that states were viable only if they conformed to a nation and its limits:

> Les *frontières naturelles*, entre lesquelles les peuples naissants se sont cantonnés, ont été la garantie de leur indépendance; c'est grâce à leur protection qu'ils ont pu grander. Ces frontières n'ont jamais été impunément brisées, soit par un ennemi extérieur, soit par une extension anormale de la nation elle-même. Les grands Empires n'ont, en effet, réussi à se fonder que sur des pays bien soudés entre eux, où la terre et la race s'accordaient dans un ensemble harmonieux et homogène. Les États qui ont englobé des pays sans affinités naturelles n'ont eu qu'une existence difficile et une durée éphémère.

This assessment, however, was limited to Europe. Niox regarded imperialism as natural, the consequence of the rise in population in Europe and the desire of its peoples to better themselves. He continued:

> Les expéditions lointaines, les aventures de colonisation sont devenues les facteurs indispensables de l'existence des nations riches. Elles donnent un aliment aux intelligences sans emploi, aux forces inoccupées, et, d'autre part, elles répandent, dans le monde, le génie de la race et sa civilisation.

Niox presented war and its casualties as a sign of vigour: 'Par l'effort qu'elle provoque, l'expansion extérieure entretient l'énergie et la virilité d'un peuple; le sacrifice, parfois nécessaire, d'une génération pour la mise en valeur des terres nouvelles, loin d'affaiblir la souche-mère, en accroît, au contraire, la vigueur.' The army was then dramatically expanding France's African empire. Indeed, at the close of the 1890s and the beginning of the 1900s the French overran much of the Sahara and Chad.

Niox added two points that reflected common views about historical atlases at that point: first, that history was only valuable if explanatory as well as descriptive, and, second, that geography was the indispensable foundation of history. The two points were related in the atlases of the period. The Vast and Malleterre *Atlas historique* began with physical maps of Europe and France. It presented France as a state with extensive natural frontiers and a great colonial past. The map of the French frontiers to north and east in the sixteenth and seventeenth centuries referred to the 'effort constant de la royauté et des hommes d'État pour donner à la France les frontières de l'ancienne Gaule (Rhin, Alpes, Pyrénées)', a view that ignored the discontinuities between ancient Gaul and early-modern France. The map of 'L'Inde de Dupleix' showed much of India in the 1740s as French and this was also repeated on the map of the world in the eighteenth century. The relevant passage of text presented France, not Britain, as the natural colonial power, but argued that French colonialism had been betrayed: 'Le gouvernement français abandonne nos colonies

2º Français. — Esprit de découverte et d'expansion. — Les hommes d'État du XVIIᵉ siècle (*Richelieu, Colbert*) conçoivent la politique coloniale et favorisent les tentatives commerciales.

1534. — Sous François Iᵉʳ, les Français s'établissent au **Canada** (Nouvelle France), en **Acadie** et à **Terre-Neuve.**

1608-1635. — *Champlain*, protégé par Henri IV et Richelieu, fonde au Canada **Québec** et **Montréal.**

Richelieu envoie des colons à la **Guyane**, au **Sénégal**, à **Madagascar** (France Orientale). Établissements à Fort-Dauphin, à Bourbon (1642-1643).

1625-1635. — Établissements des Antilles : **Saint-Christophe, Martinique, Guadeloupe, Saint-Domingue**

1656-1684. — Colbert ajoute les territoires de la baie d'**Hudson** et la **Louisiane** (*Cavelier de la Salle*), et favorise les *grandes compagnies de commerce*.

1720. — Le *système de crédit financier de Law* est fondé sur le développement des colonies. Création de la **Nouvelle-Orléans**. Tentative pour relier le Canada à la Louisiane par les postes de l'Ohio.

En 1750, la France tient, en Amérique, le Saint-Laurent et le Mississipi.

1667-1743. — Premiers établissements aux Indes (*François Martin, Dumas*).

1742-1754. — *Dupleix* exploite les divisions des nombreux princes hindous, crée des troupes indigènes (*cipayes*) et engage la lutte avec la Compagnie anglaise des Indes. — **1746-1748.** Prise et restitution de **Madras**.

1748-1750. — Conquête des côtes de **Coromandel**, des **Circars**, d'**Orissa**. Protectorat du **Dekkan**. Dupleix est à ce moment le maître d'une grande partie de l'Hindoustan.

3º Anglais. — Les Anglais ne deviennent colonisateurs qu'à la suite de l'acte de navigation (1651), et après la fin de leurs guerres civiles.

1655. Sous Cromwell, prise de la **Jamaïque.** — **1667.** Traité de Bréda. La Hollande cède aux Anglais les **nouveaux Pays-Bas** (New-York).

1713. — **Traité d'Utrecht.** La France abandonne aux Anglais **Terre-Neuve**, l'**Acadie** et les territoires de la baie d'Hudson.

En 1750, les Anglais ne possèdent encore que le territoire très limité des **13 colonies américaines** sur la côte, quelques **Antilles** et quelques comptoirs dans l'Inde (**Bombay, Madras, Calcutta, fort William**).

Le gouvernement français abandonne nos colonies d'Amérique et d'Asie. Les Anglais ne vont pas tarder à s'en emparer.

20. 'The World in the Eighteenth Century' from H. Vast and G. Malleterre, *Atlas historique. Formation des états européens* (Paris, 1900). A world very much seen in terms of European empires. The ephemeral nature of French power in India was ignored in the inset map.

d'Amérique et d'Asie. Les Anglais ne vont pas tarder à s'en emparer.' Whereas previous French historical atlases had seen the great extension of French power under Napoleon as a source of pride, Vast and Malleterre saw it as unnatural and therefore bound to fail:

> Napoléon donne à l'Empire français une extension exagérée . . . chacune de ses conquêtes provoque des résistances nouvelles, suivies de campagnes de plus en plus aventureuses pour dompter ces résistances . . . L'Empire français, ainsi constitué, ne répond à aucune conception, ni géographique, ni ethnologique; c'est une création purement factice, destinée à disparaître, comme ont disparu tous les empires violemment créés, et qui ne sont pas fondés sur l'unité de race et la communauté des intérêts.

Thus maps of imperial extent in Europe were not to be understood if divorced from those of ethnic identity, a position very different from that in the historical atlases of the previous century. Nationalism was a key to the historical process. Thus for the map of much of Europe in 1815–71:

> Les changements territoriaux . . . sont le résultat des aspirations nationales des peuples, soit qu'ils brisent violemment des liens noués par la conquête et contraires à leur constitution normale (Grèce, États danubiens, Belgique), soit qu'ils se groupent au contraire pour former des unités de langue, de race et de politique (Italie, Allemagne). La France, par l'appui de ses armes ou par le mouvement d'idées qu'elle suscite, aide les États danubiens, La Grèce, la Belgique et l'Italie à s'affranchir. Elle subit au contraire elle-même un recul dans sa formation nationale, par le fait de l'unité allemande.

Ethnicity was also seen as crucial to the history of the New World:

> Les États-Unis et le Mexique représentent l'opposition des deux races qui ont peuplé les deux Amériques, les Anglo-Saxons (race germanique) . . . les Hispano-Portugais (race latine) . . . L'Amérique anglo-saxonne cherche à absorber les deux continents américans. L'Amérique Latine défend sa nationalité.

Yet ethnic determinism could only be pushed so far. Vast and Malleterre argued that the American Civil War had left a latent hostility between the states of the north and the south and referred to 'germes de séparatisme dans une agglomération trop vaste d'États', though the reason why the USA was too large was not explained satisfactorily.

The logic was certainly not extended to French imperialism. An inset map on the plate devoted to the spread of French power in North Africa in the nineteenth century displayed journey times: Marseille–Algeria was only 26 hours. French expansion was presented as natural, necessary, beneficial and in accord with the principles of ethnic identity:

> Nécessité de ne pas laisser la Tunisie à une autre puissance . . . Prospérité croissante. Pacification absolue . . . L'Algérie n'a pas de frontières vers le sud. Pour garder le littoral, il faut tenir le Tell. Pour garder le Tell, il faut tenir les nomades des Hauts-Plateaux, puis ceux du Sahara . . . L'Algérie avec la Tunisie, est le prolongement de la France. Il s'y forme un peuple nouveau de race latine. Elle procure des débouches sérieux à notre industrie, à notre commerce, à notre marine marchande. Elle nous

assure la prépondérance dans la Méditerranée occidentale. C'est une terre d'entraînement pour notre armée et de colonisation pour notre population.

The notion of ethnic extension was employed again in the map of western Asia in the nineteenth century: the text noted: 'Les Anglais se maintennent par la force dans les régions frontières de l'Asie centrale, tandis que les Russes assimilent les peuples qu'ils ont soumis. L'avenir est du côté de la Russie.'

Ethnic assimilation was seen as a natural extension of European superiority: non-Europeans should be deracinated. Imperialism was not only for the benefit of the Europeans; it was also necessary in order for humanity best to utilize the world. Thus a notion of ethnic supremacy was linked to one of environmental adaptability. The authors argued that the European presence in Asia was necessary 'pour mettre en valeur leurs richesses immobilisées'.

Yet there was also an element of concern. A map of Europe in 1898 showing both fortresses and the division of states into the zones of army corps was accompanied by an apocalyptic warning of global struggle:

> L'union de l'Europe est nécessaire pour maintenir sa suprématie dans l'Ancien Monde, et se défendre à la fois contre les ambitions menaçantes du Nouveau-Monde et les concurrences économiques des peuples travailleurs de l'Asie, les Chinois et surtout les Japonais.[11]

The inevitability of ethnic conflict, the triumph of the 'civilized' and the absence of incorporation of the vanquished were themes in Hereford George's *Relations of Geography and History* (Oxford, 1901). He wrote of the Americans and Canadians having

> before them the prospect of indefinite expansion, at the cost of getting rid of the aborigines, thinly scattered over the whole area, whom they were neither able nor desirous to convert into slaves. Before both alike the red men disappeared: they were incapable of assimilating civilization, and have in great measure died out, there having been practically no admixture of races. The analogy is very close with many of the movements of pre-historic man, when newcomers expropriated the old inhabitants, driving them out or destroying them, but enslaving or otherwise absorbing only a few. Civilized man works by different means, and with less definite intention to destroy; but the result is the same.

Aside from writing *Relations of Geography and History* (Oxford, 1901), Hereford George was a keen wargamer who also wrote *Battles of English History* (London, 1895) and *Napoleon's Invasion of Russia* (London, 1899).[12]

Poole

The major British work of the first decade of the century, the *Historical Atlas of Modern Europe from the Decline of the Roman Empire, Comprising Also Maps of Parts of Asia, Africa, and the New World Connected with European History* (Oxford, 1902), edited by Reginald Lane Poole, was less didactic, let alone apocalyptic. It also lacked a military background. Poole praised Spruner, and his own atlas's maps of European history clearly derived from the Spruner-Menke atlas. Furthermore, unlike Droysen, who had preferred a single chronological sequence, Poole reverted to the Spruner–Menke pattern of presenting a sequence of maps of Europe as a whole before separate sections devoted to individual countries, each presented in chronological order.

However, as Poole correctly claimed, the maps of Byzantine, Asian, colonial and British history were 'in most respects independent of any previous atlas'. Work on the atlas began in 1891 and it justified Poole's claim that it was the first historical atlas of Europe 'possessing a scientific value' to appear in Britain. The stress on science reflected the academic values of the period: 'scientific history' emphasized rigour in method and research. Thus Poole criticized Pearson not only for the unsatisfactory production of his maps but also because 'they suffered from an excess of theory' and were not 'elaborated maps based throughout on critical study'. Poole's work also bore the imprimatur of academic power. Planned by the important Edinburgh map publishers W. and A.K. Johnston, it was published by Oxford University Press. The maps were by influential academics, including J.B. Bury, Regius Professor of Greek at Trinity College, Dublin, Charles Oman, Professor of Modern History at Oxford, James Tait and T.F. Tout, both important professors at Manchester, H.A.L. Fisher of New College, Oxford, G.W. Prothero of King's, Cambridge, and C. Grant Robertson of All Souls', Oxford.

Each map was accompanied by a page or two of text and the notion of the survival of the fittest was expressed early on. In his map of Europe 527–750, Bury wrote: 'The sixth century determined which of the Teutonic peoples, settled within the borders of the Roman Empire, were fittest to survive and play a part in mediaeval and modern history.' The accompanying text in the Poole atlas made relatively little of environmental conditions, but was in little doubt that imperialism was linked to a ranking in terms of civilization. Thus, for map 89 on the nineteenth-century European empires: 'Africa, as the one portion of the world not, for the most part, occupied by civilized or semi-civilized states, became the natural theatre of the new struggle.'

Nomenclature also reflected power, in this case that of England. For the map of Ireland under the early Tudors, a period when English control was in fact limited, and that of Ireland 1541–1653,

> compiled as these maps are from documents in large measure unpublished, and intended to illustrate the history of Ireland from the view of the English in Ireland rather than from a purely native point of view, the system of spelling adopted will, it is trusted, commend itself to those who depend chiefly for their information on English rather than Irish sources.

For the maps of India in 1792 and 1845, 'as these have been drawn with the object of illustrating the growth of British rule in India, the native names have been written in the forms customary among Englishmen during the period of conquest and consolidation'.

Poole's atlas also set high standards by the·fashion in which the text made comments on the problems of mapping. The text thus enhanced as well as explained the scholarship of the maps. W.H. Stevenson, Fellow of Exeter College, Oxford, who was responsible for the map of England and Wales before the Norman Conquest, a map that was weakened by the absence of any suggestion of chrono-logical shifts, warned:

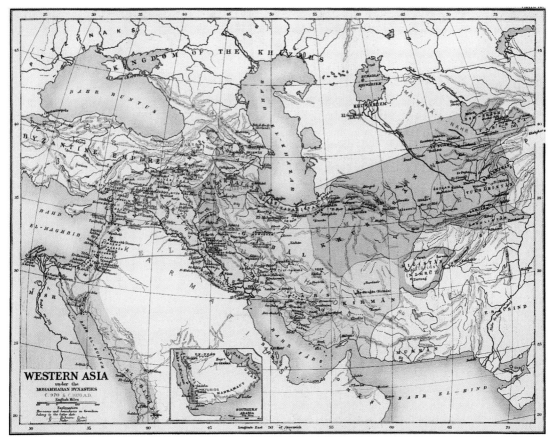

21. 'Western Asia under the Mohammadan Dynasties *c.* 970 and *c.* 1070' from R.L. Poole (ed.), *Historical Atlas of Modern Europe* . . . (Oxford, 1902). The most influential British historical atlas of the early twentieth century. The maps of this region can be related to greater academic knowledge but also to the 'Great Game'. Britain and Russia defined spheres of interest in Persia in 1907.

> The exceedingly scanty records of the history of Wales during this period do not enable us to get a clear view of the political divisions of the country at any given date. A map must be constructed, therefore, from much later evidence, which is unsatisfactory and often contradictory in nature. Under these circumstances it is somewhat improbable that we have avoided errors in laying down in the definite outlines of a map the shifting boundaries of the principalities.

Such a comment was all too rare in the historical atlases of the period. Similarly, the map of England and Wales under the House of Lancaster included a note explaining the problems of assessing boundaries within the March of Wales, and that of early Ireland commented on the limited mapping of early Irish history and the impossibility of mapping the boundaries of the septs (sub-tribes) with any certainty. As a result, 'it seemed better in general to indicate their relative positions by the positions of the names rather than to aim at a delusive appearance of greater accuracy'.

The detailed mapping of non-European lands caused even more problems. An arresting feature of the atlas was provided by four maps of western Asia between 780 and 1330, all produced by Stanley Lane Poole, Professor of Arabic at Trinity

College, Dublin. They reflected greater European historical knowledge of the area, a growth in public interest in the region that, in part, reflected imperialist concerns and the sense that historical cartography should not be restricted to Europe. The map of 'Western Asia under the Abbasid Caliphs, 780' warned: 'There are differences of a year or more among the Arab chroniclers as to many of the dates of conquest; some, no doubt, taking the first raid, others the settled annexation. There were frequent revolts in the early days of the conquest, and cities were often retaken.'

The note on the map for *c.* 970 and *c.* 1070 carried warnings that would still be valuable today, and are a caution against the assumption that historical atlases are continually improving. The map also indicates the extent to which colour had expanded the descriptive capacity of cartography:

> The present map shows the divisions of the Mohammadan dynasties at two dates. The wash-colouring and the names in blue indicate dynasties ruling about AD 970; the red boundary line marks the extent of the Seljuk empire about 1070, and the names in red distinguish the dynasties reigning at that time . . . The exact boundaries in any given year are seldom ascertainable, especially in the tenth century, when rival dynasties were constantly encroaching on each other, and an important city or province might be annexed in one year and recovered by its former possessor in the following year . . . The relations of the dynasties to each other also varied: sometimes they were rivals, sometimes one was the vassal of the other . . . Further the information concerning some of the outlying provinces, such as Muckran, Kirman, Khuwarizm and Shirwan, is often too meagre or uncertain to justify definite statements. The general outlines, however, of the dynastic divisions represented in the map are fairly established by the evidence of the coins and the statements of the Arabic chroniclers.

Discussion of specific source problems led in some cases to reflection on the process of producing an historical atlas. This had been comparatively unusual in earlier atlases and has been all too uncommon in the twentieth century, but it entailed a crucial explanatory leap, that of treating the atlas as a whole, rather than any individual map, as a device the production of which entailed issues of choice that could and would dramatically affect the message conveyed. For map seven, Europe in 1360, Charles Oman wrote:

> The date 1360 has been chosen as suitable for giving a general idea of Europe in the fourteenth century, not only because in English and French history it is marked by the important Treaty of Brétigny, but because in the rest of the continent it shows the states in their normal condition. If the date selected had been a few years earlier, South-Eastern Europe would have been shown in the unusual condition of unity to which it was reduced by Stephen Dushan, who, either as direct ruler or as suzerain, controlled not only his native Serbia, but also Bulgaria, Albania, much of Northern Greece, and the larger part of the Byzantine Empire (1346–55). If, on the other hand, the map had been made to represent the state of things a few years later than 1360, it would have exhibited Central Europe in the very abnormal state to which it was brought by Lewis the Great of Hungary, who in his elder years was possessed not only of the Magyar Kingdom, but of Poland, Dalmatia, Bosnia, Western Bulgaria, and the greater part of Wallachia (1365–82). These two short-lived empires left so little mark

behind them that it seemed well to choose a time when neither of them was complicating the political map of Europe.

Oman's particular argument can be questioned. The English presence in France as asserted and defined in the Treaty of Brétigny was even more transient than the empires of Stephen Dushan and Lewis the Great. In addition, the mapping of often ephemeral eastern European empires captured the reality of the political situation there. There was a whole series of composite states or multiple kingdoms: for example, Bohemia under Charles IV (1338–78), Poland-Lithuania from 1386, and Hungary under Matthias Corvinus (1485–90). Aside from conquest and the dynastic accumulation of territories, the elective nature of certain states led to a more transient process of accumulation. Thus, Corvinus was also elected King of Bohemia. Furthermore, boundaries in much of the Balkans remained vague, shifting according to the interests of the local potentates.

Nevertheless, the crucial point about Oman's remarks was that he brought into the open the issue of deliberation entailed in producing an atlas, the artifice in providing static portrayals of the past, specifically in selecting particular dates for mapping chronological stops. This was not completely unprecedented: several nineteenth-century atlases had discussed whether or not to follow Kruse in having maps at regular chronological intervals, but they had done so in the general terms of what best captured the dynamism of the past, rather than by drawing attention to the danger of misleading by the selection of particular dates. Oman was also commenting on his own map, not on those of others, and his remarks could be expected to affect the perception of readers of the atlas who read it sequentially and went on to consider other maps.

Text and Maps

Poole's atlas was more scholarly than its British predecessors and stood comparison with the leading German works of the 1880s: Spruner-Menke and Droysen. Like them, however, it was essentially a static work. Change was referred to extensively in the text and was shown by contrasting successive maps, but the individual maps were static depictions, generally of territorial control, and the interpretation of contrast involved work on the part of the reader. The atlas provided no help other than through the text, and that was a major reason why the text was so important. It not only commented on the problems of the information available on which the map was based, but also provided crucial interpretation by discussing the process of change of which the map captured a stage. Thus, aside from the possible role of text in explaining change, it also played a more central part in discussing it: the text was the narrative that the map illustrated.

Both of these roles were to be challenged in historical cartography during the twentieth century. Maps were increasingly to present more than one set of data with a clear explanatory message contained in the juxtaposition. This was most apparent in maps that sought to relate settlements or states to environment or states to ethnicity. Maps also came to play a greater role in providing their own narrative. This was achieved by making them more dynamic, and the particular means by which this was achieved was the use of the arrow.

Reich

Arrows had for long been used in maps of the 'Barbarian invasions', but were, otherwise, relatively uncommon in political mapping, though important in maps of exploration and warfare. Indeed, maps of the invasions can be approached as a variant on maps of journeys and war. Nevertheless, given the role of invasions in history it is striking how rarely arrows were used in late nineteenth-century historical atlases.

The need for dynamism in maps was to be pressed by Emil Reich in his *New Student's Atlas of English History* (London, 1903), a work produced by a major publisher, Macmillan. Reich (1854–1910) was a prolific writer whose works included *Foundations of Modern Europe* (London, 1904), *General History of Western Nations from 5000 BC to 1900 AD* (London, 1908) and *Handbook of Geography* (London, 1908). Intended as a cartographic complement to John Richard Green's *History of the English People*, Reich's atlas represented the fusion of environmental and military concerns with the perception that pedagogic purpose as well as analytical value dictated the use of arrows:

> Historical maps giving nothing but the locality and names of the places where events happened can not be held to project these events plastically. Considering that of all the powers of recalling things or ideas, the memory for movements and their incident places is by far the commonest and strongest; considering, further, that the events of history are mostly not static but of a decidedly dynamic nature, it is evident that any means of representing the movements of historical events by graphic methods suggesting movements give a truer and more impressive mental picture of the events . . . it is unquestionable that in colour there is a very powerful aid to memory . . . For all these reasons of practical pedagogy . . . the author has long applied coloured lines, suggesting movement by means of arrows, for the more plastic representation of historic events . . . The average student will, by the aid of such maps, acquire a firm grasp of the sequence and connection of historic facts.

For Reich military considerations demonstrated the crucial role of geography and this was brought home by imperial activity:

> The paramount importance of geography as the basis of a study of history has been brought home to Englishmen by the late war in South Africa [the Boer War 1899–1902], which has forced them to realise how impossible it is to understand events in their connection without a knowledge of such things as the relative position of towns and villages; the relative course of rivers; the nature of the frontier; remoteness from or indentation by the sea; etc. All these circumstances must be taken into account in drawing up the strategy of a campaign, strategy being in a great measure the art of adapting military movements to the geographical conditions of a given country . . . The present atlas endeavours to initiate the student into the knowledge of the strategy of events, and to accustom him to look at history from that most fertile of points of view, the geographical correlation of events.[13]

Text was added to 35 of Reich's 55 maps, and it commented on strategic and environmental questions. For example, for map three, on England 500–1066:

22. 'England from the Sixth Century AD to 1066' from Emil Reich's *New Student's Atlas of English History* (London, 1903). The map marks the 1066 campaign. Reich fails to distinguish between battles where the precise location was known and others, for example Brunhanburh, the location of which was unknown. Given the chronological range of the map, it is understandable that it does not record borders.

William the Conqueror's profoundly strategical march on London, by which he cut off the town from all sides before entering it, is given . . . The student's attention is called to the striking fact, that while several rivers, notably the Thames, the Tweed, the Ribble, and others were readily chosen as boundaries for kingdoms in Anglo-Saxon times, as for shires in post-Norman England, the Severn River never formed a boundary either to kingdoms or to shires.

Numerous maps were devoted to wars. Reich had a clear sense of national destiny. For his map on the Scottish Wars of Independence, he wrote:

King Edward I of England wanted to unite Scotland, Wales, and England under one rule, thus making of what is now called Great Britain, a political island, instead of leaving it, as it had been up to his time, and was for many a generation after his death, an island in the physical sense only. By thus anticipating the future course of British history, Edward necessarily forced and violated many an interest and sentiment but, historically speaking, he cannot be reproached with mere wanton cruelty, or land greed.

More unusually, Reich chose to map 'British Genius'. Analysing the *Dictionary of National Biography* (1885–1900), a scholarly statement of British importance, Reich found about 21,000 people whose birthplaces had been traced, and mapped them in order to establish 'many a striking correlation between locality and genius'. He acknowledged that place of birth might be less important than that of education, but argued, nevertheless, that the mapping indicated 'the prevalent tendencies' in counties. Reich considered it important that Glamorganshire produced eleven poets of note and Monmouthshire only two, or that London and Middlesex were particularly deficient in inventors and soldiers. He saw this approach as a means to indicate environmental influence, but feared that 'the influence of the locality, which is both spiritual, through its historical traditions, and physiological, through its climatic and other physical factors, has as yet been so little examined, and the whole question is so much obscured and marred by vague considerations of "race"' that his maps would be seen as interesting rather than important. Reich, however, asserted their importance and compared them to maps used in 'botanical, zoological, or pathological geography'. This was a scientific comparison that the method employed in the *DNB* maps might not seem to deserve, but that reflected the intellectual values of the period, the scientific aspirations of history and, indeed, the degree to which scientific mapping, for example of the distribution of species, also faced important problems.

Robertson and Bartholomew

Publishers saw an important market for historical atlases. In 1905 another major London publisher, Methuen, produced C. Grant Robertson and J.G. Bartholomew's *Historical and Modern Atlas of the British Empire*. As usual, novelty was asserted for both commercial and intellectual reasons, and the role of geographical factors strongly asserted. The introduction, entitled 'Relation of Geography to History', declared that the atlas was the first offering

> a correct and intelligent interpretation of the modern physical and political geography of the British empire, and will systematically connect that interpretation with, and base it upon, a geographical study of the long historic evolution through which our Empire has passed . . . no student of historical geography will learn what his subject can teach him unless at every stage he brings historical facts into intimate and vital connection with the conditions of modern descriptive and physical geographical.

A study of the history and 'geographical structure' of the British empire was presented not only as desirable but also as 'a positive duty for every British citizen'. Far from dating the British empire to the late Tudor period of maritime expansion, Robertson and Bartholomew saw a longer imperial destiny:

> since the days of Boadicea there is no period of our history in which the inhabitants of Great Britain have not been connected with or lived under a series of national and historic imperial systems . . . the theory and claims of the modern imperial crown are no pinchbeck creation of the nineteenth century.

The long procession of earlier imperial episodes thus gave modern British imperialism a legitimating history, one that made it seem natural. The earlier episodes were not an 'irrelevant' prologue, but rather 'continuously and organically connected' with modern British imperialism. Thus, one map was entitled 'Empire of Wessex'. The atlas included numerous maps of imperial growth with no suggestion that this was anything other than beneficial. Thus, the four maps of European colonies in Africa in 1800, 1850, 1865 and 1880 were entitled 'Development of Africa'.[14]

Schrader, Dow and Joppen

Three interesting atlases that appeared in 1907 reflected a sense of European destiny. F. Schrader's *Atlas de géographie historique* (Paris, 1907), published by Hachette, was a new edition of a work first published in 1896 and began with six maps on the 'Extension de l'Histoire sur la Terre'. This was essentially presented as the spread of Aryans, Semites, Hamites and Chinese. The New World was shown as largely empty until the arrival of the Aryans from Europe. History was presented as a matter of developed civilizations and these were defined in Eurocentric terms.

In the same year Earle W. Dow, professor at the University of Michigan, brought out his *Atlas of European History* (New York, 1907); again with a major publisher, Henry Holt and Co. This was a conventional work that ignored social and economic history and considered the world outside Europe only in terms of its imperialism.

The Jesuit Charles Joppen who taught at St Xavier's High School, Fort Bombay, published his *Historical Atlas of India. For the Use of High Schools, Colleges and Private Students* (London, 1907). Printed by Justus Perthes in Gotha, this was published by Longman which had branches in Bombay, Calcutta and New York as well as London, aspects of Britain's global sway and influence. The 26 maps spanned a period from one non-Indian empire to another: from Alexander the Great to the British in 1907. The atlas presented British conquest as a major episode: half of it was devoted to the seventeenth and eighteenth centuries, the last seven maps recording the progressive growth of British power from 1795 on. This was not seen in terms of British aggression. Thus, the text accompanying the map of India in 1823 claimed that in 1813–23 'the principal Mahratta states were disaffected and intriguing against the English'. Again, 'in 1845 the Sikhs made an unprovoked attack on the British possessions'.[15] There was no map of the Indian Mutiny, a striking omission. Interest in India, and the need to explain its history, led Hereford George in the 1907 third edition of his *Relations of Geography and History*, first published in 1901, to add a chapter on India. Its history was seen as an outcome of its geography and thus, in a way, necessary.

Joppen's atlas was published in a large print-run, which enabled Longman to cut the price. The second edition, published in 1910, included one more map relevant to Indian polities, the principal Mahratta states in 1795, but two more referring to non-Indian polities: Alexander's Indian campaign and 'Portuguese power in the East at its zenith'. Joppen used English, but in 1911 S.S. Chatterjee compiled and the New School Book Press of Calcutta published an Indian-language historical atlas of India; it was reprinted in 1913. Ram Swarup Vaishya produced an Indian-language *New Historical Atlas Based on the Honourable Mr. C.F. Dela Fosse's History of India for the Use of Teachers and Students* (Lucknow) in 1913.

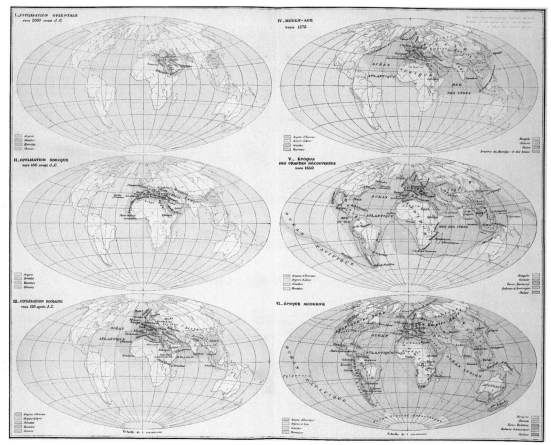

23. 'Extension de l'Histoire sur la Terre' from F. Schrader's *Atlas de géographie historique* (Paris, 1907). History was presented as a matter of developed civilizations and these were defined in Eurocentric terms. A cartography appropriate for the heyday of European imperialism.

Joppen's third edition, published in 1914, was also published in a pocket edition priced at 3s 6d (17½p). Again, there were three new maps, one showing 'the old Indian names of the chief rivers and ascertainable locations of some of the principal Aryan tribes', another the Portuguese possessions on the west coast and the third reflecting the rising interest in historical geography and environmental causation. This map, printed first in the book, covered terrain and vegetation and was derived from two maps in the *Imperial Gazetteer* atlas. Joppen's decision to combine the two was a response to the greater 'technical skill of the map-printers'. The accompanying text emphasized the role of the physical environment, but also the difficulties of mapping its impact successfully:

> The physical features of a land are responsible for much in the making of its earlier history. Yet a satisfactory method of combining physical and political features on a map has not yet been found. Sometimes the physical and sometimes the political aspect comes out more prominently, and often the whole map is lacking in that clearness which is especially desirable in school maps . . . it will not be difficult for the lecturer or teacher to explain or for the student to understand, with the help of the

map, why first settlement and conquest selected some district rather than another, and how invasion generally followed the same line of least resistance.[16]

This remained the first map in the fourth edition, published in 1938 and revised by H.L.O. Garrett, who had been Principal of the Government College in Lahore. Only two maps were added, one showing important archaeological sites, the other a map of the Indian empire in 1936. This was the final edition. India became independent in 1947 and had no need for a work whose major subject was imperial control, and at that largely the British empire from which Indian independence had had to be wrested.

The Last Years before War

The early 1910s continued to be active years for the publication of historical atlases; indeed, two works appeared in 1911 that, in various editions, were to enjoy long lives and for many were *the* historical atlases, creating expectations of what such works should be: Shepherd's *Historical Atlas* and Muir's *New School Atlas of Modern History*. In addition, the process by which more states acquired historical atlases continued, an aspect of the acute nationalism and national consciousness of these years. Where earlier works existed, new historical atlases were generally more substantial.

Prominent examples of historical atlases published in countries that had not played a major role in the field the previous century included *Li-tai Yü-ti Yen-ko Hsien-yao T'u* (Maps of the changing administrative geography of successive dynasties) by Shoujing Yang (1906–11), and the *Atlas histórico de la República Argentina* edited by José Juan Biedma (Buenos Aires, 1909). Shoujing Yang's atlas had maps drawn in the traditional style, juxtaposing the mountains, rivers and towns of earlier times (in black ink) with the geography of the last years of the Ch'ing dynasty (in red ink).

War and nationalism were linked to ethnicity. One of the influential works published in 1911, William R. Shepherd's *Historical Atlas* (New York, 1911), which drew very heavily on Putzger, included a number of ethnic maps, giving the distribution of peoples in the Austro-Hungarian empire and the Balkans, as well as the present distribution of 'European, Chinese Japanese [treated as one] and Negroes'. Published by Henry Holt and Co., Shepherd's was printed by Koerner and Dietrich in Leipzig. It expressed, at least in its American-German nature, a cosmopolitanism, though of course within Eurocentric limits, that was soon to be shattered by war.

Muir

Ramsay Muir compared his *New School Atlas of Modern History* (London, 1911) to that of Putzger as a carefully produced work issued at a price that all schools could afford, but also asserted his originality, focusing first on his determined use of physical geography:

> In the first place, great emphasis is throughout placed upon the *physical basis* of historical geography. Not only are mountain hachures inserted on all politically

coloured maps of sufficiently large scale, but a series of physical maps has been included, carefully designed so as to show the build of all the principal areas of historical importance. The periods illustrated by these maps are those in which the political divisions were sufficiently simple to be adequately shown by red lines. These physical maps have been so placed as to be capable of being used in conjunction with groups of other maps of the same area, and it is hoped that in this way the influence of the build of a country upon its history will be made readily manifest to the student.

Imperial themes were also stressed and Muir made clear that he hoped they would inspire his readers, 'prov[ing] both instructive and stimulating to the imagination'. Warfare also received considerable attention, with 22 campaign maps and battle plans in the first, black and white section of the book. None was of a British defeat. Crécy, Poitiers and Agincourt each had a plan but not the defeats of the Hundred Years' War, such as Formigny and Castillon.

The notes brought out the significance of the physical features depicted. That for Roman Britain illustrated 'the influence of physical features upon early English history. Not only the mountains but the forests and marshes exercised a profound influence, breaking up the country into isolated fragments. Observe the skill with which the Roman roads overcame these obstacles and in some degree welded the country together.'

For the Peninsular War:

Note how the campaigns were determined by the direction of the river valleys and mountain ranges, and by the greater military roads, which are shown; also how the physical barriers in which the country abounds not only prevented effective co-operation between the various French armies and thus added to their difficulties, but accentuated the strong provincial sentiment of the various provinces of Spain. Note the magnificent strategic position of the Torres Vedras lines, a vast natural fortress, commanding the best possible base for an Atlantic naval power, and also controlling the best roads into the heart of the peninsula, from which it was possible to threaten equally all the scattered French armies.

For the colonization of North America:

The two maps should be used in conjunction in order that the influence of physical factors, which is nowhere more clearly demonstrable, may be grasped by the student. Note that the barrier of the Alleghanies [*sic*] shut the English into the coastal fringe, while the St Lawrence, cutting through the mountain-line, led the French by an easy path to the Great Lakes and the Mississippi Valley.[17]

Muir reflected current wisdom not only in emphasizing the role of the environment, but also in his stress on the necessity of a particular type of statehood. For the plate on the Ottoman Empire he wrote: 'not a nation state . . . as the Empire lacked all the elements of unity, it could have no permanence; but for the jealousies of the European powers, it must have been broken up much earlier.'[18]

Muir's themes were also expressed elsewhere. *The Cambridge Modern History Atlas* (Cambridge, 1912), edited by Adolphus Ward, emphasized territorial control and warfare. Imperial conquest was also stressed, as with the map of the Mysore and Maratha Wars 1792–1804, a record of British triumphs. In contrast, previous, less glorious and unsuccessful struggles with Mysore and the Marathas were ignored. The theme of the atlas was Europe:

> The general idea of the Atlas is to illustrate, in a series of maps of Europe and of its different countries, as well as of other parts of the world associated with the progress of European history, the course of events by which the Europe of the fifteenth century has been transformed into the Europe of the present day.[19]

The Coming of War

National mission, a belief in the inevitability of conflict and fascination with war culminated in the First World War. This produced one work in 1914 that also reflected the flood of wartime patriotism and a sharp eye for commercial opportunism. Syndicate Publishing of London produced *1588 to 1914. Album-Atlas of British Victories on the Sea. 'Wooden Walls to Super-Dreadnoughts'*. Aside from the maps, which with the text were the work of the Reverend J. Featherstone Stirling, Chaplain to the Forces, the atlas itself was a tribute to British heroism. On the back cover a picture of a bulldog topped the words, 'By one of those dispensations of Providence which appeal so strongly to the German Emperor, the nose of the bulldog has been slanted backwards, so that he can breathe with comfort and without letting go.' Approved by the Official Press Bureau, the atlas included an autograph portrait of the First Lord of the Admiralty, Winston Churchill, and on the inside page 'Signatures of the Brave. A Place for the autographs of officers and men who served Britain by land and sea in the Great War of 1914', topping Shakespeare's lines 'This happy breed of men . . . this England'. The first map was of the Armada, while the text itself went back to the Saxons and Alfred the Great. Other naval conflicts mapped included the Anglo-Dutch and Anglo-French wars, and Victorian naval engagements. The emphasis was on British victories, so that topics not generally mapped, for example the campaign of 1747 or 1780 in European waters, were both covered. The atlas included details on how to join the navy and also a note on Nelson by E. Hallam Moorhouse:

> At this crisis of our destinies, there is no great dead Englishman to whom the nation's thoughts turn so surely and so proudly as to Nelson. Final victory or defeat for us is always and inevitably at sea, and the mere name of Nelson sums up all we have ever achieved there in the past, all we hope to hold and win in the present . . . men and the sea are unchanging.

Historical atlases were thus to play their part, in war as in peace, in confirming a sense of national destiny and continuity with a glorious past.

5

War, Environment and Ideology, 1914–45

Nationalism

The First World War and its aftermath greatly increased interest in political maps and mapping. Readers of newspapers became ever more familiar with campaign and battle plans. The destruction of empires and the remoulding of much of Europe, the Middle East and the European world created fresh interest in a different sort of map, which would address the questions, not only of what was happening, but also of why and what ought to be happening. The rapid pace of change and the sense that nothing was fixed encouraged demands with a definite cartographic dimension, because most of the international political debates were over the control of territory. In addition, the debates generally had a pronounced historical slant, since demands for territory were frequently expressed in terms of historical claims. The scale of the war encouraged an interest in what was in 1916 termed geopolitics by the Swedish political scientist Rudolf Kjellen (1864–1922). Kjellen regarded the nature of being as a struggle for existence, for states and nations no less than for individuals. To Kjellen the urge to gain territory was the crucial dimension of a nation or state's quest to survive. The past served to demonstrate the truth of this proposition if it was approached as a demonstration of geopolitics.

One of the most interesting aspects of the cartographic assertion and definition of nationalism occurred with Zionism. The First World War was a period in which Zionist activity increased and on 2 November 1917 the British issued the Balfour Declaration expressing support for a Jewish national home in Palestine. In that year *The True Boundaries of the Holy Land as Described in Numbers XXXIV: 1–12 Solving the Many Diversified Theories as to their Location* by the recently deceased Hillel Isaacs (1825–1917) was published in Chicago by his daughter Jeanette Isaacs Davis. The work was published before the meeting of the American Jewish Congress in order to establish a common Jewish position before the peace conference that was expected at the end of the war. As an independent state of Israel might be restored, it was necessary to establish its correct boundaries and this was especially pressing because earlier speculation, based in part on exploration in the second half of the previous century, had led to different views of Israel's boundaries; as Isaacs demonstrated with the maps in his book. Furthermore, Isaacs argued that there was a sacred duty to make the Bible explicable. His own map, drawn in 1916, gave Israel extensive frontiers, especially to the north where they extended to include all the coast to the Gulf of Alexandretta.[1] This was far more extensive than the territory sought by Zionist organizations, but it provided particularly pointed evidence of how historical claims might be extended to maximum advantage. More generally, the geography of the Holy Land was familiar to Western statesmen through maps in bibles.

The peace negotiations that followed the armistice, and the contentions that the Treaty of Versailles did not still, gave further rise to historical mapping. Thus the *Atlas de géographie historique de la Belgique*, published with government encouragement, was in part designed to assert Belgium's historical and territorial integrity after German occupation in the recent war. The first volume to be published – in 1919 – carried a notice explaining the need for the work:

> Cette lacune affecte également notre enseignement public et notre propagande à l'égard de la Belgique . . . proviennent de l'ignorance générale de son histoire politique et de ses vicissitudes territoriales. Un tel ouvrage, même inachevé, sera indispensable au moment des négociations de la paix et pour la préparation de ces négociations qui amenderont sans doute sur certains points une rectification de nos frontières. Ceux qui formeront les dossiers de la Belgique, les diplomates qui la représenteront, devront avoir entre les mains mieux que des cartes schématiques et improvisées – comme celles dont durent se servir notamment en 1830, 1831 et 1838 nos délégues à Londres – un instrument de travail sérieux, dressé scientifiquement, et jouissant par la garantie de ses auteurs d'une incontestable autorité . . . donner aux Belges comme à nos amis du dehors une image fidèle et vivante de notre formation nationale, de notre travail séculaire d'unification intérieure et d'une vitalité presque incroyable après tant de mutilations.

The Belgian maps did not emphasize ethnicity; instead they sought to give historical continuity to Belgium. They therefore contrasted with the stress on ethnicity that characterized much mapmaking, especially in eastern Europe. There were indeed serious problems in defining ethnic identity and then in mapping it. This was especially so given the interpenetration of ethnic groups in much of eastern Europe, particularly the Balkans.[2] Furthermore, mapmakers could look back to different ethnic and national traditions of discerning boundaries and mapping territory and these influenced the production of new maps.[3] The precision of cartography was thus used for propagandist reasons, as in Polish and German maps of the 1920s dealing with the Polish Corridor and Upper Silesia: ethnic categorization was used to enhance or lessen the Polish nature of both regions.[4] In Hungary the cause of frontier revision after the losses of territory by the Treaty of Trianon (1920) generated a lot of writing about the priority and evolution of national(ity) areas of settlement, which usually included cartographical material of some kind. Pál Teleki, an important politician, who became minister president in 1939–41, was by training a geographer with a great interest in the history of maps. He was responsible for a famous and original map of Hungarian nationalities presented to the Peace Conference, which was designed to overcome the problem that the non-Magyar areas, being less densely settled, appeared disproportionately prominent in conventional cartography.

War

The horrors of the war did not lessen interest in the cartography of conflict. Instead, the war increased interest in all things military, and served to underline the role of conflict in the creation of states and the development of peoples. Thus, *The Oxford Historical Wall Maps*, a set published by Oxford University Press in 1915, included numerous battles. The map of Europe to illustrate English and foreign history showed the sites of battles such as Blenheim and Fontenoy, rather than, for example, cultural or religious links. There were four maps of English possessions in medieval France, which had also been an important subject in the *Philips' Wall Atlas of Modern History* (London, 1913). The Oxford series included a map of Iberia to illustrate the Peninsular War and a map of the Low Countries in 1914, with an inset of the situation in 1702, when Britain had also deployed a major army to protect its interests there and to defeat a hostile neighbouring power, in that case France. Thus, the map asserted continuity in Britain's interests, lending the authority of the past to the commitments of the present. Like newspaper maps, wall maps helped to make historians and their public map-conscious. This was especially the case with geopolitical and military maps. They were comprehensible at various scales and the topics translated well between the different types of map.

Historical atlases published after the First World War extended their usual coverage of military history to include the war. Thus the 1923 edition of *F.W. Putzgers Historischer Schul-Atlas* featured maps not only of, for example, the German triumphs against Imperial Rome in the Teutonberger Wald campaign and against Napoleon in the 1813 Leipzig campaign, as well as the Wars of German Unification,[5] but also a section on the First World War.[6] This included a map of the western front that emphasized the German advance in 1914 and ignored the retreat in 1918.[7] The *Atlas d'histoire de la Belgique* (Namur, 1939) had a map of the First World War which underlined the role of Belgian troops.[8]

In the aftermath of the war, compilers of maps, atlases and books and their readers did not only seek to refight that conflict. Indeed, in cartographic terms, much of the First World War lacked the discreteness and finality of result that made for interesting military mapping. The nature of the war differed markedly from the way in which people sought to portray it on maps. After the war both the British and the Germans established units to produce histories of the war, which included maps. Although the units did not produce atlases of the war, the maps included in the British official history greatly influenced later cartographic presentations of the war, including historical atlases.

One of the best historical atlases of warfare appeared in the years after the war. The 120 maps of *Schlachten-Atlas zur antiken Kriegsgeschichte* by Johannes Kromayer and Georg Veith published in Leipzig between 1922 and 1929 took military historical cartography to new heights. For each battle there were usually two or more maps so that both the moves of the combatants and the different hypotheses of how the battle had developed could be depicted. This was true, for example, of Salamis and Issus. Aside from very detailed battle plans, of, say, Thermopylae, there were also maps to show the background to the battle, for example of the area round Issus or the routes of both armies to the site. For Alexander's victory at Gaugamela there were maps for the different moves and a map for the area of the battle. Hannibal's victory at Lake Trasimene was depicted in great detail and several theories of how

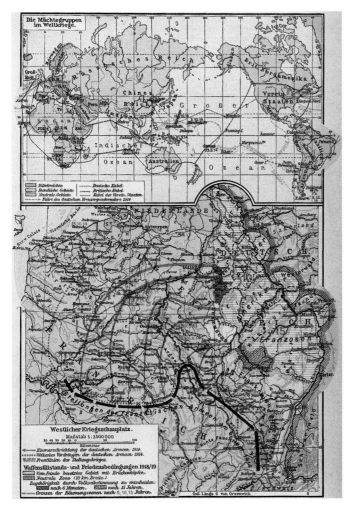

24. Maps of the First World War from *F.W. Putzgers Historischer Schul-Atlas* (1923). Treatment of the war varied. The map of the western front emphasized German success in 1914, not the failure of the German war plan. Full advantage was taken of the availability of colour.

the battle was fought were propounded. For Cannae, there was a main version of the battle, four different versions shown as insets and an area map. Throughout, the atlas was a careful and scholarly work. The map of Caesar's expeditions to England in 55 and 54 BC used the coastline of the period. The maps were accompanied by detailed text and used consistent colour symbols: blue and red for the armies clearly showing against the brown terrain.

Continuity

If continuity was displayed in the interest in national issues and warfare, this was even more true of the individual historical atlases. New editions of pre-war works were produced with few changes. This was the case with Ramsay Muir's 1911 atlas, which became the *Philips' New Historical Atlas for Students* and went through further editions in 1914, 1917, 1920 and 1923 with little alteration. The fifth edition (1923) still used the preface to the 1911 edition. Schrader's *Atlas de géographie historique*, first published by Hachette in 1896, with another edition following in 1907, appeared in a new edition with few changes in 1924. Schools appeared to want little new; certainly they were offered little. Works such as the *Historical Atlas of the British Empire* (London, 1924), published by Macmillan and the *Practical Map Exercises and Syllabus in Ancient History* by Mildred C. Bishop and Edward K. Robinson (Boston, 1921) were conventional. The last was part of a series published by Ginn and Co. that included *Practical Map Exercises in Medieval and Modern European History* (1920) and in American (1922) and European (1923) history. All were devoted to political and military topics and ignored economic history. R.C. Willard and E.K. Robinson's *Map Exercises, Syllabus and Notebook in World History* (Boston, 1927) was heavily Eurocentric. The first mention of Oriental history occurred with the map of 'the spread of European influence in the East'. This Eurocentric emphasis was retained in the new edition of 1934.

Environmentalism

Environmentalism in the 1920s and 1930s can be approached first either at the intellectual level or at that of the historical atlases themselves. The second approach may be more appropriate as it is far from clear that the atlas compilers were responding to current intellectual concerns. Instead, it rather appears that, with the lapse factor that it is all too easy to lose sight of in historiographical studies, the compilers were influenced by the ideas advanced prior to the war: they were determinists more than possibilists.

Environmentalism was combined with military interest in the *Pictorial Atlas of English History* (London, 1919) edited by J.S. Lay. Map fourteen, 'The Chief Scottish Battle-Fields', showed land above 1000 feet and readers were urged to 'notice that the battle-fields are close together in the plain between the highlands and the sea'. For map 55, a physical map of France, they were told to 'note the level country on the Belgian frontier where the Germans invaded France in the Great War'.

Physical geography was stressed more in the 1924 edition of *W. and A.K. Johnston's Historical Atlas of British and World History* (Edinburgh) than it had been in the previous edition (1917): 'fuller expression has been given to the influence of physical features upon historical development'. The map of the Roman empire in the fourth century in the 1917 edition was replaced by 'Europe showing the General Direction of the Barbarian Inroads on the Fall of the British Empire'. This depicted physical features: desert, highlands over 3000 feet and 'grassland and steppe, mainly Black Earth region, the route of Nomad Invasions from Asia'. The map of 'early explorers', a phrase that ignored millennia of exploration, also depicted land over 3000 feet, the limit of drift ice, desert and poor steppe land, and, during the northern summer, the regions of trade winds, prevailing westerlies and monsoons. Contours were marked on many maps, for example Roman Britain, India in 1857 and the American Civil War.

The 1928 edition of *Philips' New School Atlas of Universal History* included a plate, 'The Realms of Civilisation *c.* 200 AD and the Natural Conditions Affecting their Relations'. Readers were informed that it was

> intended to illustrate the relationship between the civilization of Europe and the Mediterranean and the civilizations of the East. There was very little contact between

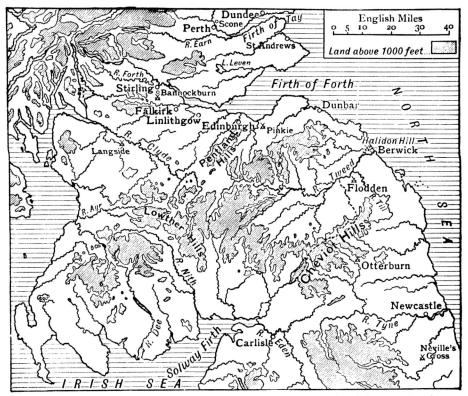

25. 'The Role of the Environment' from J.S. Lay's the *Pictorial Atlas of English History* (London, 1919). Readers were urged to 'notice that the battle fields are close together in the plain between the highlands and the sea'. Only so much could be shown. The role of a river, for example, depended on the number and location of bridging points, but these were not shown. As Halidon Hill outside Berwick indicated, local topography was crucial, and that, also, was not shown on the map.

them; and in order to show the reasons for this, the map is coloured to show the character of the soil, indicating the great desert and mountain areas which formed the main barriers to communication, and also the vast steppe regions, over which nomadic tribes ebbed and flowed, their movements often affecting the destinies of empires. This map should be used for the barbarian incursions into the British Empire.[9]

Pearson's theme of the difference between upland and lowland Britain was taken up in the Philips's atlas with the map 'The Two Halves of England' which showed land over 600 feet, navigable rivers, cathedral cities, universities, chief ports, centres of the wool trade and iron smelting, and was designed to display 'the distinction between the hilly north-western and the level south-eastern halves of England, which has profoundly influenced its history'. As if to indicate the timeless nature of this distinction, the map bore no date.[10]

Social history also made its entry, though in a diagrammatic manner rather than by mapping on a regional or national scale:

The social life of England in the Middle Ages is illustrated by a series of diagrams in the text. Fig. 27 shows the organisation of a medieval village, with its open fields, the holding of an individual villager being indicated. Fig. 28 shows how a town could be adjusted to this village organisation: Leicester – a medieval walled town in relation to its fields; while Fig. 29 gives a more detailed study of a walled town on the basis of a Roman fort: Chester.

In the 1931 edition of Putzger's *Historischer Schul-Atlas* the first map was no longer on the economy of the Ancient world, but instead depicted the climates of the world under the title 'The Natural Foundations of World History'. This was to be studied together with the second map which showed 'Old Centres of Civilization on the Earth'.[11] Thus, a cartographic historical tradition that focused on Classical roots was to be replaced by one that centred on environmental constraints and influences that were timeless (in human terms) and therefore as important for present and future as for the past.

The role of environmental factors was stressed in the *Oxford Pictorial Atlas of Indian History* by two Indians, K.S. Kini and U.B. Shanker, which was published in 1932 by the Indian branch of Oxford University Press, with new editions in 1935, 1939 and 1942. The atlas began with a physical map and a section of text explaining that the 'rugged relief' of the Decean helped it to resist invasion. British imperialism was presented favourably, the map of India in 1919 being glossed 'The additions made [since 1857] show the care of the Indian Government to maintain peace along the frontiers and defend them against European rivals'.[12] The role of the environment in history was also stressed in the works of Thomas Griffith Taylor, especially his *The Control of Settlement by Humidity and Temperature, with Special Reference to Australia and the Empire* (Melbourne, 1916), *Environment and Race* (London, 1927) and *Environment and Nation. Geographical Factors on the Cultural and Political History of Europe* (Toronto, 1930).

Environmental influence was not sought solely at the global scale. Cyril Fox, an archaeologist who greatly influenced interwar British historical geography, produced in his lengthy *Archaeology of the Cambridge Region* (Cambridge, 1923) a scholarly account of a physically based cultural zone and its historical characteristics. Fox used distribution maps that were coloured to show the physiography of the region: rivers and meres, fen and marsh, and areas probably densely forested. Fox explained 'the cultural differentiation of the eastern plain' in a way that emphasized physical factors but left room for others:

> At the commencement of this analysis the tendency to unity of cultural character in the Cambridge Region in any given Age was held to be the natural consequence of the geographical unity which a river basin possesses. The peculiar configuration of the district – a narrow belt of open country bordered by fen and forest and forming a highway into Norfolk and North Suffolk – has, however, permitted this tendency at times to be modified by military or political action.[13]

Fox went on to publish *The Personality of Britain. Its Influence on Inhabitant and Invader in Prehistoric and Early Historic Times* (Cardiff, 1932, 4th edn, 1943). This contained numerous distribution maps:

> The most convenient line of approach is to find out, by the study of distribution maps, where in this island early Man actually lived and laboured; in the process of determining, stage by stage, what conditioned his activities here . . . in pursuit of its aim, a given distributional situation may be, as here, expressed in the simplest terms

available, stripped of those complexities which made the pattern of human life and activity so interesting, and which it is the business of the prehistorian and historian to elucidate.

Fox's book emphasized the distinction between lowland and highland zones, but not in any deterministic fashion. His work greatly influenced an important generation of British archaeologists.[14] In his *Man and his Past* (1921), O.G.S. Crawford also stressed the geographical approach to history and prehistory. Crawford was responsible for a series of interwar historical maps produced by the Ordance Survey that mapped locations and distributions against the background of physical geography. Fox's use of similar distribution maps plotted against the background of a detailed map of the physical geography clearly enhanced the more conventional cartographic depictions of environmental influence. He sought to use maps to investigate relationships in detail, rather than to map them in a suggestive fashion and accompany them with text that asserted a causation that had not been demonstrated.

Fox's work was an important aspect of the process by which interwar geographers, in this case historical geographers, were demanding more from maps. This greatly influenced historical cartography, but the extent to which this process influenced historical atlases was more uncertain, because such atlases were generally produced by historians rather than geographers. Nevertheless, historical geographers and their work created a context that made demands on the mapping of the past. Thus, in his *The Geography behind History* (London, 1938), Gordon East, Lecturer in Historical Geography at the influential London School of Economics, stated:

> It is not enough, in studying history, merely to consult the atlas map in order to ascertain the position and areas of countries or the location of battlefields and cities. Yet not so long ago the geography contained in sober historical writings was either entirely lacking or assumed this jejune form. Freeman's notable and still useful work, *The Historical Geography of Europe*, included an atlas volume, the numerous maps of which showed no indication whatever of the physical features of this continent. To the uninitiated reader the inference was that the people and states of Europe developed on a uniform plane surface.[15]

Such demands could be met. Freeman was a straw man by 1938 and historians interested in geography were well aware of the role of physical environment. Many historians, however, were less conversant with the geographical perspective. The introduction to Charles Paullin's influential *Atlas of the Historical Geography of the United States* (Washington, DC, 1932) included a sentence that was relevant to historical geography, but not to most history as practised in the period: 'Historical judgment must rest on the recognition of fundamental relationships in space as well as in time, and these are often made intelligible through the medium of maps.'[16]

Historical geographers thus advanced the argument that historical cartography was not only a crucial pedagogic tool, an argument that would have been accepted a century earlier, but also a vital analytical method not simply for historical geography but also for history itself. Yet history was too varied a discipline for any single method to prevail.

Possibilism and Regions

Gordon East claimed that 'the efforts of geographers . . . converge above all on one common goal – the discovery, description and demarcation of regions – broadly uniform areas of country which can be distinguished on a scientific basis'.[17] There was indeed a branch of history, especially in France and Germany, that centred on such studies and that was a field in which historical geography and historical cartography played a major role. This regionally based historical geography, the historical geography of the *pays*, placed less of an emphasis on the environment as a determining force and more on its interaction with human society. This emphasis was particularly associated with Paul Vidal de la Blache (1843–1918). Trained as an historian, Vidal de la Blache played a major role in the development of French geography, and was appointed to the chair of geography at the Sorbonne in 1899. Geographical and historical studies were closely associated and, indeed, until 1942 the *agrégation*, the major competitive examination for admission to teaching posts in universities and high schools, entailed a joint examination in history and geography. As a result, the two subjects were each more open to the influence of the other than, for example, in Britain. Vidal de la Blache argued that the environment created a context for human development rather than determining it. It was thus a factor that set the parameters for socio-cultural developments, rather than the central issue in history. The emphasis was therefore shifted back to humanity and to the varieties of human activity, to cultural geography and the complexities of nation building. Furthermore, greater weight could be placed on influences from outside the locality, as in Vidal de la Blache's *Tableau de la géographie de la France* (Paris, 1903). When, seven years later, he published an article suggesting a new division of the French regions, Vidal de la Blache proposed they be based on the fields of influence of large urban centres, a view of the human environment that did not centre on physical geography.[18]

The role of a multiplicity of polities in German history was such that there was an historical interest in the 'regional' dimension of German historical cartography that did not depend on a more 'geographical' interest in the role of regions. Helmut Jäger suggested that the plan of an historical atlas of the Austrian Alpine lands proposed by the Austrian geographer Richter in 1896 gave the first impetus to a whole series of 'regional' historical atlases,[19] but there had been earlier developments. Aside from the *Erläuterungen des Atlas zur Geschichte der Sächsischen Länder* (Grimma, 1853), produced when Saxony was still independent, the *Geschichtlicher Atlas der Rheinprovinz* was published in Bonn in parts from the 1890s. It offered great detail with, for example, 1789 covered in seven sections (published in 1894) and a very detailed territorial map following in 1898, or the detailed treatment of the Kreis (Imperial circles) published in 1897, and of Roman roads and the religious situation in 1610 both published in 1902.

In France Vidal de la Blache's work was taken up by Lucien Febvre. Opposed to determinism and the work of Ratzel, Febvre was suspicious of the use of the notion of influences and instead preferred the idea of an interaction between man and environment. He also directed attention to the problematic nature of the sources of environmental determinism that were all too often presented in simplistic terms, referring for example to the 'complexity of the idea of climate'. Though not published until after the First World War, Febvre conceived of his critique in 1912–13, and it can therefore be placed alongside American criticism of Ratzelian notions, most obviously as expounded by Semple.[20] Similarly, in his *Relations of Geography and History* (Oxford, 1901), Hereford George of New College, Oxford, stressed the role of geographical influences and the value of geographical knowledge for historians, but also emphasized that human action could affect the environment.[21]

Febvre advanced what he termed 'possibilisme' and directed attention to the study of human regions. Distinctive *genres de vie* were seen to exist in these specific and distinct physical units, and study of them therefore became the obvious way to understand the relationship between humans and environment. A study at the regional level offered the possibility of a more detailed assessment of the relationship and directed attention to human activity, because, although the physical geography of the French regions was far from uniform, the differences, for example in climate, were not sufficient to explain regional variations in human geography. The *Annales* school of French historians, among whom Febvre was prominent, deliberately set out to fuse history and geography, and saw the future of history (as an academic discipline) in terms of its increasingly multi-disciplinary character. They stressed regional characteristics that gave places identity and that also made possible the identification of regions. The *Annalistes'* approach was therefore similar to that of de la Blache.[22]

Criticism of environmental determinism was also voiced elsewhere. In America the anthropologist Franz Boas (1858–1942) attacked the mono-causal character of environmentalism and influenced Carl Sauer (1889–1975). Sauer, a geographer interested in anthropology, criticized American geographers, such as Semple, who drew on Ratzel and instead advanced a possibilist interpretation of the role of the environment.[23]

The regional dimension was presented in a number of interwar German historical atlases, although their inception was due to a sense of political distinctness reflecting the large number of polities among which Germany had until recently been divided, rather than to a particular geographical interpretation. The role of physical features in affecting settlement and shaping development was well established in German scholarship and cartography. In his *Die Pflanzenleben der Schwäbischen Alb* (1898), Robert Gradmann had demonstrated how prehistoric settlement had been concentrated on lightly forested or open areas, especially if the soil was loess which was both fertile and easily worked.

The mapping of the relationship between settlement and physical geography was an important theme in German historical cartography. The *Geschichtlicher Handatlas der Rheinprovinz* by H. Aubin and J. Niessen (Cologne, 1926) began with a map of the area in 500 BC showing woodland and rivers before moving on to archaeological sites. The atlas included maps reflecting another source of regional distinctiveness: particular linguistic terms which were mapped over four pages. The *Elsass-Lothringischer Atlas* of Georg Wolfram and Werner Gley was published in 1931 by the Institut of Elsass-Lothringen at the University of Frankfurt am Main, an institute that kept alive a sense of German identity for Alsace-Lorraine, recently regained by France. One map depicted woodland, marshland and settled land in 500 AD, and also woodland in 800, a useful basis for the subsequent maps of Carolingian and thirteenth-century frontiers, bishoprics, monasteries, towns and castles. The *Pfälzischer Geschichtsatlas* (Neustadt, 1935), edited by Wilhelm Winkler of the provincial archives, began with a map of woodland and other physical features at the beginning of the medieval period and subsequently included dialect maps and a map of major woodlands in 1790. The last map, devoted to the French occupation of 1918–30, was a reminder of another important consequence of the recent war and an echo of the more overtly ideological mapping of the 1930s.

Keeping up to Date

Historical atlases were and are always affected by the need to respond to change, both changing means of production and change in what can be depicted. There were changes in both spheres in the interwar period, though they had only a limited effect on most historical atlases. The spread of transparent plastic in map drawing was part of an important shift in map compilation and production that put a stress on mass production, on mechanization, speed and quantity, rather than on craftsmanship. The changes threatened traditional standards of quality. There were problems with inconsistent ink cover and defective lines resulting in imperfect printing plates, and with inconsistent line weights and coarse line elements affecting precision and clarity of line and general aesthetic appeal.[24] It is not surprising that many map readers prefer nineteenth-century maps with their copper engraving or lithographic drawing to the atlases of the first half of the twentieth century.

Yet if graphic quality and appeal were compromised, most atlases were still well up to their task technically. A decline in precision of line was not too serious given the scale used in most maps. Furthermore, the advantage of having numerous maps produced was great. Not only were consumers served, and encouraged to consider the spatial dimensions of issues, but the greater availability of maps ensured that more information was spatially depicted and thus accessible to map-compilers. Historical atlases had to be kept up to date to present both recent history and its perceptions on earlier periods. The major historical atlases tended to do so in a largely perfunctory fashion. The cost and inconvenience of producing new material were important factors, but so also was a sense of continuity with the original conception of the work, a view that was especially strong if the compilers were still alive and responsible for new editions.

New editions frequently claimed a degree of novelty that consideration of their contents seldom justified, but it was clearly necessary for them to do so. Thus the preface to the seventh edition of Shepherd's *Historical Atlas* (New York, 1929) stated:

> Since the Atlas made its first appearance in 1911, new interests and methods in historical instruction have come to the fore. Marked changes also have been wrought in the map of the world. Adaptation of the material to meet the needs of the one and take cognizance of the other has been the primary object of the present revision.

In practice the changes were few. The atlas was brought up to date to include the First World War and the peace settlements, but most of the maps were unrevised. As before the war, the printer was German: in 1929 the Leipzig firm of Fischer and Wittig.

The second edition of S.R. Gardiner's *School Atlas of English History*, originally published in 1891, appeared in 1936. It contained 'a few new maps . . . in order to bring the atlas up to date'. These related to nineteenth-century developments, such as the unifications of Italy and Germany, and some in the early twentieth century, but, again, most of the atlas was unrevised, although, with an emphasis typical of the period, the plans of Bannockburn and Trafalgar were 'revised in the light of recent historical research'. Another interest of the 1930s was reflected in the map of the peoples of the Austro-Hungarian empire in 1914.[25] First World War battle-maps were added to the postwar 1930 edition of J.G. Bartholomew's *Literary and Historical Atlas of Europe* (1st edn, London, 1910).

Several new works in the interwar years broadened the cartographic horizon. The influence of Europeanization in Africa was reflected in the contents of Eric Walker's *Historical Atlas of South Africa* (Oxford, 1922) and in *Maroc. Atlas historique, géographique et économique* (Paris, 1935). Morocco was then under French control and this was fully reflected in the atlas. The editor was French – M.E. Lévi-Provençal – as was the publisher – Horizons de France – and the introduction was by the French Minister-Resident. No map dealt with recent Moroccan history. Not only was the French conquest thus ignored, but so also was the age of expansion when in the 1590s Moroccan power had reached the Niger.

Yet there was also a sense of difficulties. The three volume *Atlas historique*, published by the Presses Universitaires de France in 1936–7, responded to the economic problems of the 1930s by appearing in black and white in order to keep the price down.[26] In his introduction to the third volume A. Rébillon claimed that the most developed historical atlases had dated from decades earlier – he cited Spruner, Droysen and Schrader – and that more recent works had been more summary.[27]

This was a reasonable assessment. The interwar period was in some respects a disappointing one for European historical atlases. Whereas the nineteenth century could be said to have been a continuous period of development, the interwar years were essentially a period of continuation, and that without the amplitude of the earlier years. There was only limited innovation.

Yet it would be mistaken to push this analysis too far. First, in terms of the general pedagogic interests of the period, works such as Shepherd's were satisfactory. It was possible to use largely unrevised editions of pre-war historical atlases, such as those of Muir, Putzger and Shepherd, because they largely met the needs of the period, not least owing to the fact that pedagogic programmes had not greatly changed. There was still a heavy emphasis on international relations, warfare and territorial control, and these subjects were well covered, albeit in a conventional sense. The interests of the book-purchasing public were no different. The European empires and the USA still dominated most of the world, and thus the historical cartography of the world outside Europe and the USA continued to be addressed largely in terms of imperialism.

Second, there were new developments. The most important was in American historical cartography and the rise of overtly ideological mapping. More generally, scholarly activity was increasingly aware of cartography; this was particularly true of archaeology. The use of distribution maps became more common. Alongside the ideological and nationalist emphases of much European historical cartography in the 1930s, it is worth noting the foundation in 1929 of an international collaborative project for the mapping of the Roman world.[28]

Furthermore, whatever the limitations of the interwar historical atlases, in some countries there were important advances, at least in terms of the range of topics covered and the number of maps produced. Thus, Adolf Schück's *Historisk Atlas. Skolupplagan* (Stockholm), which was to remain one of the two main historical atlases in Swedish schools until the mid-1960s, first appeared in 1934. Though only 32 pages initially, it was a major advance on Arvid Kemple's 1897 work. Schück was an historian at Stockholm University.

Change was especially marked in countries whose political position had altered as a consequence of the First World War, although the situation varied. *Egyetemes Történelmi Atlasz* (Atlas of general history), published by the Hungarian Royal Defence Institute of Cartography (Budapest, 1920) for secondary school pupils, was mostly composed of pre-war maps. There were no maps about the wars against Habsburg rule. The new map of Europe after the peace treaties was printed on the cover at the end in black and white, while all the other maps were coloured. Of the 80 maps, only seventeen were about Hungary. The cover depicted the statue of a medieval monk, the author of the first chronicle of the Hungarians. This atlas served until the next Hungarian historical atlas was published in 1926: *Történelmi atlasz Magyarország történelmének tanításához* (Historical atlas for the teaching of the history of Hungary) with thirty-two maps. The next three years saw the publication of the following volumes in the series *Történelmi atlasz a világtörténelem tarritasahoz Ókor* (Historical atlas for the teaching of universal history): Classical world in 1927, Middle Ages and early modern in 1928, and a historical altas for secondary schools the same year, and finally the modern period in 1929. In conjunction with the atlases, new wall-maps were also produced. During 1927 eight maps depicting Hungarian history were published, while in 1929 four maps on ancient history appeared. They were followed during 1930–31 by a further eight wall-maps on the medieval, early modern and modern period of European history. In 1931 the Hungarian Geographical Institute published another historical atlas containing thirty-two small format, but high quality maps. In newly independent Poland a whole series of historical atlases was published in the interwar period.[29]

The United States

'No important subject connected with American history has been so neglected as the historical geography of the United States.' That had been the verdict of Albert Bushnell Hart and his colleague Edward Channing in their *Guide to the Study of American History* (Boston, 1896). They criticized the inaccuracies of most textbook maps and the data they relied on, and stressed the 'great need of an elaborate historical atlas of North America, worked out from the documentary sources'.[30]

The historical mapping of the USA was to advance greatly in the interwar period. To a certain extent this mapping was more complex than the conventional agenda of historical atlases, for whereas readers of most European historical atlases were apparently satisfied with that agenda – international relations, empire and warfare – and the history of these countries could be largely presented in those terms, that was. less true of the USA: domestic history was seen as more important.

Hart

A number of important historical atlases appeared in interwar America. The first was Hart's *American History Atlas* (1918). Illustrating the danger of excessive compartmentalization to subsequent analysis, in this case of separating atlases from wall maps, Hart's atlas was based on the series of large wall maps he had prepared for the Chicago publishers Denoyer Geppert and Co. It contained 60 colour maps, and, aside from the conventional cartographic agenda – both in American terms and with reference to the historical cartography of the period – the atlas ranged widely. Thus, in addition to maps of war and territorial gain – the development of the USA as a state, there were also maps of its development as a country, for example of pre-independence trade and industry, of land and water routes and of land grants to the railways. There were maps on the development of manhood and female suffrage, on the end to slavery and on liquor regulations. Neither the map on the War of American Independence nor the accompanying text made any reference to the Loyalists who had resisted independence.

Hart's atlas was a great success. Further editions appeared in 1924, 1930, 1940 and 1942. The third (1930) edition contained twice as many maps and considerably more text. Hart was influenced by the environmentalism of the period, and drew attention to the role of physical geography:

> The close relationship between the lines of the railroads and the old trails and roads (see Maps 7 and 10) should be noted. They testify to the fundamental influence of topography in fixing the lines of communication, which in turn influence the establishment of cities and towns as commercial, industrial, or cultural centers.[31]

Fox

Two years after Hart's first edition, Dixon Ryan Fox, Assistant Professor of History at Columbia, produced the largest American historical atlas hitherto: *Harper's Atlas of American History* (New York, 1920), with its 128 maps, many of which were taken from 'The American Nation' series, a 28-volume collection published by Harper and Brothers in 1904–18, for which Hart was the general editor. In his foreword Fox claimed that teachers had frequently regretted the absence of a cheap and convenient collection of maps 'which adequately show the progress of American life'. Fox accompanied the maps with an essay on 'American History and the Map' and with a series of map exercises designed to teach American historical geography. In the first, he discussed the problem of environmental influence, rejecting the notion that 'human history, like ecology, is a science which concerns itself only with how environment conditions life growth', in favour of a possibilist interpretation. Fox also argued that 'human influences can be indicated on a map'. One of his maps indicated the routes of the Underground Railroad, and Fox pointed out that some of them ran 'near Quaker settlements'. He also pressed the need for learning where men 'acted': 'Historical facts are localized facts, and precision in this respect is especially essential in American history, which is so much an evolution in space as well as time.'

Fox's essay is also valuable because he engaged directly with the meaning of maps. He saw their value as dependent not simply upon cartographic skill, but also upon the meanings that their readers brought. To Fox the map was not an independent force, and, in a significant passage, he questioned the notion of cartographic progressivism:

> Something may be said for the old maps which pictured ships, sea serpents, bears, woods, and houses, for they prodded up the laggard fancy to some conception of the regions that they indicated. The map to have a meaning must be regarded as a symbol. When the student, drawing in a line to mark the route of Daniel Boone, comes to the pass through the Alleghanies, he must be forcibly reminded of that important day in the history of America, when this resolute pioneer looked out upon a billowy sea of tree tops, with the . . . thrill at scanning boundless space.

To Fox the reader must have 'the type of mind to which a map can mean more than black lines printed on white paper'; but it was far from clear how and with what consequences that end was to be obtained, questions that were to be of increasing importance to those who thought about the purposes of mapmaking.

For Fox the particular lesson of American history, 'impossible to understand without the map', was sectionalism and the way it was overcome, particularly by the improved communications that the atlas mapped. His was an optimistic account: 'the land seems formed for a great and united people'. Although Fox's account was essentially one of European Americans, he did include a map that acknowledged the earlier inhabitants: 'Distribution of American Indians about 1500 by Linguistic Stocks.' The impact of the Native American presence was, however, lessened because the information was printed against the background of a state map of America and the state names were printed at the same size as those of most of the Indian names. There were subsequent maps of Indian cessions, of the 'Western Indians' and the trading posts in 1820–35 and of the 'removal of Southern Indians'. In contrast, the maps of American history in the third edition of W.R. Shepherd's *Historical Atlas* (New York, 1923) essentially ignored Native Americans. The maps of 'European exploration in the United States' and 'Territorial Expansion of the United States since 1803' marked on state boundaries and names, but not tribal areas or names.

Fox devoted due space to the American Civil War (seven pages), and to the processes of American territorial expansion and trans-marine imperialism, but his atlas was also interesting for its acceptance of division in American history. Aside from maps recording a number of presidential elections – 1800–1, 1824–25, 1836, 1840, 1844, 1848, 1856, 1860, 1884, 1892, 1912 and 1916 – there were also maps of house votes, for example on tariff legislation in 1816, 1824, 1828, 1890, 1894 and 1917, on the Bank Bill of 1832 and the Force Bill of 1833. Fox devoted more space than any earlier atlas to contentious issues in American history. Concerned to use maps so that students might 'discover and indicate the forces which have interplayed to make this nation',[32] Fox's emphasis on environmental possibilism led to a cartographic account of American history that put a stress on human division.

McElroy

Fox's historical atlas was the best published in the 1920s to cover American history, but it was not the only historical atlas published in the USA that decade, although the Americans drew heavily upon foreign works for their mapping of the history of other countries. The Muir/Philip's atlas was published without change in New York by C.S. Hammond and Co. as *Hammond's New Historical Atlas for Students*. *Philip's Historical Atlas Medieval and Modern* (London, 1927) was also used for *Putnam's Historical Atlas Medieval and Modern* (New York, 1927), although with the addition of an American section by Robert McElroy, Professor of American History in Oxford. This consisted of a number of colour maps in the main section of the atlas, including three to show the Civil War, as well as maps of the USA in 1860 and 1927 in order to show shifts in population density and the spread of railways. McElroy also contributed an essay on American economic history that included black and white maps of roads and westward trails, early post roads and canals, trails to the Far West, cotton production and slavery, changing centres of population 1790–1920 and Indian reservations in 1876 and 1926. McElroy did not ignore what he termed 'the scandals of an age of progress', but his essay closed with a powerful paean of praise to America that is also a reminder that those seeking to chart intellectual history or to find historiographical texts would be wise to consider historical atlases:

> the building of railroads toward the setting sun, the expansion of highways, canals, tram lines, automobile routes to meet migrations unrivalled in all history; the enormous expansion of factories and of trade, internal and external; the interpretation of laws meant for an age of small things to meet an age of great things; the growth of credit, perfecting of banking systems, stabilization of currency by the education of public opinion against the heresies of the ages; the building of schools enough to educate not a class, but every class, regardless of wealth, race, creed, or place of birth; the assimilation of millions of immigrants from almost every stock on earth; the harmonizing of religions so that the bells of one village church will not sound discordant as the rest chime in.
>
>   With all its faults, America's economic expansion is an epic of glory; and as we see its steady acceleration there is an added sense of satisfaction in the thought that the end is not yet.[33]

It is worth stopping to consider this passage because it exemplifies the point that it is mistaken to distinguish between a tradition of objective historical cartography and a cartographic 'other'. More specifically, the notion that ideology was and is only present in works that can be clearly defined as 'biased', and thus that 'bias' can be segregated in order to leave objectivity as an unquestioned reality, or at least as a workable goal, is suspect.

This was true of the period after the Second World War that will be considered in chapter seven, but was also the case with the interwar years. It is all too easy to present 'distorted' mapping as the product of ideological societies and then discuss the question in terms of Fascist and Communist states, as if they were the sole states with ideologies or in which ideological issues influenced mapping and historical atlases and as if it is clear how to assess distortion in historical cartography.

It is apparent, however, from McElroy's prose that there was a distinction between the American historical imagination as presented in historical atlases and that of most Europeans. The emphasis on ethnicity was different. American historical cartography of the 1910s and 1920s underplayed the role of African Americans, Asians and Hispanics and scandalously neglected that of Native Americans, but, within the confines of an essentially white and male-dominated society, it did not use race to define American identity. The history of the Americans was the history of America and the two could not be distinguished. Interwar German cartography was very different and far more exclusive. Racial identity, continuity and interests were central to the German cartographic agenda.

Paullin

The population section of Charles O. Paullin's *Atlas of the Historical Geography of the United States* (Washington, DC and New York, 1932) mapped African Americans, emigration to the USA and the foreign-born population, but it did not do so with any sense of threat or confrontation. The genesis of this atlas was a long one, unsurprisingly as it was the best historical atlas of the USA to be published. In 1903

J. Franklin Jameson, soon to be Director of the Department of Historical Research at the recently founded Carnegie Institution of Washington, drafted an outline of contents for an atlas at the request of his predecessor, Andrew McLaughlin. Jameson took the major role in the atlas project from 1912, when it was launched and an ex-student of his, Charles Paullin, was given charge of it, until 1927, when the Carnegie Institution began to wind up its Historical Department. Jameson selected the contributors and had the crucial say in which maps were to be included. In 1927 the American Geographical Society of New York came to play a major role in the project, in 1929 the project was moved to New York and the American Geographical Society eventually co-published the atlas with the Carnegie Institution. John Wright, the Librarian of the Society, took over the supervision of the work and appears on the title-page as the editor.[34] The introduction began in bold terms that reflected the work's achievement:

> This is the first major historical atlas of the United States and probably the most comprehensive work of its kind that has yet been published for any country. Its aim is to illustrate cartographically, in manageable compass and yet with considerable detail, essential facts of geography and history that condition and explain the development of the United States.[35]

Although including a plate on 'Indian Tribes and Linguistic Stocks, 1650', the atlas ignored the long earlier history of the Native Americans and, by beginning with European exploration and settlement, marginalized the Native Americans. The section of the atlas devoted to them was short – 3.2 per cent – and, aside from the plate referred to, all the other maps related to Native Americans as affected or controlled by the European Americans: successive plates were devoted to 'Indian Battles', 'Indian Reservations' and 'Indian Missions'. Little of the pre-Columbian history of Native Americans could yet be mapped. Native American economic activity, settlement patterns, religious and cultural life were also all ignored. However, there were reasons for some of the omissions. Relative chronologies of separate Native American cultures were only worked out between *c.* 1900 and *c.* 1950, and it was only with the development of Carbon-14 dating from 1947 onwards that absolute chronologies could be established.

Instead, the principal players in the history of the settlement of the USA were the European Americans and the environment. This did not reflect the environmental determinism that had been influential at the time of the initial planning of the inception, for there had been a reaction against Semple and environmentalism.[36] Instead, the influence of Frederick Jackson Turner was prominent. Turner, professor at Harvard and an advisor to the *Atlas*, had made a great impact with his interest in the role of the frontier in American history.[37] His approach, with its stress on human dynamism, social factors and interaction with the environment, was not that of a crude environmental determinist; indeed, he was chairman of the conference on the relation of geography and history in 1907 in which historians had severely criticized Semple's work. Turner used maps extensively in his research, employing them both for analytical and descriptive purposes.

The introduction to the *Atlas* explained the prominence devoted to the frontier in terms that reflected both Turner's views and a sense of American exceptionalism that explained why its historical cartography should be different from that of the European model:

In Europe the foundations of national life were laid far back in the Middle Ages or earlier. America is nearer its beginnings. The chronicle of material is a large part of its record. The nation has just emerged from the pioneer epoch, and it is fitting that stress should be laid upon the frontier aspects of its history: the story of the exploration and charting of mountains, rivers, lakes, and plains, of the spreading tide of settlement into vacant lands; of the friendly and hostile contacts between settlers and Indians; of the progress of settlement as it was fostered here and thwarted there by the great facts of nature; of the use made of natural resources; of the apportioning of land among individuals; of the adjustment of conflicting political claims to territory; and of the marking out of new administrative units. The sections of the *Atlas* dealing with the Natural Environment, Cartography (1492–1867), Explorers' Routes, Indians, Settlement and Population, Lands, and Boundary Disputes illustrate these topics and fill more than half of the plates.[38]

Indeed, the percentage was 56.9. Furthermore, these maps were placed first. Traditional cartographic topics, especially military history, were relegated in importance by being placed later and receiving less attention. The introduction claimed that 'most maps illustrating wars and campaigns are confused and difficult to follow, especially when a tangle of lines on them is intended to show troop movements',[39] but disinterest, not difficulty, was the crucial issue. The *Atlas* was also different from its predecessors in that its emphasis was thematic rather than chronological. The essential organization of the work was by topic, a process that underlines the importance of editorial imagination and direction, whereas with chronology the issue of organization is far less problematic.

The thematic maps included appreciable sections on economic history and 'cultural development'. The first – 13.7 per cent of the atlas – included maps that reflected the available wealth of statistical information; they were not impressionistic. For example, the development of industry was mapped in terms of the in-crease in the number of wage earners, and also the increase in value added by manufacture, by states, in 1849, 1880 and 1927. Individual industries were mapped for different dates. Again the emphasis was statistical, for example the number of cotton spindles, not impressionistic. Improvements in communications were again presented in quantifiable terms: maps recording the length of time taken in 1800, 1830, 1857 and 1930 for passengers to reach different areas from New York by the ordinary means of travel then in use. There were also detailed maps for individual forms of transportation, such as railways, and the spread of the motor car was represented by two maps recording the number of people per car in 1913 and 1930. Aside from the obvious agricultural maps on crops grown, there were also maps of farm tenancy since 1880 and farm values since 1850. Even the more obvious agricultural topics were presented with considerable detail, not least in terms of the chronological spread: a series of maps revealed the total acreages and the changes in the acreages of improved land and of land in harvested crops at decennial intervals from 1850 to 1930. Maps also revealed the production of particular crops since 1839. Foreign trade was mapped in similar detail.

The *Atlas* represented a considerable advance in the mapping of wealth. Drawing on information on the value of houses and lands in 1799, 1912 and 1922, maps were produced showing total and per capita wealth by states. Income taxes, bank capital and bank distribution by states were also mapped. The detail in the political maps was increased by using the smallest possible territorial units: counties for Presidential elections and Congressional districts for votes on 36 major Congressional measures. There was also a series of maps of reforms that were largely brought about by state legislation: the abolition of slavery, the elimination of property qualifications for suffrage, female suffrage, prohibition, labour legislation and school education.

The Paullin *Atlas* was far better than any hitherto published in the USA and was arguably the best hitherto in the world. It is unfashionable to make such judgments, but it is difficult to reach any other conclusion on the basis of the range of the material mapped, the statistical basis of the information and the size of the country covered. The scholarly nature of the *Atlas* was indicated by the text and biblio-graphical references that accompanied the maps. Furthermore, although individual maps did not draw relationships between different subjects, the introduction invited just such a process. For example, for the maps on the locations of cities: 'These maps will repay careful comparison with the maps showing relief, physical divisions, climatic factors, and mineral resources, all circumstances upon which the location and grouping of cities are closely dependent.'[40] The *Atlas* was also far more sophis-ticated than most, because of its self-awareness: the manner in which issues of inclusion and representation were discussed. This was most obviously the case with the table listing the number of half plates and percentage of total space by topic, but there are other examples that reflect awareness that particular methods would have different effects:

> On Plates 61–67A space was economized by marking on the same maps both colonial and state boundaries and the locations of towns and cities . . . Perhaps somewhat more graphic effect might have been achieved had it been practicable to separate the two elements – political units and cities – and to employ a greater range and variety of symbols to distinguish the towns and cities according to size.[41]

Yet an open response to issues of choice of topic and method of representation cannot simply be regarded as an 'objective', 'scientific' or 'progressive' characteristic, for that neglects the extent to which an engagement with method also characterized historical atlases not usually seen in such a light, but, instead, seen as products of overtly ideological and authoritarian societies.

There are of course problems with the Paullin *Atlas*. The relative neglect of the Native Americans was compounded in the introduction when their stake in the land was referred to as 'shadowy claims'.[42] There were also problems posed by the mapping of social and economic history, problems that were to become more prominent when the subject was increasingly mapped in the last quarter of the century. It is probably anachronistic to suggest that the maps of economic history could have been accompanied by one of environmental damage. This was provided to a certain extent by maps of virgin forest in 1620, 1850 and 1926. However, given acute American concern with trusts, by which companies co-operated to create monopolies, it is clear that the depoliticized way in which the economic history was mapped could have been broadened by consideration of economic regulation. Maps of employment and wealth could have been matched by others of unemployment and poverty. Four plates were devoted to plans of the country's seven major cities at the end of the eighteenth century in order to illustrate different systems of early town planning. There was nothing comparable for the close of the following century to indicate, for example, indices of poverty.

Poverty would have been revealed even more acutely if more mapping had been done using territorial units smaller than states. The *Atlas* was of course dependent on the available data, but another factor was at work. This was very much an atlas of the entire USA. There were very few sectional maps, and, instead, there was an emphasis on depicting the entire USA and dividing it up on a state basis: state lines were marked on most maps. Thus, the prime categorization of information in the sources – by state – was strengthened in the maps. This emphasis clearly minimized differences within states, yet these were as acute, if not often more so, than those between states. For example, as the introduction noted, 'expenditures for schools by states indicate roughly (as shown on Plate 131B–D) nation-wide tendencies and sectional divergencies in primary and secondary teaching',[43] but local differences were even greater and, for the bulk of Americans, it was these that were most significant.

Another distinctive feature of the atlas was the reproduction of 48 maps from the period 1492–1867. These revealed developing cartographic knowledge of the USA, an important aspect of the process of *European* discovery. In recording past mapping, the *Atlas* also thus served to underline the transience of cartographic images and therefore, possibly, of the *Atlas* itself. Yet the *Atlas* is still referred to. Much that it mapped has not been subsequently treated in historical atlases of the USA and its determined espousal of thematic mapping, non-political topics and a non-chronological organization was to be of considerable influence after the Second World War.

Ideologies

Paullin's *Atlas* can be taken as the high point of historical atlases produced in a liberal-national ideological context in the interwar period. It was recognizably different from the European historical atlases not only for the reasons already given, but also because it was a national historical atlas that did not need to encompass the imperial experience. For Britain or France in the interwar period, their overseas possessions were not separate or detachable but part of the state and crucial to its geopolitical identity and interests. This assumption even underlay the treatment of British dominions such as Australia. Thus national historical atlases had to devote considerable space to the process of imperial growth. This was far less the case with the USA, although that was largely because of the different nature of American imperialism, a point captured in 1902 in plate 89 of Poole's *Historical Atlas*. This map of European empires 1815–97 showed the north-west of the USA as colonized from the eastern states, the text noting:

> In the marking of the United States the endeavour has been made to bring out a fact which is often forgotten. The geographical continuity of the United States, as well as its federal form of government, serves to obscure the truth that the western states are, for the most part, colonies in one sense of the word, insomuch as they owe their population to emigration from the Eastern States. This is wholly true in the case of the extreme North-Western States while in those states which once formed part of the Spanish or French dominions the original stock has been almost completely swamped by the flood of Anglo-American immigration.[44]

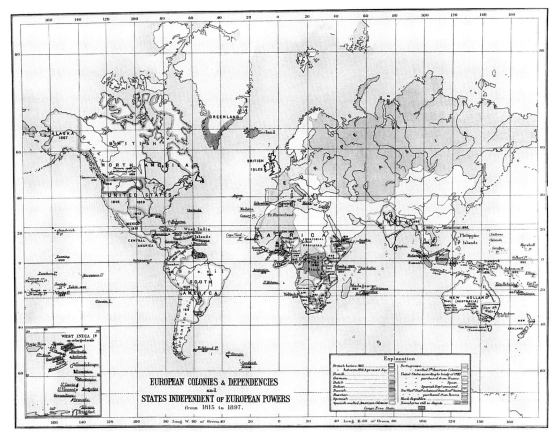

26. 'The Progress of Colonialization' from R.L. Poole's *Historical Atlas* (Oxford, 1902). A projection that minimized the relative extent of the tropics, and therefore Britain's gains in India and Africa. Canada, in contrast, seemed a vast acquisition. The expansion of USA was brought out as part of the imperial process.

Paullin's *Atlas* was not like the historical atlases produced in European authoritarian societies in the 1930s. It is possible to draw attention to comparisons, not least the stress on immigration as an aspect of interest in ethnicity, and the emphasis on the frontier as a variant on European concerns with conflict and confrontation. More specifically, the maps in German historical atlases of the medieval expansion of Germans into eastern Europe can be compared with the American emphasis on the frontier.

It is necessary, however, to strike a balance. Comparisons can indeed be made. Objectivity was elusive and it can be argued that it is a potentially misleading concept given the need for selection and abstraction in mapping. More specifically, there is a degree of teleology, not to say triumphalism, in all interwar historical atlases. Yet any consideration of Nazi historical atlases indicates that comparisons between works produced in authoritarian and democratic societies should not be pushed too far. Contrasts are even clearer if due weight is placed not only on the graphic images, but also on accompanying captions, keys and text. The historical atlases of authoritarian societies employed more dynamic graphic imagery, appropriately so for cultures that put an emphasis on the inevitability and role of conflict. Thus, Nazi works frequently used arrows while their Communist counterparts favoured clenched fists or red flames. In addition, the accompanying prose was didactic.

Nazi Historical Atlases

Henryk Kot and David Murphy have drawn attention to what they see as the degeneration of German geopolitical maps in the 1920s and early 1930s, as objective geographic standards and values were abandoned in favour of tendentious presentation in response to the aggressive and racist conservatism of geopolitical circles in this period.[45] Geography and cartography served Nazi purposes, as with the use of town directories to manipulate urban images.[46] Geopolitics in general became more important in the 1920s and 1930s and influenced Nazi ideas from early in the party's history. German geopolitics was to affect Nazi foreign policy,[47] although the process was not free from tension.[48] The quest for an Aryan geography had some surprising aspects. In *Die Entdeckung des Paradieses* (The discovery of paradise) (Brunswick, 1924), Franz von Wendrin argued that the Garden of Eden had been in Germany but that the Jews had falsely claimed it for Asia. His cartographic claims were accompanied by statements on the need to liberate Germany from the inferior races.

Murphy did not discuss historical atlases, but the latter were also affected by the definition of a geopolitics of racial conflict and national destiny; although works of a more conventional type continued to be produced or appeared in new editions, for example the *Atlas zur Kirchengeschichte* by Karl Heussi and Hermann Mulert (Tübingen, 1937), while G. Lüdtke and L. Mackensen's *Deutscher Kulturatlas* (5 vols, Berlin, 1928–38) represented a broadening out in the range of historical cartography. If the principal German theme in late nineteenth-century historical atlases had been the political unification of Germany by Prussia, a process accomplished by military victory, in the 1920s and 1930s outrage over the Versailles settlement and concern about the Germans outside Germany hardened into a cartographic obsession with Germany's relations with and in eastern Europe, Germany being understood primarily as the political representation of the Germans. The enemy without was matched by the enemy within: the Jews. This racial perspective had a clear historical dimension that lent itself to cartographic depiction. Alongside the traditional emphasis on conflict with foreign states could be found a concentration on ethnic rivalry between Germans and others. Conversely, the Nazi vision of the German past was, to an extent, depoliticized: internal divisions were largely a matter of the Jews. Once they were defeated, the race would be united. Thus, Nazi mapping of domestic political, social and economic divisions and differences was deficient.

Ethnographical themes could be seen in works such as the 1931 edition of *F.W. Putzgers Historischer Schul-Atlas*. This included a map of German linguistic and cultural territory that offered a vista of a greater Germany. Another similar map included the western boundary of the Holy Roman Empire in 1500, a boundary to the west of the German frontier in 1931; while the first page of maps included one of Germany as the bulwark of European culture against the Asiatic hordes, the latter depicted in terms of Huns, Avars, Arabs, Magyars, Turks, Mongols, Jews, Tsarist Russia and Communism. The *Saar-Atlas* of H. Overbeck and G.W. Sante (Gotha, 1934) supported the German case for the reintegration of the Saarland. Map one offered on facing pages a territorial map that placed the Saar on the Franco-German border, and a linguistic map that showed both the Saar and Alsace as clearly German.

The *Atlas zur Deutschen Geschichte der Jahre 1914 bis 1933* (Bielefeld and Leipzig, 1934), by Konrad Frenzel and the Nazi intellectual Johann von Leers, combined ethnic hatred and international confrontation. The atlas was essentially a work of propaganda and the very organization of the book underlined its polemical purpose. Thus successive pages were headed 'Versklavung' (the enslaving of Germans as a result of the post-war peace conferences), 'Die Ausbreitung der Juden' (the spread of the Jews), 'Verjudung' (increasing Jewish influence) and 'Chaos', the last dealing with reparations and inflation. The book opened with a passage from Hitler's *Mein Kampf.*

Arrows were employed extensively in Alfred Pudelko and A. Hillen Ziegfeld's *Kleiner deutscher Geschichtsatlas* (Berlin, 1937). This black and white atlas emphasized confrontation in its essentially territorial account of German history, an account that was clearly aimed at the contemporary situation. The atlas had, inside the cover, a map of the current distribution of Germans showing how many were outside Germany. The maps began with the creation of the German homeland. The third map – of German tribes in 58 BC – showed them as covering Germany, the Low Countries, Alsace and most of Poland and Bohemia, but the element of conflict was present: the Germans were shown as clashing with Julius Caesar near Strasbourg, which was printed using the German name, Strassburg, as any German publication in any era would have done. In the following three maps the conflict continued, first with Roman arrows advancing into Germany in AD 9, the year of German victory at the Teutonberger Wald, and then with the invasions of the Roman empire.

The emphasis then shifted to the German struggle with the peoples to the east. Slav attacks on the Germans in AD 600 were mapped. The map of the foundation of the first German empire under Henry I showed the beginning of the advance to the east. The 'Sicherung' (securing) of the eastern frontier in 1000 was followed by a map of attacks on Europe from the east in 451–1683, showing Hun, Arab, Mongol and Turkish assaults. This preceded a map of German expansion east in the Middle Ages, and the theme of struggle dominated the mapping of the medieval period. One map showed the German knightly orders resisting attacks from the east – by Poles, Lithuanians, Mongols and Kumans. The last were shown being repelled by the Germans in Transylvania. Similarly, the map of the Hussite wars emphasized the threat to Germany, in this case Hussite advances out of Bohemia towards German centres such as Vienna, Linz, Regensburg, Nürnberg and Magdeburg.

Similarly, conflict was the major theme in the early modern period. The theme of Germany being invaded by foreign powers was underlined in the map of the Thirty Years' War. The section included an ahistorical map of challenges to Germany from east and west: from Hussites, Turks, Poles and French.[49] This suggested a continual struggle: the French were shown as attacking in 1302 and under Louis XIV. In addition, it endorsed current ambitions for territorial aggrandizement by indicating past losses, for example to the Poles at Tannenberg in 1410, and by presenting the need for bulwarks against attack. Arrows were also used in this map to show German forces concentrating on Vienna to defend it from the Turks. Similarly, the map of the Seven Years' War depicted Prussia resisting attacks from all sides: she had indeed done so, but the map served to reiterate the themes of struggle and foreign aggression.

The mapping of recent history centred on the losses of the Versailles settlement and these losses were scarcely explained by the maps of the First World War. For example the map of the southern zones of operation depicted Austrian and German advances in the Balkans and Italy in 1916–17, but not subsequent defeats. The map of German losses at Versailles was followed by maps of German commercial interests in eastern Europe, Germans in Europe and German frontier disputes in 1919–35. The map of the western frontier showed what Germany had lost in 1919, but also the imperial frontier in 1000 and the linguistic frontier, the latter two establishing historical frontiers to the west. A similar view of past greatness emerged from the map of the Holy Roman Empire in context in 1250, a map that gave Germany a prominent position. It also referred to England as a vassal state, a claim that had little political meaning.

The *Neuer deutscher Geschichts- und Kulturatlas*, edited by Fritz Eberhardt (Leipzig, 1937), was lengthier and more ambitious, but the themes were the same. Conflict was stressed, whether between 'Indogermanic' peoples, and Hamites and Semites in the Ancient world, or between the Romans and the Germans. There were four pages of maps of the eastward expansion of medieval Germans. In marked contrast to the static depictions of territorial power in late nineteenth-century historical atlases, the Nazi works introduced an element of dynamism, indeed made it central. Thus the map of the Counter-Reformation presented a Paris–Rome axis advancing its cause in Germany through the foundation of Jesuit colleges. The Great Elector of Brandenburg was shown as advancing against Poles, Swedes and France. The European map of the 1870s and 1880s depicted Germany and Austria-Hungary as threatened by arrows from Russia and France: panslavism and *revanche*. The atlas presented other threats to Germany: the Jews, described as an excrescence, and political Catholicism. The map of how the latter had affected German history presented France, Austria and Poland as its proponents. The last map of the book, one of Germany and the Germans, indicated that there were large numbers of Germans outside Germany.[50]

Present dispossession was therefore set in the context of past threats, and the range of these was far wider than any simple emphasis on the challenge from the east. Political Catholicism as a threat provided both a means to present France and Poland as a threat and an interpretation of German history that combined secularism and North German Protestant suspicion of the conflation of Habsburg interests and Catholicism. This was a Prussian reading of German history in which traditional antipathies were sharpened and fused by a powerful new ideology and geopolitics. Again, the force of Nazi historical atlases was provided by the intertwining of ethnicity, ideology and geopolitics, the spatial depiction of Nazi beliefs and concerns in an historical context.

The Nazi approach can be contrasted with the universal pretensions of Communism and Socialism which resulted in mapping which lacked the spatial specificity of Nazi mapping. For example, the *Atlas of Empire* by the British Socialist James Francis Horrabin (London, 1937), a work published by the left-wing house of Victor Gollancz, depicted the globe on its cover as encircled by a chain that included the symbols of the dollar, pound and French franc. Horrabin, the first Labour MP for Peterborough and a member of the National Council of the Socialist League, argued that modern imperialism rested on economic penetration: universal forces were responsible for specific advances. Sandor Radó's *Atlas für politik Wirtschaft Arbeiterbewegung. I. Der Imperialismus* (Vienna and Berlin, 1930) stressed the global nature of struggle in the contemporary world. It was a geopolitical atlas, based on Marxist ideology, that favoured axes of influence as a device.[51] Communist historical atlases were very different from those of the Nazis in that they were primarily concerned to show how the whole of human history could be interpreted in accordance with Communist beliefs.

The Nazis in contrast presented the history of the Germans in a dramatic fashion. A people, not the proletarians of all nations, were the heroes. In his *Werden und Wachsen, Ein Geschichtsatlas auf völkischer Grundlage* (Brunswick, 1938), published by the major publishing house of Westermann, Bernhard Kumsteller began with ethnographical maps intended for clearly racist purposes. The first page was devoted to the races of modern times, the second to 'Die Nordische Rasse und die Germanen als Kulturträger' (the northern races and the Germans as upholders of civilization). Again there was the theme of conflict with the east, as in the map of Germany in 600 showing attacks by Czechs, Slovenes and Poles. Inset maps provided a more didactic element to that of the main cartographic narrative. Thus, the inset on the map of Germany from the thirteenth to the fifteenth century presented losses in the fifteenth: to Poland, France and Denmark; the inset on the map of the Reformation and Counter-Reformation was of 'Deutschland als Bollwerk gegen Asien' (Germany as the bulwark against Asia): Huns, Avars, Magyars, Mongols, Turks, Russians and Bolsheviks were shown as the assailants, Lechfeld, Tannenberg and Berlin 1918–33 as the sites of resistance. Thus the contemporary struggle against Communism was presented as a necessary continuation of the glorious past. Similarly, there were echoes of the nineteenth-century victorious military past in maps of the battles of Leipzig (1813) and Königgrätz (1866) and of the 1813 campaign to clear Germany of the French. Waterloo was not thus honoured, but Frederick the Great's victory over the Austrians at Leuthen (1757) was, and this indicated the manner in which Austria was separated from the true, i.e. Prussian, German legacy.

Kumsteller's mapping of the more recent past again emphasized the threats to Germany. A map of nineteenth-century nationalism showed panslavism and panrussianism like tentacles with arrows coming out of St Petersburg. There were other maps of Germany's vulnerability to France, Czechoslovakia and Poland, Soviet imperialism 1913–36, of Communist influence, and of the spread of the Jews. A map comparing Germany in 1250, 1800, 1871 and 1919–21 dramatized its recent losses. Readers could, however, turn from threats and losses to the growing influence of the Nazis, their agricultural and regional policies and their autobahns:[52] strength through straight lines.

The German people were therefore the protagonists in Nazi historical atlases, and the emphasis was very much one on their mission, the need to triumph through blood. This was the case whatever the market, as for example with Albert Höft's *Geschichtsatlas für die Jugend*, and with successive editions of already existing atlases. Thus the 1944 edition of *Neuer Deutscher Geschiches- und Kulturatlas* added essentially more of the same: maps of German gains prior to the Second World War, and the 1939 conquest of Poland.

Germany's Allies

Had the Nazis won the Second World War their historical cartography would doubtless have been complemented by that of their client states. This cartography would presumably have entailed a heavy emphasis on ethnographical themes and

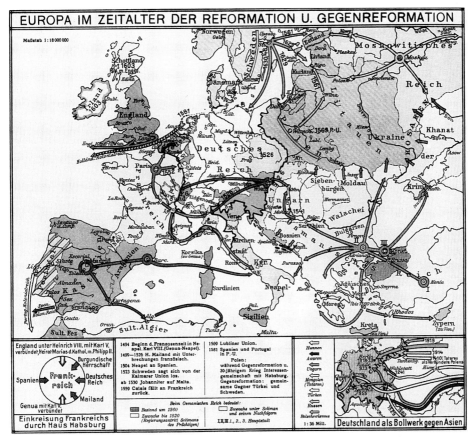

27. 'Europe in the Age of Reformation and Counter-Reformation' from Bernhard Kumsteller's *Werden und Wachsen, Ein Geschichtsatlas auf völkischer Grundlage* (Brunswick, 1938). Thanks in part to the use of arrows, the map emphasized war and conquest, not least Turkish expansion. The inset map, 'Germany as the Bulwark against Asia', presented an expanded Germany, that included much of the medieval empire and Prussia, as the eternal target of challenges from the East. No other European resistance was allowed for. Thus, the Poles appeared not as resisters of Russia and Communism but as assailants at Tannenberg linked to the Tatars. Only the Germans appeared able and willing to protect civilization, and thus their leadership seemed natural.

anti-Semitism and would have also served to make the redrawing of Europe's frontiers in the shadow of the swastika appear consistent with traditional territorial and ethnic aims and interests. Nazi supremacy was fortunately too short-lived to encourage an outburst of historical cartography on the part of allies and conquered peoples. The extent to which Hitler was inconsistent in his treatment of conquered and allied areas, altering their status and frontiers as for example with the short-lived nature of the Vichy government, could not have encouraged such work, while there were presumably more pressing calls on resources.

Yet there are hints of what might have happened. In 1937 the prominent Ukrainian geographer Volodymyr Kubijovyč (1900–85), then lecturer at Cracow University, had prepared and edited an *Atlas Ukraïny i sumerzhnykh kraiv* (Atlas of the Ukraine and adjoining countries) in Ukrainian and English, which included an historical section. It was published in what was then Lvov in Poland, i.e. outside the Soviet-controlled Ukraine. In 1940 Kubijovyč was appointed professor at the Ukrainian Free University in German-occupied Prague, and was elected head of the newly formed Ukrainian Central Committee, an officially accepted, largely social welfare agency created in German-occupied Poland. Kubijovyč helped to raise Ukrainian consciousness, establishing, for example, a publishing house, and in 1943 agreed to the German suggestion that a Ukrainian division be formed in the German army – the SS Volunteer Galicia Division.[53] Two years earlier Kubijovyč had prepared an atlas in German based on his 1937 work: the *Handschrift-Karten zur Geschichte, Volkstumskunde und Wirtschaft der Ukraine*. This was to have been published in Berlin but remained in typescript. It was not published until 1993, and then only thanks to a grant from the Kubijovyč fund of the Canadian Institute of Ukrainian Studies:[54] the sponsorship of the Reich replaced by that of the Ukrainian diaspora, although, as in 1941, there was a common theme: institutional support was required.[55]

The Nazis and their allies sought the redrawing of eastern Europe, in large part on supposed ethnic grounds. This involved, therefore, ethnic maps, both contemporary and historical. Germany's ally Hungary gained much of Transylvania from Romania in 1940. The following year Imre Lukinich (1880–1950), a reputable and prominent professor at Budapest University, edited the *Documenta Historiam Valachorum in Hungaria Illustrantia usque ad annum 1400 P. Christum*, a work published by the Institute of Central and Eastern European History in Budapest University. This gave a history of the Romanians in Transylvania, arguing that far from being the original population, they had only appeared in the area relatively late and in small numbers; only arriving *en masse* in the fourteenth century. His map of the Romanians in Transylvania in the thirteenth and fourteenth centuries used different symbols for settlements by period in order to demonstrate his argument.[56] The *Documenta*, though with an axe to grind, is a scholarly volume still representative of the Magyar view. The institute which published it was a short-lived institution, like others called into being in Hungary in the war years.

Fascist Historical Atlases

In Fascist Italy and Fascist Spain, the Nazi emphasis on race and long-lasting rivalries was largely absent. Instead, atlases produced in these countries could be seen as examples of the more general European historical atlases that pushed national identity and pride hard. Ethnic mapping played a role, though far less than in Nazi atlases, and was again more in tune with the general European pattern, not least with maps of Spaniards or Portuguese territories and people abroad.

In his *Atlas histórico español* (Madrid, 1941), published soon after the Spanish Civil War, Gonzalo Menéndez Pidal essentially ignored the nineteenth and twentieth centuries. Modernization and domestic politics were denied in favour of a more heroic and united past. The *reconquistà* received much attention. A page was devoted to industry and commerce in Habsburg Spain, another to maps of the journeys of four saints, and several pages to early modern cultural history. The Jews and the Moriscos were ignored; a racial statement by omission.

In Mussolini's Italy, geopolitics, imperialism and Fascist culture were all closely linked.[57] Fascism was presented as a revival of Italian greatness,[58] and historical cartography played a role in this process. In 1935 the Consiglio Nazionale di Ricerca embarked upon a major project to map the Classical Roman empire. L. Visintin's

Piccolo atlante storico. III. Evo moderno (Novara, 1934) included a map of the triumphant campaign of 1918, not of the 1917 disaster; no mention was made of the important role of Italy's allies. In G. de Agostino's *Dal Risorgimento all'impero atlantino storico con testo illustrativo* (Milan, 1938), Mussolini's march on Rome was presented as regenerating Italy. There were maps of Italian expansion under Mussolini and of Italian voluntary heroism in the nineteenth and twentieth centuries.[59]

The Second World War

As with the previous global conflict, the Second World War led to a great increase in mapping. Conflicts around the world, on land, sea and air, had to be mapped, both for military purposes and for civilian populations. A great effort was made to sustain the support and encourage the morale of the latter, and maps were particularly suited to what can be variously described as information and propaganda. Most of this mapping was contemporary, not historical. A multitude of newspaper maps reveal no historical element. However, some works did offer a historical dimension. *The War in Maps. Its Background and Course* (London, 1940), edited by George Goodall, in part offered what was considered relevant historical information, with maps of Germany in 1870, 1914 and the 1930s and of Poland in the eighteenth century, 1919–21 and 1939, and sought to explain what had happened hitherto in the conflict. Thus a map of 'Belligerents and Neutrals' in September 1939 carried the caption, 'Though the map presents the appearance of "encirclement" of Germany, Poland was a negligible factor, and could not be helped by Britain and France.' Maps and text stressed the role of economic factors, such as the Lorraine iron deposits.[60] Natural resources and trade similarly played a large part in the *Atlas of the War* by J.N.L. Baker, first published in November 1939 in the series of Oxford Pamphlets on World Affairs. The maps in *The War in Maps. An Atlas of New York Times Maps* (New York, 1943) went back to the First World War.

The war was also important because it involved the redrawing of many frontiers. Again, most of the maps, of actual and possible changes, involved no historical cartographic dimension, but there were exceptions. Thus the single-sheet map of *East Prussia, Pomorze* [Royal or West Prussia] *and Danzig* prepared by the British Foreign Office in April 1944 included not only relevant contemporary details, such as double-track and single-track railways and canals, but also pre-1772, 1914 and 1938 frontiers and areas Polish until 1657.[61] The maps in A. Brecht's *Federalism and Regionalism in Germany: The Division of Prussia* (Oxford, 1945), a book about dividing up Germany after the war, used the voting trends of Weimar Germany in the 1920s in order to map democratic and nationalist regions.

The disruption of the war also affected mapping. Production facilities were put at the disposal of war efforts. Bombing and bombardment brought destruction, as with the German bombing of the British Ordnance Survey in Southampton. In 1944–45 Hungarian cartographic institutions and facilities were either moved to Germany or destroyed during the Russian invasion.[62] There was also disruption outside Europe. The Centennial Historical Atlas planned in New Zealand from 1937 as part of the centennial celebrations in 1940 fell victim to a number of problems including the difficulty of the task, delay and the eventual removal of government support, but the loss of draughtsmen during the war was also important.

The process of research was also interrupted, especially in Europe. Archives and libraries were destroyed or evacuated. Scholars were conscripted. The evacuation of the Finnish Public Record Office ensured that although plans were made for a Finnish historical atlas before the Second World War, research was not begun until after the armistice in 1944. The atlas was also affected because of the loss of Finnish territory to Russia and the transfer of its population.[63] Neighbouring Sweden, in contrast, was neutral, and in 1944 appeared the first edition of a work that was to be one of the two main Swedish school historical atlases until the late 1960s, Sture Bolin and Josef Carlsson's *Historisk Atlas*.

Thanks to the war, historical cartography was partly concentrated in one country that did not suffer from invasion or bombardment, the USA. American historical atlases did not only map the USA. The first major work to tackle Latin America, A.C. Wilgus's *Latin America in Maps, Historic, Geographic, Economic*, was published in New York by Barnes and Noble in 1943. Yet it was the USA that received most attention. In large part this was a matter of new work, though in 1942 the fifth edition of Hart's *American History Atlas* appeared. It carried a publisher's note that emphasized the work's social value and national purpose:

> The students in our schools today are the citizens of tomorrow. On them will fall the burden of conducting the affairs of the nation. They must, therefore, be educated for citizenship in a democracy. To carry on intelligently, the electorate must be well informed. In addition to love of country, Americans must 'know' their country. They must possess a knowledge and understanding of American history and government. Certainly there is no better means of accomplishing this end than by supplementing the flags and textbooks in our schools with fine, colorful, and instructive maps; maps which cover, in graphic and easily understood form, a fairly complete history of the development of the American nation and its institutions.
>
> The Hart-Bolton American History Maps contain a wealth of information. When correctly interpreted they open the door to the principal political, economic, and social problems that have faced the United States. No other group of maps cover so adequately all of the phases of our history. They aid materially in bringing out all the important element of continuity in history.

The following year a new atlas was published, the *Atlas of American History* (New York) edited by James Truslow Adams and R.V. Coleman. This black and white work emphasized conventional territorial and military topics, rather than those of the Paullin atlas, for example its economic topics. However, an important element of continuity reflected the influence of the Turner thesis. As the second edition, published in New York in 1978, noted of its 1943 predecessor:

> The heavy emphasis of that edition was on the frontier – broadly considered. The Atlas was particularly strong on boundary disputes during the Colonial period, on battles of the American Revolution and the Civil War, on early routes to the West, and on the American Indian.

Adams and Coleman stressed the importance of precision, writing that they had sought to produce maps 'that would interpret our history through the location of places as they actually existed and exactly where they existed at a given time'.[64] Their stress on war, territoriality and nation-building seemed particularly appropriate to the period of the Second World War. The following year the *Historical Atlas of the United States* by Clifford L. and Elizabeth H. Lord was published by the New York house of Henry Holt and Co. This offered 300 fairly simplistic maps. The Lords' atlas certainly did not compare to that of Paullin, but it was more accessible and less expensive, an aspect of the diversity of historical cartography and the role of the marketplace as well as that of academe.[65] These were to be important themes in the post-war world.

6

Commercial Context 1945–

Choices

In writing about historical atlases one faces some of the same problems as are encountered in compiling them. One of the most obvious parallels is that provided by the tension resulting from chronological narrative. Is it best to depict, describe and discuss the past in the order in which events occurred, or atlases were published, or is it more appropriate to adopt a thematic approach? If the latter route is taken a number of important issues are raised. First, there is the danger of a deceptive simultaneity, of discussing together events, issues and works that it is misleading to juxtapose and that can only be understood in their chronological context. Second, there is the problem of deciding how best to define themes, how far they should be differentiated, how far they should be treated as discrete topics, how much space to allocate to individual themes, and how they are to be ordered. These questions involve not only analytical issues, but also those of representation. Any ordering automatically suggests a hierarchy of concern and interest, a sense of progression and a degree of causation, and these cannot be readily separated or countered. These issues are especially important in the post-war period, for it was then that the volume of historical atlases produced greatly increased and their range became more pronounced.

A thematic approach also risks losing a sense of chronological development and divisions. It is now over half a century since the end of the last world war and the habit of treating these years as a unit – the post-war period – is misleading. It is not simply that there were major shifts: politically, the changes in the Cold War in the mid-1950s and early 1970s, the decolonization of the 1960s or the collapse of Soviet and eastern European Communism in 1988–92; economically, the oil crisis of 1973 and the rise of the 'tiger' economies of east Asia; culturally, the rise of relativism in the Western world; and socially, the collapse of deference, the cult of youth and novelty, and the consumerism that all gathered pace from the 1960s. In addition, historical cartography was not immune to these changes. They were not simply new issues and events that had to be mapped: historical mapping was greatly affected by them. Decolonization, for example, meant not only that maps of the dissolution of European empires had to be produced, but also that newly independent countries wished to map their history in a new fashion. Economic shifts have affected the economics of publishing and, even more clearly, technical changes have transformed the potential of mapping, particularly in the 1990s.

Thus the chronological dimension cannot be ignored. Nevertheless, that does not imply that it is best to present historical atlases after 1945 in terms of a chronological narrative. Not only were many problems common throughout the period, but, in addition, the growing diversity of historical atlases is such that this approach risks creating confusion by juxtaposing very different works; however necessary the last is. Furthermore, it is misleading to assume that developments in different countries or in work produced by different publishers or authors necessarily occurred with similar chronological trajectories and are therefore best presented with reference to a chronological organization.

There is no guide book on how to produce an historical atlas: the field is too diverse and inchoate. Instead, each historical atlas is an individual work, reflecting the intellectual assessments and priorities of its creators, though obviously the compilers are affected by widespread academic and intellectual developments, most clearly with environmentalism at the beginning of the twentieth century. Equally, there is no guide as to how best to write about the subject, no developed corpus of literature to build on. Thus, this discussion of the post-war situation is very much a personal account.

Commercial Pressures

The 'structural' features commonly emphasized in explaining the direction and nature of academic work generally omit one of the most crucial: the impact of publishers' strategies. The experience of all academics is that publishers play a major role, and not simply a passive one. Far from it being the case that publishers only evaluate typescripts that they receive, they shape the scholarly agenda with active commissioning policies. These reflect both a sense of commercial need and opportunity and the intellectual views of publishers themselves, and the latter often influence the former.

These comments are especially relevant to historical atlases. They are unusual in that the customary constraints placed on the author by the publication process are far more overt, direct and active from the outset. Historical atlases are very expensive to produce. For most, the cost of the cartography is far greater than the amount paid to the authors, both compilers of maps and writers of text, involved, and this naturally conditions the attitude of the publishers. In addition, factors of cost and organization are such that it is usually the publisher, rather than the author, who takes the decision to begin a project, and who thus sets its parameters and provides a framework for the contents. Authors are then commonly hired to produce work to set specifications and terms, rather like the other individuals and companies involved in the production process. Thus, historical mapping repeats the experience of contemporary mapping for, as has been noted of the eighteenth century, 'the maps produced represented the publishers' sense of demand at the time'.[1] Indeed in the case of historical atlases, the editorial and production costs are so complex and variable that publishers frequently find themselves out of their depths.

The views of publishers are crucial both in determining what is to be produced and in controlling its contents and appearance. It is easy then to move to the statement that their rationale is overwhelmingly commercial. Yet such a statement is misleading, not because it implies an economic determinism, but because it ignores the political economy of publishing in much of the post-war world. Publishing in North America and Western Europe has throughout been capitalist, but in Eastern Europe and many other parts of the world it was a totalitarian system that sought to overcome commercial pressures by means of planning and the state direction of resources; and in other parts of the world that lacked a clear policy of state direction publishing was nevertheless an aspect of a society and economic system characterized by privileges. In this context it is not surprising that many publishers had an official or semi-official character. Authoritarian societies were frequently directed to ideological purposes and this lent fresh reason for ignoring capitalist pressures.

Thus, if we agree to ignore the degree to which the economies of authoritarian societies were indeed affected by commercial pressures and motivation, it is possible to qualify any emphasis on capitalism by presenting a more varied publishing world. If a typology of post-war historical atlases is to be attempted from the perspective of publication or politics, the distinction between capitalist and control societies must come first.

The historical atlases produced by control societies will be considered in the next chapter. Suffice it to say at this point that in terms of international appeal and impact it is the products of capitalist societies that have been most successful. This is not intended as a triumphalist point and in part reflects a complex mix of factors, including the global reach of the English language as a means of communication. Yet commercial considerations also play a major role in global publishing. However successful historical atlases produced by control societies – for example, China – have been in serving a domestic market, they have been of very limited appeal to foreign consumers and publishers, and translation has rarely been attempted; although there are exceptions: for example, the Polish Communist historical atlas, which was also published in Poland by the State Cartographical Publishers in Wroclaw in an English edition, as *The Historical Atlas of Poland* (1981). The economics, ideologies and governmental practices of control societies have combined to minimize the international appeal of their historical atlases and that in a period when the cost of producing such works has increasingly encouraged a global publication strategy on the part of capitalist publishers.

Capitalist publishers of historical atlases not only seek global sales, especially through co-publication deals, but also rely on utilizing the differences in production costs and skills between particular countries in order to lessen costs. Thus, the *Atlas of Classical Archaeology* by Moses Finley, which was designed and produced in London by Rainbird Reference Books in 1977, was printed and bound in Italy. It was published in New York by McGraw-Hill. Bloomsbury Publishing Ltd had the copyright to Charles Messenger's *Chronological Atlas of World War Two*, but DAG Publications Ltd were responsible for the design and co-ordinated the project, the atlas was printed and bound in Spain, and published in New York in 1989 by Macmillan.

By the late 1980s atlas publishers were increasingly tapping into production facilities in the Orient, part of a general trend in book publishing that reflected the development of skill bases and production facilities there, advantageous currency exchange rates, differential labour costs and more rapid communications. *The Atlas of the Christian Church* edited by Henry Chadwick and Gillian Evans (1987) was planned and produced by Equinox in Oxford, and the maps were drawn there and in Hornchurch. The atlas was originated in Singapore, the film produced in Stafford and the work printed in Spain and published by Macmillan in London. Anton Powell's *Cultural Atlas for Young People. Ancient Greece* (Oxford, 1989) was planned and produced by Equinox in Oxford and printed in Italy, but the origination was by J. Film Process of Bangkok. Colour processing was done in Singapore and printing in Hong Kong for *The Times London History Atlas* edited by Hugh Clout (London, 1991). Margaret Oliphant's *Atlas of the Ancient World* (1992) was conceived, edited and designed by Marshall Editions, a London packaging house, typeset in Manchester, originated in Singapore, printed in Frome and published in London. Antony Mason's *Children's Atlas of Exploration* (London, 1993) was designed, produced, typeset and published in Britain, but manufactured and printed in Singapore. Anne Millard's *Atlas of Ancient Worlds* (1994) was designed and published in London, but produced in Singapore and Milan.

Thus global specialization came to play a major role, especially in the case of British historical atlases, which were the basis of the majority of co-publication deals. As British industry failed to cut costs or modernize, printing moved abroad, to Portugal, Spain, Italy, Hong Kong, China, Singapore and Malaysia, but the publishing dimension of atlas production remained in Britain. In the latter there is a wealth of academic and other talent willing to write for popular markets and costs are cheaper than in Germany, which has an excellent cartographic tradition, but, in the 1980s and 1990s, has not played a major active role in the production of historical atlases for non-German markets.

Economics, ideologies and governmental practices interacted to underline another crucial aspect of the publication of historical atlases in control societies: the infrequency of new works. Thus, it is striking that in China the publication of new historical atlases increased as economic decision-making was decentralized in the 1980s and as there was a greater emphasis on the consumer.

In contrast to the situation in control societies, the financial resources produced by global publication strategies and the inherent competitiveness of publishers in the capitalist world encouraged the production of new works and the probing of the market by an increasing diversity in type. Thus the assessment of the market is all-important. Times Books decided not to follow their *Atlas of the Second World War* (London, 1989), edited by John Keegan, with a similar work on the First World War, because the cost of the project was such that they needed commitments from other publishers for co-publication deals in their countries, but found no real interest when they made approaches at the Frankfurt Book Fair.[2]

Publishers generally have fixed ideas about what they want and what they can sell and what will or will not be ruinously expensive to produce. They put atlases together and have to take a view on the commercial potential of projects. Most publishers and purchasers have no particular interest in scholarly apparatus, such as commentary, footnotes, authorities, and sources for individual maps, without which it can be very difficult to evaluate and interpret them. Instead, most publishers see atlases as visually attractive to potential buyers who are themselves on the look-out for visual aids. Historical atlases became more visually appealing from the 1970s. This had much to do with design conventions and also with popular expectations of illustrative material, whether in atlases or elsewhere. Readers are used to seeing information on television packaged in exciting graphic forms and maps cannot be too static: they have to respond to that kind of expectation.

The Role of Text

In the 1980s and 1990s, publishers, particularly in Britain, France and the USA but not Germany, have shown increasing support for atlases which are in fact books in atlas format: illustrated popular history books of a slightly different kind, rather than atlases which accord with the conventional definition, i.e. page after page of maps. For example, Donald Matthew's *Atlas of Medieval Europe* (Oxford, 1983) is 240 pages long, but contains only 64 maps, far less than the number of pictures, while the text is about 75,000 words. The work was published by Phaidon as part of a cultural atlases series of historical atlases that were equally strong on pictures and text, but had only a relatively small number of maps. The quality of the maps varies considerably throughout the series, according to the interest of the volume's author in the cartography, his abilities in cartography and the availability of source material. There were one or two full-time professional in-house cartographers working on the series, so the editorial organization and design of maps was always strong, some of the maps are extremely good and some of the mapping is important, as in Caroline Blunden and Mark Elvin's *Cultural Atlas of China* (Oxford, 1983).

For both author and publisher seeking co-publication deals, the constraints are even stronger for series. In such cases the publisher devises a formula which is imposed on all new ventures: the publisher will only allow so many plates and generally insists on their size and the range of colour printing that can be employed. In the Matthew atlas, Switzerland as a small country was deemed unworthy of full-scale treatment by the publisher. In his preface to his *World Atlas of Military History I to 1500* (London, 1973), Arthur Banks noted 'whereas authors obviously want as many maps as possible in their books, publishers try to keep these to a minimum for economic reasons'.[3]

Though not in a series, *The Atlas of the British Empire* edited by Christopher Bayly (London, 1989) contains only 39 maps in its 244 pages, far less than the number of illustrations. In 1990 Mike Corbishley's *The Middle Ages: Cultural Atlas for Young People* (Oxford) was produced by Phaidon's sister-imprint Equinox. It contains 26 maps (excluding small insets) for 87 pages, again far fewer than the number of illustrations.

In a thoughtful review of Matthew's *Atlas of Medieval Europe*, P.D.A. Harvey argued that 'we might reasonably think that an atlas in which maps do not predominate is not an atlas at all'.[4] Furthermore, although not in the case of Matthew's atlas, a relative lack of maps is sometimes linked to an absence both of cartographic quality, in particular clarity, and of scholarly information in those that are produced. This is true of Bayly's atlas, while *The National Trust Historical Atlas of Britain Prehistoric and Medieval*, edited by Nigel Saul (Stroud, 1994), has an excellent text and well-chosen and produced illustrations, but the unambitious maps are a disappointment. There are only 31 and some are weak. The map of 'The Anglo-Saxons and the Vikings' lacks locational specificity: not only are place names missing, but it is also unclear which places are being indicated. That of the arrival of the Gothic in England is overly crude in its depiction of the diffusion of architectural style, while

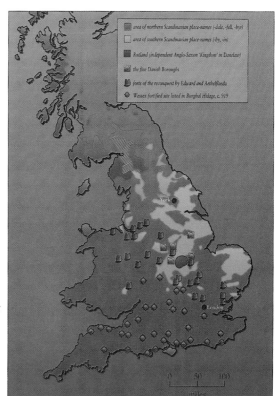

28. The atlas as consumer product. 'The Anglo-Saxons and the Vikings' from *The National Trust Historical Atlas of Britain: Prehistoric and Medieval* edited by Nigel Saul (Stroud, 1994). This map carries far less information than it can or should. Aside from the failure to name fortified positions, there is no guidance to the chronology of the reconquest. The black and white maps in David Hill's *Atlas of Anglo-Saxon England* (Oxford, 1981) provide far more information.

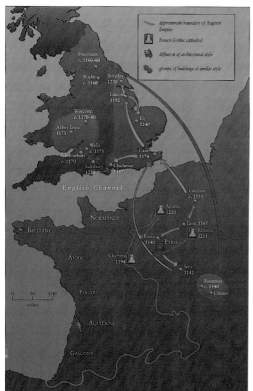

29. 'The Arrival of the Gothic' from *The National Trust Historical Atlas*. Cultural influence is difficult to map and it is far from clear that the ubiquitous arrow conveys the complexity of the situation.

30. 'Late Medieval Economy' from *The National Trust Historical Atlas*. A simplistic map that provides no indication of relative importance, quantity or changes. For example, there is no indication that until the end of the thirteenth century Boston in Lincolnshire exported more wool than any other English port before experiencing a decline. Such information is difficult to map but is also crucial to the subject.

that of industry and trade in the late Middle Ages would have benefited from some attempt to suggest quantities. Saul was limited both by the cost and by what the publisher could do. Nevertheless, this work was commercially successful and a Book Club Choice in Britain in 1994.

A prominent role for text in historical atlases is not new, but, although the text can be of the highest quality, it sometimes characterizes atlases that fail to provide sufficient maps to offer much real cartographic assistance to the reader. If combined with photographs, the maps are often relegated to a secondary form of illustrative material. The emphasis on photographs and text reflects two aspects of financial pressure. First, there is a commercial distinction between essentially scholarly atlases which are, to some degree at least, new and different, usually being therefore more specialized in focus and more expensive, and atlases in colour for the general market and book clubs. The latter are generally synthetic and broad-brush, and depend for their viability on being marketed, usually at the Frankfurt Book Fair, for international publication in a string of different language editions. They demand an international perspective in order to enjoy worldwide sales. In addition, it is easier and less expensive to translate text and picture captions than the lettering on maps.

Thanks to commercial pressures, publication policies and the nature of the historical atlases increasingly available, the understanding of what constitutes an historical atlas shifted in the 1980s and 1990s away from the heavy emphasis on maps that characterized most works produced earlier in the century. In part this reflects a commercial judgment on the marketability of maps. A book composed solely of them no longer seems so marketable and, instead, three disparate elements – text, pictures and maps – are brought together to make an attractive marketing package. The glamorous pictures attract people to buy the books. The maps and text then work independently or interdependently upon them, but the whole enterprise depends upon more people purchasing the product than are ever likely to use it. Second, it is less expensive to create an atlas that employs text and illustrations extensively than one that is largely composed of maps. The production of maps to book quality was and still is a specialized and expensive process. Highly labour-intensive cartography is expensive, as are intricate photomechanical processes and production. It was and is very tempting to fill an atlas by other methods.

In addition, in some recent atlases, for example *The Times Atlas of World Exploration*, many of the maps are considerably smaller than the page size. Such books are therefore unnecessarily large, and are punished by being shelved where few browsers will find them.

There is also a tension about the nature of the maps between the very diagrammatic images favoured largely by non-geographers, for example, large arrows moving in a general direction, or Norse longboats, and the traditional techniques of area, line and point favoured by geographers. The former are more pictorial and more readily understood and have much greater popular appeal, but their value for analytical purposes and the degree to which they describe events or processes at the scale used are both limited. In contrast, the more traditional cartography maps information using methods such as dot distribution or choropleth maps that may be more difficult to understand. However, it would be misleading to present the issue in terms of too rigid a contrast. Choropleth maps which use a scale of colours or shades to suggest different densities are also found in more popular works.

Costs

Bold new departures requiring extensive research and much new cartography are very expensive. They either require considerable commercial investment, which implies a production agenda with an emphasis on global sales appeal, or large-scale financial support. For example the scholarly case for an atlas of late eighteenth-century American history was made in the early 1970s[5] and, after major efforts, the resulting *Atlas of Early American History* (Princeton, 1976) obtained extensive sponsorship. It took twelve full-time historians and cartographers more than five years to produce; and it was revealed in *Publishers' Weekly* on 21 June 1976 that the volume had cost close to $1,600,000 provided by 44 foundations, organizations and individuals for research and development. The most important source of funds was the National Endowment for the Humanities, but there were other important institutional donors including the Bicentennial Council of the Thirteen Original States. Princeton University Press spent at least $250,000 on publication, and the press and the Newberry Library spent an additional $115,000 on sales promotion. There were 7,500 copies printed but only 2,500 bound. The atlas sold at $125 each compared to a real cost of $600–700. The cost of the project had originally been estimated at $600,000. It is not surprising that only one volume of what had been intended as a series going up to the 1830s appeared.

The costs of research and production affect the contents of historical atlases in a number of ways. A major new historical atlas requires extensive research and that takes time and expenditure. The necessary research work for the first Finnish historical atlas, *Suomen Historian Kartasto* edited by Eino Jutikkala (Helsinki, 1949), depended on grants from the Werner Söderström Foundation. Nine cartographers, as well as a large number of scholars, worked for six years to produce the first Australian historical atlas, as most of the maps and diagrams had to be created for it.[6] The Tübingen Classical historical atlas project has cost over $10 million and its Princeton counterpart's projected final cost is $3.5 million.

The large majority of the 121 maps published in the *Maps, Genealogies and Lists* companion volume of the *New History of Ireland* (Oxford, 1984) were derived from primary sources, many of them thus the product of research specifically undertaken for the project. The selection of topics was partly determined by the 'state of research on the materials for Irish historical cartography'.[7] This was also true of the *Historisk Atlas Danmark* (Copenhagen, 1988), which involved work by 45 scholars.

Given the costs of such research, it is not surprising that most atlases re-use familiar material, and that this is especially the case with works produced by commercial publishers lacking institutional support. The same maps recur frequently, with very little variation. Many maps in British historical atlases can be traced back to that of Poole. The practice of recycling older maps goes back to the sixteenth century. Even when the need for new maps is admitted, cost factors can prevent such a step. It took more than a decade of scholarly work to produce the 650 well-researched maps in the *Historical Atlas of South Asia* (Chicago, 1978); by 1967 the project had a staff of eighteen. The second edition published in New York in 1992 essentially offered only new text, and the editor admitted that the new maps that were most needed, specifically relating to the prehistoric period, could not be afforded.[8] Even so, the published price of this work is £175. A resulting problem is that maps copy each other's mistakes, which are terribly difficult to eradicate, and more generally repeat the emphases and agendas of past compilers.

Financial constraints also affect the timetable of projects. Thanks to cash-flow considerations and the need to earn a return on capital, commercial publishers face severe restraints, which in effect demand extremely rapid production, a limited number of maps and a very straightforward presentation. Costs are high. Multi-colour printing, for example, is expensive.

Since the war, and particularly in the 1980s and 1990s, many historical atlases were produced by 'packaging houses', companies that conceived and created works which they then sold to the publisher, which then published them under its own imprint. For example, the *Atlas of the 20th Century* published by Facts on File in New York in 1982 was produced by Bison Books, a packaging house then based in Greenwich, Connecticut, and London. Nicholas Hooper and Matthew Bennett's *Cambridge Illustrated Atlas of Warfare: the Middle Ages 768–1487*, published by Cambridge University Press in 1996, was produced by a London packaging company, Calmann and King. Packagers specialize in highly illustrated volumes that usually are only viable in a range of national markets. So there is little point in having publicity sales, warehousing and distribution departments for the home market, i.e. just one market among several. Many packagers are led by a partnership of a designer and an editor. The formation of such companies was sometimes a reaction against the small scope for designers within more traditional publishing houses.

One of the most important packagers was Swanston Publishing Limited, a company founded on the entrepreneurial energy and graphic direction of Derby-based

31. The Swanston Style. Part of the spread on 'Kleindeutschland' from Eric Homberger's *Historical Atlas of New York* (New York, 1994). Produced by Swanston Publishing Limited in Derby, with maps designed by Malcolm Swanston and edited by Liz Wyse, the atlas was published in New York, by Henry Holt. The publicity emphasized the American character of the book, including the American birthplace of the author, but the layout of the atlas and the style of the maps were familiar to those used to Swanston books.

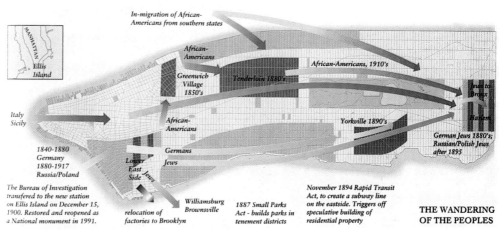

32. 'The Ethnic City' from *Historical Atlas of New York City*, an example of impressionistic maps that gives no guidance to quantities or sources. In contrast, Bruce Macdonald's *Vancouver. A Visual History* (Vancouver, 1992) mapped the single highest density of each ethnic group that made up more than fifty per cent of a census tract's population. The percentages given in brackets, showing the percentage of each group over the whole city, served to indicate the degree of concentration or assimilation of each group shown on the map when they are compared with the percentages of the most dense area.

Malcolm Swanston. His historical atlases are distinctive for their extensive range of colour, frequent employment of arrows and plentiful text. Swanston carried out cartographic work for many British publishers, such as Penguin, which launched a major new series of historical atlases in 1995. Other distinctive Swanston works include Michael Kidron and Dan Smith's *New State of War and Peace* (London, 1991). Swanston was also responsible for the cartographic work of historical atlases published in the USA: for example, William H. Goetzmann and Glyndwr Williams's *Atlas of North American Exploration* (New York: Prentice Hall, 1992), and Eric Homberger's *Historical Atlas of New York City* (New York: Henry Holt, 1994). Swanston began as Swanston Graphics – a contracting cartographic design company – before becoming a packager.

Such packagers are generally small companies with limited financial resources, and cannot afford long production times for individual volumes. Their cash-flow and profitability depend on the rapid production of atlases once the publisher agrees to the project, usually on the basis of a synopsis and a mock-up of several page spreads. The time pressures resulting from this commercial system limit the time available for innovative mapping and increase the possibility of error.

More generally, even publishers that do not use packagers frequently contract out many of the processes involved in the production of historical atlases because they lack the necessary specialized in-house production facilities. This again ensures the constraints of time, cost and profitability already referred to. Production facilities and skills are relatively uncommon. Little new expertise is available easily or cheaply. Four-colour printing of historical atlases was beyond the means of publishers in much of the world in the 1980s; not possible, for example, in Africa. Specialized mapmaking facilities and skills depend for their profitability on continual work, which again encourages time pressures and a hectic pace with an emphasis on the speedy production of maps far removed from the slow deliberative weighing of cartographic options.

The complexity of production arrangements, with all that that entails for possibilities of error, pressures of time and cost, and the presence of a number of production stages each of which has to be paid for, can be illustrated by the *Atlas of Ancient America*, one of the series of Cultural Atlases that were produced by Equinox and later Andromeda and many of which were published by Phaidon in Britain and Facts on File in the USA. For the *Atlas of Ancient America* by M. Coe, D. Snow and E. Benson (1986), the text and captions were written by three Americans and edited by an Englishman. The preparation of four-colour film of illustrations was carried out in Singapore, the maps drawn by outworkers in three locations in southern England, the film typesetting was the responsibility of a Midlands subcontractor and the printer was Portuguese.

The situation may change with technological developments, especially the desktop mapmaking of the 1990s, and it may be the case that the commercial constraints and context of the post-war production of historical atlases are in the process of dissolution; but these constraints certainly defined the parameters of much production in the half-century after 1945. Outside authoritarian societies, it was generally publishers that controlled the budgets. The size and duration of the expenditure required for the production of new research-based historical atlases and the slow rate at which large-scale investment could be recovered were and are such that institutional sponsorship is necessary. For example, the Newberry Library in Chicago is both headquarters and sponsor of the United States *Atlas of Historical County Bound-*

aries project. Aldo Dami's *Les Frontières européennes de 1900 à 1975. Histoire territoriale de l'Europe atlas* (Geneva, 1976), a valuable work not least because it records frontier changes during the Second World War, was published with help from the funds of the Swiss Council of Scientific Research. The cartography in J. Langton and R. Morris (eds), *Atlas of Industrialising Britain 1780–1914* (London, 1986) depended on a grant from the Nuffield Foundation. The *Carte archéologique de la Gaule*, begun in 1930 by the French Académie des Inscriptions et Belles-Lettres, has displayed more progress since 1992 when the Ministère de la Culture agreed to support it.

The need for such institutional support has further encouraged the concentration on the historical mapping of Europe and North America that is also such an obvious feature of unsubsidized historical cartography. Few countries would choose to spend the 14.6 million Canadian dollars that the three-volume *Historical Atlas of Canada* (Toronto, 1987–93) received from donors – 6.1 million alone from the Social Sciences and Humanities Research Council of Canada, and even with that sum the project encountered many financial problems.

Compromises

Institutional support rarely ends anxieties about finance. Even with such support the production of the *Atlas of Early American History* was affected by the need to secure more funds: the dialectic of money and maps that affects so many atlas projects. This affected the choice of maps to work on first. As Barbara Petchenik, the cartographic editor, recorded in reflections that are all too rare:

> it was not considered expedient to work exclusively on the general reference maps during the first few years of the Project. Had this been done, there would have been little to show for our efforts when additional funding for continuing work was sought. As it was, the funders were sufficiently encouraged by our apparent progress to allow us to continue; such long-term inefficiency produced short-term gains that were simply essential.

Conversely, it has been argued that subsidies are problematic because they lessen the need to accommodate the interests of general readers.[9]

Compromises are necessary, compromises that are rarely referred to in the atlases and that leave only infrequent traces in the scanty records that survive for such atlases. The preface to the atlas volume to the New Cambridge Modern History series began 'The Making of any atlas is an exercise in compromise' and specifically referred to the reasons why there were not more maps of economic history: 'To have increased such economic maps by even a small number would have involved extensive research programmes impossible within the limits within which we worked.'[10] The compromise between academic integrity and the demands of the market-place as mediated by the publisher is one that authors are familiar with and frequently complain about, but it is a compromise that is necessary to make any book viable. Far from reducing him to hack status, acceptance of this reality is a sign of an author's genuine ability to communicate his ideas.

The demands of the market-place are prescriptive as well as proscriptive. Atlases that have a totally commercial rationale are inherently more conservative in content. Their publishers cannot afford to present potential purchasers with contents that are so novel that the work is rejected. A novel projection that may be seen as bold and interesting in one market may be regarded as silly or unacceptable in another. In order to make the historical atlas more attractive there is an emphasis on the visual appeal of the maps. This can entail a bold use of colour printing, a stress on clear boundaries, as opposed to the caution, if not vagueness, that might be accurate, and, in the 1980s and 1990s, the plentiful use of arrows in order to suggest dynamic elements. For commercial reasons, there is also still an emphasis on the mapping of military events. Geographically, the allocation of page space in atlases reflects commercial as well as academic priorities. The former entail both a sense of what the market will expect – which parts of Europe, for example, American or Japanese readers expect to see well covered – and the specific nature of the anticipated sales: historical atlases sell better in North America than in sub-Saharan Africa, better in Japan than in Malaysia. As co-publication deals and often book club agreements precede publication and are a vital part in the planning of historical atlases that seek global sales, they can play a role in the allocation of space.

Global Publishing

Much of the emphasis hitherto in this section has been on problems. It is also important to note the opportunities that have developed and the positive role of publishers. A number of technological and marketing changes in publishing since the 1960s made the production of atlases and four-colour printing much easier and cheaper. The marketing systems of the book trade have become increasingly sophisticated and, more generally, there has been a globalization of publishing, especially of illustrated book publishing. A fair number of publishers have thought it worth their while to publish atlases, a high-cost commodity which might readily sell a large number of copies, possibly 150,000 or more. This compares well with the numerous books of which publishers would be lucky to sell 1000 or 2000 copies.

Sales have in some cases been considerable. The Penguin series compiled by a hospital psychiatrist, Colin McEvedy, has sold in total over 650,000 copies.[11] The *Times Atlas of World History* has been the most important of the global historical atlases, not least because with its innovative use of interesting perspectives and coverage of much non-political material, it has altered the general perception of what an historical atlas of the world should contain. English editions appeared in 1978, 1984, 1989 and 1993 and concise English editions in 1982, 1986, 1988 and 1992. Planning for a fifth edition began in 1996. By 1995 the main atlas was available in seventeen languages, including Chinese, Croatian, Hebrew and Portuguese, and had sold 1.1 million copies. The publisher sold the film to other publishers or printed it for them. Times Books provided black film with boxes around the maps, the co-publishers translated the text and sent back their own black film to which Times Books added the maps. The atlas cost £½ million in the mid-1970s to produce, an enormous sum that would not be risked today, but the return has been considerable.

The foreign-language editions of the *Times Atlas* repay attention, as some contain additional material. The French publishers insisted on changes for their version, *Le Grand Atlas de l'histoire mondiale* (Paris, 1979), while *Atlante Storico Mondiale* (Milan, 1993), which is based on the third edition of the *Times Atlas*, includes an Italian section with 23 large pages of text and illustrations, offering a miniature history of Italy, followed by a largely political and military cartographic section with 107 maps. The *Grande Enciclopédia Portuguesa e Brasileira Atlas Histórico* (Lisbon and Rio de Janeiro, 1992), which was also based on the third edition, included at the end a history of Portugal illustrated with maps, but none dealt with the eighteenth, nineteenth or twentieth centuries.

Co-publication deals spread the heavy costs of initial outlay. Important initiatives were taken by the Dutch in the 1950s. The small size of their domestic market encouraged Dutch publishers to look for foreign sales and they had considerable experience in so doing. Thus F. Van Der Meer and C. Mohrmann's *Atlas van de Oudchristelijke Wereld* (Amsterdam: Elsevier, 1958) appeared that year in London as the *Atlas of the Early Christian World. Elseviers Historische Atlas* was published by Thomas Nelson and Sons as *An Atlas of World History* (London, 1965). R. Roolvink's *Historical Atlas of the Muslim Peoples* (Amsterdam: Djambatan, 1957) was published in London in 1964 by George Allen and Unwin. Elsevier, a Dutch publisher with a strong tradition of producing reference series, played a major role in financing what was to become Equinox, the major British packager of historical atlases in the 1980s. The Equinox Cultural Atlases were originally conceived as a replacement series for the older Elsevier atlases. The latter comprised maps, text and many illustrations. In the Cultural Atlases series it was decided to integrate these elements rather than have them as separate sections.

The *dtv-Atlas zur Weltgeschichte* of Hermann Kinder and Werner Hilgemann (Munich, 1964), a work that devoted a reasonable amount of space to extra-European themes, has been translated into English, French, Italian, Japanese, Spanish and Swedish, appearing for example as *Atlas historique* (Paris: Stock, 1968 and 1977) and the *Penguin Atlas of World History* (London, 1974) and *The Anchor Atlas of World History* (Garden City: Anchor Books, 1974). The *Historical Atlas of the World*, published in 1970 by Chambers in Edinburgh and Barnes and Noble in New York, was an English edition of a Norwegian work published in 1962. Other editions included *Kansojen Historian Kartasto* (Helsinki, 1962). *The Hamlyn Historical Atlas* edited by R.I. Moore and published in London in 1981 appeared that year in Chicago as *The Rand McNally Historical Atlas of the World*. A second edition was published in London in 1992 as the *Philip's Atlas of World History* and in Chicago as the *Rand McNally Atlas of World History* (1993). Planning for a very much revised third edition began in 1996.

In the 1980s and 1990s the co-publication of historical atlases was dominated by works produced in Britain and British packagers or publishers played a major role. Other publishers, however, have also been important. The vivid graphics of modern French cartography, the interest of French scholars in global history and the presence of major French publishers have ensured that French works have been sold abroad. *Le Grand Livre de l'histoire du monde*, published in Paris in 1986 by Hachette, became *The Harper Atlas of World History*, published in New York in 1987 by Harper and Row. Pierre Vidal-Naquet and Jacques Bertin's *Atlas historique* was published in Swedish translation in *Atlas till Mänsklighetens Historia* in 1991. The *Historical Atlas of the Jewish People*, published in London by Hutchinson in 1992, was the translation of a work produced by Hachette.

There have also been British editions of other foreign historical atlases. For example, the *Atlas of World History* by Giorgio Bombi *et al.* (London, 1987) was translated and adapted from *Il Grande Atlante Storico Illustrato* (Milan, 1985). Thanks to their cost, German works have had less of an impact, though, for example, the *Atlas zur Kirchengeschichte* edited by H. Jedin *et al.* (Freiburg, 1987) was published as *Atlas d'histoire de l'église. Les églises chrétiennes hier et aujourd'hui* (Paris, 1990). Helmut Pemsel's *Von Salamis bis Okinawa* (1975) also appeared as the *Atlas of Naval Warfare* (London, 1977). There were four Swedish editions of Westermann's historical atlas – in 1958, 1963, 1967 and 1978 – all under the name *Atlas till Världshistorien.* Additional maps on Swedish topics were included.

A number of publishers from smaller countries with limited domestic markets made an impact in the late 1980s and 1990s. The most successful was Carta, the Israel Map and Publishing Company, which benefited from the close links between Israel and New York. Works originally published in Hebrew by Carta were then published in New York in English. Thus, Dan Bahat's *Illustrated Atlas of Jerusalem* was published by Simon and Schuster in 1990, and Evyater Friesel's *Atlas of Modern Jewish History*, originally produced in Hebrew in 1983, was published by the New York office of Oxford University Press the same year. Haim Beinart's *Atlas of Medieval Jewish History* (New York: Simon and Schuster, 1992) was another translation of a Carta original, but Carta also produced historical atlases for Simon and Schuster that were not originally published in Israel in Hebrew: G.S.P. Freeman-Grenville's *New Atlas of African History* (1990) and his *Historical Atlas of the Middle East* (1993). There has also been increased Scandinavian activity. The *Rand McNally Historical Atlas and Guide* (Chicago, 1993) is based on a 1991 work by J.W. Cappelens Forlag of Oslo and Maps International/Liber Kartor of Stockholm.

Sponsorship

To turn from the commercial to the subsidized sector, it is clear that an unstudied aspect of the latter is the way in which the academic and institutional politics of the search for subsidy structures or affects the contents of historical atlases. The role of subsidies is repeatedly mentioned, but not the process by which they were obtained and whether compromises had to be made, and, if so, how and to what extent. The support of prominent individuals is clearly crucial, for what is ascribed to institutions is generally the work of particular individuals. In her introduction to *Historic Towns. Maps and Plans of Towns and Cities in the British Isles I* (London, 1969), Mary Lobel noted that it was crucial that Sir Ian Richmond had agreed to become chairman of the sponsoring committee and had obtained a generous British Academy grant that helped towards both research work and publication.

The Historic Towns project was an international collaborative scheme launched in the 1960s that in part reflected the optimism of the decade. As more generally with the whole of higher education, this was a period of expansion and bold projects. Economic growth and investment in education created a context in which it was easier to obtain grants for scholarly projects and increasingly common to seek them. For much of the 1960s most funded projects were still small-scale, essentially a continuation of the position in the 1950s. Thus, for example, F.W. Jessup's *Kent History Illustrated* (Maidstone, 1966) was written mainly for educational use at the request of the Kent Education Committee and published for it by Kent County Council.[12]

By the end of the decade bolder projects were on the planning board. The Société de l'Atlas Historique Français was founded in 1969 to oversee the creation of a series of regional historical atlases covering all of France. Sponsored by the President of the Republic, the first volume, devoted to Provence, Orange, Nice, Monaco and the Comtat Venaissin, appeared in 1969, followed in 1973 by Anjou. This was not the limit of French sponsorship. For example, the two-volume *Atlas d'archéologie aérienne de Picardie* by Roger Agache and Bruno Breart (Amiens, 1975) received considerable aid from public funds including from the Secretary of State for Culture and the Établissement Public Régional de Picardie. The atlas was published by an official body, the Société des Antiquaires de Picardie. It was far more common for subsidies to go to such bodies than to commercial concerns, but, as already suggested, the very emphasis on non-commercial criteria in such searches for subsidies instead led to a reliance on institutional and individual affiliations.

The 1970s witnessed the first of successive crises in sponsorship. More projects came forward for subsidy in the context of an institutional and academic society that took such subsidies for granted. Yet, at the same time pressures on budgets stemming from the oil crisis of 1973 and the subsequent recession had baleful consequences. The French project for regional historical atlases had initially intended that each volume of maps should be accompanied by another devoted to textual information: for example, bibliographies, episcopal and abbatial lists, and dynastic genealogical tables. However, for *Savoie* (1979) and *Agenais* (1979) only the volumes of maps were produced, and the atlases for Franche Comté, Alsace, Limousin and Marche were finished but not published because of the budgetary crisis that brought the project to an end.

The ambitious nature of major projects and the increasing costs of cartography in the 1970s and 1980s were such that as subsidies became more difficult to obtain they were, nevertheless, more necessary. Costs were such that it was important to seek multiple sources of sponsorship. Thus, the *Scandinavian Atlas of Historic Towns. IV Uppsala* (Odense, 1983) was supported by the Nordic Cultural Fund, the Swedish Council for Research in the Humanities and Social Sciences and the Institute for Urban History in Stockholm, while volume six, on Reykjavik (Odense, 1988), received grants from the city, the Nordic Cultural Fund and the Icelandic Science Foundation.

Aside from sponsorship, it was also important to absorb some of the costs among supporting institutions and individuals. A grant from the Australian Research Grants Scheme to provide funding for a chief cartographer in 1980–85 with some help for travel and technical issues was crucial to the production of *Australians: A Historical Atlas* edited by J.R. Cram and J. McQuilton (Broadway, New South Wales, 1987), but so also was the direct support of the Division of National Mapping in Canberra, which housed the volume's cartographic staff and provided technical facilities for the production of the atlas.[13] The Irish Historic Towns Atlas project had a cartographic editor, K. Mary Davies, appointed in 1982 and paid by the Irish government. The project was sponsored by the Royal Irish Academy, which provided a financial structure, accommodation and a publisher.[14] *The Atlas of Industrialising Britain 1780–1914* edited by John Langton and R.J. Morris (London, 1986) depended not only on a grant from the Nuffield Foundation but also on the resources of the two editors' departments and of Langton's Oxford college. The editors noted the difficulty of the editorial process when they referred to it as 'a splendid experience in the relationships of industrial production as we, the putting-out masters, negotiated between contributors who had all the ethic of craft producers controlling the work process, and the merchant princes of the' sponsorship societies.[15] In most cases publishers impose more direct controls and constraints.

The use of an institutional publisher can be crucial to the finances of historical atlases. Thus, the *Atlas de la Sardaigne rurale aux 17e et 18e siècles* by John Day, Serge Bonin, Itria Calia and Aline Jelinski (Paris, 1993), a work that revealed the possibility of using maps and text to recreate the agrarian world of the past, was published by the École des Hautes Études en Sciences Sociales, and the maps and graphics were produced in-house. Such support is taken to its logical conclusion when historical atlases in the 'free world' are produced by government agencies. Work on a New Zealand historical atlas began in 1990 with the project funded by the Lotteries Board and under the management of the Historical Branch of the Department of Internal Affairs in Wellington.[16] Even when assistance is far less direct, it is, nevertheless, also possible to suggest a political purpose. Joseph Schwartzberg, the editor of the *Historical Atlas of South Asia*, wrote:

> To the extent that the peoples of South Asia take cognizance of the fact that the elected representatives of the citizens of the United States, actively assisted by the staffs of the federal agencies concerned, thought enough of South Asia to fund and sustain a project as difficult and costly as that which created this atlas, the gulf of misunderstanding that at times looms so large between South Asians and Americans may be significantly narrowed. Should that fervently desired end be attained, we shall feel that our great debt to the American public will have been honorably discharged.[17]

Rising costs are a particular problem for atlases that anyway are not going to make a profit. There is a lack of comparable buoyancy in sales. As a result, the extent of available sponsorship has become a more acute problem in the 1980s and 1990s.[18] Writing in 1988 about the need to find the substantial funding necessary for the drafting of a map of Belfast in 1838, a major task, Mary Davies noted: 'We have not until recently thought of any kind of sponsorship, but the increasing cost of drafting the 4-colour maps may soon make this necessary even for medium-sized towns.'[19] Again, it is unclear how the technological changes and possibilities that gathered pace in the 1990s will affect the situation. As with commercial atlases, however, it is clear that it is mistaken to see the contents of historical atlases simply as a project of the intentions of the compilers, or of these intentions compromised only by problems of mappability and representation. Instead, it is necessary when approaching the contents to bear the general financial context and the generally shadowy details of financial exigencies and pressures in mind.

7

Politics and Post-war Historical Atlases

The most obvious impact of politics on post-war historical atlases is evident in those produced by Communist states. It would be misleading, however, to present those works as the only example of political intervention. Instead, politics can be seen at work in a number of respects. Communist historical atlases were countered by explicitly anti-Communist works, although the latter were very much in a minority among works produced in the 'free world'. Aside from the historical atlases of the Cold War, the political dimension can be seen in the increase in the number of states producing their own historical atlases, or general atlases with historical sections, as a result of decolonization. This process also interacted with specific issues that led to mapping, for example the Arab-Israeli conflict. Lastly, aside from explicit politics, there is the more general case of the ideological and political assumptions present in works that lack explicit and readily analysable cartographic and textual statements but can nevertheless be in part interpreted in a political light. It is not so much that maps are about *mentalité* not reality, as that the depiction and representation of realities reflect *mentalités*.

Historical atlases can also serve to reflect political shifts, for example with the movement of societies away from authoritarian politics, as in the case of Spain after Franco or states that abandoned Communism. In addition, they can be studied in terms of their depiction of both domestic and foreign history.

The Cartography of Communism

Communist historical atlases were different from their Western counterparts, both in contents and in methods of depiction. Their characteristic features were maps of people's warfare, such as 'struggles for national liberation', and class struggle, and the use of symbols, such as red flames and clenched fists, to indicate this tension. Thus, the development of states and a states' system in terms of homogeneous blocs of territory – the classic features of historical atlases at the beginning of the century – was subverted by an emphasis on divisions within these blocs. In addition, Communist historical atlases carried maps of economic development and, in accordance with Communist ideology and historiography, adopted a periodization related to different modes of production.

Class struggle was a major theme of the Hungarian historical atlas for secondary school pupils, *Történelmi atlasz* (Budapest, 1961). There were special maps for Spartacus, the Hussites, the Peasants' War in Germany (1524–25) and in Hungary (1514), for the English 'Bourgeois Revolution' 1640–89 (*sic*), the Paris Commune, a big whole-page map for the not terribly significant movements of Socialist workers and peasants in 1867–1918, two maps for the Russian Revolution, two for the Hungarian Soviet Republic of 1919 and one for the struggles of Tito's partisans. Other maps included the uprisings of Mukama, Babek and the black slaves against Arab rule in the eighth and ninth centuries, the French Jacquerie (peasants' rising) of the fourteenth century, the English Peasants' Revolt, the uprisings against Richelieu and Peter the Great, the centres of the Chartist movement, the workers' uprisings in the nineteenth century and the Indian Mutiny.

Conversely, there were no maps about the rise of Christianity, the empires of great medieval Hungarian kings – Louis the Great and Matthias Corvinus – or about the growth of the Austrian monarchy and its dissolution after the First World War. Instead, six of the 89 maps were about risings against Habsburg rule. The greatest taboo was the territorial aggrandizement of Hungary at the time of the Second World War. There was a map about the 'liberation of Hungary in 1944–5' by the Red Army, but the borders were those of Hungary after 1945: earlier gains of northern Transylvania and parts of Slovakia and Yugoslavia in 1938–41 were ignored. Whereas previous Hungarian historical atlases had reflected national traditions, the cover depicting the statue of a medieval monk, the author of the first chronicle of the Hungarians or a horseman of the Magyar conquest, the cover of the 1961 atlas carried a big, Communist-style coat of arms with a red star.

The mapping of resistance to the Habsburgs was part of a tradition in Communist historical atlases of seeking to conflate popular consciousness and warfare with national identity and activity. This conflation could be seen, for example, in Czech treatment of the Hussites, as in the *Skolní Atlas Československých Dějin* (Prague, 1959), an atlas that also reveals another characteristic: the detailed mapping of economic history. Economic themes were also prominent in Yugoslavia's *Povijesni Atlas*, edited by Zvonimir Dugački (Zagreb, 1971). This included maps of the economy of the Hellenic and Roman world, of the Serbian economy in 1459, that of Bosnia in 1463 and Slovenia in the sixteenth century, of medieval European trade routes, the early modern European economy, Ragusa's trade routes, the world economy in 1800, and those of Serbia and Croatia in the nineteenth century.[1]

The emphasis on radicalism and people's warfare abroad served to universalize the Communist message. In the *Atlas i Historise se Kohes se Mesme* (Tirana, 1963) attention was directed to popular risings in maps of the German Reformation, sixteenth-century England, early modern Iberia, and seventeenth-century Europe, and a full page was devoted to 'Revolution in the Netherlands 1566–1609'. Thus the map of the Reformation showed prominently areas affected by the Peasants' War, that of sixteenth-century England areas affected by risings in 1549 and 1607 and that of Iberia the regions of the Communeros and Germania revolts. The Hussite wars were also mapped, while the map of seventeenth-century Europe included popular risings. Similarly, in the map in *Povijesni Atlas* of the English Revolution (Civil War), substantial areas were shown as affected by Leveller and Digger action.[2] The *Atlas Historik. Koha e re dhe e sotme* (Historical atlas for the recent and contemporary period) (Tirana, 1974) begins with the 'Bourgeois Revolution' in England (the Civil War).

Wherever possible, the atlases emphasized positive relations with Russia and minimized or ignored problems. Thus, the role of Russian forces in driving both the Turks from the Balkans and the Germans from eastern Europe was mapped. Romania's *Atlas Istoric* edited by S. Pascu (Bucharest, 1971) included a map of the liberation of the Balkans by Russian and Romanian forces in 1877. It also mapped interwar strikes, the anti-Fascist insurrection of 1944 and the subsequent operations of the Romanian army in helping to liberate Transylvania, Hungary and Czechoslovakia.[3] The *Atlas Po Bulgarska Istoriia* (Sofia, 1963) emphasized Russian campaigns, especially those of 1876–78. These were very significant in Bulgarian history as the Russians liberated the country from 500 years of Ottoman control.

The *Atlas Historyczny Polski* (Wroclaw, 1967) concluded with a map of territorial changes of the Polish state that compared the frontiers of 1018, 1634, 1939 and post-1945, in order to show that the first and last corresponded most closely, in short that Poland's eastward expansion had been an aberration. A similar map appeared in *Nasza Ojczyzna. Atlas historyczny dla klasy IV* (Wroclaw, 1981–82). The *Atlas Historyczny Polski* (Warsaw, 1973) ignored the Russian role in its four maps of the German conquest of Poland in 1939. The maps appeared on the same page as one of the Spanish Civil War, implying a misleading degree of similarity.[4] Likewise, Polish historical atlases did not emphasize Polish resistance to Russia's role in the earlier Partitions of Poland of 1772–95. The East German *Atlas zur Geschichte* (Gotha and Leipzig, 1976) also suppressed the geopolitical results of the Molotov-Ribbentrop pact of 1939. It included maps of 1939 and 1941, but no arrows or explanations to draw attention to how the Soviet frontier moved several hundred miles westwards in the intervening period. However, the *Atlas Historyczny Polski* did show the 1919–20 Polish-Russian war.

One important cartographic device that presented Russia in a favourable light was the publication of maps of Europe that included most or all of European Russia. This ensured that the country did not appear as an area outside, and a force alien to, Europe. It also had the effect of making Eastern European states appear more central in Europe. This was true for example of the maps of tenth- and fourteenth-century Europe in *Povijesni Atlas* (Zagreb, 1971).

The mapping of popular uprisings ensured that topics that were not generally treated in Western, or indeed other Communist, historical atlases received attention. Thus the *Školní Atlas Československých Dějin* (Prague, 1959) included maps of the 1680 and 1775 Bohemian rising as well as those of 'bourgeois' revolutions: England in the 1640s and Russia in 1905.

The *Atlas Po Bulgarska Istoriia* (Sofia, 1963) included not only good maps of the Bulgar-Byzantine wars, but also maps of interwar radicalism in Bulgaria. The maps of the early history of Bulgaria appropriated the powerful and dynamic Bulgars for the historical context of modern Bulgaria, and the latter was presented in heroic terms. Interwar radicalism was followed by the mapping of resistance in 1941–44, of liberation in 1944 and of subsequent operations in Yugoslavia and Hungary. A separate atlas of the Bulgarian resistance in 1941–44 had already been published in 1958. More generally, Communism allowed cartographic depictions of nationalism in order to further its own purposes.

Although the Communists mapped the prehistoric, ancient and medieval past, they were particularly interested in those sections of the past that could be readily interpreted in Marxist terms and in the history and prehistory of Communist agitation. At a conference on the production and use of historical maps held in Budapest in 1972, B.G. Galkovic stated that 'Historical maps in the Soviet Union . . . are compiled according to the methodological directives of V.I. Lenin', and M. Bárdosi stressed the need 'to give a picture of the route of social development'.[5]

The emphases of Communist ideology ensured that in the *Historický Atlas. Revolučního Hnutí* (Prague, 1956) the earliest map was that of the Hussites. This Czech work, which had the globe with a red star underneath on the front cover, was divided into four sections. The first was of revolutionary crisis and activity from the mid-nineteenth century on. These maps, for example of Europe in 1905–7 and of the world in 1917–23, created a sense of widespread disorder. There was a lack of precision in the mapping of discontent: anti-colonial demonstrations were treated alongside industrial strikes. There was also a powerful element of bias. Disputes within the Communist bloc were ignored. The second section was devoted to the history of Russia from the late nineteenth century on, with an emphasis on the 1917 revolution and the subsequent civil war. An extensive treatment of Russian history was a characteristic feature of Communist historical atlases. The third section – on Czechoslovakia – proceeded by popular violence: after the Hussites, there were maps on risings in the early modern period and the Bohemian revolution of 1848–49 before a lot of attention to twentieth-century revolutionary activity.

The fourth section was devoted to colonization and resistance. This was clearly anti-Western, and careful not to present Russia as one among many imperialist powers. Thus, in the global map of economic expansion Russia was not treated as one of the states exerting pressure. The map of Afghanistan and Britain did not include Russian expansion in the region. Cartographic devices were also used to emphasize the positive role of the Soviet Union. Thus, in the map of the war in the Far East in 1931–45 a prominent role was accorded to the war in China and to the Russian invasion of Manchuria in 1945, whereas the American and British role was shown as comparatively insignificant. The most striking colours – orange and red – were used for the former, grey and purple for the latter. For the map of the expansion of Fascist states, the Soviet Union was coloured differently from the other non-Fascist states in order to stress its clear resistance to Fascism.[6]

Aside from the portrayal of the major powers, the atlas also emphasized the extent of hostility to imperialism, thus providing a historical lineage to the anti-imperialist agitation of the 1950s. There were for example maps of Indian opposition, including strikes and demonstrations, to the British in 1900–8, of the Mahdi's struggle against the British in the Sudan, of Philippine opposition to the Americans in 1899–1900, and of Socialist agitation in the South Asia in 1919–31,[7] all preludes to the maps of struggles against imperialism in Asia and Africa from 1945.[8]

Thus both content and representation were used to make points. Conflict was a clear theme in both. This was true not only of the maps of popular radical and anti-colonial action, but also of the town-maps published in order to show revolutionary moments. Thus the *Atlas Historik. Koha e re dhe sotme* (Tirana, 1974) included street plans for Paris and Prague for 1848 and a map of the Paris Commune. The dramatic arrows of the Communards advancing from Paris had a greater visual impact than those of their more numerous and successful assailants. Similarly, the map of Revolutionary France exaggerated the extent of revolutionary support.[9]

As with Nazi historical atlases, Communist works stressed the continuous nature of struggle and thus looked for episodes in the past that could be seen as similar, an ahistorical process that failed to place enough weight on the specific contexts of particular episodes. Thus, Budapest's War History Institute issued four wall maps in 1968–70 showing first the 1848–49 war of independence, second the 'patriotic war' of the Hungarian Soviet Republic in 1919, third Hungarians against Fascism, with an inset map of Resistance operations in Budapest in 1941–45, and fourth a map of the liberation of Hungary in 1944–45.

The emphasis on the Second World War was not restricted to Hungarian wall maps, but was a more general feature of Communist historical atlases. Three of the twenty-four maps in *Nasza Ojczyzna* (Wroclaw, 1981–82) were devoted to the war. *Povijesni Atlas* included a map of the invasion of Yugoslavia in 1941 with an insert map of the bombardment of Belgrade, six maps of partisan operations and four of the clearing of Yugoslavia.[10]

The pursuit of Communist ideology did not entail the abandonment of traditional territorial and geopolitical interests and ambitions, though these had to be shelved if they involved gains at the expense of the USSR. The *Atlas of the Slovak Socialist Republic* (Bratislava, 1983), produced in English and Slovak by the Publishing House of the Slovak Academy of Sciences, included a map of Great Moravia in the ninth century that emphasized its territorial extent at the expense of Hungary:

> Contrary to other conceptions, the author of this map considers eastern Slovakia, together with the territory between the Danube and the Tisa rivers (reaching as far as Szolnok in the south) a basic territory of Great Moravia, and not merely an annexed territory. Similarly he intrudes into Great Moravia also a part of the Transdanubian region (Pannonia), between the Danube and near Vyšegrad.

In terms of extensive and detailed coverage and cartographic quality, the best historical atlases produced in Eastern Europe under Communist control were those from East Germany. They can be seen as examples of perfectly acceptable maps being used to sustain a questionable approach. The East Germans continued the earlier German tradition of historical cartography and mapped both German and world history. They were able to benefit from a measure of institutional continuity. Thus in 1952 the great Gotha cartographic house of Justus Perthes was nationalized. In 1955 it was renamed VEB Hermann Haack in honour of Haack (1872–1966) who had worked for the company since 1897 and played a major role in its post-war redevelopment.

East German historical atlases maintained the cartographic qualities of their predecessors, for example precision and full use of colour, but also reflected the Communist intellectual agenda. Thus the *Atlas des Saale-und mittleren Elbegebietes* edited by O. Schlüter and O. August (Leipzig, 1959–61) covered revolutionary opposition to the First World War and post-war revolutionary activity.[11] The *Historisch-geographisches Kartenwerk . . . Wirtschaftshistorische Entwicklung* edited by Edgar Lehmann (Leipzig, 1960) reflected the Communist interest in socio-economic history. The maps were prepared and printed by VEB Hermann Haack.

The company, in combination with the Zentralinstitut für Geschichte der Akademie der Wissenschaften der DDR, was also responsible for a two-volume atlas of world history that was the best produced by a Communist state. The very organization of the atlas reflected the impact of Communism. The first volume, published in 1973, covered history up to the October 1917 revolution, the second, published in 1975, history thereafter until 1972. The emphasis of the atlas was very much in accordance with Marxist views on history. There was considerable coverage of economic history with, for example, maps of the second-century Roman economy and the medieval European economy, with separate maps for the eleventh–thirteenth and thirteenth–fifteenth centuries, and the Hansa economic system. However, the treatment of Classical and medieval Europe did not neglect popular action.[12] Red flames indicated slave risings in the Roman empire. Greece was referred to as a slave society. The slave rising under Spartacus received a map of its own. The Peasant's Rising of 1381 featured prominently in the map of England in the thirteenth and fourteenth centuries. There were maps of class warfare in Germany from the mid-ninth to mid-fifteenth century, and from 1470 to 1517.[13] The Hussite wars received two maps, while there was another on medieval European heresies.[14] For the Reformation attention was devoted to the more radical Anabaptists who were shown as fairly widespread.[15]

The emphasis in the mapping of early modern Europe was on the dynamic of popular revolution. The map of the German Peasants' War of 1524–25 depicted not only the well-known uprising in south-west Germany, but also widespread activity, for example in Thuringia. The map of the Dutch revolt included peasants' revolts in 1567, 1572–76 and 1579–80 and centres of the 'democratic-plebian' movement in the south in 1576–85. The map of France in the period showed a rising of 1548 against the salt tax and peasants' uprisings in 1592–98, and that on Spain depicted the Communeros and Germania risings, both as very widespread, and another on Majorca. The net effect was of extensive discontent.[16] Similarly, the map of the Counter-Reformation included uprisings in Austria in the late sixteenth and early seventeenth centuries and that of the English 'Bourgeois Revolution' (the Civil War) included signs for Leveller and Digger activity. The pro-Russian agenda was hinted at in the map of the Great Northern War which depicted a Russian popular uprising against Swedish invaders in 1708–9. The map of the Ottoman empire from the late seventeenth until the late nineteenth century included the anti-Habsburg rising in Hungary in 1703–11, the Transylvanian peasants' rising of 1784, the anti-French uprising in Cairo in 1799, revolutionary committees of the 1870s in the Balkans and 'anti-feudal' risings in Syria and Lebanon in the mid-nineteenth century. Similarly, the map of the Austrian empire included sites of uprisings. The map of South America in the eighteenth and nineteenth centuries showed an extensive area as subject to slave and Indian revolts, and that of the Industrial Revolution in Britain includes strikes.[17]

Support for Russian territorial ambitions was reflected in the map of eighteenth-century Siberia which presented the Amur valley as belonging to nobody, rather than the Chinese control that the Russians had been forced to accept in the 1689 Treaty of Nerchinsk.[18]

For the nineteenth century the atlas presented an even more intensive degree of popular agitation, as with the maps of Europe in 1789–1871 and 1815–47 and of the world in 1789–1871. There were detailed maps of the Mainz Republic of 1793, an untypical episode of German radicalism, and of the rising of Parisian workers in 1848. The German revolution of 1848–49 was shown as very widespread, the map of western Europe in 1850–70 displayed strikes, Fenians, Spanish radicalism and anti-Bonapartist action in France, that of the *Risorgimento* included the popular risings of 1859–60 and the map of Germany in 1850–71 depicted radical agitation there. For

France in 1871 there was not only a map of the Paris Commune, but also one of other places in France affected by revolutionary activity.[19] The life and work of Marx and Engels and the development of left-wing organizations were also mapped.[20]

A similar agenda was maintained for the extra-European world. The map of the world in 1871 was itself interesting as it included African states; as had *Povijesni Atlas* (Zagreb, 1971), with its map of the global economy. That of South America showed slave, Indian, peasant and worker agitation; the Taipang, Boxer and 1911 risings were also mapped in the case of China; worker risings were recorded in Japan; anti-colonial uprisings in Africa and violent responses to European expansion in the Middle East and North Africa; the Madhist movement in the Sudan, the Young Turks and action in Persia. The stress throughout was on the response to colonialism, as much as on colonialism itself.[21]

Thus the extra-European world served to parallel the two major sources of confrontation in the 'first' world: the struggle for social justice as shown in strikes and other activity in Russia, Germany, Britain and North America,[22] and the battle for national independence, as depicted for example in the Balkans, where the struggle against the Turks in 1875–78 was seen as a people's war, and partisan activity in 1875–76 was mapped, as well as the more conventional military moves by Russia.[23]

Though tendentious, the atlas contained much of value. Much that it mapped was not treated in, for example, West German historical atlases. Furthermore, some of the mapping was imaginative. The social structure in 1900 of Chemnitz, a German industrial town, and of Potsdam, a garrison town, were both mapped.[24]

The second volume also reflected Communist views. There was much mapping of Soviet developments and a clear-cut view of the rest of the world. German Communist activity was covered extensively, as was resistance to the Nazi regime. This was presented as continuing during the war, so that the post-war East German regime was given an anti-Fascist pedigree that accorded with an important strand in German history. Anti-imperial struggles elsewhere, for example in Africa and Latin America, were mapped, as was the concentration of capital and social tension in interwar Britain, France and America.

American aggression and intervention was emphasized in the mapping of the post-war world, for example in China, Korea and Cuba. The map of the Chinese Civil War also depicted popular anti-Kuomintang activism in southern China, so that the Communist triumph did not appear as resting on conquest. Maps of Britain, Canada, France, Germany, Italy and the USA between 1945 and 1970 emphasized class conflict. Thus, for the USA strikes and anti-war demonstrations were both presented as aspects of a wider crisis.

To celebrate the 200th anniversary of the foundation of the firm of Justus Perthes, VEB Hermann Haack, again in validating association with the Zentralinstitut für Geschichte der Akademie der Wissenschaften, in 1985 published a third volume, designed to cover the period up to 1980, the *Atlas zur Zeitgeschichte* (contemporary history). The atlas offered some historical context, beginning with maps of the world in 1923, the Second World War and 1980. They distinguished between Socialist, i.e. Communist, imperialist/capitalist and independent states. Nevertheless, the mapping was essentially contemporary, presenting the Communist powers as successfully advancing the cause of peace in the face of the aggressive policies of their rivals. The military, especially nuclear, strength of the latter was depicted in detail, whereas the Warsaw Bloc was presented as a force for peace.

Historical atlases played a role in the Soviet school history curriculum. Soviet historical atlases had an agenda that reflected Communist ideology and a positive view of Russian power. They were concerned mainly with expansion of the Russian and Soviet states (often characterized as 'voluntary' or 'fraternal union' or even reunion), economic development (locations of factories, industries, etc.), class struggle (with regions 'enveloped' by peasant and worker disturbances), the location of underground Communist cells and printing presses and the life of Lenin. Soviet historical atlases therefore reflected the strengths of Soviet historiography – concern to highlight social and economic as well as political history, regional history as well as developments at the centre, but more so the weaknesses: the limitations imposed by the narrow and rigid official ideology combined with Russocentrism. This led to ahistorical perceptions and often exaggerations of what they took to be developments in the 'forces of production' and manifestations of 'class struggle'. Far too much attention was devoted to Lenin and the Bolsheviks, with the assumption that all history was building up to their inevitable victory in the Great October Socialist Revolution. Soviet historical mapping of the revolution was therefore particularly limited.

In general, Soviet historical atlases and maps in monographs and textbooks were good on details for a limited range of subjects, but not as interesting as the broader scope and sweep of, for example, the *Times Atlas of World History*.

Soviet historical atlases were naturally under state control, and this control was very tight.[25] This reflected both the military aspects of cartography and belief in its ideological value. Lenin had pointed out that visual aids, including maps, could be important for political education.[26] This was particularly so as literacy levels were low. Visual aids were used to portray Soviet propaganda and maps can be seen alongside posters, murals and cinema trains as part of the strongly visual nature of interwar didacticism. The role of central control was such that standardization in presentation and style was taken further than under the Nazis.

The major Soviet interwar atlas, the *Bolshoi Sovetskii Atlas Mira* (Great Soviet world atlas) (Moscow, 1937–39), established the principal cartographic themes. It offered clear-cut contrasts and teleology: a conflict between the 'world of conquering Socialism' and that of 'dying and decaying capitalism'. Historical cartography also served to demonstrate the process. Thus the atlas included maps of the Russian economy in 1913 and 1935 in order to indicate the pace of industrialization.[27] The first Soviet historical atlas was Konstantin V. Kudriashov's *Russkii Istoricheskii Atlas* (Russian historical atlas) (Moscow, 1928). It was clearly different from its predecessor, Egor Zamyslolvskii's *Uchebnyi Atlas po Russkoi Istorii* (Student atlas for Russian history) (St Petersburg, 1887), because it not only contained more maps – 58 instead of sixteen – but because it also had an economic emphasis in accordance with Communist views on history.

The Second World War was followed by the publication of the longest Russian historical atlas hitherto, the *Atlas Istorii SSSR dlia srednei shkoly* (Historical atlas of the USSR for high schools) (3 vols, Moscow, 1949–54). This was an attractive atlas, making extensive use of colour. The emphasis was very much on the Communist interpretation of history and on more recent history. One volume, the last to be published, containing 27 maps, covered the period to 1700, another, with 21 maps, covered 1700–1900, the third, with 52 maps, tackled 1900 to 1950. Unsurprisingly, in the aftermath of the Second World War, much of the mapping was of military campaigns. Thus, for example, there was a detailed map of Ivan IV's campaigns in the eastern Baltic in 1558–83, and another of Peter the Great's campaigns. The Russian operations in France in 1813–14 were depicted, the map of the Crimean War included Russian campaigns in the Caucasus and Balkans and there was a detailed map of Russia's advance in central Asia. The Second World War was extensively covered and episodes such as the Russian clash with Japan in 1939 and the Russo-Finnish war were mapped.[28] The Soviets had a very strong tradition of military mapping, including extremely informative and dynamic wall charts of the Second World War and component operations.

In the *Atlas Istorii SSSR* the radical pedigree was presented with, for example, detailed maps of the Decembrist uprising of 1825 and a map of Communist travels and activities including Lenin's movements.[29] The benefits of Communism were also presented with, for example, maps of interwar industrial expansion and improvements in communications.[30]

Other Soviet atlases of the 1950s similarly adopted the Communist agenda, the sole agenda that could be adopted. Thus the *Atlas Istorii Srednyth Vekov* (Atlas of the history of the Middle Ages) (Moscow, 1952), which in fact covered European history up to 1648, did not ignore economic history. There was a double-page map of the medieval economy.[31] Popular movements and risings were covered with, for example, maps of the Hussites, the German Peasants' War of 1524–25, English agrarian risings in 1549 and 1607 and the Dutch revolt. The last map in the atlas, devoted to the mid-seventeenth century crisis, showed the rebellions of the 1640s.[32] In general, the extent and importance of popular risings were exaggerated in order to serve the notion of class war.

It is of course easy to draw attention to questionable emphases, but it is also worth noting the degree to which Soviet works differed from their conventional western European counterparts by devoting more attention to Eastern Europe. Thus, the Atlas of the history of the Middle Ages included maps of seventh- to tenth-century Bulgaria, tenth- to eleventh-century Russia, a good map of the southern and eastern Baltic in the twelfth to fourteenth centuries and maps of the campaigns of the Times of Troubles and the Ukraine in 1648–51.

Similarly, the *Atlas Istorii Geograficheskikh Otkrytii i Issledovanii* (Historical atlas of geographical discoveries of Russia) (Moscow, 1959), an atlas of exploration, provided much information on Russian explorers whose journeys were ignored in Western historical atlases. This was particularly so with Russian exploration in Asia, northern Siberia and the northern Pacific in the seventeenth to nineteenth centuries, all of which were covered extensively. Thus, there were good maps of eighteenth-century Russian exploration in the north Pacific and Arctic and of Russian expeditions into Sinkiang.[33] Raids and missions for plunder, such as that of Yermak in Siberia in 1581–84, were treated as 'exploration'. The atlas also reflected Communist views in making it clear that European exploration did not impact on an empty world. Thus, African states were depicted in maps covering the exploration of the continent.[34] The second edition of the volume of the Soviet school historical atlas covering the twentieth century, published in 1959, included a big map of new industrial activity in 1928–40.[35] It was less problematic to depict industrialization than collectivization.

Yet, there were also serious inaccuracies in Soviet historical cartography. Thus, the map 'Growth of the Russian State up to the end of the Eighteenth Century', published in the textbook *Istorii SSSR dlia 8-ogo klassa* (History of the USSR, pt 1, for eighth class) (Moscow, 1957), depicted 'lands lost to China by the Treaty of Nerchinsk, 1689', an entry in the key that should rather have read 'regained by China' or 'acknowledged as Chinese' (due to the rigorous censorship process, Soviet works rarely contained printing errors), omitted the Kalmyks of the lower Volga and marked the Chukchis of north-eastern Siberia as under Russian control, which was not the case. The map of the situation in 1689–1800 published in *Istorii SSR dlia 9-ogo klassa* (History of the USSR, pt 2, for ninth class) (Moscow, 1957) included, besides these faults, Kamchatka as Russian under Peter the Great when it was only under limited control, and a dubious frontier line for the Altai, exaggerating gains under Catherine II. The flame device in the map in the same atlas for Russia in 1800–61 exaggerated the seriousness and extent of opposition. The impact of such maps was increased by the very rigid nature of the Soviet national curriculum: every school was supposed to teach the same thing to the same class at the same time.

The Soviet school historical atlas published in 1960–63 also emphasized the range of popular agitation as in the map of the peasant uprising in the 1660s and 1670s and that of nineteenth-century disorder.[36] There were detailed maps of Petrograd (St Petersburg) and Moscow in 1917[37] and the map for the first stage of the Russian civil war opposed red to black and brown arrows; the former were more dynamic.[38] The impact of Communism was revealed in a map showing how a small area changed, especially with alterations in control over the land.[39]

An emphasis on Russian territorial interests was maintained in Soviet historical atlases. Thus, in the *Atlas Istorii SSSR, 7-oi klass* (Atlas of the history of the USSR, seventh class) (Moscow, 1982) the late-medieval formation of the Russian state was depicted in terms of the 'struggle of the Russian people for overthrow of the Mongol-Tatar yoke'.[40] Russian gains were presented in part in terms of assimilation, as in western Siberia in the second half of the sixteenth century, and Kamchatka, Sakhalin and the southern bank of the Amur in the seventeenth century. The latter map also wrongly included the Chukchis and Tuva in Russia and made no mention of the Treaty of Nerchinsk.[41] It was not therefore surprising that the volume for the eighth class published that year made no mention of the annexation of the Amur in the nineteenth century:[42] the longevity of Russian control was therefore exaggerated. The volume for the ninth and tenth classes, also published that year, omitted the native peoples in its map of Socialist construction in the USSR in 1926–40.[43] This was a reversal of the Soviet mapping of, for example, Africa, which made it clear that imperialism did not operate in a vacuum.

Communist ideology and traditional territorial interests also affected the historical maps produced by the non-Russian republics within the Soviet Union. This was seen in the case of the republics of the Caucasus. Armenian historical maps tended to show Armenia at its periods of greatest expansion. The first Armenian historical atlas was published under the Communists: *Atlas hay žotovrdi patmut yan* (Atlas of the history of the Armenian people) (Yerevan, 1952). It was by the distinguished Armenian historical geographer Suren Eremyan (1908–93) and was intended for use in Soviet high schools. Eremyan also produced a large number of Armenian historical wallmaps and most of the historical maps that accompanied the official history of Armenia and that appeared in the Soviet Armenian encyclopedia. A different impression of Armenian power and history was presented by the historical maps in the *Atlas Gruzinskoi SSR* (Atlas of the Georgian SSR), produced by the Georgian Academy of Science (Tbilisi/Moscow, 1964). These maps have been reproduced in French in *Histoire de la nation géorgienne* by K. Salia (Paris, 1980). They did not show Armenia at its periods of greatest expansion.

The content and coverage of Soviet historical atlases changed little during the period of Communist rule. A heavily didactic note continued to be struck. For example, the *Atlas Istorii SSSR* (Historical atlas of the USSR) (Moscow, 1990) for fifth-year students carried maps with rousing titles such as 'Struggle of the peoples of our country against alien aggressors in the thirteenth century'. This depicted resistance to the Teutonic Knights and to the Mongols, the latter interestingly shown as invading what was in 1989 Soviet Central Asia as well as European Russia. The very first map addressed the presence of 'southern', 'western' and 'eastern' Slavs, with pictures of marauding horsemen to the south-east, but has neither caption, nor shading nor even pictures to suggest that there was any inward movement from the north, only a ship to show trade routes through the Baltic. This was an instance of the practice in Soviet historical atlases of consistently defending the ideologically based and factually inaccurate 'anti-Normanist' line on the foundations of the Rus state. Instead of accepting that Scandinavian raiders/traders/conquerors in effect created the Rus state by subduing scattered Slav tribes, the Soviets had to create a myth which fitted their nationalist and ideological prejudices. They emphasized a largely mythical organic rise in Slav self-awareness and thus statehood in the pre-Kievan era.[44]

A defeat of the Mongols in 1380 near the river Don was shown as the product of the united action of Russians, while the map of the seventeenth century carried an unsympathetic picture of Cossacks attacking peasants. The Pugachev rising was prominently displayed in the map of the eighteenth century and the peasantry were shown as taking a major role against Napoleonic invasion in the 'patriotic war' of 1812. In the maps of the Second World War in Russia and eastern Europe, heroic symbols were used for the Russians in retreat, but not for their German counterparts.[45]

Historical atlases were seen as part of a wider whole that encompassed both Communist ideology, especially historical materialism, and a view of Russia's role in the world; not as a specialized form of literature. Maps and atlases were intended to help create Soviet men and women.

Yet there were changes in Communist historical cartography, and there were differences between some of the historical atlases of the 1980s and their predecessors. In Hungary the Kádár regime became less autocratic and in 1985 a new and larger edition of *Történelmi Atlasz* (Historical atlas) appeared. This included, along with such new maps as the Cuban revolution and the Vietnam wars, a two-page map of Hungary in the second half of the nineteenth century, when it was very much part of the Habsburg system, as well as maps about the dissolution of the Austro-Hungarian monarchy and the aggrandizement of Hungary in the Second World War. Most of the maps were political, but they were better quality and less biased than those in the 1961 atlas and the red star on the cover was replaced by a painting from a Greek vase and pictures of a ship and a Hungarian civil aeroplane.

Nasza Ojczyzna (Our fatherland) (Wroclaw, 1981–82) presented an heroic account of the Polish past and for 1939 showed both the German and the Russian invasions. The map of the liberation of Poland stressed the role of the Poles, rather than the Russians, and that of Poles fighting the Germans in the Second World War in Europe depicted the activities of Poles who had not been under Communist control.[46]

Dějepisný Atlas 6 (Historical atlas) (Prague, 1982) included maps of Europe that made Russia appear marginal. It also carried maps of the Czech cultural tradition – Gothic, Renaissance and Baroque Czechoslovakia with inset maps for Prague that contrasted with the earlier emphasis on socio-economic issues. Furthermore, most of the sites indicated were palaces, churches and monasteries, suggesting that the social elite and the Church had played a major role in developing and sustaining cultural activity.[47]

Peasant uprisings, such as that in Bohemia in 1775, were of course still indicated, and the map of Europe in 1920–39 in *Dějepisný Atlas 7* (Historical atlas) (Prague, 1982) showed the activity of the Czech International Brigade in the Spanish Civil War, but these atlases were very different in tone from those that could be more accurately described as Cold War. Thus the map of Europe 1914–20 in the 7 volume made no reference to social discontent in, for example, Red Clydeside, while that of Europe 1815–1914 was a long way in its limited depiction of radicalism[48] from the East German *Atlas zur Geschichte*. The 6 volume closed not with the triumph of the proletariat, but with a map of Czech vernacular architecture.

There was therefore a measure of variety and development in European Communist historical cartography; its non-European counterpart will be considered later in the chapter on non-European historical atlases. Communist historical atlases played an important role in widening the agenda of political maps away from simply territorial control and in directing attention to socio-economic issues. However, they became somewhat repetitive and derivative in their contents, and mapping that had seemed biased but interesting in the 1950s appeared far less promising in the 1980s, especially as Western historical cartography had become more varied and visually interesting in the meantime.

In the latter period radical atlases began in the West, and sought to use issues of relative wealth and health, armaments and environmental concerns in order to criticize Western states and aspects of their societies.[49] Though *Marxisante* at times, they were not Marxist in any strict sense. It remains to be seen whether a Western radical historical cartographical tradition will develop. There are a few signs. In *The New State of War and Peace* (London, 1991), Michael Kidron and Dan Smith provided a survey of the 1980s that used maps. Some of the mapping was innovative, for example the map of war space as a multiple of the biosphere,[50] an index of potential destructiveness. It is possible that a radical mapping will develop based on the notion that radical opinions are most fittingly expressed on maps that are not only cheap, but also look cheap, i.e. crude and ugly, in order to subvert conventional notions of cartographic content. Nevertheless, such signs are still limited. Until then, however problematic they were, it will be the Communist historical atlases that will serve as reminders that the traditional agenda of historical atlases had grave limitations.

Against Communism

Few historical atlases during the post-war period were produced in accordance with a coherent ideology and in as didactic a fashion as the Communist examples. Yet, albeit from differing political positions, there were historical atlases that sought to foster an anti- or non-Communist viewpoint. Propaganda elements were readily apparent in Iwo Pogonowski's *Poland. A Historical Atlas* (New York, 1987), a work devoted to demonstrating that a free Poland was essential for European civilization. The acknowledgments and the plaudits on the back cover helped to establish the alignment of the book. They included Zbigniew Brzezinski, National Security Advisor under President Carter, and Richard Pipes, Director of East European and Soviet Affairs in the National Security Council 1981–82, both opponents of Soviet power, and Ian Nowak, National Director of the Polish American Congress and former Director of the Polish section of Radio Free Europe.

Pogonowski presented Poland as a country that was praiseworthy in itself and crucial to the fate of Europe, 'the middle ground of Europe'. He emphasized the democratic aspects of Polish history, and was also concerned to refute allegations of anti-Semitism,[51] a serious charge in the USA. A series of maps presented Poland as the crucial frontier of Western civilization, its shield and bastion, and, in the interwar period, the main barrier against Communism.[52] The multiple pressures of the 'vultures' – German, Russian, Swedish, and Turkish aggression – were a repeated theme. There was no need to share the susceptibility towards Russia of the Communist Polish historical atlases. Thus, it was possible on the map of Poland in 1480 to write of the 'maturity of Muscovy political engineering, a beginning of a 500-year tradition of empire building by coercion, deportations and despotism'.[53]

Pogonowski used black and white maps with didactic titles and captions and text in boxes on the maps. For example, a frequent theme in Polish historical atlases, the battle of Tannenberg (Grunwald, 1410) was presented as 'Defeat of the aggression by German Monastic State against Poland and Lithuania'. The box included praise of the Poles and a complaint about the views of the Western Europeans, a frequent theme in the atlas: 'Pontoon bridge prefabricated earlier by the Poles for a surprise crossing of the Vistula River was a technological feat of medieval military engineering . . . Teutonic Order escaped the full consequences of the crushing defeat thanks to Western support obtained by deceitful propaganda covering up the crimes of the Brethren.'[54]

Pogonowski took pains to emphasize a heroic and praiseworthy past as a suitable backdrop to more recent history. Thus, for example, there were battle plans of Polish victories at Orsha (1514) and Obertyn (1531) not otherwise depicted in historical atlases.[55] No fewer than four maps were devoted to Sobieski's relief of Vienna in 1683. However, in part such mapping continued a long-standing refusal by all too many of the peoples of Eastern Europe to face up to the fact that their 'nations' had been their own worst enemies. In the case of Poland there has been no mapping of the use of the *liberum veto* by which attempts at reform were thwarted. The *veto* was a more important part of Polish-Lithuanian history than battles such as Tannenberg and Vienna. Victories such as Orsha and Obertyn, which are rarely heard about, arguably deserve their obscurity because the 'victors' were unable to take advantage of them. Battle plans enabled Communists and anti-Communists to find common nationalist ground.

Aside from his views on international relations, Pogonowski advanced his opinions on Poland's domestic position, preferring what he termed the 'Jagiellonian' concept of Poland as the leader of a multinational federation between Germany and

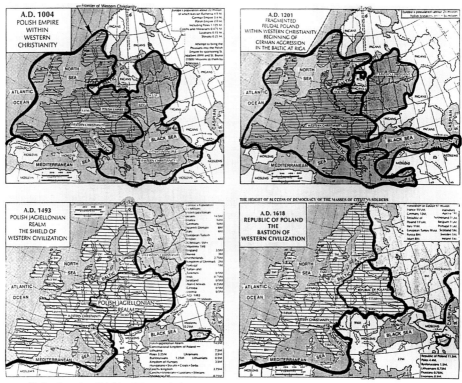

33. 'Poland as the Shield of Europe' from Iwo Pogonowski's *Poland. A Historical Atlas* (New York, 1987). Successive maps presented Poland as an integral and necessary part of Europe.

34. Keeping the Russians at bay. This map allows Pogonowski to suggest a modern arrangement that gives Poland a place in Europe.

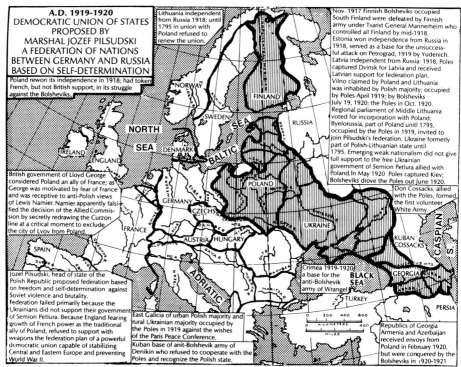

Russia to the 'Piast' concept of an ethnic Polish state.[56] Pogonowski also favoured democracy over magnate oligarchy.

The heroic account of the Polish role in saving Vienna and therefore Christendom in 1683 was matched by another of the similar role of the Poles in blocking the Red Army in 1919–20. This stretched over sixteen maps, and provided an opportunity for Pogonowski to second-guess history.[57] A map of the 'Democratic Union of States' proposed by Marshal Pilsudski, a federation of nations between Germany and Russia based on self-determination, was printed with a caption explaining its failure in terms of a lack of Ukrainian and British support leading to a vacuum that encouraged the onset of the Second World War.[58]

The military-political emphasis of the atlas was indicated by the fact that only two maps were devoted to the interwar period before Pogonowski turned to his account of the 1939 invasions by Germany and Russia; in it he severely criticized Anglo-French inaction. His interesting might-have-been mapping led him to depict Sikorski's 1942 Confederation plan for a pro-Western federation along Russia's western border, a scheme that he presented as having been betrayed by the USA.[59] Titles on individual maps were clear-cut, for example '1944–1947. Civil War and Gigantic Deportations, the People's Poland'.[60]

Garbis Armen's *Historical Atlas of Armenia* (New York, 1987) was a shorter work, intended in part for school use, also produced in an anti-Communist diaspora. Although it did not present Armenia as the saviour of the West, it likewise sought to emphasize the continuity of Armenia and to stress its importance. Published by the Armenian National Education Committee, the atlas was scarcely a Communist work, but it shared with Communist Armenian historical cartography a concern to extend Armenian territoriality, unsurprisingly so not least because Armen, an architect, did not seek to develop any original cartography. Thus Armen's work exaggerated the Armenian nature of north-east Anatolia.[61] The absence of a distinct diaspora version of Armenian historical cartography was further emphasized by Gary Poghosyan's *Hayasdani Badmutiun Kardesnerov* (History of Armenia in maps) (Burbank, 1995). Thirteen of the fourteen maps were based on those by Suren Eremyan in works such as the *Soviet Armenian Atlas* (Yerevan, 1961) and the *Soviet Armenian Encyclopedia* (Yerevan, 1974–90).

Ivan Tesla, Evhen Tiut'ko and Lubomyr Wynr produced a *Historical Atlas of Ukraine* that was published by the Ukrainian Historical Association in Montreal, New York and Munich in 1980. The atlas included maps of Ukraine when its extent had been considerable and also a map of Ukrainian lands in 1815–1914 that indicated a far-flung Ukrainian presence. Paul Magocsi's *Ukraine: A Historical Atlas* (Toronto, 1985) was another product of the diaspora, in this case of the large number of Canadians strongly conscious of their Ukrainian descent. Magocsi was from 1980 Professor of Ukrainian Studies in the University of Toronto and the atlas owed much to the generosity of Peter Jacyk, a Canadian Ukrainian who wished to commemorate 'the beginning of the second millenium of Christianity in Ukraine-Rus with this cartographic survey of three millennia of Ukrainian history'.[62]

Although Magocsi himself was suspect to some Ukrainian nationalists – because in his *Rusyn-Ukrainians of Czechoslovakia* (Vienna 1983) he had minimized the Ukrainian nature of Trans-Carpathia and Prešov, instead seeing its people as Rusyns (Ruthenians) – his atlas was not a Communist work, although it was nowhere near as anti-Communist as Pogonowski's *Poland. A Historical Atlas*. The inside flap of the

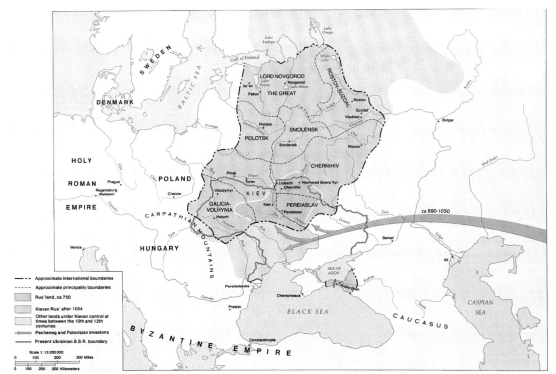

35. 'Kievan Rus' in the Eleventh Century' from Paul Magocsi's *Ukraine: A Historical Atlas* (Toronto, 1985). The history of Kievan Rus' was a matter of controversy in Russian, Soviet and Ukrainian works. Magocsi was careful to note that boundaries were approximate. His inclusion of the then modern Ukrainian boundary provided a frame of reference that could be employed by readers searching for historical parallels or seeking to assert territorial claims.

cover carried a clearly partisan statement by George Demko of the US State Department: 'A beautiful, valuable, and all too rare historical atlas of a suppressed region and people.' Magocsi's emphasis was on the continuity of the Ukraine and it was treated both as a country and as the area occupied by Ukrainians rather than simply the present-day Ukraine, then the Ukrainian Soviet Socialist Republic. In his preface he stated that 'Like most other countries, Ukraine has experienced varying periods of political discontinuity. This means that, like Belgium, Poland, Italy, or Germany, for instance, Ukraine might not have existed in its present form, or even as a concept during long periods in the past. Yet, the histories of those countries from earliest times according to their present-day boundaries – and Ukraine is no exception – are legitimate subjects of study.'[63] Thus Ukraine (not *the* Ukraine in Magocsi's book) was compared to other countries that were independent of Russia.

In contrast to Pogonowski, Magocsi was careful to draw his readers' attention to lacunae in the evidence and was particularly cautious in describing large medieval polities as if they were like modern states. Thus, the map of Kievan Rus' in the eleventh century marked its boundaries as 'approximate' and the facing page of text noted:

> Like most medieval political entities, Kievan Rus' was not a unified state in the modern sense of the term, but rather a loosely knit group of principalities. Consider-ing its political nature, neither the boundaries of the realm as a whole nor those of its

individual principalities should be considered as definitive or fixed at any one period of time as the visual effect of historic maps would suggest. Rather, these boundaries might more appropriately be viewed as the farthest extent of a sphere or spheres of influence radiating from one or more centers of authority. Not surprisingly, these spheres of influence often overlapped, and they were continually expanding and contracting, depending on the ability of rulers at the center to enforce their authority over the inhabitants.[64]

Magocsi's comment is appropriate to many periods and countries, but all-too-few historical atlases juxtapose maps with such warnings or label their boundaries as approximate.

The need for unity and strength was a lesson that readers could take from this as from many other historical atlases. For example, the collapse of Galicia-Volhynia in the fourteenth century was traced to internal dissension and external intervention.[65]

Magocsi's treatment of the twentieth century lacked the anti-Communist diatribes of Pogonowski. Sufferings at the hands of the Soviets, especially during the 1930s, were ignored or minimized. In part this was because the twentieth century was presented as the latest stage of a centuries-old process of external pressure. It may also have reflected a contrast in age and circumstances. Born in 1921, Pogonowski left Poland. Magocsi was born in Englewood, New Jersey, in 1945. V. Daugirdaite-Sruogiene's *Lietuvos Istorija* (History of Lithuania) (Chicago, 1956) contained only few and simple maps, but they presented Lithuania when it was powerful and far-flung. Roman Pavlovčič's *Zgodovinski Atlas Slovenije* (1960) was published by the Slovenian Cultural Centre in Buenois Aires. It was not explicitly propagandist but was a reminder of Slovene identity.

Conservatism

Magocsi's was a diaspora atlas centring on national consciousness rather than anti-Communism. In contrast to the extensive Communist historical cartography, there has been relatively little explicitly anti-Communist historical cartography since the Second World War. There is no coherent body of literature to turn to in looking for an active conservatism in the content (rather than method) of historical atlases. The depiction of the less attractive aspects of the history of Communist states can be seen as anti-Communist or in a more 'objective' light. For example, the map of anti-Russian activity in the Soviet zone of Germany on 17 June 1953 published in the *Grosser Historischer Weltatlas* (Munich, 1957) both depicted events that occurred and in showing such activity as very widespread[66] presented the Communist nature of Soviet-occupied East Germany as un-German.

The historical cartography produced in 'right-wing' states was more obviously conservative. This was true, for example, of both Portugal and Spain. The second edition of the *Atlas de Portugal* by Aristides de Amorim Girão, Professor of Geography at Coimbra (Coimbra, 1959) included as a prologue a section on how Portugal was 'born' and 'spread over the world' that had not been in the first edition (1940). The preface to the second edition, published in facing columns in English and Portuguese, expounded the Portuguese theory of colonialization:

The second edition of the *Atlas of Portugal*, whilst still addressed to the author's countrymen, has a special purpose: to make better known to foreigners a country which many people still regard as merely a Spanish province ... There are also many fallacies concerning the geography of Portugal – alike of Portugal at home and of Portugal overseas – circulating in foreign books. For some minds are still influenced by mistaken ideas of colonialism and are unable to understand how a nation may be a complete entity although dispersed throughout the world without continuous land boundaries.

Portugal was described as a nation 'whose lot it was to fulfil an exploratory and civilising mission without equal' and cartography was seen to have a role in showing 'the organic whole that ... overseas provinces ... form with the Mother Country':

the cartographical presentation of certain little-known facts will perhaps help towards a better understanding of how these different plots of land are, finally, just so many other members of a huge national organisation with a maritime base, which, in obedience to an essentially Christian and humanitarian idea of unity, and in the geo-political realisation of the evangelical mandate, Euntes in mundum universum, struck deep roots in the soil of four continents.[67]

The section on 'How Portugal was born' consisted of nine maps mostly devoted to the *Reconquistā*. The facing text ended: 'Portugal thus comes into being; and its worldwide missionary call is immediately confirmed in St Anthony of Lisbon (1190–1231) ... making his voice heard over nearly the whole of Europe, as may be seen by the journeys he undertook.' These were depicted on map nine. Portugal's historic Christian mission was further revealed in the five maps and facing text of the section 'How Portugal spread over the World'. The fourth map directly compared the Lisbon of sixteenth-century overseas exploration to Classical Rome. The map depicted Roman roads and Portuguese maritime routes. The fifth map showed the journeys of St Francis Xavier, a Spaniard in Portuguese service, who 'typified ... the great missionary and civilising activity of Portugal'.

As ever with cartography, especially historical cartography, the lacunae were most instructive. There were no maps of Portuguese conquests in Africa or Brazil: the empire was presented as natural and organic, not as the consequence of conquest.

The *Atlas Historico Español* by Gonzalo Menendez Pidal (Madrid, 1941) has already been discussed.[68] It remained important after the Second World War, although the Catalan historian J. Vicens Vives produced a more vivid historical atlas under the title *Atlas y sintesis de Historia de España* (Barcelona, 1944, and in many editions since).[69] Due to the Franco regime, Vicens Vives had to be cautious in what he tackled politically, but his atlas eventually covered crucial episodes of Spanish disunity – the Carlist and the Spanish Civil Wars – and was more willing than Gonzalo Menendez Pidal to present Spanish history in its European context. There were also no maps of the travels of saints in his atlas.

An important aspect of conservatism outside Europe was the use of the atlases of colonial powers in their colonies and the production by these powers of atlases of their colonies. Thus, for example, the Spanish government and the Spanish Instituto de Estudios Africanos co-operated to produce the *Atlas Histórico y Geográfico de Africa Española* (Madrid, 1955). The situation in South Africa was a variant, in that atlases

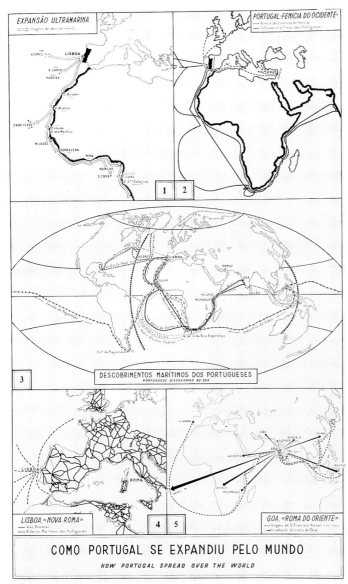

36. 'How Portugal Spread over the World' from *Atlas de Portugal* by Aristides de Amorim Girão (2nd edn, Coimbra, 1959). This curious map suggests that Lisbon had taken over Rome's role and that the Portuguese base Goa was the Rome of the East.

produced for the minority white population necessarily served the entire country. In South-West Africa (now Namibia), which had become a mandated territory administered by South Africa after the First World War, a national atlas incorporating a historical section was edited by J.H. van der Merwe and published in 1983. Sponsored by the Administrator General of South West Africa, it was published in matching columns of English and Afrikaans; no native language was used. The historical section did not ignore the precolonial period, but its emphasis scarcely subverted the existing political situation. The text accompanying maps 37, 38 and 39, which dealt with settlement in 1921 and 1937 and the Odendaal Plan for the country drawn up in 1962–63, emphasized government care for the 'general welfare' of the population and for 'tribal life'.

After the Fall of the Wall

The role of politics in the content of historical atlases was indicated by the changes that occurred in the 1980s and 1990s after the collapse of autocratic regimes in Iberia and Eastern Europe. Spanish historical atlases of the post-Franco period were more innovative in their cartography and bolder in their projections than their predecessors had been. Thus Juan Roig Obiol's *Atlas de Historia Universal y de España I, edades antiqua y media* (4th edn, Barcelona, 1992) and *II. edades moderna y contemporánea* (2nd edn, Barcelona, 1992) were striking works that compare well with non-Spanish counterparts. Africa and Asia received more attention and there was a map of nineteenth-century European Socialism and syndicalism. There was information on the Spanish parliamentary elections of 1931, 1933 and 1936 and a page on those of 1977, including details of the Basque and Catalan parliaments. In contrast to the views of the Franco regime, this atlas was not an overly centralized account of Spanish history. Similarly, the *Atlas Histórico. Edad moderna* (Madrid, 1986) of E. Martínez Ruiz, A. Gutíerrez Castillo and E. Díaz Lobon did not disguise the depth of the crisis in Spanish power in the seventeenth century. Due to state sponsorship via the education system, changes in the content of atlases provide a guide to shifts in the political system, for example towards provincial autonomy.

A similar liberation occurred in Eastern Europe. After the political changeover in 1989–90, a new edition of *Történelmi atlasz* appeared in Hungary in 1991. The cover depicted a medieval woodcut featuring János Hunyadi, a prince of Transylvania who had played a crucial role in resisting the Turkish advance in the 1440s and 1450s; an image of Christian Hungary resisting the heathen from the East. The maps of the Paris Commune and Hungarian workers' and peasants' movements disappeared, as did the global map showing Socialist countries as pink (not red), capitalist countries as blue and the Third World as yellow. In place of the four maps about the Russian Revolution in the 1985 edition, there were now only three, and all of them were smaller. A less didactic view was taken of the Second World War. The map entitled 'The Liberation of our Homeland 1944–1945' was now retitled 'Military Operations in Hungary 1944–1945'. New maps included 'Movements of Peoples 1939–1952', which showed how many Hungarians were carried off to Russia after 1945, a map of Hungary in the 1850s and one of Hungary between the world wars.

That year, 1991, also saw the publication of an Hungarian historical atlas for the general public: *Történelmi Világatlasz* (Historical world atlas). Clearly based on the example of the *Grosser Historischer Weltatlas*, this was a varied work, including maps on social movements and economic links and without obvious ideological or political bias. The new atlas, however, was concerned to tackle the contentious subject of Hungarian aggrandizement in 1938–41, when Hungary was allied to Nazi Germany, and did so by explaining Hungary's losses after the First World War. *Történelmi Világatlasz* emphasized the losses at the Treaty of Trianon (1920), and a subsequent map drew attention to the size of the Hungarian population in neighbouring countries after 1920: the cartography of *revanche*. There was still, however, the map of the 1956 anti-Communist rising. Lajos Pándi's *Köztes-Európa 1763–1993* (Budapest, 1995) is the most comprehensive historical atlas yet published on central and Eastern Europe. The scale of the work is a testimony to greater interest in mapping the region's history: the 798-page book includes over 300 full-page maps and numerous insets, leading to about 800 maps. Only 'European' Russia is included and the atlas does not present Russia as the necessary *deus ex machina* of European history or as a geopolitical equivalent of any inevitable triumph of the proletariat.

The changes in Eastern Europe at the end of the 1980s also allowed the region to play a role in the globalization of historical atlases. Western works circulated and some were translated. Donald Matthew's *Atlas of Medieval Europe*, for example, was translated into Hungarian.

The abandonment of Communism also allowed Eastern European historical atlases of the 1990s to adopt a more critical approach towards Russia. Thus, one of the global maps in *Történelmi Világatlasz* placed Russian, Cuban, Libyan, Indonesian and Indian military interventions in foreign countries after 1945 alongside those of the USA, Britain, France, South Africa, Israel, Argentina and Turkey; an arresting map. *Atlas Historyczny Świata* (Warsaw, 1992) included a map marking Polish prisoner-of-war camps in the Soviet Union after the Nazi-Soviet pact, a map that included the site of the Soviet massacre of Polish prisoners at Katyn, and maps and plans that made the role of Free Polish forces during the Second World War clear. The map of territorial changes of the Polish state that had concluded the standard Communist Polish historical atlas was dropped. The post-Communist Lithuanian secondary school historical atlas, *Mokyklinis Visuotines Istorijos Atlasas* (Vilnius, 1993) was able to depict Lithuanian greatness in the later Middle Ages – again covering part of the later Soviet Union, while the map of Europe in 1939–41 placed Soviet and Nazi gains in the same image. *The Concise Atlas of the Republic of Croatia and of the Republic of Bosnia and Hercegovina* (Zagreb, 1993), edited by Mladen Klemenčić, included a chapter on history supported by seven maps. The maps indicated periods when Croatia had had a measure of identity if not autonomy or independence and had been more extensive than under the Yugoslav republic, thus demonstrating the 'historically forced disjunction of the Croatian lands' referred to in the book's preface. *Atlas Historyczny dla klasy VII-VIII* (Warsaw, 1995) did not hesitate to map episodes of Russian aggression, including in 1939. There was a picture of Sikorski on the map dealing with the military role of expatriate Poles in the Second World War.

Liberalism and Selection

It would be easy to conclude the chapter at this point, to present bias and distortion as defeated, or at least in retreat, and then to press on, possibly in a teleological and optimistic fashion by discussing the post-war expansion in the number of topics covered and the future prospects offered by technological change. Yet it would be foolish to imagine that problems of bias arise only in totalitarian states. Selection is an issue in all historical atlases and the range of possible subjects for a general historical atlas is now greater than ever before. The Hungarian situation clearly displays from a political perspective what is readily apparent in states that have escaped the experience of totalitarianism: namely, that the historical agenda is far from constant.

In addition, it is necessary not to forget that historical atlases produced in the Western 'liberal' tradition have their own emphases and conventions of content and representation that can also be regarded as distorting. First, it is clear that a teleological approach to the past leads to an assessment of historical alignments in terms of progressive and reactionary; these can be highly misleading. Thus, for example,

Europe in 1848–52 was presented in simplistic terms of liberalism versus repression in *Atlas historique. Histoire de l'humanité. De la préhistoire à nos jours* (Paris, 1987).[70] This partisanship tended to support liberal movements in the nineteenth century and more left-wing ones in the twentieth. Thus, in his *Caribbean History in Maps* (London, 1979), Peter Ashdown claimed:

> Castro's Cuba was at first shunned by the organisation of American states, but his achievements have made his policies respected in many other West Indian states. Jamaica and Guyana are presently pursuing strong socialist policies in an effort to redistribute wealth and create greater social justice.[71]

The teleological approach in Western historical atlases is generally less politically obvious, partisan and tendentious, but a progressive ideology, nevertheless, was and is very common. This can be seen in atlases of world history. For example, the *Times Atlas of World History* (London, 1978) offered a clear, differentiated notion of civilization, one that was organic, readily separable from an uncivilized barbarian 'other', and open to spatial depiction. The spread on the commercial and cultural bonds of Eurasia was preceded by a section introduction that stated:

> By AD 100 . . . an unbroken zone of civilised life from the Atlantic to the Pacific . . . The area of civilisation was still narrow and exposed to unrelenting barbarian pressures, and development in the different regions was still largely autonomous; but with the expansion of the major civilisations and the elimination of the geographical gaps between them, the way was open for inter-regional contacts.[72]

The *Hamlyn Historical Atlas* (London, 1981) made it clear that the selection of maps was linked to a clear theme:

> the maps have been selected to present highlights of historical periods and to give the reader a broad view of human history as a whole . . . The theme we offer in this Atlas is simple and straightforward: humanity's gradual progress from isolated societies to a world that is rapidly becoming a single global community. More than in any other period of history people today are bound together in their political destinies and connected in an expanding network of communication. Distances between people have been bridged by the expansion of communities . . . Differences among people have been broken down by conquest, cooperation, the spread of universal religious and political ideals, and the rise of dominant civilizations. One has only to compare the maps of early scattered settlements with the maps of industrialized nations to see a graphic illustration of our basic theme.[73]

The notion of pattern and theme in the past is generally present. The nineteenth-century emphasis on national growth, the late nineteenth-century stress on environmentalism and the twentieth-century search for socio-economic development are all present in modern historical cartography, sometimes interdependent and related, though often separate. The depiction of pattern and theme is presented as having analytical and pedagogic value, as, for example, with the production of an historical map of the south-western USA:

setting forth . . . the essence of the American experience in map form attractive to and readily understandable by a broad readership. Our purpose is to provide a fresh perspective on the continuous and dynamic development of the United States emphasising a geographic interpretation of our history and focusing on how each region owes its special character to the changing human geography of its past and how the imprint of former inhabitants is often still there to be read in the landscape.[74]

Thus the notion of Western historical atlases as value-free is mistaken. The text may give vital clues to the values of the work, indeed is designed to do so in expounding and amplifying the analytical and pedagogical meaning of the maps. However, there is rarely precise guidance as to why particular topics have been included, or, more commonly, excluded. With every historical atlas it is possible to point to omissions or to suggest a different basis for compilation and then to speculate as to whether the choices reflect 'bias'. This is readily apparent on the global scale. The *Times Atlas of World History*, for example, largely ignores the history of Abyssinia/Ethiopia, Armenia, Georgia and Ireland,[75] although they are all important and their history is readily mappable.

Important lacunae can also be readily discerned in atlases that range less widely. *An Historical Atlas of Wales* by William Rees (Cardiff, 1951) did not map politics after the Civil War, Methodism and the rise of Labour. Its emphasis was thus on unity. The *Historical Atlas of Lincolnshire* edited by R.S. and N. Bennet (Hull, 1993) ignored post-1931 politics and unemployment trends. Possibly modern politics is seen as too contentious or at least divisive a topic for works that are supposed in some way to represent the unity of their subject. This must be a particular problem with works in receipt of public subsidy. *Addressing the Twentieth Century 1891–1961* edited by D. Kerr and D.W. Holdsworth (Toronto, 1990), the third volume of the *Historical Atlas of Canada*, failed to address post-war politics and such sensitive issues as the rise of Québecois separatism.

The nature of matching ideological standpoints is captured in J.M. Lambin and J.L. Villette's *Atlas des collèges* (Paris, 1993), when they depicted both 'La menace américaine vue de l'URSS' and 'La menace soviétique vue des États-Unis'. In the keys, the terms 'monde libre' and 'encerclées' were printed in inverted commas, a process of authorial distancing and commentary.[76] However, a greater awareness of the regional perspective is a distinguishing feature of Western historical cartography. It reflects the extent to which, in comparison with autocratic political systems, Western societies are far less centralized. Not only, therefore, is there greater interest in the regions, but funding and institutional independence also exist at that level.

It would be mistaken to imagine that the role of authorial choice can be discounted in the compilation and presentation of maps. Any schematic basis for the choice of contents that might limit such a role faces problems, and Armin Wolf's attempt to suggest one does not really proceed beyond generalities.[77] It can be seriously misleading to attempt to lessen the scope for authorial choice by having all maps drawn for a standard base and a regular sequence. For example, Paul Magocsi's valuable *Historical Atlas of East Central Europe* (Seattle, 1993) included eleven full-page maps showing 'the changing boundaries at certain key historical dates': *c.* 1050, *c.* 1250, *c.* 1480, *c.* 1570, 1648, *c.* 1721, 1815, 1910, 1918–23, *c.* 1950 and 1992, while the other maps, such as the Second World War, 1939–42, the Second World War,

1943–45, and east central Europe after the Second World War, have a similar effect. Such a scheme, with the authorial choice it reflects, could be replaced by maps at, for example, fifty-year intervals – 1750, 1800, 1850, 1900, 1950, or 1740, 1790, 1840, 1890, 1940, 1990, yet this limitation of authorial independence would gravely restrict the flow of information offered to the reader: the first would omit the two world wars and the impact of the Versailles settlement, the second the Napoleonic world and the Versailles settlement. Both the latter were short-lived, but this selection would seem remarkable to most readers and scholars. Similarly, periods of population growth or decline can be masked if particular intervals for mapping that emphasize contrary longer-term movements are chosen: scale is a matter of time as well as space.[78]

The teleological approach is misleading and can be readily shown to be thus. However, there are also problems with the historical cartography that appears to have no obvious teleological dimension. R.R. Palmer, a distinguished historian who was the editor of an important historical atlas of the 1960s, the *Rand McNally Atlas of World History* (New York, 1965), claimed that 'political facts such as the size of states, the location of boundaries, and the territorial changes brought about by wars and treaties, are the most susceptible of all historical facts to representation by mapping'.[79] This was in fact very much the view of a modern Europeanist, for there were and are major problems in locating and mapping boundaries, or what would be understood as boundaries in late twentieth-century terms, in medieval Europe and for most of history in many other parts of the world. Palmer exaggerated the importance of political borders in history. Even when they could be readily mapped, such a process would still omit much.

That was a problem with many Western post-war historical atlases, particularly in the 1950s and 1960s. They concentrated on issues of territoriality at the level of the state and international system and devoted less attention to issues of power that could be depicted spatially but that did not relate to this agenda. Thus, and in marked contrast to Communist historical atlases, relatively little attention was devoted to the political aspects of social relations in terms of spatial differentiation and rural and urban disaffection. Questions of choice recur and it is necessary to consider more broadly the contents of post-war historical atlases. However, before doing so in chapter nine and discussing the broader range, it is also important to direct attention to the greater number of countries that have historical atlases since 1945, particularly outside the 'first world', and to assess how far this led to change.

8

Remembered Histories

A less Eurocentric approach was a major feature of post-1945 historical cartography. This was true both of historical atlases produced in Europe and of those from other continents. The process can be examined in a number of ways. One is by considering the production of historical atlases, or atlases with historical sections, in countries that had hitherto lacked such works. Another is by assessing changes in the historical atlases produced outside Europe before and after 1945, in for example Canada.

Indigenous Peoples

A major aspect of recent criticism of historic (not historical) cartography was that it followed a course of ethnic cleansing. J.B. Harley claimed that cartography was 'a discourse of power', the silences of which commonly reflected minority or subject populations. Denis Wood complained that in 'mapping – but not mapmaking – peoples get lost in the process'. Harley supported his point by considering English expansion in New England. Helen Hornbeck Tanner commented that 'Maps of frontier areas conventionally showed newly established white towns and omitted long-existent Indian communities. Maps of military expeditions recorded the location of forts but not the Indian towns that were targets for attack. The successive sites of Indian communities seemed particularly elusive and difficult to trace.'[1] This thesis can be amplified by noting the chauvinist nature of Spanish mapping of the discoveries and conquest of the New World, and Russian mapping of their expansion in Siberia.

Yet there was also an important shift after the Second World War: growing interest in non-European peoples. The first volume of the three-volume *Historical Atlas of Canada: From the Beginning to 1800*, edited by R. Cole Harris (Toronto, 1987), reflected a determined attempt to engage with and map the history of Canada's non-European peoples. This was also related to the wider range of disciplines that some post-1945 historical atlases readily called upon. Archaeology played a major role in the Canadian atlas, and the prehistory section was not only visually arresting, but also offered interesting information not hitherto available in an historical atlas; although the fragmented nature of the evidence was a major problem. For example, archaeological data permitted only a partial picture of subsistence patterns in late prehistoric Canada. Furthermore, as a consequence of the difficulty of establishing locations and the absence of statistical series, maps concentrated on broad patterns of distribution, as in the map of ecological regions *c.* 1500, and routes of movement, as in the maps of native trade, warfare and epidemics in the St Lawrence Valley in the sixteenth century and the Great Lakes Basin in 1600–53.

The Maori

A Maori Committee was set up for the Centennial Historical Atlas planned in New Zealand from 1937 and *He Korero púrâkau mo; ngâ taunahanahatanga a ngâ túpuna/Place Names of the Ancestors. A Maori Oral History Atlas* (Wellington, 1990) was produced under the sponsorship of the Department of Survey and Land Information as part of the sesquicentennial. A Maori Committee was again established when work on a government-sponsored New Zealand historical atlas began again in 1990. A major section of the planned atlas is devoted to 'The world of the Maori': it will map for the thousand years before the arrival of Europeans the economic and social frame-work of Maori society, the record of migration, of encounter and of conflict and the related toponymy.

Major efforts have also been made to appreciate and communicate the Maori view of history. It is not simply that different events and places are mapped, but also that they reflect a specific view of the connectedness of the past and of the relationship of past and present. The *Maori Oral History Atlas* explained that many Maori names could only be understood through their connection to other names and places and that such connections commemorated historic events, such as journeys. Such group-ings relate therefore to stories; they are oral histories that can be cartographically depicted because they sought to explain and appropriate particular landscapes.[2]

The attempt to depict the experience of the colonized population from their perspective is easier in New Zealand than in most of the world. Colonization is relatively recent and much of the indigenous population survives. Maori oral history is very specific geographically, with great attention being devoted to the rivers, lakes and mountains of particular tribes, and the oral tradition is accessible, both from nineteenth-century European records and because it is still alive today. In addition, the large degree of cultural and complete linguistic homogeneity of the Maoris helps in bringing their history into the mainstream of the atlas.

Latin America

The situation is less favourable in, for example, Latin America, although differences in national sensitivity to indigenous peoples are also clearly a factor. This has obvious cartographic implications, as in the historical section of Mercedes Perena's *Atlas IberoAmericano* (Mexico City, 1991), a work published by the Mexican foreign ministry. Nevertheless, the *Atlas Historico de Chile* produced by the Chilean Institute of Military Geography (Santiago, 1992) devoted three of its 23 pages to the pre-Columbian situation. In contrast, the historical section in the *Atlas Historico-Geografico del Ecuador* (Quito, 1990), which was produced by the Institute of Military

Geography, was limited to text and maps relating to territorial disputes with neigh-bours. All the maps in the *Atlas del Ecuador* (Paris, 1982) edited by A.C. Delavaud show the 1830 and 1942 frontiers, a reminder of past losses and present claims.

Before criticizing the historical mapping of Latin America, by both Latin Ameri-cans and outsiders, for underrating the pre-Columbian era, it is necessary to draw attention to the problems of mapping the period. These are readily apparent with regions, such as Amazonia, where state structures were apparently absent. These areas receive very little attention in works such as the *Atlas of Ancient America* by M. Coe, D. Snow and E. Benson (Oxford, 1986). Hunting and gathering communities are poorly documented in the archaeological record, but the tropical lowlands of the Amazon basin had complex societies with intensive agriculture, large settlements and extensive chiefdoms.[3] Nevertheless, they are generally ignored in historical atlases. There are also problems with mapping regions where state structures were present; although historical cartography was not unknown. Early forms of Mesoamerican cartography depicted journeys and historical narratives and were used to explain pre-Spanish civilization and expansion to Spanish chroniclers.[4]

To take the case of the Incas, the first problem concerns the lack of indigenous writing in the region. All Inca history derives from oral accounts written down in the Spanish colonial era. Accordingly, the available accounts have gone through several filters: translation, cultural misunderstandings, differences in the conception of time and space between natives and Europeans. These points are clear, but there is also a debate over the degree to which the Inca versions of history told to the Spaniards provided a historical account that is trustworthy with respect to actors, events and sequences of events. The Incas treated their histories as statements of sociopolitical hierarchy and cosmology rather than as event-based histories;[5] a familiar situation in non-European cultures and, indeed, in medieval Christendom. Thus, histories were compressed, actions were invented and past acts were recast in terms of contemporaneous political power structures.

The Inca method of recording history was through the use of the *khipu* knotted cords. These mnemonic devices were apparently structured in such a way as to give geographic space priority over time in reporting events. Furthermore, different *khipu* accounts told to the Spaniards attributed the same conquests to different rulers. Spanish chroniclers complained about the variety of accounts that they were told, ostensibly about the same history. A specific myth and dynastic history affected the earliest of those accounts.[6] In addition, radiocarbon dates and the conventional Inca history, as synthesized by the chronicler Cabello Valboa and reworked by John Rowe,[7] do not accord. Carbon dates assign the empire at least twice the duration that the conventional history does.

It is difficult to reconstruct Inca history spatially as well as temporally. The Incas conquered areas by taking control of pockets of territory and repeatedly had to reconquer regions. Frontiers varied in nature considerably, as military, political, economic and cultural perimeters did not match well. It is awkward to record the control of societies in space under such circumstances, and the most recent work to deal with the problem in detail[8] is more expansive in its acceptance of Inca control than other studies.[9]

There are also problems with mapping the Aztecs. Most Mesoamericanists simply copy Robert H. Barlow's classic map.[10] He based his 'provinces' on his reading of the Codex Mendoza and the material in the *Relaciones geográficas* of 1577–86.

Barlow's map provides the readily recognizable boundaries that most readers seek, but the sources are limited. In practice the Aztecs organized their empire in a hegemonic fashion and never created an integrated infrastructure that would make it readily possible to map imperial extent. Rather, they just drew tribute from subdued or submissive cities, but the tribute varied considerably. It is unclear whether cities that sent the Aztecs 'presents' or entered into agreements to permit unobstructed passage to Aztec armies should be regarded as independent, as Barlow saw them, or as within the empire, and it is difficult to decide how best to map the situation. Most of the towns paying tribute to the Aztecs – especially smaller towns – were not conquered but as tributaries to larger towns that were conquered became *de facto* part of the empire without ever having to see an Aztec.[11]

Ethnicity and the USA

In the USA greater historical cartographic interest in Native Americans is in part an aspect of the greater interest in the histories of particular ethnic groups or peoples that can be seen not only in many general historical atlases, but also in many specialist works. Ethnic awareness and assertiveness in the USA are combined with a commercial publishing industry seeking new opportunities and a market combining a large and affluent book-purchasing public with public institutions willing to purchase works that focus on particular ethnic groups. This has led to works such as *We the People: An Atlas of America's Ethnic Diversity* (New York, 1988), Evyater Friesel's *Atlas of Modern Jewish History* (New York, 1990), a work that emphasized the American experience and was a revision of a Hebrew edition published in Jerusalem in 1983, and Molefi Asante and Mark Mattson's *Historical and Cultural Atlas of African Americans* (New York, 1991). Lubomyr Luciuk and Bohdan Kordan's *Creating a Landscape. A Geography of Ukrainians in Canada* (Toronto, 1989) was a Canadian equivalent, concerned to map the internal morphology of Ukrainian settlements in Canada as well as the general pattern, and also interested in the impact of home-country geography on settlement choices, for example in encouraging location in woodland environments even if of limited agricultural potential.[12]

Like other historical atlases, such works had their own agenda. Arguing that 'no other ethnic group in the United States has been under such intense pressure to forget origin and cultural past as African Americans', Asante and Mattson's book was committed to demonstrating the contribution of African Americans to the history of the USA and the extent to which 'African-American culture is also African at its most elemental and fundamental level' and thus not dependent on European culture.[13]

As with other 'ethnic' atlases, that by Asante and Mattson can be criticized for underrating differences within the ethnic group, in this case within Africa and between African Americans. However, it is valuable in that it draws attention to a people or consciousness that is generally underexplored. Many American historical atlases neglected or minimized ethnic issues and this situation has not ceased. For example, they play little role in the state historical atlases produced by the University of Oklahoma Press. That of Texas, by A. Ray Stephens and William Holmes (Norman, 1989), is typical in ignoring the movement of African Americans and modern Hispanics into the state. Such an omission can be regarded as an aspect of a more widespread failure to map issues that divided America. The Stephens and Holmes atlas devoted three pages to maps of military installations in the world wars, but had nothing on unemployment, labour disputes or poverty in the interwar period.

Native Americans

Despite these problems there was a considerable advance in ethnic historical mapping in the 1980s and 1990s and this has been particularly marked in the American treatment of Native Americans. There are still atlases and maps that reveal a lack of sympathy, interest or understanding. *The Making of America. Deep South*, a map published by the *National Geographic* magazine in August 1983, marked in tribes such as the Chickasaw, but the map was essentially organized round European Americans. They were responsible for the boundaries that defined the map, and the Native Americans were depicted as a subject for these boundaries or as obstacles to them. Thus, the Creek were divided between the French and the Spanish zones of control, and on the map the Chitimacha were similarly written across European divides.

Yet a change of attitude can also be detected from the 1970s on. The Native Americans were no longer simply people to be fought. Milton B. Newton's *Atlas of Louisiana* (Baton Rouge, 1972) noted: 'Indian occupancy patterns reveal much about the usefulness of the state . . . Man's relations with nature, mediated by culture, seems to be the appropriate focus for cultural geographers.' To Newton there was no moral difference between Native and European-American settlement, nor any sense of progress involved in the analysis:

> Geographers' interest in European settlement is no different in theory, from their interest in Indian settlement. The main difference lies in the great increase in the volume of data and its greater reliability . . . the main concern is in accounting for the areal associations observed in the constantly varying cultural landscape.[14]

The *Atlas of Oregon* edited by W.G. Loy (Eugene, 1976) that was published by the University of Oregon both acknowledged the importance of Native American history and made a serious attempt to explain the difficulties of mapping it. Oregon was not seen as a creation of European Americans. Instead, 'the Pacific Northwest was an Indian land for more than 10,000 years before the first European explorers sailed along its coast . . . Their history were Oregon's first history.'[15]

The dangers of treating all Native Americans as similar, specifically of adopting the classification method employed further east, were also explained:

> Tribes as political entities had virtually no relevance in aboriginal Oregon. Oregon's Indians were divided into dozens of bands, groups, villages and families. These groups sometimes shared a similar life style, dialect, or language, but they acknowledged no overarching authority or identity. The listing of names of Indian bands or groups on the map of the facing page is necessarily incomplete.

The records of the Oregon Superintendency of Indian Affairs and the accounts of treaty sessions were therefore flawed because there was a misleading attempt to discern tribes. Similarly, there were problems in using linguistic classification, in part because of changing theoretical views about such classification, but also because of a lack of records and the degree to which European Americans found it difficult to distinguish linguistic differences.[16] In addition, there was a warning about the danger of neglecting the dynamic nature of Native American settlement patterns.[17] Nearly all tribes, even the more urbanized, moved at least once every generation, as they wore out fields. Ideally, the farming communities could burn, plant in fertile ashes, then move to do the same again quite soon. As a result the mapping of Indian tribes would be very difficult. Colin Calloway has recently mapped the migration of specific Shawnee bands.[18]

The depiction of Native American migration reflects a common problem with mapping, which tends to be a static representation of changing entities, but also a more specific difficulty with the conventional mapping of indigenous peoples, not least Native Americans: their presentation in essentially passive terms with dynamism being instead the characteristic of colonizers. This situation is exacerbated by the use of European American nomenclature. It would be more useful to see settlements named as their possessors named them, presuming that a time-series of maps would indicate change.

The *Atlas of Utah* (Provo, 1981) included a map of Native Indian cultures in about 1840, designed, as maps in other atlases also sought to do, to indicate the situation on the eve of the direct impact of European Americans; the role of the horse ensured that their indirect impact had been considerable. The accompanying text argued that Native Indian territoriality was in no way inferior to that of European Americans:

> The myth that aborigines were migratory and aimlessly nomadic, having no definable territories, is refuted by known permanent living and farming areas, consistent patterns of travel, permanent sacred places, and group or tribal names given to themselves or to others which signify a land feature or a particular food-stuff. Although concepts of individual ownership of land parcels were alien to most native peoples, love of land and place and respect and appreciation for land resources were basic to native cultures and life styles.

There was also a clear warning to be drawn about the permeability of the tribal boundaries.[19]

It is not surprising that the mapping of 'Indian–White' encounters was relatively sympathetic to the Native Americans, a sympathy that was clearly displayed in the text, for the text offered a way to approach Native American attitudes that maps could not do:

> The native life patterns were destroyed forever and hostility became common . . . the Indians increasingly raided the Mormon cattle herds . . . though deemed by cattle owners to be outright theft, [they] were deemed by the Indians to be justified on the principle that the earth's bounty, cattle as well as deer, should be shared by all.

The killing of surrendered Native Americans and of their women and children was mentioned and there was reference to 'white usurpation' of their land.[20]

In the same year Jack D. Forbes produced a striking *Atlas of Native History* (Davis, 1981). This was a dramatic repudiation of the conventions of American historical

37. 'The United States Area as it really was in 1820' in Jack D. Forbes's *Atlas of Native History* (Davis, 1981), a rejection of conventional historical mapping of North America. The role and control of European Americans was minimized, and, instead, the Native Americans were emphasized. Aside from the treatment of the USA, the Spanish presence was also minimized.

cartography. Forbes consciously rejected the appropriation of the Native American past, an appropriation that was true in both nomenclature and territoriality. He employed the 'names used by the native people themselves' and sought to 'present real political conditions', ignoring 'the claims of white governmental units', which, Forbes argued had come to compose a 'mythological map'. He also represented his atlas as part of an intellectual process that the country had to go through, 'discovering truth free of ethnic bias and colonialist chauvinism'.[21]

The very titling of the maps represented a conscious rejection of past cartographic traditions; titles that matched the contents of the maps. The map of 'The United States Area as it really was in 1820' depicted Native American groups as well as states, for example the Maskogi Confederation between Georgia and Alabama. The map for 1845 did not carve up North America into, for example, Mexico, Canada and the area gained for the USA by the Louisiana Purchase of 1803. For the 1845 and 1861 maps no European frontiers were shown west of the line of white settlement; instead, forts and isolated areas of settlement were depicted.

Alongside the attempt to present a general cartographic history that centred on the Native Americans, there were also attempts to produce atlases for individual tribes and these involved some historical maps. Thus J.M. Goodman's *Navajo Atlas* (Norman, 1982) included a map for 'prehistoric Navajo inhabitation'.[22] J.J. Ferguson and E.R. Hart produced a *Zuni Atlas* (Norman, 1985) that applauded their care of the land: 'the exploitation of resources in the area was undertaken in a non-depleting manner. In fact, the Zunis treated the area with great reverence at the same time that they used its resources to sustain life.' In contrast, modern non–Zuni activity, such as ranching, was seen as deleterious to the environment.

The matching map of non–Zuni settlement in the area of Zuni sovereignty could not be used to demonstrate the point, and the text and map were thus both necessary.[23] The theme of environmental balance was also taken up in the *Atlas of Colorado* by K.A. Erickson and A.W. Smith (Boulder, Colorado, 1985). Its map of native population and subsistence in *c.* 1500 was accompanied by the comment: 'theirs was a relatively harmonious relationship with the harsh environments of Colorado', while Europeans had 'initiated a process of environmental modification'.[24]

Ferguson and Hart addressed the problem of reconciling traditional oral culture and the more 'scientific' knowledge produced by modern research, a central problem for the mapping of indigenous peoples with active oral cultures. A map of 'major archaeological sites and culture areas in the Zuni region' was glossed:

At the present time archaeologists can only trace the cultural antecedents of the Zuni people on a broad regional basis, because the data and analytical techniques necessary to trace the movement of a particular group of people from site to site in the long prehistoric era have not yet been developed. Given this limitation and the essentially symbolic nature of the Zuni origin account, it is not possible to specifically correlate archaeological culture history with the Zuni accounts of origin and the migration. In general, however, the Zuni origin accounts and archaeological culture history share certain basic and major themes, including an economic shift from hunting and gathering to corn agriculture, the prevailing movement of people across the landscape, occasional violence and hostility between groups of people, and the assimilation of two cultural traditions with Zuni culture.[25]

The area of Zuni sovereignty in 1846 was mapped, part of the argument that tribal boundaries were clear,[26] and it is possibly relevant to note that though the authors were not Zunis, much of the work on which the atlas was based was done at the request of or under contract to the Zuni Tribal Council, and a lot of material was used in a case filed in 1979 by which the Zunis sought to gain compensation for lands. Again, as part of the positive impression created by the atlas, the map of significant incidents of violence in the Zuni area was glossed with the statement that the Zunis fought only in defence of their territory or people; indeed, they were presented as allies of the USA.[27]

Carl Waldman's *Atlas of the North American Indian* (Oxford and New York), also published in 1985, was sympathetic to the Indians. They were seen as relatively in tune with themselves and the environment and Waldman was careful to point out the implications of the use of analytical devices that were alien to the Indian tradition:

It should be pointed out, especially in light of the particularly holistic Indian world view, that the various categories and classification systems in the book are heuristic devices, applied for the sake of convenience and understanding, and not absolutes . . . many terms and concepts have evolved from, if not an outright cultural bias, then at least an implicit cultural vantage point – that of the dominant European/ American tradition.[28]

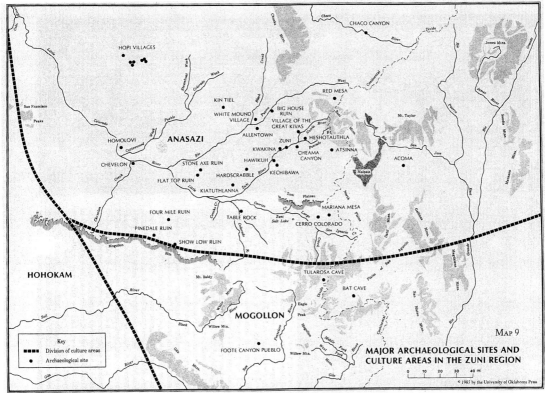

38. 'Major Archaeological Sites and Culture Areas in the Zuni Region' from J.J. Ferguson and E.R. Hart's *Zuni Atlas* (Norman, 1985). Mapping the history of native peoples offered a different perspective on the areas seized by the nineteenth-century imperial powers. What had been blanks in their maps or spaces organized by territorial structures and new rail links were, instead, filled with reference to the native peoples.

Waldman's atlas was nonetheless produced within the constraints of the Phaidon/ Equinox series of cultural historical atlases. This was not true of Helen Tanner's *Atlas of Great Lakes Indian History* (Norman, 1987). Tanner had been a commissioner for Indian Affairs in Michigan and her project was based on a National Endowment for the Humanities grant approved in 1976. The sequence of maps in the atlas traced the changing patterns of Native American village locations, a more helpful approach than dividing up territory between undifferentiated blocs, not least because the European concept of sovereignty was alien to Native American leaders. She collected data on over 1500 village sites. Tanner's atlas revealed a number of points that suggested a degree of bias in more conventional mapping. Aside from indicating the persistent Native American element in Great Lakes history, the maps of conflicts in which Native Americans had been caught up, for example the French and Indian War (1754–63) and the war of 1812, devoted greater attention to this involvement and indicated the extent of conflict distant from the St Lawrence, the Hudson River corridor and the lakes east of Detroit. Tanner also benefited from extensive archaeological research which permitted more mapping of Native American history prior to the European arrival than had been possible earlier in the century. Tanner drew attention to dynamic features in Native American society, such as population pressure and tension, and indicated that these affected location.[29] Thus, she presented a way of life that was not static when the Europeans arrived. Tanner also echoed

Waldman when she stressed the difference between Native American and European American concepts of property.[30]

There has therefore been considerable development in the historical mapping of Native Americans. However, it is still the case that much of the data derives from European Americans. For example, thanks to the arrival of French colonizers and traders, it is possible to provide detail for the situation in south-eastern Louisiana in the late seventeenth and early eighteenth centuries that is lacking earlier. Yet increasingly such information is interpreted in a way that is sensitive to the particular characteristics of Native American culture and is supplemented by material derived from research that is directly on this culture rather than on earlier non-Native intermediaries. Thus, the distribution of Paleoindian projectile points has been used to develop a series of phase maps that reconstruct prehistoric settlement distributions in eastern North America.[31]

Native Canada

The same is true for Canada, though maps in which Native Canadians do not feature are still produced. In his *A Country So Interesting: The Hudson's Bay Company and Two Centuries of Mapping 1670–1870* (Montreal, 1991), R.I. Ruggles included four maps entitled 'Retreat of the Unknown'. They depicted the retreat of a *terra incognita* that was coloured black. Given this Eurocentric view, it was not surprising that the names of Native Canadian cultures were not marked.

However, research into pre-European and early Native Canadian history gathered pace from the 1960s. The research was intimately linked with mapping, not so much because it produced information that could be depicted in historical atlases as because the past itself was reconstructed from the patterns produced by the information. Conrad Heidenreich, an historical geographer, and Bruce Trigger, an anthropologist, played a major role in interpreting native history in the early European period and both were to contribute to the *Historical Atlas of Canada* (3 vols, Toronto, 1987–93). Heidenreich used the accounts of Jesuits to reconstruct the location of Huron missions and villages in 1615–50. Large sections of Huronia had not been archaeologically investigated and thus his research was of particular value. Heidenreich also offered a crucial contextualization of archaeological research by pointing out the need to recall that Hurons changed the location of their villages about every decade, as soil and firewood were exhausted.[32]

Trigger experimented with the mapping of native–European relations in his work. For the sixteenth century he distinguished between regular and sporadic penetration of European goods on the basis of archaeological sites which can be dated to approximately 25-year intervals. The frequency of European goods on these sites, together with the variety of such goods, and the extent to which it could be established that only fragments of European goods, not whole items, were reaching sites in various areas were used to distinguish these two categories. Warfare among native groups proved difficult to assess. Alien pottery styles turning up in different regions had been interpreted by archaeologists as carried there by female potters who were either refugees or prisoners of war. The two alternatives produced different patterns of warfare and were included by Trigger as evidence of a problem unresolved for lack of enough direct historical data and of sufficiently unambiguous archaeological criteria.[33]

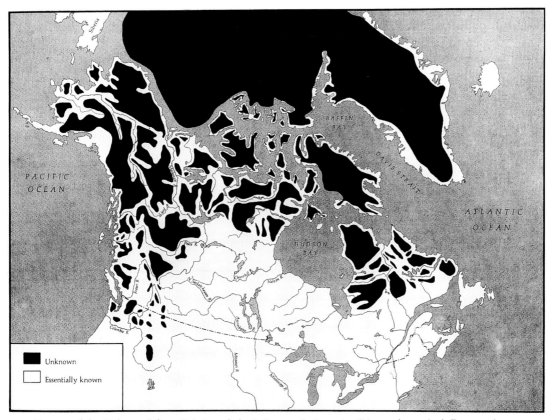

39. 'Retreat of the Unknown' from R.I. Ruggles's *A Country So Interesting* (Montreal, 1991). A Eurocentric account of knowledge of Canada in 1870. The choice of black for the 'unknown' echoed traditional assumptions. Edward Quin had used black clouds in his *Historical Atlas* (London, 1830).

The *Historical Atlas of Canada* made a serious attempt to incorporate the Native experience but was affected by the Eurocentric emphasis in the archival record and research.[34] Nevertheless, the first eighteen spreads in volume one were devoted to the pre-European period and, although the remainder of the volume covered the years up to 1800 in far greater detail, the Native experience was not forgotten once the Europeans had arrived. Due allowance was made for problems with the data, as in Trigger's spread on Native Resettlement 1635–1800, but efforts were made to summarize, map and explain the available data.[35] The extensive use of colour-coding for all forms of symbol ensured, for example, that it was possible to distinguish linguistic families, native economies and patterns of movement on the map of Native Canada at the end of the period, a period when, as the text pointed out, natives were still the predominant and, over much of what was to become Canada, the only population.[36]

For the nineteenth century, reference was made to the prevalent ideology about land use, an ideology that was related to the more general interest in territorial control on the part of states. Control and progress were equated with settled agriculture and the development of communications. They defined agrarian progress and justified control by European peoples. Thus, nomadic peoples were primitive

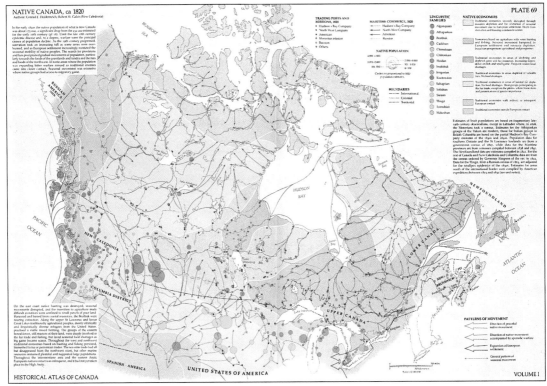

40. 'Native Canada *c.* 1820' from the *Historical Atlas of Canada* (Toronto, 1987–93). A determined attempt to incorporate the Native experience characterized this atlas. This for example ensured that the European-imposed international frontier was not used to limit what was shown. Crucial inclusion of Native population numbers prevented any sense that the Canadian environment was under human control.

and mapping of them was redundant: mapping of the past not as it led towards the future but the past as the dead hand of obsolescent practices. As this ideology was questioned in the last quarter of the twentieth century, it became easier to praise the ecology, economy and culture of native peoples; not that they left the environment in a pristine state.

The plate on 'Native Reserves of Western Canada to 1900' was essentially locational, but it included a text that created a very different impression from the maps in many atlases of native reserves:

> A major preoccupation of government agents in the nineteenth century was to make a farmer out of every Indian. The ideology of the time viewed cultivated land as a cornerstone of civilization . . . Together with the Christian religion and the English language, the adoption of farming was seen as the basis for the assimilation of native populations . . . a complete cultural transformation.[37]

Thus, although it was not *mapped*, the atlas offered a guide to the character, use and consequences of power that was far more profound than maps of native–European contact that focused on conquest, and then treated the natives with an essentially static depiction of reserves.

The *Historical Atlas of Canada* further qualified the conventional treatment of native peoples by mapping the governmental view of native reserves in a portion of British Columbia in 1922 alongside native claims of territorial control. Similarly, the

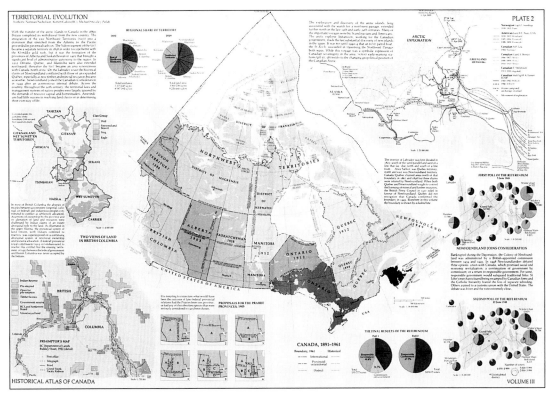

41. 'The Territorial Evolution of Canada' from the *Historical Atlas of Canada*. A plate that made clear the controversies that underlay territorial development. The governmental view of native reserves in a portion of British Columbia in 1922 was mapped alongside native claims of territorial ownership and resource allocation. Similarly, the polls on the referendum by which Newfoundland joined the Confederation in 1949 made clear its close nature.

extent to which education was employed to try to enforce cultural norms, and the unsuccessful and destructive nature of this process, were not ignored.[38]

Native Australians

The historical cartography of Australia has recently paid more attention to its Aboriginal population, to their history before European arrival and to their subsequent fate. *Australians: A Historical Atlas*, edited by J.R. Cram and J. McQuilton (Broadway, 1987), which is the closest Australian work to an official historical atlas, considered different theories of Aboriginal settlement in detail and also mapped Aboriginal language families.[39] Aboriginal art was also discussed, and the role of regional variations in systematic research effort in affecting the available data was mentioned: thus, for example, there is little surviving data for Tasmania.[40] There was also a valuable section of maps and text discussing one particular Aboriginal people, the Wik, their ritual, clans and spatial organization. The text pointed out that using different criteria for mapping, for example language, provided different impressions of spatial organization. Furthermore, the civilization versus barbarism debate was addressed with the map showing density of sites:

Clearly this landscape is not a 'wilderness'. It has been humanised and domesticated by the human tendency to intellectualise and to explain, to transpose into religious and

artistic imagery the mundane elements around us . . . The Wik . . . organise and maintain their land with care and affection.[41]

These maps and remarks were far different from the earlier tradition of largely
ignoring the Aborigines. A more positive account of Aboriginal culture was linked
to an awareness of the extent to which they were dispossessed,[42] although, as was
pointed out in connection with the map of population in Victoria in 1891 in the
Atlas of Victoria (Melbourne, 1892), maps could not show the cost of the process.
Greater knowledge of current aspects of Aboriginal life, for example language and
territoriality,[43] offers more guidance to the interpretation of Aboriginal history.

Decolonization and Cartography

Greater interest in and sensitivity towards the mapping of native peoples can be seen
as an aspect of the displacement of a teleological account of past, present and future.
The notion of 'the ladder of civilization'[44] appears increasingly redundant in a
Western culture that preaches relative values and is unsure of its own purpose. That
is true not only of intellectuals, but more widely, and helps to ensure that the
historical process is understood far less as the triumph of the West.[45] Thus in the
West there is greater interest in other cultures and societies, and not simply from
the point of view of their contact with Western societies. Outside the West there is
more pride in national histories, not least on the part of countries affected by
decolonization. This process can also be observed in former colonies that received a
large number of European emigrants, such as Australia, Canada and New Zealand.
Their sense of their own history is now less focused on the mother colony, and this
also affects their cartographic imagination, most dramatically with maps of the world
in which the meridian line passes through Australia and the southern hemisphere is
depicted at the top. In terms of historical cartography, this new interpretation of the
past leads to an emphasis not on the process of state formation, a process in which
the colonial power was dominant, but on subsequent history, particularly social
history. That was a major theme in the *Historical Atlas of Canada*.

The cartographic processes and devices employed elsewhere in the world are very
much those of the West. Western science and techniques remain central, and there
has been no real attempt to revive or devise different cartographic methods, no more
than there has been a serious challenge to the Western understanding of time. Thus,
an historical map produced in Ethiopia or Mongolia can be readily interpreted and
assessed by those familiar with, say, Italian or American historical maps. The
language of the text is different and the message may be specific and require careful
decoding, but the language of the map – its symbols – is similar, if not identical,
although the resonances may vary.

Historical atlases produced by nations and peoples that have thrown off European
political control, or the political control of peoples of European descent, since 1945
have varied from Western historical atlases in topics covered rather than cartographic
approach or technological method. They have sought to present their histories in
cartographic form, but the ability to do so has reflected the nature of available
information, while another constraint has been the habit of seeking to portray the
long-term history of states whose territorial extent and ethnic composition were
often the work of European conquerors and therefore relatively recent.[46] More

generally, modern concepts of space are essentially those spread by Western powers, and delimited by their surveyors, in the nineteenth century.[47] Non-Western peoples seeking to understand their history have to cope with the problem of describing cartographically a pre-Western period when indigenous notions of space were different and are therefore difficult to depict in terms of the modern cartographic-territorial language of clear lines.

Mapping African History

The recovery of African history and its cartographic depiction are major develop-ments of the post-war world. Prior to 1945 African history received little attention in world historical atlases and there were very few historical maps produced specifi-cally for Africa. The most important were the maps in Eric Walker's *Historical Atlas of South Africa* (1922) which was published in Oxford. Much of the mapping of African history has drawn on Arab and European sources. For example, European maps of 1602, 1629 and 1746 were used to indicate a 'historical and spatial continuity of towns' in the Gold Coast.[48] Such sources, however, are limited in their geo-graphical scope and also represent the views of outsiders.[49] On the basis in part of such sources, much can be mapped, as, for example, Devisse's maps of the develop-ment of trans-Saharan trade from 900 to 1100 reveal,[50] but Arab sources provide relatively little information on sub-equatorial Africa and European knowledge of the interior of the continent was limited prior to the mid-nineteenth century.

Non-political maps of sub-Saharan Africa are difficult to construct for any period prior to European colonization because of the lack of data. Maps showing political processes taking place over time are difficult to construct for any society, and for 'prehistory' one is arguably no worse off in Africa than for most other continents since archaeological artefact distributions can be mapped and it is possible to use arrows to suggest trends and relationships. However, for the millennium prior to colonization there is either no information or the evidence available, for example from oral traditions, is difficult to use as a basis for maps. One response to the difficulties that is noticeable in many historical atlases or in the maps used to illustrate textbook histories is to plot various European activities in Africa for which there is often more tangible evidence. This creates a misleading impression of African history. Certainly, it is more pertinent to start with an understanding of the role of geography and of environmental shifts.[51]

The mapping of sub-Saharan African history has reflected differing interpretations of the nature of African polities. There are the problems of determining if bound-aries as currently understood existed at all, and second, of locating through historical sources where boundaries actually lay. The difficulty of the latter has led to the frequent practice of using floating names on African maps. Many of the more durable cartographic conventions derived from the maps produced by John Fage in his *Atlas of African History* (London, 1958). Fage began with the contention that African sovereignty was vaguely defined and had a tendency to fade – strong at the centre near the capital and weaker near the peripheries. African states, in addition, ruled over people and not over land, so that the concept of a territorial boundary was not important. Fage argued that these conditions made the drawing of discrete boundaries anchored on fixed points or even geographical features inappropriate.

Instead, Fage opted for 'bubble' and circle maps, where a circle would be drawn with its centre on the capital and its radius a rough estimate of the extent of the power. 'Bubbles' were a product of circles with allowances made for other circles or for geographical features that clearly hindered control.[52]

Fage's approach has been challenged more recently by an American scholar, John Thornton, in his *Africa and Africans in the Making of the Atlantic World, 1400–1680* (Cambridge, 1992). Thornton argued that African concepts of boundary were similar to those of early modern Europe, though certainly not those of the modern world. He presented the basic unit of African politics as a fairly small, discrete and well-bounded entity, which he termed the 'mini-state'. As African law did not recognize landed private property and states did not assess land taxes (hence Fage's contention that they ruled people and not land), state jurisdiction became critically important in defining who was taxable and who not. Jurisdiction was ultimately territorially bounded, so that subjects of states could, and often did, cross the borders to escape taxation, though usually this only put them within the taxable boundaries of another similar state. The essential mapping problem lay with the larger units which typically agglomerated mini-states, either by charging them tribute or by interfering in their institutional, judicial or leadership functions. The point at which such a state lost sovereignty and became a part of a larger unit is problematic: was it when one recognized the supremacy of another with nominal presents, or when significant tribute was assessed, or when judicial functions or leadership positions were taken over and appointed from outside, or when boundaries were completely redrawn?

Thornton demonstrated the possibility and value of establishing boundaries in an area where they are difficult to map in the three maps of West and Central (in fact only western-central) Africa in *c.* 1625. The maps were supported by 22 pages of source notes, evidence of the degree of research and discussion required to support maps for regions hitherto poorly mapped. Even so, Thornton did not pretend that it was possible to offer comprehensive maps: 'Mali's southern border is a complete mystery . . . Gurma. Its location is inferred from passing references . . . but its size cannot really be told, the boundaries being simply a guess and fixed in reference to neighbouring states.' Thornton's notes also drew attention to the variety of polities that are difficult to map with precision:

> The boundaries shown here represent the maximum extent of Loango's effective control but include a number of tributary states who exercised considerable internal control and who were bound to Loango by tributary payments more than administrative fiat . . . The term 'Jaga' in sixteenth- and seventeenth-century sources describes, in general terms, a rootless, usually cannibal group of raiders . . . The Dembos (Ndembu region). The politics of this area was quite unstable, with many small states . . . Larger states . . . made claims and campaigns in the area, and most of the region was nominally a part of one or another (or several simultaneously) of these states. Moreover, the larger Ndembu states built up confederations with the smaller ones, but these were often no more stable than the claims of the larger states. The boundaries drawn on the map simply make a guess at the political configuration at any given time.[53]

Thus, apart from important methodological problems, a tremendous amount of basic research is necessary if African boundaries are to be drawn with confidence.

Post-war historical cartography of and for Africa has reflected a number of developments, several of which mirror those in late nineteenth-century Europe. In particular, nationalism has been displayed in the publication of national atlases which tend to have an historical section, while growing literacy and the demands of the educational system have had an impact. The latter were initially largely accommo-dated within the historical cartography judged appropriate for European students. Thus *Philips' Intermediate Historical Atlas for West Africa* (London, 1964) consisted of the 21st edition of *Philips' Intermediate Historical Atlas* with eight inserted pages, which were not included in the table of contents. These were devoted to West Africa, and highlighted the extent to which in the remainder of the atlas no states were depicted in the interior of West Africa on the maps of the world. European influence was also readily apparent in the *Historical Atlas 1789–1964 for South African Schools* by R.R. Sellman and C. de K. Fowler (1965). Published in Cape Town and by Edward Arnold in London, this was largely derived from Sellman's *Historical Atlas 1789–1962*, which Arnold published. Of the fourteen pages of maps on the history of South Africa published at the end, six were from Fage's *Atlas of African History*, which was also published by Arnold.

Intended for secondary schools in British Africa, *The Map Approach to African History* (London, 1959, 3rd edn, 1965) was written by two former Education Officers in Kenya, A.M. Healy and E.R. Vere-Hodge. Educational priorities and European influence both remained important in the *History of West Africa in Maps and Diagrams* by Brian Catchpole and I.A. Akinjogbin (London, 1986). Published by Collins Educational and intended for the school certificate syllabus in West African history, the atlas covered the four sections of the West African Examination Council's syllabus. The introduction, by Akinjogbin of the University of Ife in Nigeria, made the purpose of the work clear. It had been 'drafted to give students a good idea of the diversity of the peoples of West Africa while at the same time showing the similarities in their historical experience and their essential cultural homogeneity'. 'Unity is strength' was a theme and lack of African unity was seen as partly to blame for European conquest. Colonization was criticized and colonial ideology refuted. Thus for Portuguese Guinea: 'a mere 1% of Africans were *assimilados*: the rest were low paid workers exploited so that Portugal could sell the colony's palm oil and ground-nut products on world markets at highly competitive prices. . . .'[54] The last spread was on worldwide recognition of Nigerian art.

Locally produced historical atlases are uncommon. Brian Catchpole's *Map History of Africa South of the Sahara* was published by Longman Zimbabwe in Harare in 1992, but many copies were pulped owing to editorial and production faults. National atlases, however, contain much of interest, not least because the historical sections, however brief, generally include material not found elsewhere. The *Atlas of Uganda* published by the Department of Lands and Surveys in 1962 was designed to be ready at the time of independence. It included a spread on both archaeology and history. The former, tackled by the Curator of the Uganda Museum, marked sites; the latter included a section of text by the British former Director of the Department that downplayed pre-colonial history:

The period assigned to 'History', which in Uganda can hardly be stretched back beyond the beginning of the nineteenth century, is almost equally barren [of artefacts]. In general terms it may be said that it is not possible to point to any structure or monument of man's handiwork that is certainly a hundred years old. For the most part the Historical Sites shown on the accompanying map illustrate the progress of European exploration in Uganda and the subsequent organisation of the forts.[55]

A very different work was published in Madagascar seven years later. The *Atlas de Madagascar* (Tananarive, 1969), prepared by the country's association of geographers and with a foreword by the President, included maps of exploration and archaeological sites, but also a spread with eight maps covering stages of political unity. The accompanying notes explained that the theme was one of the formation of the Madagascan nation, a 'unité morale', which had followed on from the earlier stages of the formation of a united people and a united state. The maps depicted this tripartite process and used the colour green to represent the forces of unification proceeding from Tananarive, then the capital city. Unification and unity were and are central themes in Madagascan government and education.

The *Atlas de Burundi* (Gradignan, 1979) also made a serious effort to map pre-colonial history. One map, dealing with the late nineteenth century, made a good attempt to show the nature of the sacred monarchical system. It included the royal necropolis, sacred places and ritual itineraries, and the text described the ritual of sacred monarchy with reference to places.[56] The plate for German colonization in 1896–1916 qualified the military moves depicted in the map by explaining in the text that local German officials justified military actions 'pour "pacifier" le pays', the quotation marks indicating a judgment that it was difficult to show on the map. In the same fashion the spread on 1804–1915 in the *Atlas d'Haiti* (Bordeaux, 1985) referred to the racism of American occupying forces and described the first years of occupation as a 'pacification' with the word in inverted commas.[57]

A similar technique was employed in *Nigeria in Maps* edited by K.M. Barbour *et al.* (London, 1982). Though published by a British publisher, most of the contributors were Nigerians, as were the draughtsmen and typists, according to the introduction.[58] The historical section sought to create the impression of a pre-colonial world that was far from weak. For example, alongside a map of pre-colonial polities and societies, the text, having mentioned the size of the polities in the sub-Saharan Sudanic Belt, discussed the Guinea Savanna to the south:

> The factor of environment has been a major impediment in the way of the emergence of large kingdoms and empires in this region of Nigeria. The area is, on the whole, sparsely populated, made up of small, fairly isolated and fragmented groups. Yet, paucity of historical attention must not be taken as evidence of unimportant and insignificant static societies. The region is known, for example, to have been the seat and source of some very ancient civilizations.[59]

As with the *Atlas de Burundi* and with the Marxist John Horrabin's *Atlas of Africa* (London, 1960), quotation marks were used to qualify the colonial control depicted on the map: 'the growing imperialist stranglehold was justified on the basis of a "humanitarian" concern for the "unfortunate" peoples of the area . . . By 1897 the British had successfully "pacified" war-torn Yorubaland and imposed their "protection".'[60] The section on post-independence Nigerian history was used, as in the case of other states, to assert the values of unity. Four maps of the administrative regions into which Nigeria was divided in 1955, 1963, 1967 and 1976 were published with the gloss:

in the long and difficult process of nation-building in Nigeria, internal boundary changes have been used to create easily manageable administrative units coinciding where possible with geographical, socio-cultural, and historical reality, and so assisting the achievement of national unity. Right from its formation as a political unit, the main question has been whether Nigeria does indeed constitute a durable, workable, political community . . . the steady determination with which the Biafran attempt at secession was quashed by the rest of the federation stands also as a warning to any state that might seek to follow suit.[61]

The text thus made a slighting reference to the single topic in post-independence Nigerian history that was and is most marked in historical atlases, if anything is indicated for Nigeria at all: the civil war of 1967–70 stemming from the attempt by the Ibo homeland to become an independent state under the name of the Republic of Biafra. There was no map of the war nor, more generally, of separatism.

A clearly anti-Western line was taken in the historical section of the *National Atlas of Ethiopia* that was produced by the Ethiopian Mapping Authority (Addis Ababa, 1988). The foreword asserted that Ethiopia had 'existed as an independent country for over 3000 years' and the historical section emphasized Ethiopia's history of external challenge and proud independence. It did so, however, in a fashion that reflected the militantly left-wing nature of the then Ethiopian government and its longstanding rivalry with the Somali Republic. The Somalis were presented as a continuation of earlier invasions going back to the Sultan of Adal and the Turks in the sixteenth century. Portuguese intervention in that century was also criticized; these were 'the Portuguese maritime pirates'. The key to the map on the second half of the nineteenth century included 'The Great Battles of the National Resistance against the forces of aggression and imperialism'. British imperialists were blamed for inventing the notion of a 'Great Somalia', which was seen as continued by the contemporary Somalis. Thus the leading modern rival was following an agenda laid down by an imperialist manipulator. Reference was made to the 'successful liberation and reunion of Eritrea with the Motherland in September 1952', a view that made little sense of the separatist movement launched there the following year.[62]

Post-war historical mapping of Africa has therefore provided opportunities for the expression of ideological positions. In general, works produced within Africa or to serve an African market have made little or no reference to the problems of mapping the continent. In part, this reflects the degree to which a number of the atlases have lacked text and have clearly been intended for schools. In such works as *Atlas for the Republic of Cameroon* (London, 1971) and *Atlas for Botswana* (Gaborone, 1988) little space was found for historical maps (two and four respectively).

The series of national atlases published by the Paris house of Éditions Jeune Afrique similarly included few historical maps, but did discuss the nature of the sources. For example, *Atlas de la Haute-Volta* by Y. Peron (Paris, 1975) only included one historical map – of Haute-Volta (Upper Volta, Burkina Fasso) at the end of the nineteenth century, mapping places, tribes and commercial routes. Yet Peron also explained that very little was known about the pre-colonial period.[63] Other volumes in the series offered more maps. Paul Pélissier's on Senegal included a map of prehistoric and protohistoric sites and another on pre-colonial Senegal which used wide lines to depict frontiers. The Niger volume similarly covered archaeological sites and included a map showing colonial polities and trade routes. Pélissier drew attention to source problems.[64]

There is of course no obligation on national atlases to include an historical section, and to do so is a particular problem in the case of a state created by colonization during the late nineteenth or early twentieth century, as was the case with most African states. There are contradictory pressures: one to search out a heroic pre-colonial past; the other to ignore the past and concentrate on the present, on the cartography of the new state. Thus, for example, the *Atlas de Côte d'Ivoire* (Abidjan, 1975), produced by the country's Ministry of Planning, included as historical maps only the development of administrative regions after 1895 and the creation of military or administrative posts by the colonial power (France).[65]

Such a limited historical cartography reflected a colonial mentality in the sense of a world-view framed by colonialization, not least in publishing in the language of the colonial power and in taking governmental boundaries and control as the central theme of cartography. It did, however, ensure that the problems of mapping pre-colonial African history could be avoided.

The depiction of pre-colonial Africa has also been affected by Western concepts of identity and political authority, although these have been used to particular ends by African nationalists. The extrapolation of the Western model of the nation state had and has immediate value for African nationalists, but it may be very misleading. It is possible that the states and especially the political identities that were first charted in any detail in the nineteenth century have had their longevity exaggerated by our own assumptions and by the agendas of ethno-genesis which lie at the heart of proximate cultural nationalism. Not simply has tradition been invented, but even possibly states, for some revisionist archaeologists have thrown doubt on the extent and even existence of certain pre-colonial states. Furthermore, modern concepts of nationality have been used misleadingly, to interpret the polities and politics of the past. Instead, there appears to have been considerable movement for centuries across what have since been constructed as national borders in almost every sphere of human activity. There were multiple civil and sacred identities and it would be misleading to ignore the complexity of African thought on these matters. Thus, and more generally, modern Western thinking about what we are and what we belong to yields something very far short of a universal taxonomy.

Mapping African kingdoms is often an act of unacknowledged analysis, rather than the cartographic rendering of a clear-cut reality. It is right to try to do this as it matters to any historian where things approximately were. However, the mapping itself reifies ideas in a way that makes assumptions about the actual nature of pre-colonial organizations. Thus, independence has not solved the problems of mapping Africa's past, nor has it freed the cartography of the subject from Western influences.

Communist Historical Cartography outside Europe

Communism is another aspect of the European legacy. Moreover, Communism did not dissolve the state, but rather came to power by gaining control of it. Thus the Communist cartographic inheritance can be seen as an aspect of state-directed nationalist cartography, with of course an emphasis on Communist ideology, rather than a completely separate cartographic tradition. The *Atlas de Cuba* (Havana, 1978) was published by the Cuban Institute of Geoscience and Cartography in order to commemorate the twentieth anniversary of the Cuban Revolution in 1979. The brief history section began with the more recent past, a big map of the Cuban revolution and 'Imperialist aggression' in 1953–59. The Cuban republic of the first half of the century was referred to as neo-colonial in a map of the situation in that period. The map depicted American economic penetration and murders of workers. The map on wars of independence 1868–1902 referred to the American intervention of 1898 as a military occupation by American imperialism. Last, the map of discovery and colonization in 1492–1868 included acts of rebellion against colonial domination.[66]

This historical section thus combined traditional Communist themes with nationalist defiance of the USA. The two were linked in the portrayal of the USA as an imperial power seeking economic domination. Indeed, the USA was very useful in Cuban propaganda precisely because it linked the notion of a domestic threat with that of a foreign challenge.

China

Nationalism also played a major role in Chinese historical atlases. The Communist takeover was followed by the publication of four atlases of Chinese history; by Shoushi Wan in 1954, Guangy-Cheng and Shengmo Xu in 1955, a five-volume work by Jiegang Gu and Xu Zhang in 1955, and by Tan Qixiang in 1975–82, the last an eight-volume work. Each of the volumes in the last contains maps of China under one or several dynasties. For each dynasty there are province-by-province maps showing rivers, towns and administrative boundaries. Historical and contemporary features, distinguished by colour, are juxtaposed. Administrative and political boundaries are the major topic of the atlas.

In addition, there have been a number of specialized historical atlases. These have included the *Historical Atlas of Beijing City* edited by Renzhi Hou (Beijing, 1985) and two atlases of historical earthquakes. The latter were presented in a utilitarian fashion. The *Atlas of Historical Earthquakes in China* (Qing Dynasty Period), compiled by the Institute of Geophysics, State Bureau of Seismology, and Institute of Chinese Historical Geography of Fudan University (Beijing, 1990), included an English preface explaining that it was necessary to examine the degree of seismic activity in order to determine the best location for industries.

The essential divide in Chinese historical mapping was between atlases of the twentieth century and those covering earlier periods. The former reflect the details of Communist historiography, while the latter are mostly of interest for their territorial pretensions: nationalist grandeur through territorial extent. The revolutionary war in which the Communists gained power has been treated in two historical atlases, both compiled by the Military Museum of the Chinese People's Revolution.[67] They were both published by the Cartographic Publishing House in Beijing, a publisher that reflected the role of state direction in Chinese cartography. The Chinese were open to new technology,[68] but more resistant to Western concepts of intellectual freedom. The Cartographic Publishing House also published an atlas of Chinese history covering 1840–1918 that, unsurprisingly, was hostile to the interventions of Western powers in that period.[69]

Maps dealing with earlier periods tend to emphasize China's territorial extent, especially with reference to regions subject to territorial disputes or tension in the decades after the Second World War, for example Sakhalin, Turkestan and the Amur valley. This impression of territorial extent was created both by producing maps of China when it was most powerful and, even then, by advancing question-able claims. The historical maps in *Information China I* (Beijing/Oxford, 1989), a volume produced by the Chinese Academy of Social Sciences and published by it and by Pergamon Press, depicted China during the Western Han and T'ang dynasties, when it extended widely.[70] Other periods were ignored. There was a map of Chinese expeditions across the Indian Ocean in the fifteenth century, and a series of maps of the twentieth century. That of the 'Revolution of 1911' marked Taiwan as Japanese-occupied and Hong Kong as British-occupied, in order to lend historical depth to Chinese claims on these territories in the 1980s. This process was selective: Tibet was not shown as Chinese-occupied. The map was also designed to show how much of China was affected by the 1911 rising. The map of the 'Northern Expedition 1926–7' similarly stressed the radical nature of China in the period. The key included an entry for major cities affected by the labour and anti-imperialist movement. The map of the Long March of the Red Army commemorated a crucial episode in Chinese Communist history. The map showed the march as more complex than was sometimes suggested: the various routes were depicted, as also the area of guerilla activity. The map of 'The General Counter-Offensive from bases in the occupied areas during the war against Japanese aggression 1945' included guerilla areas on the eve of the general offensive. This included much of China south of Manchuria that otherwise appears as occupied by Japanese invaders in historical maps of the period. The subsequent civil war was presented as a war of liberation and depicted in two maps. China itself was shown as including all the islands in the South China Sea.[71] Thus, the two key features of modern Chinese historical cartography – territorial claims and a Communist account of the recent past – were combined.

A different tradition of Chinese historical cartography is offered by Taiwan, where Communist historiography and ideology play no role. Interest in pre-Communist cartography is indicated by the reprinting of Shoujing Yang's 1906 historical atlas of changing administrative geography in 1975. The two-volume *Chung-kuo Li-shih Ti-t'u* (Historical atlas of China), published in Taipei in 1984 by the Chinese Culture University Press, lacked the separate provincial maps for each dynastic period published in Tan Qixiang's volume, but valuably attempted to extend the range of Chinese historical cartography by mapping more than administrative geography. It had maps of the distribution of industries and natural resources at various points in China's history, maps of water conservancy and communications, of population distribution and of major military campaigns.

Mapping Chinese history faces a number of problems and it is instructive to note the contents of works produced outside China. The most important is Albert Herrmann's *Historical Atlas of China*, first published in 1935 by the Harvard-Yenching Institute, reissued in 1964 by the Literature House of Taipei and in a revised edition in 1966 by the Aldine Press of Chicago. This was a set of colour maps with one map for each major dynasty. In addition to the basic physical geography, imperial and provincial boundaries and major cities were also indicated, as were some military campaigns. Herrmann, Professor of Historical Geography at Berlin, was cautious about bold claims for early Chinese territorial extent.[72] Brian

Catchpole's *Map History of Modern China* (London, 1976) was a lively, varied and illustrated work essentially for students; it was not a work of scholarship.

The *Cultural Atlas of China* by Caroline Blunden and Mark Elvin (Oxford, 1983) was a far better work, as well as being one of the more impressive of the Phaidon/ Equinox series of historical atlases. Its historical maps were not a static account of administrative geography, but were instead more imaginative and, with the assistance of text and captions, more interpretative. The dynamic contrasts of Chinese geography, for example between Inner and Outer China, were brought out,[73] and the authors were properly cautious about the need not to exaggerate the importance of provincial boundaries.[74] Instead, they drew on William Skinner's idea of macro-regions each containing an economic core area to propose a system of functional regions,[75] and used them to indicate 'how dramatically the "real" China . . . differed from that depicted in the familiar historical maps based on political boundaries'.[76] Aside from this important cartographic reconceptualization of the Chinese past, the Blunden and Elvin atlas was also instructive for mapping anti-Chinese resistance and independence movements,[77] a topic very different from the radical risings favoured in Communist historical cartography.

The treatment of Chinese history in historical atlases of the world has serious limitations. First, it is generally inadequate given the importance of China in world history. Pierre Vidal-Naquet acknowledged this fault in the *Atlas historique* (Paris, 1987) he edited. It is true of all other world historical atlases.[78] Second, the mapping on the whole lacks the detail employed for European history. Third, it is often limited in its interpretation, in part reflecting the use of Chinese provincial divisions, as in the map of Tang China in the *Times Atlas of World History*.[79] French scholars, however, have produced some interesting maps trying to capture dynamic interactions in Chinese history. Alain Reynaud has depicted relations between the statelets of ancient China using the graphic methods of much late twentieth-century French historical cartography – circles and arrows – in order to lay bare what he saw as their essential interrelationships.[80] Similarly, Chaliand and Rageau's *Atlas politique du XXe siècle* (Paris, 1988) includes an unusual map of the Cultural Revolution of 1965–69 depicting not only the areas of Red Guard agitation, but also the essential axes in the diffusion of the revolution.[81]

There are a number of problems in producing historical maps for China, not least the limited nature of the existing maps, both historical and otherwise. For a long time, China did not make available medium- and large-scale topographical maps. Furthermore, although China has a long administrative tradition, there are surprising limitations. Aside from the general point that paper, the writing material in China for near 2000 years, lacked the durability of parchment and papyrus, the surviving written sources are often too unclear or unreliable to provide a basis for accurate mapping. For example, the vague and often contradictory nature of the sources makes it difficult to pinpoint the exact location of particular towns in the medieval period. Tan Qixiang's maps show prefectural boundary lines for the middle years of the T'ang dynasty, but their exact location on the map was largely a matter of guesswork, since the information is not to be found in any T'ang source; instead, these provide only the locations of the seats of the subordinate territorial units. It is indeed a common problem in historical cartography: the desire to mark in boundary lines places a misleading weight on the edges rather than the centres of units.

As the accuracy and even the meaning of early Chinese census data have been hotly contested, there are also problems in mapping aspects of Chinese demographic history, for example the transfer of population from north to south China during the Middle Ages.

External boundaries also pose problems. For example, the movable picket and 'karun' system makes it very difficult to depict China's north-western frontier and also ensures that whatever is depicted has to be explained.[82] There are illustrative maps of picket positions during the Qing period, but the task of locating these points in terms of longitude and latitude is very difficult. The first detailed Chinese map to cover north-west China was probably the *Shisan pai ditu* (*c.* 1770), which the Jesuits worked on.

More generally, the nature of the relationship between China and its neighbours varied. It is possible to present it in adversarial terms, but it has also been argued that most of the nomad rulers who controlled the northern borderlands wanted to extract resources from China rather than conquer it, that this extraction was most efficient if relations were peaceful and that intervention was usually a response to political fragmentation within China.[83] It is unclear how best to indicate these relationships on maps. Nevertheless, the historical study of Chinese geography is fairly well developed. William Skinner has divided China into nine macro-regions using central-place theory analysis. He and Robert Hartwell have proposed treating the history of China as really several separate histories. By dividing China into macro-regions, a more precise model of historical trends becomes clear. While some areas experienced economic growth, others were in decline.

Japan

The mapping of Chinese history is a formidable challenge, but it is not alone in Asia in posing problems for historical cartography. Japan has a long cartographic tradition. *Ban sei tai hei zu setsu*, a manuscript historical atlas of Japan compiled by Kitajima Choshiro (Tokyo, 1815), consisted of eleven territorial maps.

In the twentieth century, Japan's position in the world and specifically in east Asia has been a matter of great controversy. Nationalist feeling was replaced after the Second World War by a vastly changed appreciation of Japan's position in the world. This led to the production of a new historical atlas: *Nihon Rekishi Chizu* (Japan historical atlas) (Tokyo, 1952) by the Japan Map Study Society. The atlas was rather short and simplistic, but it served the needs of the moment by offering a cartographic account of Japanese history that did not centre on conflict with other states. Most obviously, Japan was defined with reference to its post-1945 boundaries and most of the maps were restricted to a coverage of this area. The map of the distribution of bronze vessels from the Stone and Iron Ages did include most of the Korean peninsula and that of the administrative divisions of successive periods included an inset map of the 'Conditions on the Korean Peninsula in Ancient Times', but such an inclusion was not the case with, for example, maps of the distribution of stone implements and of Chinese-made mirrors found in tombs, and of feudal Japan. There were numerous town plans, an uncontentious topic. Japanese history over the previous century was presented in terms of Commodore Perry's 'opening up' of the country, the establishment of the modern state in the late nineteenth century presented in terms of administrative reconstruction and the path to constitutional democracy, and industrialization. The cartographic section of the atlas closed with a map of modern Japan and the world that concentrated on trade. Thus, topics such as the Russo-Japanese War and both world wars were ignored.

This atlas was frequently reprinted but not significantly revised, and was still the most common choice of historical atlas in Tokyo bookshops in 1995. In 1982 a two-volume *Nihon Rekishi Chizu: Genshi Kodai-hen* (Japanese historical atlas: primitive and ancient) was published in Tokyo. It was followed in 1985 by *Nihon-Shi Sogo Zuroku* (Comprehensive illustration of Japanese history) by Haruo Sasayama and others. An expanded version of the last appeared in 1995. The principal themes were the extension of political authority, economic development, the spread of Buddhism, the growth of education and Japan's international position. The atlas included numerous illustrations, but was far larger than the 1952 work. For example, the maps of early archaeological finds were both more numerous and were complemented by site maps. This reflects the tremendous expansion in Japanese archaeology after the Second World War. Prior to that, archaeological discussion had been limited, in part out of respect for the national myth tracing Japan and its emperor back to a legendary past.

Compared to *Nihon Rekishi Chizu*, *Nihon-Shi Sogo Zuroku* gave greater prominence to Japanese relations with East Asia, particularly China, and this included, for example, the Mongol attacks on Japan. Other interesting maps, not found in non-Japanese works, mapped the routes taken by Japanese embassies to Europe in the 1580s and 1610s and voyages by Japanese to Europe and Mexico in the period. The Japanese invasions of Korea in the 1590s, a topic ignored in the 1952 atlas, were also mapped. Maps of peasant riots in the 1780s and of peasant uprisings from 1590 to 1867 also added an element that undercut the unity of pre-modern Japan. This was matched more generally by a depiction of civil strife that extended into the twentieth century with a map of the 1918 rice riots, another of peasant uprisings after the First World War and one of army movements in Tokyo during the attempted coup of 1936. The successes of Japanese imperialism were also depicted, with maps of the Sino-Japanese War of 1894–95, of the Russo-Japanese War of 1904–5 and of the expansion of Japanese power in 1895–1910. Involvement in the First World War, and subsequently in Siberia, was also the subject of a map, another dealt with expansion in China after 1931 and the Second World War was the subject of a spread. This included a map of Japan's Great East Asian Co-prosperity Sphere in 1943 and another depicting Japanese casualties of Allied bombing, alongside more conventional maps of the Pacific War and of the battle for Okinawa.[84]

Elsewhere in Asia

Many Asian states lack detailed historical atlases, but there are important works, nevertheless, and they offer much information not found elsewhere. Thus, the Korean historical atlas of the world published in 1983 includes important maps of Korean history. Other such maps can be found more accessibly in Ki-baik Lee's *New History of Korea* (Seoul, 1984). Much of early Korean history is still disputed, and it is clear that the boundaries of the early kingdoms are not perceived in the same way in the South and the North.

Irfan Habib's *Atlas of the Mughal Empire: Political and Economic Maps* (Delhi, 1982) was a more detailed work, informed by his deep knowledge of the relevant Persian sources. Financial constraints played a role. The maps could have brought out more of Habib's research had they been printed in colour, but Oxford University Press in Delhi felt that this would make the book too expensive; it was dependent for its printing costs on a grant from the Indian Council of Historical Research. However, the atlas was particularly impressive for its inclusion of a map showing how the inability to identify 28.4 per cent of *mahals* (local seats of administration) varied geographically. Habib then pointed out that the map emphasized lacunae where *mahals* were very small and offered another map showing the number of places depicted in the atlas per 1000 square miles. The combination of the two and information on population density are used to suggest that most towns and townships with populations of 5000 and above during the Mughal period are shown on the maps. Similarly, the maps of economic information are presented with an explanation that much of the material comes from the accounts of travellers and thus that areas not crossed by major routes may be under-represented. Although the atlas has its deficiencies, particularly in the mapping of economic data,[85] it is all too rare to see diagrams in historical cartography that provide guidance to the reliability of the basic information given in the atlas.

Another important historical atlas produced within Asia was the *Historical Atlas of Iran*, the first of that country, produced by Teheran University and the National Cartographic Laboratory on the occasion of the 2500th anniversary of the Persian Empire and published in 1971 by Teheran University Press. The atlas employed Arabic, English and French, but it was made less helpful by an absence of pagination. Maps and text emphasized the importance of the monarchy. Thus the monarchs of the early tenth to the mid-eleventh century 'put great effort into reviving national traditions, preserving the customs of their ancestors and providing for the welfare of their subjects. This is true to such an extent that it can be said that the era of the greatest attainment of Iranian civilization and of the Islamic sciences and literature is the period of these same noble and magnanimous men.'

Subsequent problems were blamed on 'domination by savage yellow-skinned tribes from Central Asia', who created a dark age from the eleventh century to the start of the sixteenth. Rebirth was associated with a dynasty, the Safavids, and they were described in terms of a prospectus for the necessary government of Iran: 'a strong and independent central government' and the extension of Iran to its 'natural frontiers'. The maps were glossed to the greater glory of Iran. For that of Iran in the second and third millennia BC 'the archaeological evidence . . . shows that the people of Iran possessed an extremely advanced civilization as long ago as 7000 years'. The maps also served to justify the territorial pretensions of the Pahlavi dynasty. Map 21, for the Safavids, showed the Persian Gulf as surrounded by Iranian territory, and the text added 'Bahrein was Iranian territory and even Basra was sometimes under Iranian control'. It was in fact held by the Ottoman Turks from 1535 until 1776. Similarly, map 22 misleadingly extended Persian control over all the shores of the Persian Gulf during the reign of Nadir Shah, who indeed overran most of Oman in 1737–38, but abandoned his occupation of it in 1744.

Territorial ambition also played a role in an historical atlas of Thailand published by the Royal Survey Department of Thailand in 1935 or 1936. Five maps each claiming to present conditions during the reign of a successful monarch were presented in sequence. They failed, however, to note intervening periods of more modest territorial extent, if not defeat, displayed a false precision in the use of boundary lines, exaggerated the extent of Thai dominions and failed to differentiate between nominal vassals and the kingdom itself.[86] The territorial ambitions reflected in the atlas prefigured Thailand's role as a Japanese ally from 1941.

Asia: Conclusions

It is easy to point to lacunae or bias in individual maps and particular atlases, but there are also more general problems. First, modern approaches to Asian history both on the part of Europeans and on that of Asians are apt to concentrate on states, especially powerful states, and to ignore the more complex and varied political nature of much Asian history, not least 'the proliferation of localized areas of authority'.[87] Second, and relating particularly to the period before European colonization, there is the question of the very applicability of modern notions of space. Historical understandings are difficult to evaluate, but it seems clear that cultural assumptions about the nature and dynamisms of space were distinctive. Joseph Schwartzberg has suggested that Indian traditions of learning had little need or place for visual imagery and that 'a cosmically attuned society' attached 'relatively little importance to the mundane concerns to which most terrestrial maps relate'.[88] Denys Lombard's recent study of Javan culture contrasts the cartographic realizations of the Dutch colonial power with local assumptions.[89] It is far from clear how modern historical mapping should relate to these assumptions, whether historic or modern. Given that the traditional agenda of historical atlases – clearly demarcated territorial control – seems to be of limited relevance for the pre-colonial period, and the nature, role and relevance of that period are under challenge as decolonized peoples assess their history, it is clear that the processes of questioning and expanding the agenda that have affected historical mapping in the 'first world' should be extended elsewhere. Thus, for example, the most important historical atlas of Asia produced outside the continent, Schwartzberg's *Historical Atlas of South Asia* (Chicago, 1978, 2nd edn, New York, 1992), has been criticized for concentrating on geopolitics, rather than economic or environmental questions.[90]

Eurocentrism and 'First World' Historical Atlases

The problem of Eurocentrism in mapping has been increasingly recognized since 1945,[91] and major attempts have been made to adopt a less Eurocentric perspective. This is pre-eminently true of atlases of the first world, most clearly as a consequence of controversies over projections. Arno Peters criticized Mercator's projection and in 1972 employed an equal-area projection that subsequently led to the *Peters Atlas of the World* (London, 1989). This made the Third World more visually prominent. So also, though less strikingly, did the optimal conformational projection of the *Oxford-Hammond Atlas of the World* (Oxford, 1993). These maps still retained north at the top, but this convention is increasingly questioned in Australasia: MacArthur's *Universal Corrective Map* published in Artarmon, New South Wales, in 1979, had south at the top and the central axis running through Canberra.

The topics covered in historical atlases have been affected less by shifts in modern mapmaking than by increasing pressure in the historical profession for 'global' history. The covers, contents and texts of historical atlases are now less Eurocentric. Whereas the cover of the first edition of R.R. Sellman's *A Historical Atlas 1789–1962* (London, 1963) reproduced a photograph from the British Imperial War Museum of Churchill and Montgomery, the second edition, updated to 1971 and published that year, carried a montage of five pictures, including the death of Nelson, but also a prominent picture of African freedom fighters.

The influential atlas companion volume to the *New Cambridge Modern History* (Cambridge, 1970) offered nearly as many maps dealing with non-European lands and the world as a whole as those devoted to Europe. Such staples as *Putzger* now include more maps on regions outside Europe, although it is necessary not to be complacent. It is still possible to read modern historical atlases, for example *Atlas till Historien* (Stockholm, 1993 edn), which is currently used at the secondary school level in Sweden, and be surprised by the weight still placed on European topics.

The greater stress on non-European topics has been paralleled in historical atlases of the Islamic world. There has been a trend away from an emphasis on the central Islamic lands, towards placing more weight on south-east and central Asia, Africa and China. This is particularly true of Francis Robinson's *Atlas of the Islamic World since 1500* (Oxford, 1982).

The *Times Atlas of World History* (London, 1978) made a definite attempt to break away from Eurocentricity and this was seen as one of the defining points of the atlas, designed to make it both intellectually and cartographically distinctive and more attractive commercially. Geoffrey Barraclough, in an editorial introduction that was substantially reprinted in successive editions, stated: 'Our aim has been to present a view of history which is world-wide in conception and presentation and which does justice, without prejudice or favour, to the achievements of all peoples in all ages and in all quarters of the globe.'[92] In fact, the balance was still in favour of the history of European peoples, and has remained so. While one double-page spread in the fourth edition of the concise version (London, 1992) was devoted to Africa *c.* 900–1800, ten were entirely devoted to Europe in this period, and Europe also played a major role in another two. Moreover, Asia received far more attention than Africa or America before the European impact, while there was a relative lack of south Asian compared to east Asian coverage. Nevertheless, the atlas sought to demonstrate global relationships, 'links and interplays . . . it is not simply a series of national histories loosely strung together . . . it is concerned less with particular events in the history of particular countries than with broad movements . . . spanning whole continents'.[93]

In the *Times Atlas of World History* and the *Philip's Atlas of World History* a number of maps combine much of Eurasia and part of North Africa. Such coverage is especially appropriate for demonstrating the impact of nomadic peoples on settled societies. The *Times* includes an effective map of the 'barbarian' invasions, entitled 'The crisis of the Classical world', that covers the Eurasian world from western Europe to China, a similar map of medieval trade routes and a map of the resurgence of Muslim power that combines the rise of Ottoman and Mughal power.[94] Use of this perspective enables the extent to which the Mongols impinged on China, Persia and Europe to be readily seen.[95] The perspective is particularly useful for polities based on western Asia, such as those of Alexander the Great and his successors,

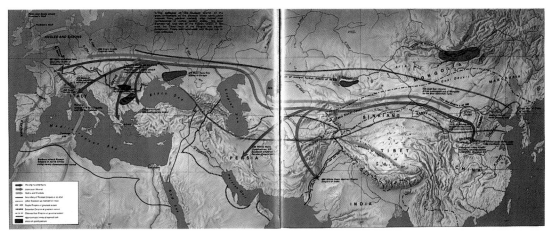

42. 'The Crisis of the Classical World' from the *Times Atlas of World History* (London, 1978). Rather than seeing the 'barbarian' invasions as an assault on the Roman world only, this map brought together a series of related crises. As with many of the maps in this influential atlas, this one offered novelty and visual appeal rather than precision. Dynamism was provided by the ubiquitous arrow.

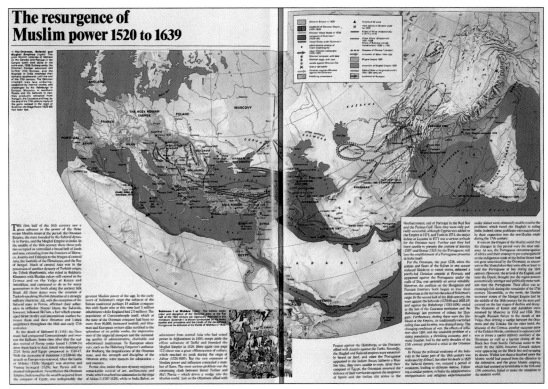

43. 'The Resurgence of Muslim Power 1520 to 1639' from the *Times Atlas of World History*. Ottoman and Mughal expansion were skilfully combined, although other important expanding Muslim states, such as Adal in the Horn of Africa and Aceh in Sumatra, were ignored. The importance to the Ottoman Turks of Persia emerged clearly and helped prevent the habitual concentration in maps on Ottoman expansion in Europe.

I/THE EASTERN FRONT
Nov. 1942 – May 1943
Russian front line Nov. 1942
Russian operations:
19-30 Nov. 1942
1-31 Dec. 1942
1-31 Jan. 1943
2-18 Feb. 1943
18 Feb.-31 Mar. 1943
German counter-attacks
1-4 Jan. 1943
18 Feb.-31 Mar. 1943
FINLAND
Baltic Sea
Gulf of Finland
Gulf of Riga
LENINGRAD FRONT
GOVOROV
12-30 Jan. Leningrad blockade broken. See page 64
VOLKHOV FRONT
MERETSKOV
NORTH-WEST FRONT
TIMOSHENKO
KALININ FRONT
SOKOLOVSKI
NORTH
KUECHLER
5 Feb.-30 Mar. German withdrawal from Vyazma and Demyansk salients. See page 64
Moscow
U S S R
WEST FRONT
KONIEV
BRIANSK FRONT
POPOV
CENTRE
KLUGE
VORONEZH FRONT
GOLIKOV
Pripet Marshes
SOUTH-WEST FRONT
VATUTIN
see map 5
see map 2
becomes Army Group Centre later
WEICHS
19-30 Nov. Stalingrad counter-offensive. See page 104
Stalingrad
DON FRONT
YEREMENKO
U K R A I N E
see maps 3 and 4
becomes Army Group South later
DON
MANSTEIN
NORTH CAUCASUS FRONT
MASLENNIKOV
Sea of Azov
CRIMEA
1 Jan.-4 Feb. N. Caucasus Operation
A
KLEIST
RUMANIA
BULGARIA
Black Sea
Caspian Sea
Caucasus Mts.

44. A conventional mapping of war from the *Times Atlas of the Second World War* (London, 1989), edited by John Keegan. Different projections and perspectives were also used to effect in the atlas. Maps such as that reproduced here helped to anchor more detailed treatments that were frequently more innovative. The greater number of army groups on the Russian side contributed to a sense of German weakness, although the size of such groups varied greatly.

Byzantium and most of the major Islamic states.[96] Maps of Europe, Asia and much of Africa in AD 100, 600 and 1300 that make Europe appear less central than is usually shown are presented in Anders Røhr's *VerdensHistorien* (Oslo, 1991).

Thus historical atlases of the world increasingly seek to take a less Eurocentric approach. The extent to which they succeed in this aim is of course questionable, but it is also necessary to make allowance for the difficulties in assessing how best to treat global history. An approach based on relative demographic weight would lead to an overwhelming concentration on east and south Asia. Furthermore, relatively little space would be devoted to North America and Australasia before European colonization. It is unclear what other basis for the allocation of space should be employed; certainly none could command general, still less universal, assent. The combined influence of perspective and selectivity is demonstrated in the *Times Atlas of the Second World War* which offers a number of very different global battlefield perspectives, for example 'The American War'. 'The Polish War' is also presented, ably making the point in the caption that 'the experience of war was neither clear-cut nor decisive for many peoples and nations, especially those chosen by the major powers as targets for ideological policies'.[97]

Even if a more truly global note is struck in atlases of world history, there are still two other important sources of imbalance. First, the concentration of 'territorial' historical atlases – national, regional, provincial, state and town – in Europe and North America ensures that these areas are best treated and that, in addition to the emphasis in atlases of world history, their history dominates the field of historical atlases. Second, the widening of the agenda of historical studies since 1945, in particular in social and cultural history, introduces the danger of a new Eurocentric perspective. Most historical research is conducted by North American or European scholars, and in those continents, and it will be difficult to match their findings by comparable work elsewhere. For example, Andrew Cliff and Peter Haggett's *Atlas of Disease Distributions* (Oxford, 1988) covers diseases both past and present and offers a comprehensive exposition of epidemiological mapping techniques and analysis. A range of approaches to the mapping and statistical analysis of medical data is employed, as in the use of choropleth and isopleth maps and a block diagram to depict the deaths in London during the 1849 cholera epidemic. However, most of the maps are of north-west Europe and, in particular, of Iceland, the country where the two authors have both worked longest. Data availability varies greatly. For example, Meron Benvenisti and Shlomo Khayat noted in their *The West Bank and Gaza Atlas* (Jerusalem, 1988) that, whereas two censuses had been conducted in Israel between 1967 and 1988, none had been conducted in Israeli-occupied territories. More generally, they suggested that the very absence of vital statistical data for these territories was linked to a lack of interest in 'rational planning' for them.[98]

The distribution of data, research activity and publication has important implications for historical atlases, especially in terms of what can be mapped. Similarly, resources are concentrated in the 'first world'. Thus, the Atlas of European Towns project adopted in 1968 by the International Commission for the History of Towns had already led to the establishment of national publication programmes, such as the *Irish Historic Towns Atlas* (since 1986), and Austrian (since 1982), British (1969), Dutch (1982), French (1982), German (1972), Italian (1986) and Scandinavian (1977) equivalents. At its annual meeting in 1993 the Commission decided to extend its membership to representatives of American and Japanese urban history groups. By 1994 maps and research on about 230 European towns had been published.[99] The effort and resources have not been matched elsewhere. If the new agenda threatens to exacerbate Eurocentrism, the same is also true of the expensive march of technology, but it is first necessary to look at the former.

9

A New Agenda: Post-1945 Historical Atlases and the 'Non-political'

The agenda of post-1945 general and national historical atlases has broadened greatly. No historical atlas published before the Second World War would have tackled the topics covered in Michael Dockrill's *Collins Atlas of Twentieth-Century World History* (Glasgow, 1991). He covered desertification, sea pollution, acid rain and tropical forest clearance in two maps devoted to the global environment, and incidence of AIDS cases in one of the maps devoted to health. Social, economic and cultural data are now mapped in all general historical atlases (although the essential logic of most remains geopolitical), while there has also been a major development in the number and importance of thematic historical atlases. Whereas late nineteenth-century historical atlases frequently closed their map section with a world map depicting the European colonial empires, it is now more common to close with a map showing the state of the world that incorporates information on crucial social-economic indicators. The *Philip's Atlas of World History* (London, 1992) closes with a double-page spread 'Foundations of a Post-Imperial World', showing, on a national basis, life expectancy at birth, and gross national product (GNP) in aggregate terms and per capita. The *Times Concise Atlas of World History* (4th edn, London, 1992) closes with a similar spread on 'The World in 1990' showing GNP per capita, international debt and overseas development aid. One of the supporting diagrams contrasts the life expectancy, birth, infant mortality and literacy figures of eight countries. The sheer mass of information is one of the greatest problems with which mapmakers today contend.

Culture

Cultural and intellectual influences within Europe from the sixteenth century can, in part, be readily displayed by maps concentrating on printing and publication. The spread of artistic styles, especially the Romanesque, Gothic and Baroque, is increasingly mapped. The two maps on the spread of Baroque architecture in the Westermann *Grosser Atlas zur Weltgeschichte* (10th edn, Brunswick, 1978) made the growing importance of southern Germany clear. In seeking to define Europe, Michel Foucher's *Fragments d'Europe* (Paris, 1993) maps cultural indicators, such as the spread of opera and the Baroque.

The cultural information mapped can also be presented in a way that explains and comments on perceptions of cultural development. For example, the map of art commissions 1280–1550 mentioned by Giorgio Vasari, published in the *Atlas of the Renaissance* (London, 1993), is accompanied by a caption that makes the point that his work overemphasizes the relative importance of Tuscany and the artistic poverty both of northern and southern Italy. Yet, as is pointed out, Vasari's *Lives of the Artists* has coloured perceptions of Renaissance Italy until modern times. Scholarly interest in the nature and role of perceptions and current work on 'mental maps' suggest that the compilers of historical atlases may soon show greater interest in the mapping of perceptions and ideas. The *Atlas of the Renaissance* also includes maps of the spread of printing and universities, while for France, a map combines the royal progresses of François I and the châteaux of the period. The map 'The Enlightenment in Europe' in the *Philip's Atlas of World History* (London, 1992) includes palaces modelled on Versailles, the correspondents of Voltaire and the travels of Mozart and Dr Burney, alongside territorial acquisitions by Austria, France, Hanover and Prussia, though the use of arrows to represent both travels and 'direction of expansion of powers' is somewhat problematic. The *Histoire de l'humanité* (Paris, 1987) also depicts Mozart's travels.

In cultural history, the powerful role of the culture of print as a force for and expression of social change, political consciousness and economic development can be displayed in maps. Thus, *An Historical Atlas of South-West England* edited by Roger Kain and William Ravenhill (Exeter, 1997) contains maps of the distribution of book trade firms *c.* 1800, of towns where a printing press is known to have been located before 1801 and the number of imprints, of the spread of newspaper production down to 1860 and of the probable routes of newsmen delivering *Trewman's Exeter Flying Post* in 1772. The growing comprehensiveness of print emerges clearly in spatial terms. *The Historical Atlas of Canada. II The Land Transformed, 1800–1891* (Toronto, 1993) includes a double-page spread on 'The Printed Word' as well as another, reflecting recent interest in the spatial ordering of social relations on 'Parades and Processions'.

Until very recently, scholarly work on cultural history related largely to elite activity. There is little doubt that cultural consciousness and activity at the popular level is far harder to evaluate and thus map.

Religion[1]

This is also true of other spheres. It is easier to map religious affiliations than to map religious fervour, to provide reliable indications of the strength of religious sentiment and, in particular, the nature of popular religion. There are major problems with the reliability of religious statistics.[2] Mapping religious affiliations, one is often mapping evidence that is equivocal. For example, maps of areas that were prone to heresy are only maps of places where heresy was found by visitational officials or reported by local inhabitants. The attempt to map orthodox piety often means indicating where church building was undertaken or where chantries were founded: these may be a measure of wealth rather than piety. The sources tend to impose a rather clerical view on the subject, for example by making the parish the central focus of lay piety. Thus, there are problems with the evidence used for the maps, rather than the maps themselves, that can distort the attempt to plot religious life and affiliation. There is

SAINT JOHN
ORANGE DAY PARADE
12 JULY 1849

Parades frequently resulted in the breakdown of civic order. On 12 July 1849 Saint John, NB, experienced one of the century's worst riots. Protestant-Catholic tensions exploded into death and destruction during an Orange Day Parade. In consequence, such processions were banned from the city's streets.

The urban parade served many purposes. In May 1872 an extremely well organized and orderly parade proceeded through the principal thoroughfares of Hamilton, and past the leading places of employment. Designed to enforce the demand of organized labour in the city for a nine-hour working day, the parade demonstrated the potential of such public demonstrations to attract attention without creating disorder.

THE PARADE SEASON

Other
Labour
Circus
Visitors
Religious
Fraternal
Military

M J J A S O N   M A M J J A S O N
Toronto May–Oct 1880   Hamilton Mar–Nov 1872
Each block represents one parade

HAMILTON
'NINE-HOUR MOVEMENT' PARADE
15 MAY 1872

Important points along the route
1 Johnson's Marble Works
2 Great Western Railway General Office
3 Beckett Machine Co
4 Mayor Chisholm's Residence
5 Residence, Gen. Superintendent of GWR
6 The Standard Office
7 Pryke's Store
8 Mr Watkin's Store
9 Wanzer Sewing Machine Co
10 Wilson, Lockman & Co
11 Gardner Sewing Machine Co
12 Mechanics' Hall
13 St Patrick's Society
14 Iron Moulders' Union
15 Crystal Palace

Known locations involved with the movement
A Shakespeare Hotel
B Dan Black's Club House
C Schuck's Saloon
D L.D. Sawyer & Co Implement Works
E H. Hennessey

Nine-Hour Movement Parade, 1872

Some events of 1872 in Hamilton

45. 'Parades and
Processions' from *The
Historical Atlas of Canada II*
(Toronto, 1993). Political,
social and ethnic
distinctions were and are
mirrored in the use of
public space for collective
action and demonstration.
Disputes over where
marches can proceed
reflect perceptions of
spatial identity.
Cartographically, however,
it is difficult to capture a
moving spectacle.

a general bias towards the religious life of the elite and literate. Detailed work has been carried out on the reliability, comparability and continuity of some religious sources,[3] for example the 1851 religious census of England and Wales, but this is not true of most such sources.

There are also major problems with definition. For example, it is possible to map South America in 1900 as largely Catholic but there were (and are) enormous differences between, for example, pious Italians in the Argentine and members of various syncretic faiths in the Andes. The mapping of religious history is of more than ecclesiastical interest. The mapping of Catholic Easter communions undertaken by Gabriel Lebras and his successors led to the establishment of areas of high and low church attendance across western Europe and the realization that these corresponded closely with the maps of conservative and radical voting established by political cartographers.

Most historical atlases do not seem particularly concerned with mapping 'Christian practice'. Instead, they focus on institutional developments, such as the creation of dioceses, the spread of particular religious orders and schisms. There is very little mapping of more mundane features of practice, such as pilgrimage sites, liturgical uses and types of artefact. These would, however, be difficult to map effectively, because of losses of evidence over time, and also because of the difficulty of collecting the information in sufficient quantity. Furthermore, the constantly changing patterns of religious experience limit the value of maps to represent a long-term picture other than for the institutional structures.

The treatment of the relationship between different faiths is a major problem with the mapping of religious history. As with maps of states and peoples, maps of religious affiliation provide no guidance to the degree of harmony and conflict.[4] For example, the relationship between Jews and Christians in Spain varied greatly, and, indeed, it is not clear how best to distinguish them, especially in the sixteenth century when there were officially no Jews in Spain. This issue is particularly a problem at the global scale as religions adopted dissimilar positions on exclusiveness and tolerance.[5] Furthermore, religions have different needs of fixed structures, and this again affects mapping,[6] as does state patronage.[7] At another level, it is unclear whether and how best to map the mythic worlds that play such a major role in many religions; especially if they are in fact a mythologized account of the real world. Cosmology involved sacred movement that was transformed into cartography in many societies.

Shifts in the mapping of religious history reflect more general changes in historical cartography. Thus, in the mapping of Christian history there has been a move away from the Eurocentrism of earlier works such as the *Atlas zur Kirchengeschichte* of Karl Heussi and Hermann Mulert (Tübingen, 1937), and there is also more interest in mapping the history of other religions. Furthermore, local and regional historical atlases are paralleled by works that are quite restricted in their scope, such as Frédéric Van Der Meer's *Atlas de l'ordre cistercien* (Paris, 1965) and William Schroeder and Helmut Huebert's *Mennonite Historical Atlas* (Winnipeg, 1990). In addition, a broader and less conventional agenda of relevant aspects of religious history has been matched by recent trends in conceptualizing and representing space as in the spread 'Defining Sacred Space' in the *Historical Atlas of Canada* (3 vols, Toronto, 1987–93).[8]

Transport

Transport forms an obvious contrast to religion as a cartographic subject. It lends itself readily to mapping: not only routes and volume, but also changes with what they suggest about shifts in perception of space. Thus, a simple map of the 'Transport Revolution 1765–80' in Anders Røhr's *VerdensHistorien* (Oslo, 1991) draws attention to the dramatic shrinking of France prior to the railway age. There have also been atlases specifically for transport history: for example, S. Maxwell Hajducki's *A Railway Atlas of Ireland* (Newton Abbot, 1974) which included opening and closing dates for every line, as well as the changing structure of companies, Michael Freeman and Derek Aldcroft's *Atlas of British Railway History* (London, 1985) which brought out the geographically fragmented nature of control and the *Atlas zur Verkehrsgeschichte Schleswig-Holsteins im 19. Jahrhundert* by Walter Asmus *et al.* (Neumünster, 1995), a detailed study of transport links and flows which clarifies a number of subjects such as the impact of the railways and the continued role of coastal shipping. The atlas also depicts what is commonly ignored, the interrelationship of systems too often presented as competing. Instead, a series of maps focuses on links, for example between railways and canals, and sea ports and railways.

The mapping of transport history is greatly dependent on data availability, not least because quantifiable information also throws light on the qualitative nature of the system. Different indices of density of usage can, for example, be mapped: numbers of trains or passengers per day, freight tonnage or income turnover per mile. Such analysis is much more difficult for the nineteenth century as the data is less sophisticated, but is necessary in order to provide some indication of the success or failure of particular routes. The same is true of canals. This is an issue in which text can be a valuable complement to maps. Thus, the maps of railways in 1850, 1885 and 1914 in the *Atlas of Portsmouth* reveal steady expansion, while the text suggests a more hesitant development.[9] In his *Historical Map of the Birmingham Canals* (Kidderminster, 1989), Richard Dean warns that not all the canals shown existed at the same time. A similar warning attaches to the Roman roads indicated in the *Tabula Imperii Romani Lutetia* (Paris, 1979).[10] Similar problems with simultaneity and 'quality' affect other forms of mapping. For example, the excellent historical *Atlas of Food Crops* by Jacques Bertin *et al.* (Paris, 1971) was unable 'to show degrees of intensity of cultivation'.[11]

It is difficult to depict slow improvements and periodic upgrading in existing systems, so that maps of transport links tend to place an undue weight on new routes. As a result, rail and road improvements in the first half of the twentieth century are generally underrated.[12] This is especially the case because there is an emphasis on the length and general direction of routes rather than on the time taken to accomplish particular journeys. It is also valuable if the supply-side of links is depicted alongside some indication of demand. This can be simply achieved by including area of settlement, but population density is more useful. Maps of public transport in Berlin in 1890, 1910, 1933 and 1960 in the *Deutscher Planungsatlas. Atlas von Berlin* (Berlin, 1956) included a choropleth background of population density.[13]

There is also an increasing realization of the role of transport as a creator and facilitator of power, both in integrating areas economically and politically and in extending power. Thus, the *Historical Atlas of Islam* edited by W.C. Brice (Leiden, 1981) presented railways as 'instruments of conquest and control'.[14] Government postal routes were another expression of control and greater integration.[15]

Transport, however, is not the only aspect of social and economic history that lends itself readily to mapping. For example, geographies of banking have been recreated using mapping.[16] The mapping of historical demography is primarily a post-Second World War phenomenon. Mapping procedures were extensively adopted in G.M. Howe's *Man, Environment and Disease in Britain. A Medical Geography through the Ages* (Harmondsworth, 1972).

Gender

The literature on gender and space in the modern city might give rise to maps of the male and female areas of a city (in terms of gender-preponderant population and employment) depicting spatial segregation along gender lines. The suffrage movement with its umbrella of sister organizations would be eminently mappable, and the same is true of female trade unionism and modern feminist groups. In the 1990s there has been a growing interest in the spatial dimension of homosexual activity.[17] However, mapping sexualities in the past is very difficult given that until the post-war period there has been little record of the spaces and communities of sexual dissidents.

Topics

The increased role of non-political items can be seen by considering individual historical atlases. For example, the early modern section of *Suomen Historian Kartasto* (2nd edn, Helsinki, 1959) includes, besides separate maps for individual Swedo-Russian conflicts, maps of settlements in the 1540s, the rural linguistic situation, the distribution of population in 1749, seventeenth- and eighteenth-century forestry and internal trade, schools in the second half of the seventeenth century and administrative districts.

The *Historisk Atlas Danmark* (Copenhagen, 1988) similarly includes, besides a thorough treatment of Denmark's wars, very detailed maps of fiefs in 1662, of counties and districts in 1682–83, witch trials in 1616–87 and provincial courts and provincial court districts in 1751. The mapping clearly reveals differences, as in the maps of the percentage distribution of lower court judges according to their education by county in 1750 and 1807, the number of farms per square kilometre by district in 1682–83 (higher density on the islands), the number of householders per farm by district and the number of small-holdings and cottages per farm by county in the same years. Thus, the structure of rural society and its regional variations are treated in detail. Paul Magocsi's *Historical Atlas of East Central Europe* (Seattle, 1993) includes a full-page map of the Counter-Reformation that depicts Catholic and orthodox universities, academies and schools; another shows the foundation of universities up to 1794 and the establishment of print shops prior to 1700.

'What the Renaissance was to the 15th century and the Reformation to the 16th, the French Revolution was to the 18th, and its results are as impossible to map as theirs.'[18] This statement, from the introduction to *Philips' Junior Historical Atlas* (5th edn, London, 1929), reflected the views of a period that placed an emphasis on the feasibility and desirability of mapping territorial boundaries. Its cartographic trace is still very much present today. Partly this arises from the genuine need for such information: at a pedagogic level, students wish to know where Lusatia was or what the frontiers of Poland were. Nevertheless, teaching increasingly emphasizes broad social and cultural themes. Unfortunately, maps tend to treat the same subjects – for example, for early modern Europe the Peasants' War, the spread of printing, the expansion of the Baroque (represented by the spread of imitations of Versailles) and the travels of Mozart. Yet information exists to permit the mapping of other themes and issues. For the Enlightenment, it might be instructive to map changes in the legality of torture or the spread of freemasonry, though the first would be a map of political units. Intellectual links in the seventeenth century could be depicted by mapping places of student origin for selected universities and the accompanying text could discuss the degree to which religious differences were an obstacle. The establishment of printing presses is a limited measure as it offers no indication of quantity of activity. A map depicting approximate numbers of books published by centre or country in a given period might be useful.

Dynamism

The selection of topics for mapping clearly relates both to the data available and to the purposes of the atlas. These are increasingly understood in dynamic terms, entailing not static territorial or distribution maps, but maps designed to highlight and explain processes such as centralization, decentralization and the creation of national identity.

An emphasis on a depiction of change, and on maps as reflecting ideological suppositions rather than as uncomplicated, neutral accounts of the past, accords with current theoretical discussion about the nature of map appreciation. In 1993 David Turnbull advanced the then commonplace view about the selective nature of maps and their dependence 'on the understanding of a cognitive scheme' and wrote:

> At base there is something more than merely metaphoric about maps and theories; they share a common characteristic which is the very condition for the possibility of knowledge or experience – connectivity. Since we cannot have a pure unmediated experience of our environment, that experience is better understood as an active construction resulting from a dialectical interaction between the 'lumps' in the landscape and our imposed connections of those lumps. Our experience and our representations are formative of each other and are only separable analytically.[19]

Indeed, there is a double dynamism. Maps take on their meaning in terms of an interaction with their viewers/readers, and, second, it is necessary to appreciate that even as static representations they depict processes of change. Even in terms of location of industry or territorial boundaries at a given moment in time, the past is more fluid and ambiguous than is suggested by the flat colours and apparently precise lines and positions of conventional mapping. Furthermore, the moment takes on much of its meaning in terms of its context in change: are the frontiers of the state advancing, contracting or static? Is industrial location constant and if not, why not? The mapping of finance is another field that benefits from an ability to depict change: this is partly a matter of indicating whether countries, regions or other entities were becoming wealthier or poorer, and if so in absolute or relative terms, but also of the degree to which finance has meaning as processes, for example, of monetary circulation and investment. In seeking to represent flows of money, it is often difficult, however, to explain a process by using a map, which is essentially a snapshot. The *Philips' Atlas of World History* used pie-charts to express the movement of exchange rates of major European currencies against Dutch guilders on the Amsterdam market in the century 1609–1709. Heavy devaluations in Poland and Portugal emerged clearly, as did a rise in sterling. The growth of bank assets by head-office location in Ontario and Quebec from 1861 to 1891 was mapped in the *Historical Atlas of Canada*. The concentration of resources and decision-making in Toronto and Montreal was also demonstrated by the diagrammatic map of changing locations of bank head offices in 1891–1931.[20]

Given the degree to which distribution maps are affected by the extent of the available research it can be very important to complement them by indications of trends, which tends to mean the depiction of zones and movements.[21] Even when the research is fairly complete, it can be argued that a suggestion of dynamism is crucial to the understanding of the phenomena mapped:

> L'atomisation de la réalité associative constitue une seconde difficulté. Autant de points sur la carte, autant d'entités inertes, sans relation apparente l'une avec l'autre. Or, la force des société ne réside pas seulement dans les activités qu'elles développent

au sein de leur propre commune; elles tirent aussi leur dynamisme des relations qu'elles entretiennent entre elles par les affiliations qu'elles ont contractées, par les correspondances et les informations qu'elles s'échangent.[22]

The sense of change is not one that is catered for by most historical atlases, other than by turning the pages and hopefully noting alterations. A significant problem for all static graphic depictions of historical change is that they lack a dynamic dimension and so depict change as a series of stages or 'stills', rather than as a continuum. This can be either a conscious or unconscious way of depicting the past, and it is interesting to see where the sequence is 'frozen', but historical atlases tend to encourage a very stilted view of change.

Text can therefore be very valuable, while there is much to be said for the cartographic devices that represent developments, notably arrows, however simplistic they may seem. A number of devices, which can be dignified as a distinctive cartographic language, were increasingly used in the 1980s and 1990s, especially in French and Spanish historical atlases. For example, the *Atlas Histórico. Edad Moderna* (Madrid, 1986) uses circles to represent powers, a process that lends itself to another characteristic feature, the depiction of axes. Circles and arrows are also used extensively in Joan Roiy Obiol's *Atlas de Historia Universal y de España. II: Edades Moderna y Contemporánea* (Barcelona, 1993). Thus, the map of the Habsburg empire distinguishes bases of Habsburg power with circles and centres of anti-Habsburg resistance with triangles. Arrows, circles and lines representing barriers help to make the territorial maps dynamic, although it cannot be said that they offer the expert much additional information. Similar devices are employed in the *Atlas de História de Portugal* by A. de Carmo Reis (3rd edn, Lisbon, 1988). French cartography was influenced by the work of Jacques Bertin on graphic symbols and the language of maps. He sought ways of displaying dynamism and conveying graphic messages.[23] However, his impressionist methods sacrificed graphic precision.

The compilers of the *Philips' Junior Historical Atlas* in 1929 might have felt domestic, particularly non-political, developments difficult to map, but, as the historical agenda has widened, it is increasingly clear that such mapping is expected, while the range of research is such that the information exists to map many phenomena. Certain subjects, however, are difficult to map: political thought does not lend itself to cartographic depiction. With others there are problems of the significance of what can be mapped, or of lacunae in the relative material. In addition, the criteria of classification vary. Different archival practices, especially in the retention and organization of material and varied historiographical traditions, affecting not only the treatment of questions but also the very subjects that have been studied, pose problems. In addition there were major differences in the use of writing in administration, both public and private, between and within states. Furthermore, methods of measurement varied greatly.

There are therefore important difficulties in expanding the conventional repertoire of subjects for mapping and, in particular, in moving from the national to the international scale with such subjects. Yet, the vast expansion of historical research in the last 30 years is such that there is far more available data that can be mapped. This not only increases the range of subjects that can be mapped; but also the quantity of information available for individual topics. As a consequence, maps can become 'denser' as information systems. This both increases their advantage over other forms of exposition that cannot display so much information simultaneously or in comparable space, for example the printed page, but also adds to the problems of how best to present data.

The challenge is to alter the contents of historical atlases. That will inevitably be a slow process. The cost of cartographic work and printing encourages an essential conservatism in content, as does the degree to which the vast majority of historical atlases are produced without subsidy by the trade divisions of publishing houses.

Technology and the possibilities of the future will be considered in the next chapter, but before that it is necessary to assess the developing agenda with reference to the problems and possibilities of mappability.

Units

First, at whatever level information is gathered and presented, there are problems with the level and nature of the unit that serves as the basis for analysis and presentation. The consistency of units can pose major problems. For example, the number of counties in the province of Quebec increased dramatically between 1851 and 1901 and this poses problems of data adjustment.[24]

The makers of atlases first need to identify their levels of reference. For example, is a British county or American state atlas simply providing a wider context for indigenous parochial historians, or is it, in some sense, hoping to summarize some of the key peculiarities of the country's history? In which case, how can we tell where (and how far away) those peculiarities fade into other spatially definable areas of cultural distinctiveness on either side? Exactly the same points could be made at the level of nations or states whether presented within insular *or* continental contexts.

Historical atlases of particular regions are apt to assert that the individual regions were both an entity and distinctive.[25] In Britain a county approach either covering just one county or dividing some larger area into counties and using these as unit areas for choropleth maps, etc., implies that a county is a self-contained unit[26] and can lead to the neglect of important regional variations within counties.[27] Alternatives have been mapped: the 42 'farming counties of early modern England [and Wales]', and the fourteen 'cultural provinces' of England;[28] but if these units are not the basis for the collection of information there are obvious problems with data acquisition. Data standardization is a major problem when mapping at greater than the national level. Even when there is a partly shared history, such as between England and Scotland, there can be different legal and institutional frameworks that affect the data, in this case for example for the poor law. Furthermore, even when data standardization is less of a problem, the extent of research is likely to vary between different regions. For example, the reconstruction of human settlement during the last glaciation in the northern hemisphere in the *Atlas of Paleoclimates and Paleoenvironments of the Northern Hemisphere* (Stuttgart, 1992) was necessarily incomplete because of the 'equivocal state of research in different regions'.[29]

Relevance

Another problem that affects all historical mapping is the question of the significance of what is being mapped. The *Pergamon General Historical Atlas* (Oxford, 1970) included the location of nuclear power stations on its map of industrial development in the United Kingdom in the twentieth century, but with a national grid their distribution is less instructive than that of coal mining in the map of the Industrial Revolution. Wilhelm Schier's *Atlas zur Allgemeinen und Österreichischen Geschichte* (Vienna, 1982) uses the same map to show the movement of Jews in the Middle Ages and the spread of plague,[30] but there is no connection between the two. More generally, there is no point mapping activities that occur throughout a given geographical space either with a fairly uniform density or in close correspondence with the size of population. Thus, it is valuable to map bank deposits, but the location of branches is less instructive.

Simultaneity

It is necessary for map compilers to consider how their maps will be read. They are faced with a dilemma: how to present complex and perhaps controversial information and its interpretation in a visual form which is simple and easily comprehended but yet also makes clear the limitations as well as the virtues of the material and its treatment. However, even if the limitations are clearly indicated, it is not clear that map users 'will incorporate data quality information in map-based reasoning'.[31] To believe that relationships can be easily and intelligibly read off from visual evidence is in part a refusal to contemplate the real complexities of explanation, but it has the great virtue of accepting that visual evidence is the best form of displaying how change took place in space. Maps are abstractions that largely hide their abstract quality and that can offer a powerful means of locating and thus making concrete descriptions and explanations that would otherwise be overly abstract. In his preface to the French edition of the *Times Historical Atlas of World History*, Emmanuel Le Roy Ladurie claimed that 'L'extraordinaire puissance visuelle des cartes, coloriées et fléchées, permet, mieux qu'un long discours, d'énoncer une synthèse.'[32] Maps offer a simultaneity of events or developments, something that is not possible in text and that enables the readers of maps to devise their own patterns of association and explanation without the textual ordering of precedence. The sequential nature of writing is a problematic way to convey spatial simultaneity,[33] and, more generally, the unilinear form of language has limitations for the assessment and transmission of two-[34] and three-dimensional images.

 Visual representation in a map is a more effective way to suggest patterns of distribution and causation than talking or writing.[35] In one sense, readers can take in the contents of a map at a glance. In another, they have to teach themselves to study maps – as art historians do with paintings – very carefully indeed, and this takes time. Thus, the simultaneity has an element of delusion about it. Furthermore, it is generally limited to two dimensions. Yet this simultaneity is also particularly instructive if it entails the juxtaposing in the same image of events and developments that are not commonly linked, and this can be facilitated both by unfamiliar projections and perspectives and by using the same map to cover a wide chronological sweep. To take the first example, by centring its maps of Burgundian state formation near Verdun, the Westermann *Grosser Atlas* makes the process appear more probable and less peripheral than if it is depicted as part either of a general European map or a map of the development of the French state. The map of the Thirty Years' War in the

Atlas Historyczny Swiata (Warsaw, 1992) extends sufficiently far east to include much of Poland and thus to depict the Swedo-Polish battles of 1627–29. Due weight is given to the 1626 Silesian campaigns of Mansfeld and Wallenstein.[36] Thus, Poland does not appear as marginal, as it frequently does in maps of the war.

Conversely, Persia was the major threat to the Byzantine empire at the time of Justinian, but as maps of that empire are commonly centred on the Mediterranean or to the west of Byzantium, or presented as part of a map of Europe at that period, the threat appears peripheral. Similarly, it would be easier to illustrate the Turkish threat in the early modern period by maps centred on Vienna than by those in which the Turks lie on the edge of Europe. More generally, Persian history is underrated by the common failure to centre any maps on Persia, other than those of Alexander the Great's conquests. Unfamiliar perspectives and projections can be employed to add to what maps are doing. For example, Chinese expansion in the eighteenth century and on earlier occasions could be shown more vividly by adopting a north–south base line. The use of novel perspectives and projections is very important both in enhancing maps' pedagogic value and in increasing the competitive appeal of individual atlases.

Any departure from familiar images enlarges the cartographic repertoire and offers room for reflection about maps as graphic rhetoric and 'ways of seeing' and as 'texts' that require unpicking. Some compilers are explicit in their intentions. In his *World Atlas of Revolutions* (London, 1983), Andrew Wheatcroft commented on the spread of the American Revolution: 'The American colonies were dependent not on the interior of North America but on Europe. They have been given an Atlantic perspective which also emphasises the linearity of the colonies.'[37] Michael Freeman presented his view of the spatial nature of Nazi Germany with clarity. He wrote of

> *relations* in geographical space; in plainer terms . . . the tensions and dissonances that incongruent administrative areas generate . . . the Third Reich as a geographical or spatial entity was so riddled with discordant and disintegrative tendencies, either deriving from the character of its administration or from the forced exigencies of massive territorial accretion and the productive and operational demands of war.[38]

Braudel showed how the Sahara dominated the Mediterranean by putting north at the bottom.[39] In the *Historical Atlas of Canada* the process by which explorers found land but no sea route around it was demonstrated by putting North America on its side.[40]

Using one map to cover a broad chronological sweep also offers the possibility of creating a novel and arresting visual image and of suggesting a connection or parallel between events or developments not generally considered in such a light. It therefore implies that time should be treated with a degree of flexibility, not least that different societies followed similar patterns but at varying timescales. Some of the resulting combinations can be queried. In *The Times Atlas of World History*, a full-page map opposite the text 'The Rise of the Modern State in Northwest Europe 1500 to 1688' includes the British Isles, France and the Low Countries, a valuable combination, but, whereas the Dutch Revolt, French rebellions between 1568 and 1653 and British counterparts between 1497 and 1638 are included, there are separate maps for the French Wars of Religion and the British Civil War.[41] Thus, readers are offered neither a map of the wars of religion nor one on the mid-seventeenth century crisis. Similarly, in 'The Emancipation of the Peasantry', a valuable map of a generally unmapped issue, the situation in the early nineteenth century is confused by including the German Peasants' Revolt of 1525.[42] In *Atlas Historyczyny Swiata* (Warsaw, 1992), the latter shares a page with a map of the Dutch Revolt, a juxtaposition of two very different rebellions.[43] Maps that cover a long timescale sometimes exaggerate the impact of events that were only infrequent, for example rebellions.

Alongside questionable combinations, conflations and juxtapositions, there are others that are more appropriate and interesting. The map of 'Convulsiones en la Europo oriental' in *Atlas Histórico. Edad Moderna* (Madrid, 1986) offers an interesting perspective, covering Eastern Europe, Russia and the Turkish empire in the period 1549–1610.[44] Maps are designed to provoke and answer questions, excite curiosity and stir the imagination, and novel mapping of whatever type can help with all of these. Thanks in large part to television and video games and instruments, graphic images are of greater importance as conveyors of information and moulders of taste and opinion than at any time since the onset of mass literacy in the West. Visual symbols and systems provide direct links to readers that are more immediate and effective than the printed word.

'Reading the text' may present problems for those who wish to assess historical atlases, but deciding the best way to represent what is to be mapped involves cartographic, conceptual and historical issues. Nevertheless, makers of historical atlases relating to quite different periods and themes individually face similar problems. They all need to think about costs, colour, which themes can usefully be mapped and which can't, and how sophisticated the cartography needs to be in each case. Liaison with professional mapmakers can often be difficult. Many scholars are not map-conscious, and often leave the work to mappers who have not always understood the text. There is an important distinction between cartographers, who can devise and plan maps, and cartographic draughtsmen who can only draw maps from cartographers' drafts. Mappers need to appreciate that the scholars' location of names in space and desired typeface are not personal whims, but often attempts to show selected geographical features in a limited space. In turn, authors have to be aware of the limitations of mapping and in particular of the amount of information that a map will bear.[45]

Obvious difficulties in mapping include the nature of continuity and relationships between maps,[46] the level of abstraction involved in mapmaking and problems of scale. All maps are highly selective in content.[47] A 1:1,000,000 map can only crudely represent detail from 1:250,000 sheets.

Precision and Purpose

The degree of precision required and possible are also serious problems. Rather than assuming a perfect model, it is more appropriate to suggest a typology of different kinds of historical cartography, seeking dissimilar, though sometimes overlapping, markets, and with disparate intellectual goals. There are clearly different criteria for teaching and reference functions, and a 'need-to-know' map has to be judged quite differently from one that claims to be comprehensive. For example, it is true that atlases are essentially about place and location, historical atlases adding location in time to location in space. What is generally required is to know exactly where a place or territory is situated in a specific historical context. Precision in location, not least the inclusion of graticules, makes it easier to compare different maps and atlases and to interpret information in other sources alongside maps. Yet, the density of such information that is required varies, and it is therefore necessary to be cautious before criticizing many modern historical atlases for lacking sufficient information. The *Times Atlas of World History* is seriously lacking in detail, more interested in presenting the spatial character of historical events in a way that does not focus on showing space-relations as accurately as their scale allowed, and cannot serve for those interested in administrative and, in many cases, political boundaries, but it was not seeking an academic market and its pedagogic purpose focused on the broad sweep of world history and major currents of change, rather than static depictions of detail.

More generally, postmodernist geography has ensured that in the 1990s it is difficult to rank differing assumptions about space and spatial relationships, and competing geographical imaginations.[48] Thus, the *Times Atlas of World History* is more interested in space as an aspect of and sphere for dynamic historical changes, in space as process, rather than in space as place, an account of location, and it is no longer possible to assume a clear hierarchy of cartographic quality that can be used to judge such an aspiration.

Colour

The desirability of colour is also an issue. The use of solid colour for states can be very misleading, since it implies that governments controlled all the areas within their boundaries, which was often not the case. Instead, they generally had shifting spheres of influence. Employing colour, however, it is possible to convey more information in an individual map, although an examination of the use of colour suggests that frequently it does not serve that purpose, providing no more informa- tion than could be obtained by using black and white with different shadings. Indeed, colour is generally used without any capacity for phased shadings, although some atlases, such as the *Historisk Atlas Danmark* (Copenhagen, 1988), employ a sliding scale of colours. Instead, colour often serves mostly to help in the production of a more attractive book. Commonly judged essential for the illustrations, colour is often used to make maps more striking rather than more informative. Given its cost, colour often yields a surprisingly poor return in scholarly terms, and good black and white may even be preferable. Black and white maps are used with success in Martin Gilbert's series of historical atlases, for example his *Atlas of American History* (London, 1968, 3rd edn, 1993), *Atlas of British History* (London, 1968, 2nd edn, 1993), *Atlas of the Arab–Israeli Conflict* (London, 1974, 6th edn, 1993), *Atlas of the Holocaust* (London, 1988, 2nd edn, 1993), *Atlas of Jewish History* (London, 1969, 5th edn, 1993), *Atlas of Russian History* (1972, 2nd edn, 1993), *Atlas of the First World War* (London, 1970, 2nd edn, 1994), and *Jerusalem. Illustrated History Atlas* (London, 1977, 3rd edn, 1994).

Colour is not necessary for the location of places, which is a major factor for many scholars, especially medievalists, who require maps that accurately locate sites, par- ticularly those that have disappeared or changed their names. Nevertheless, colour can be of great assistance if different stages of locational development are to be

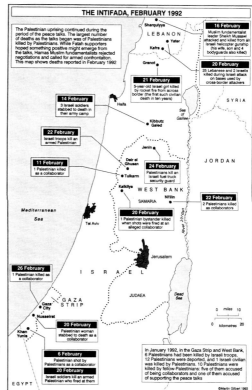

46. 'The Intifada, February 1992' from Martin Gilbert's *Atlas of the Arab–Israeli Conflict* (6th edn, London, 1993). Gilbert's atlases with their black and white maps enjoyed extensive sales. Gilbert's committed Zionism emerged in his atlas. In this map he made the reasonable point that Palestinians were killed by their fellows as well as by Israeli troops, but mention of the Lebanese-Israeli border was made without reference to the Israeli-backed occupation of part of southern Lebanon, the use of Judaea and Samaria was questionable and the West Bank was presented as part of Israel.

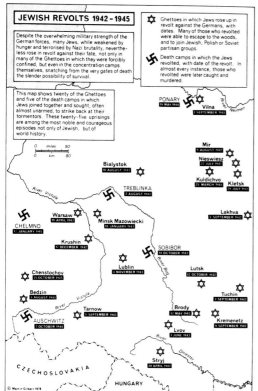

47. 'Jewish Revolts 1942–1945' from Martin Gilbert's *Atlas of Jewish History* (5th edn, London, 1993). In contrast to the usual treatment of the Holocaust, Gilbert directed attention to Jewish resistance; the previous map was of Jewish partisans and resistance fighters. The maps provided no guide to the numbers involved but achieved their purpose of demonstrating that the Jewish response to persecution was not always passive.

shown on the same map. Furthermore, the use of colour increases not only the density of information that a map can carry, but also the number of relationships it can present: thus, in addition to locational and quantitative material, correlations such as densities, proportions, ratios and trends can be depicted. Colour is also important in the educational process, increasingly so in societies used to colour imagery and graphics.

Frontiers

Like shading, colour can enhance depiction of territorial gradations. This is important in both political and non-political history. Clearly contrasting primary colours and firmly delineated frontier lines do not describe adequately or accurately problems of multiple allegiances, overlapping jurisdictions and complex sovereignty or societies that lacked a sense of rigid and clear-cut territorial units. In his foreword to the excellent *Atlas of the Crusades* (London, 1991), Jonathan Riley-Smith noted:

> it is well known that even when the course of a frontier can be accurately plotted –
> and that is rare for the Middle Ages – it meant less than it does now, being more often
> than not simply the boundary between the lands of two villages which owed returns
> to lords who were the subjects of different powers. In some regions, indeed, frontiers
> were characterized by broad belts of *condominia*, in which lords of different national
> ities, and in Palestine and Syria of different religions, shared the ownership of great
> swathes of villages. Customs posts were sometimes to be found . . . but they were
> often not on the border itself.[49]

The same was true of many other cultures.[50] Regions with shifting peoples, such as northern Europe and the Balkans from the third to at least the seventh century AD, are obviously difficult to map in terms of frontiers, but this is also true of the world of Imperial Rome with which such peoples are frequently contrasted. Not all parts of the empire had frontier structures such as Hadrian's Wall, the role of which is anyway debated, and it is argued that the Roman frontiers should be understood as permeable and shifting frontier zones.

Similarly, Byzantine frontiers are best understood as the shifting consequence of a number of dynamic elements that include the role of tribal transhumance. Thus, the mapping of its territories can be presented in 'maximal' and 'minimal' terms.[51]

In Europe in the later Middle Ages and the early modern period the general trend towards more defined frontiers ensures that it was then (and obviously also now) increasingly possible to draw maps with reasonable certainty that they corresponded to political reality at any given point. That was and is a statement that has to be qualified, first by factors of detail and scale, and, second, by an awareness of the continued problem posed by multiple allegiances, an issue that may recur in modern Europe with the move towards federalism within the European Union. For example, the 'gradualist' methods of conquest used by the Ottoman Turks in the fifteenth and sixteenth centuries pose cartographic problems. Christian territories on the borders of lands fully assimilated into the empire (in the sense that the provincial system of government was implemented) might be compulsorily allied to the Sultan, or endure tributary status to the Turks. The territories coming into the latter

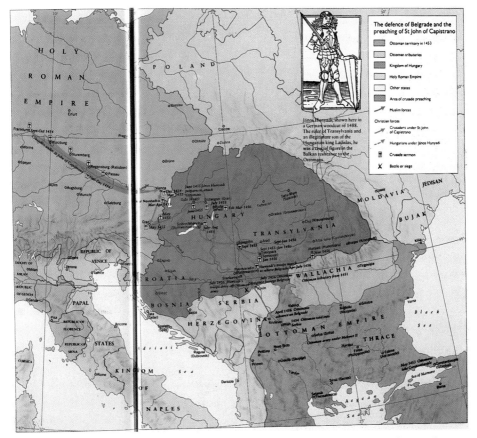

The defence of Belgrade and the preaching of St John of Capistrano

Ottoman territory in 1453

Ottoman tributaries

Kingdom of Hungary

Holy Roman Empire

Other states

Area of crusade preaching

Muslim forces

Christian forces

Crusaders under St John of Capistrano

Hungarians under János Hunyadi

Crusade sermon

Battle or siege

János Hunyadi, shown here in a German woodcut of 1488. The ruler of Transylvania and an illegitimate son of the Hungarian king Ladislas, he was a crucial figure in the Balkan resistance to the Ottomans.

48. 'The Defence of Belgrade' from *The Atlas of the Crusades* edited by Jonathan Riley-Smith (London, 1991). This atlas valuably served to enlarge the cartographic understanding of the Crusades by extensively mapping the period after the fall of Acre. In this map Ottoman territory was distinguished from Ottoman tributaries. Although published by Times Books, the atlas was produced by Swanston Publishing, and had their characteristic bold colours and campaigning arrows.

category were in practice under the Sultan's control: he could move his armies there at will, and demand resources and manpower on the same level as within the empire proper.[52] This situation is very difficult to depict cartographically. The map 'The Defence of Belgrade' in *The Atlas of the Crusades* shows that the tributary principality of Wallachia constituted a substantial part of the Ottoman presence in Europe. It would be necessary to give a large amount of detail about relations between the Prince and the Sultan to offer a realistic impression of how powerful the Turks were at any given point beyond the Danube. The same is true for the subsequent relations between the Sultan and both the Crimean Tatars and the Barbary states. Similarly, most historical atlases also show as Byzantine territories some areas that were really client states, for example Croatia and Serbia in the eleventh century.

Given such problems, it is not surprising that modern historical atlases face difficulties if they are trying to be accurate, or mislead by suggesting the uniform sovereignty of single-tone colours within sharply demarcated boundaries. Even where shared sovereignty was not an issue, modern maps can be misleading if they imply a high degree of precision in boundaries and control by different governments.

Instead, as Paul Magocsi noted, for a map of Ukrainian lands after 1569: 'the international boundaries between the lower Dnieper and lower Donets rivers as marked on this map were really only symbolic, because this whole region was a kind of no-man's land dominated by nomadic and free-booting communities of Zaporozhian Cossacks and Nogay Tatars.'[53] Similarly, the region between the Taurus and Antitaurus in eastern Anatolia in the eighth and ninth centuries was a frontier zone, under the control of neither Byzantium nor the Caliphate, and largely uninhabited; it is very sparsely settled even today. There has also long been a tendency to show Byzantium (and other states) in control of territory in Syria, Egypt and North Africa that was (and is) almost totally uninhabited desert, controlled by no one.

Thus, colour and other devices that suggest gradations or zones rather than lines, such as air-brushed lines, play an important role in the depiction of political control and the same is also true of other aspects of mapping, for territorial affinities and allegiances are of central consequence whatever the subject. Graphic fuzziness is useful in the representation of shifting or uncertain frontiers.

More generally, problems of defining and thus mapping frontiers reflect not just different patterns of political action but differing notions of territoriality and space. This point, already made on a number of occasions, has to be reiterated as it clashes with the general practice of historical atlases, and specifically with the treatment of certain themes that are frequently mapped. One is the expansion of Roman power, generally shown in terms of a series of provincial 'annexations'. This is misleading, since it has little connection with contemporary perceptions of the *imperium populi Romani*. It is also unclear how far the *provinciae* were thought of as territorial entities or had clearly defined boundaries.[54] The notion of a political boundary for the empire has been questioned,[55] and, more generally, Rome poses the problem of the value of subsequent cartographic analysis of a society that had a different, and by twentieth-century standards, limited[56] cartographic practice.

Mapping boundaries for 'prehistory' or 'protohistory', terms that themselves are problematic and invite debate, creates even more problems. Maps are crucial to almost every stage of archaeological research, but when once the mapping proceeds beyond the basic plotting of an archaeological site on a topographic map, major issues of cultural interpretation arise. These have been the subject of extensive discussion by archaeologists, and much of this discussion is of direct relevance to mapping in historical atlases.

The physical act of drawing boundaries around the known distribution of an archaeologically defined culture, prehistoric or otherwise, indicates a degree of cultural cohesiveness and contemporaneity of any locality's occupation that cannot be substantiated by the data. Especially within the context of a historical atlas, this practice suggests a validity to such boundaries comparable to those based on non-archaeological historical records, and this is not accurate.

For example, the boundaries usually drawn for the Harappan culture or Indus Valley Civilization span seven centuries, and would incorporate one million square kilometres and thousands of archaeological sites, or ancient settlements, thus representing one of the largest archaeological cultures in the ancient world. However, the physical representation of this area as a distinct region with boundaries would omit archaeologically significant synchronic and diachronic variations that existed. Equally important, it also implies a level of social, political and economic organization comparable to other mapped politico-geographical distributions, which is simply not true.

A central factor is the limited ability to control chronological issues. In the absence of historical documents, it is necessary to depend upon radiometric dating techniques, which in most instances means radiocarbon dates. Therefore all that is available are 'ranges' of dates from a limited number of sites which will vary in their degree of reliability by hundreds of years. Archaeologists attribute a range of dates to the Harappan culture, currently *c.* 2600–1900/1800 BC, but cannot determine which or how many of those thousands of sites were occupied at any given time. This problem raises fundamental questions, including whether the Harappan culture had one or multiple urban centres at any given point in time. British colonial records indicate that more than 25 per cent of the settlements in any given district in south Asia could be abandoned within any five-year period, a degree of mobility that has significant cultural ramifications, but archaeological data cannot detect such mobility. Yet the dating of archaeological remains, such as pottery, can be used to indicate the progress of colonization, as with maps of the spread of the Lapita civilization in the south-west Pacific.[57]

The archaeological database is nevertheless generally very incomplete. The absence of sites in a given region may reflect incomplete or non-existent field research. Since relatively few sites are ever excavated, archaeologists rely upon material collected from the surface of a site for most regional information; indeed, what is found on the surface influences which sites are selected for excavation. In addition, later can obscure earlier deposits. Even with excavation there are significant sampling problems. Seldom is more than 0.5 per cent of a site sampled. Second, it is difficult to project what is to be found beyond the limits of the actual excavations. More generally, modernity has a Janus-like relationship with archaeology: endowing it with identity, resources and technological progress, while destroying sites at an ever-more rapid rate, dramatically altering the database upon which an archaeologist would attempt to make geographical and, ultimately, cultural interpretations.

Mapping Change

Within mapping there is always a tension between the solidity, rigidity and, at times, simplicity with which territorial relationships are generally depicted and both the more complex nature of other relationships and the extent to which they are composed of dynamic actions, generally repetitive acts such as purchases of goods, attendances at religious meetings or taxes demanded and paid. Changes in the latter are difficult to depict. For example, it is unclear how best to depict the centralization of governmental, economic and cultural power in most twentieth-century states. At the level of locality and region it is easier to map administrative boundaries than the erosion of power.

The potentially misleading nature of clear lines in maps is not restricted to their role as bonders of territory – boundaries and frontiers – but also relates to their role as representations of links. This is the case, for example, with communication links. Modern maps are apt to be misleading, because they generally depict only the major routes, but these are fixed on land; although far less so in the air and at sea. However, for most of history land routes varied and this poses problems for

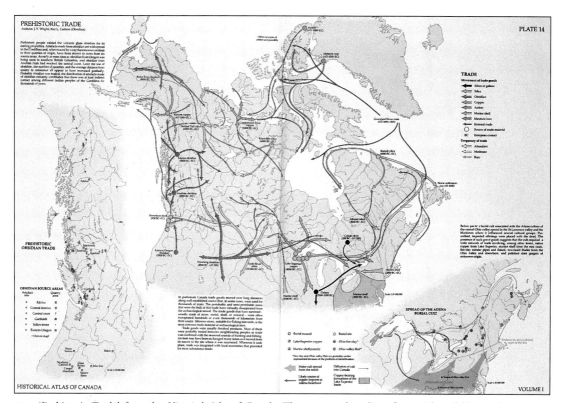

49. 'Prehistoric Trade' from the *Historical Atlas of Canada*. The range and quality of material available on the prehistoric economy was suggested here. The absence of frames for the individual maps contributed to the fluid feel of the plate and maps of different scales were included, again adding to the visual interest, each bearing an appropriate quantity of information. The movements shown represented general directions, rather than detailed paths. This accords with a widespread tendency in modern historical cartography.

mapping. It is unclear whether maps of itineraries, for example in medieval Asia or Europe, are of physical roads or of routes taken by travellers not constrained to exact trackways.[58] Archaeological evidence is of little value on this point because few new roads were built and the routes of the period have since been built over or ploughed up. The map of Native American and Explorer trails in the *Atlas of Kentucky* included physical features, and the text noted:

> These trails, so clearly defined on the map, were really 'flow lines' rather than single well-defined roads. The trail would be in one place in wet weather, in another in dry periods. And in peace-time certain routes would be used that were unsafe during war. Topographic features such as Cumberland Gap would constrain the travellers' use of alternate routes even in times of stress. Once the trail was free of topographic restraints, however, a series of essentially parallel trails and traces could be used at the travellers' discretion.[59]

Until the introduction of the motor car, the precise routes of many 'roads' in Australia changed as a result of local conditions.[60]

Arrows can also be used to suggest direction and volume of flow. Thus, the width of the arrows in the plate on prehistoric trade in the *Historical Atlas of Canada* were intended to convey an impression of the relative intensity and direction of transportation of materials from source. For example, truly massive amounts of Lake Superior copper and Ramah quartzite from northern Labrador were mined, fashioned and distributed while, in contrast, the Greenland Norse trade arrows generally pertain to single items. In the case of the Ramah quartzite, the decreasing thickness of the arrows is intended to indicate that most of the material was transported to the south along the Labrador coast and into the Lower St Lawrence River valley with minor amounts moving further south along the Atlantic coast and into the interior of the continent. An understanding of the map depends upon an appreciation that the thickness of the arrows is relative to the *individual* materials being plotted and does not represent an absolute scale for the trade map as a whole. In addition, the calibration of the width of the arrows in terms of 'abundant', 'moderate' and 'rare' is all that it is reasonable to expect. The use of eight colours permits the crucial distinguishing of the most important items traded and thus a portrayal of a much more complex situation than the aggregate trade links which is all that the use of black and white would have allowed.[61] The depiction of such material is an instance of how mapping both adds an extra dimension to research and makes it more accessible. In both cases, however, it is best to see historical maps as graphic theories seeking to express relationships, rather than as photographic replications.

Arrows are also useful for maps of prevailing winds and currents. Once standard in general atlases, they are now scarce enough to warrant inclusion in historical atlases. Oceanic maps should also include a colour gradient that indicates continental shelves and areas of upwelling, and it is necessary to indicate major fisheries: seas and oceans were not a uniform blank for previous generations.

Regions

By indicating comparisons and contrasts between and within regions, at given moments of time and over time, historical maps set the scene for and suggest analyses of cause and effect. An emphasis on comparisons and contrasts also makes it possible to identify, or refine, regions and boundaries, both of which are necessary for illustrative and analytical purposes. The stress in the 1980s and 1990s on a dynamic presentation of regions – of regions as systems of activity, their boundaries defined by the reach or intensity of such activity – facilitates a more multiple reading of regional identity. This is an accurate reflection of the multifarious nature of regionalism, but it presents problems for cartographic depiction and also ensures that the consistency of mapping is far less than when the emphasis was on historical international boundaries. A stress on regions as complementary spheres that are functionally interrelated[62] can be seen in economic regionalism and mapping,[63] rather than its cultural, political and social counterparts. Thus, Maryanne Kowaleski, in her study of trade and markets in medieval Devon, explained why she departed from a recent map of agrarian regions in that period:

> I have enlarged Fox's Dartmoor region . . . for the purpose of this study, which concentrates above all on trade, the commercial relationship between the moorlands of Dartmoor and the surrounding border parishes is more significant than their agricultural differences . . . Similarly Exmoor (a separate region in Fox) has been included in north and mid Devon because both their commercial ties and their distance from Exeter were similar.[64]

Likewise, industrial production is generally misrepresented if shown in terms of static plant and processes, for most manufacturing involves a degree of out-work and assembly, or at least of the movement of raw materials and energy. An emphasis on towns and their surrounding hinterlands can also serve to direct attention to important elements in other spheres of history. Migration patterns, for example, are of significance as cultural and social links. Even when considerable allowance is made for the impact of physical geography and of related socio-agrarian arrangements, especially the difference between upland and lowland areas, it is still clear that regional consciousnesses are affected by political structures and history,[65] the nature and impact of which were far from universal in extent and effect within any region, however defined.

The nature of 'cultural landscapes' and of cultural regionalism has also attracted considerable attention. This reflects greater interest by both historians and geographers from the 1970s and also the issue of how best to present the USA,[66] a large country whose regionalism cannot be satisfactorily explained and mapped with reference to its political history: the lands of the Louisiana Purchase, for instance, do not form a distinctive region. The extent to which 'cultural regions' create the context for political history is a major theme in Schwartzberg's *Historical Atlas of South Asia* (Chicago, 1978, 2nd edn, New York, 1992).[67]

The mapping of historical regions clearly faces major problems. The concept of a region may not be a historical chimera, but what constitutes a region cannot be held within the same set of boundaries over a period of time, as patterns of government, socio-economic development and cultural identity and activity also change. Yet, if this creates problems for mapping, the departure from the concentration on international political boundaries and a largely undifferentiated presentation of states can only be seen as broadening. Changing regions themselves indicate shifts in spatial organization and perspective. Unfortunately, the nature and role of regions can only be fully displayed in large-scale maps, and these are generally lacking in atlases of world history. That leads to the mapping of global regionalism, for example types of agriculture in the first millennium AD or degree of industrialization in the nineteenth century. Such maps have considerable value and provide a degree of explanation lacking in maps of global political power, but the research on which they rely is more limited than that in the case of many smaller regions, and it is far harder to produce consistent information once a degree of quantification is required.

Conclusion

In the foreword to his *Penguin Historical Atlas of North America* (London, 1995), Eric Homberger argued that

> Atlases are among the most conservative of historical forms, and remain . . . quite insistent upon the old concerns. I have been intrigued by the general difficulties of mapping certain kinds of historical experience. There are detailed maps of the battle of Midway, and of Pickett's charge at Gettysburg, but not of the changing configuration of domestic space.[68]

This is true of most historical atlases, but decreasingly so. Historical studies, historical geography and historical cartography have all become more varied and adventurous in their interests. There are, of course, major problems. Aside from serious conceptual issues affecting mapping in some fields, it may also require a considerable amount of additional research to generate the data that are required,[69] assuming they exist. The temptation may be to stick with readily available data, or that which can easily be extracted from, for example, published statistical tables.

More generally, there can be the problems that an intelligentsia faces in assessing the views and experiences of others,[70] and, in addition, it is necessary to be careful in assuming that the latest development is the last, or at least the best hitherto, word: that, for example, increased attention to social, economic and religious factors, questions and spatialities over and against their political counterparts unambiguously represents a gain. In retrospect it can be seen to be, but earlier compilers and cartographers were doing what was appropriate in their own time. Not only is historical cartography concerned with time as well as space, but the passage of time will also inevitably affect how spatial differences are and will be perceived. Maps become obsolete, not only because mapmakers may become more sophisticated in their approach, but because events are seen as more or less important as mindsets change and because events, processes and trends have effects that change the way the past impinges on the future.

10

Technology and the Spaces of the Future

As the range of cartographic approaches developed during the twentieth century, new techniques and production methods offered fresh opportunities for understanding and exposition. This process was not restricted to the world of computerized cartography in the last quarter of the century. Rather, change has been a constant feature of the last century with innovations in both design and reprographic technique, a product of the role of experimentation and application in modern science and industry, of the synthesis of new materials, of the information revolution and of the pressure for improvements in cartography and graphic analysis, modelling and display that arises from military competition.

From the late 1920s cartographers turned again to engraving. Instead of using metal plates, however, they employed first glass plates and then transparent plastic sheets.[1] In the late 1940s and early 1950s there was a rapid spread in the use of transparent overlays of plastic material for drawing and scribing. In the 1950s and 1960s photography replaced lithography in the main process of map reproduction.[2] Maps were compiled as a multilayered system of overlays, with information registered on a base map on which typographers had placed type. Photomechanical laboratories then produced colour negatives for the preparation of printing plates.[3]

Both changing techniques in graphic display and the expectation among the reading public that a range of techniques will be employed in mapping have encouraged innovation, altering the look of maps. For example, iso-mapping, in which places of equal value were linked by lines, such as isodemographic maps, can present material far more vividly and clearly than any text.[4] Isolines originated in the seventeenth century and became familiar in the nineteenth. They were drawn to illustrate 'mean public-information time-lags to Boston and Philadelphia in 1790' in the *Atlas of Early American History* (Princeton, 1976).[5] The mapping of isochrones illustrates the nature of communications in a vivid fashion. In his study of the Amsterdam insurance market, Frank Spooner made excellent use of isokindunes to depict risk spatially, providing a sequence of monthly maps representing monthly insurance premiums. The response to threats of war was clearly indicated, as was the role of the United Provinces in co-ordinating commercial flows.[6]

Australians: A Historical Atlas, edited by J.R. Cram and J. McQuilton (Broadway, New South Wales, 1987), included facsimiles of nineteenth- and twentieth-century maps to show how cartographic styles and techniques have changed alongside its use of contemporary methods such as pie charts, computer mapping and flowline maps. The development of mapping, culminating in high-quality computer-generated maps, was also demonstrated in Hal Empson's sumptuous *Mapping Hong Kong: A Historical Atlas* (Hong Kong, 1992).

The use of a variety of cartographic techniques expressing dynamic relationships or offering a guide to quantification can give modern historical atlases a range and visual quality that are strikingly different from earlier works. For example, *L'Armée et la guerre* (Paris, 1989), in the series *Atlas de la révolution française* (Paris, 1987–), is a world away from traditional military historical atlases such as the West Point series, most obviously the *Military History and Atlas of the Napoleonic Wars* by Vincent J. Esposito and J.R. Elting (New York, 1964). The difference in content – a move away from only tackling strategy and tactics in order to include subjects such as logistics and desertion – is matched by a more varied use of techniques.

Computer technology has transformed and given greater flexibility to the printing of maps. Prior to computers, maps were printed from a master printing copy that was made up of several flaps or overlays, each containing part of the relevant copy. Computers store material previously divided between several flaps in a database, and maps are produced as a raster that consists of many minute dots. These record symbols as dots, lines or surfaces and the information can be presented on screen, where it can be edited, and the entire map printed out in one process. Geographic base maps are stored as digital images and the separation of storage (the digital map) and display makes the analysis and presentation of the data more flexible.[7] Manuscript and printed maps can be added to the computer databank by digitization, using either a cursor that traces the lines on the map, with the position of the cursor being recorded by an electronic co-ordinate system, or an automatic scanner,[8] though scanning can be expensive.

Digitization has totally transformed correction and updating. On old-fashioned coloured maps, there were two methods of producing the map, both of which were very difficult to correct. In one style, which was usually reserved for simple maps, you produced a coloured (painted or airbrushed) baseboard, with the linework either painted in position or supplied as overlays for reversing out at the reproduction house, and with each piece or type stuck down by hand on a further overlay. If you wanted to change the coloured base, you had to repaint the base, which was clumsy and then produced inferior results. You had to hope that the type did not fall off during handling.

Alternatively, in the method used for more complex maps, you prepared a set of 'peelcoats' (photographically opaque films), in which the information you wanted for each colour on the map was 'scribed' (cut) away, so that the reproduction house could expose each peelcoat, make a suitably coloured printing film, and then combine them for proofing. Since you had one peelcoat for each tint on a map, a single map might require ten or twelve peelcoats. This was expensive in materials, and meant you could not see any colour effects until you got your proof. Any correction to lines or colour might involve changing several of these peelcoats; you had to stick something opaque over your old line, and scribe a new one. This created serious problems in matching up the old and the new.

Both methods of correction were so clumsy, slow and expensive that you tried to limit corrections to the barest minimum. There was often neither the budget nor the time in the schedule for this correction phase for anything that was not absolutely wrong.

With digitization, everything becomes a lot easier. You can change your mind endlessly. Colours and typestyles can be changed, individually or globally through a project, literally at the touch of a button; and line and colour work can be modified almost as easily. There is no problem in getting the old and the new to marry up, and you supply a completed map to the reproduction house confident that you know exactly what you will get back. If you want to update the map in two years time (even if you want to re-draw pie-diagrams, for example) this can be done in a matter of moments, for the cost of the new film involved.

Design and cartographic processes can be integrated more easily. It is possible endlessly to modify bases to fit the design requirements. The entire world coastline and drainage are available on databases. They can be output in different projections, chosing different sizes and centrepoints. This saves the endless process of drawing coastlines for individual maps. It also makes it easy, for example, to rescale a map by 10 per cent while designing the spread on which it goes. This was complete anathema in the 1980s. Also, it is easy to design, use and modify complex and pictorial symbols, and to achieve fades and blends which were very clumsy or downright impossible. All of this makes it much easier to design a map that not only looks good and is accurate, in its own right, but looks good integrated with other elements such as timelines, photographs, text, artwork and so on.

Likewise the cartographic and editorial process. The editor now has the final say. In the 1980s the cartographic process was so complex and unwieldy that the editor had little control. He would be presented with a symbol design, for example, or a way of presenting a particular piece of information, as a *fait accompli*. Instead of concentrating on the exigencies of the production processes for maps, and being ruled by them – in the context of schedule and budget constraints – editors are now able to devote more attention to how best to communicate information. This increases the commercial value of the atlases.

Digitization also makes it far easier for the translator. Translation is a crucial process in global publishing. Instead of supplying map proofs for the translator to fit his type to, as in the 1980s, modern map producers can supply an electronic file, into which he fits his text. This means that all the problems of fitting the type have already been resolved. All he has to do is apply (instantly) any style changes he requires to the type; and to key the foreign language terms over the top of the English copy; then adjust the position of particular words or blocks that have significantly changed their length.

Computer mapping packages are used both to produce atlases, as in Stéphane Sinclair's striking *Atlas de géographie historique de la France et de la Gaule* (Paris, 1985), and to present maps on screen. Computers rapidly construct spatial information systems containing diverse, interrelated layers of data in contrast to the paper map with its essentially static character and its two-dimensional ability which offers only a range of perspectives and relationships. Maps drawn on computers are very easy to change. However, especially initially, they looked like maps produced by just such a method: angular and awkward in places. Eventually many atlases will probably be generated and stored digitally, and presented differently for the particular require-ments of individual users: an atlas will more clearly be a database.[9]

The depiction of movement and change remains a particular problem with the conventional format. Paullin suggested as early as 1932 that 'the ideal historical atlas might well be a collection of motion-picture maps, if these could be displayed on the pages of a book without the paraphernalia of projector, reel, and screen'.[10] The impact of the cinema was echoed in the preface to the second edition of Clifford and Elizabeth Lord's *Historical Atlas of the United States* (New York, 1953):

> The startlingly rapid growth and development of the United States make its history particularly susceptible to visual portrayal. The animated cartoon-map is certainly the most vivid way of showing, for instance, the tentacles of our railroad system reaching out year by year across the country, or of portraying the spread of our crop areas, the development of manufacturing regions, the westward advance of population . . . But movies have their limitations. They may be seen and heard, but they are difficult to study, even in classrooms. Those who lack photographic memories (and they are many) are more apt to carry away a vague impression than definite knowledge. By mapping developments in particular fields every few years, so that one can almost see them grow or shift, this atlas tries to combine the usefulness of the animated map with the advantages of being able to sit down face to face with the moving panorama of American history . . .[11]

In 1972 it appeared best to use a slide projector and rotatable disc in order to show developments.[12] In 1978 George Kish offered 203 slides and a cassette tape in *The Discovery and Settlement of North America, 1500–1865: A Cartographic Perspective* (New York). In 1982, by which time computer-generated maps were becoming more common, slides were still seen as the best way to advance beyond the traditional atlas when Aragonese history was mapped by Agustín Ubieto Arteta in his *Como se formé Aragón* (Zaragoza).

The first computer-aided maps to appear in a scientific journal were weather maps generated by the first ENIAC numerical calculator in 1950. By the 1980s powerful desktop computers were making the routine visualization of data on screen readily available, and the first prototype of an electronic atlas was developed in Canada in 1982.[13] The great increase in the power of personal computers and the appearance of relevant software and hardware packages enhanced the cartographic applicability of computers. By 1989 MundoCart/CD, the digital map of the world on CD-ROM, was commercially available. This made interaction with the data used to compile modern maps much easier. GIS (Geographical Information Systems) have also come to play a major role in cartography, including historical cartography. GIS are automated, digital information systems concerned with data relating to locations stored on computers; they are a by-product of the use of computers in the Cold War arms race. Information is converted into numbers and can then be mapped through an automated system.[14] More generally, computerized methods offer new approaches for harmonizing different historical sources, and mapping is a possible consequence. Many projects now rely on the technology of GIS and CD-ROM. It is planned that the *Atlas of the Greek and Roman World*, currently being edited by Richard Talbert and due for publication by Princeton University Press in 1999, will be made available on CD-ROM; the maps themselves rely on a GIS. In 1993 the National Endowment for the Humanities Research Tools and Grants Program began funding a project to produce an *Archive of North American Indian Maps* on CD-ROM.[15]

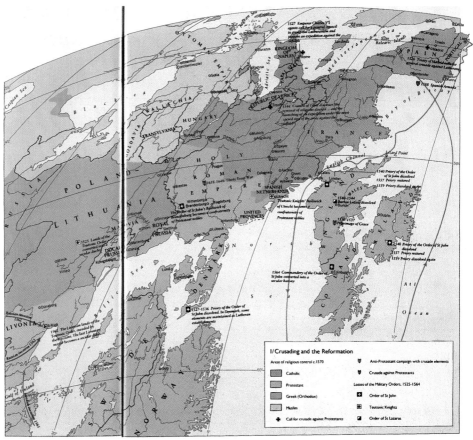

I/ Crusading and the Reformation

Areas of religious control c.1570

Catholic
Protestant
Greek (Orthodox)
Muslim
✚ Call for crusade against Protestants

⚑ Anti-Protestant campaign with crusade elements
⚑ Crusade against Protestants
Losses of the Military Orders, 1525-1564
✚ Order of St John
✚ Teutonic Knights
✚ Order of St Lazarus

50. 'The Reformation' from *The Atlas of the Crusades*. The distinctive perspective arrests the viewer. By mapping 'religious control', the map does not allow for religious minorities.

The use of new technology makes it easier to provide novel perspectives. Such perspectives reflect a combination of technological application, cartographic imagination and a greater willingness, indeed eagerness, on the part of the public to see the world in a new light, a willingness that owes much to the impact of air travel and satellite photography. A crucial figure was Richard Edes Harrison, who in the mid-1930s began creating maps that employed an aerial perspective. He regarded these maps as the 'missing link' between two-dimensional maps and the reality of a globe on which distances are very different, especially in higher latitudes, and, in order to create an impressive three-dimensional image, Harrison was willing to sacrifice mathematical precision. Harrison's work excited a lot of attention in the Second World War when interest in geopolitics and maps grew and the aerial dimension was of greater concern; his atlas *Look at the World* (1944) was a great success.[16]

Harrison charted the path for the unconventional perspectives, projections and map styles that became more common from the 1940s. They first made a major impact in historical cartography with the *Times Atlas of World History* (London, 1978). A major project in which about £500,000 was invested,[17] an enormous sum for the period, this was one of the first historical atlases to make use of computers, and its innovative approach and methodology were reflected in its perspectives:

special computer-derived map projections were used. As Geoffrey Barraclough noted in his introduction: 'We have sought . . . to emphasise different historical situations by employing a variety of different projections . . . the results may not always be familiar, but we believe they may open new insights.'[18] The map of the rise of the Ottoman empire helped to stress the importance of trans-Pontine Europe and of Turkish gains at the expense of the Mamelukes. Similarly, that of the resurgence of Muslim power 1520–1639, stretching from Bengal to Morocco, offered a perspective that brought the centres of the Muslim world into prominence. The map of the Adriatic with the south at the top threw considerable light on Venetian strategic problems[19] and indicated the importance of John Cole's observation that, by thinking of each country or region as having a right way up and as being mapped on a particular projection, we may limit our perception of past problems.[20] However, in the fourth edition this map was replaced by a more conventional one – 'Italy divided' with north at the top of the map[21] – because the perspective was felt to be too novel for many readers.[22]

As, until the spread of the railway in the nineteenth century, landmasses were generally less easy to cross than seas, and water united rather than divided, it would be valuable to have more maps that reflect the importance of maritime links by being centred on them. Maps of military campaigns frequently represent the strategic problems generals faced by using different perspectives, though the very act of mapping is misleading as it reveals the dispositions of both sides in a way that was denied to generals and thus removes the vital elements of uncertainty, surprise and confusion. It is also possible to provide a three-dimensional illustration of the topography of battlefields by the use of computer graphics.[23] Distortion, however, can arise with military mapping – failing to take into consideration changes in military technology that reduce or alter the significance of space.

Initially, computer maps were rather limited and therefore limiting of cartographic possibilities. Routes, for instance, could only be shown by lines of uniform thickness; colours could not be overlaid or made, in certain combinations, to fade into one another; some maps, once chosen, could not be changed except at ruinous cost. Computer graphics did not always deliver the quality or the basic understanding of the good draughtsman.

They have since greatly improved and the use of computers for the depiction of information has become much more common. In part, this reflects the falling real cost of computers and their hardware and software, the decline in what used to be a more substantial time-lag between technological development in fields related to mapping and its full-scale implementation in cartography, and, more specifically, the geo-coding of digital databases and the digitization of the earth, so that conventional cartographic and other information and the new technology can be integrated.[24]

As a result, it is possible to combine data files, cartographic co-ordinate files and statistical mapping software in an automated statistical mapping system. This not only produces the map but also performs necessary statistical calculations, such as classing the data, and can also integrate non-graphic material, for example scaling, positioning and centring text for titles, captions and keys.[25]

Historical cartography responded to the new production technology, and this was very much a change of the 1980s and early 1990s. Whereas the *Historical Atlas of Newcastle-upon-Tyne* (Newcastle, 1980) was produced by hand using stencils, the same group of authors produced *Newcastle's Changing Map* (Newcastle, 1992) by

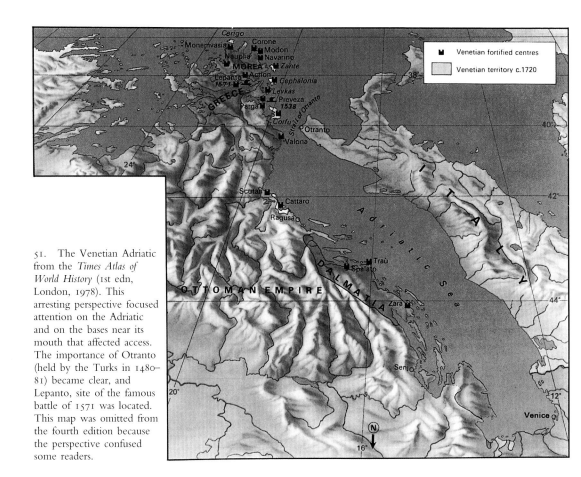

51. The Venetian Adriatic from the *Times Atlas of World History* (1st edn, London, 1978). This arresting perspective focused attention on the Adriatic and on the bases near its mouth that affected access. The importance of Otranto (held by the Turks in 1480–81) became clear, and Lepanto, site of the famous battle of 1571 was located. This map was omitted from the fourth edition because the perspective confused some readers.

computer. Bruce Macdonald found that his ambition of an atlas history of Vancouver was not feasible in 1985, but that the development of desktop computers changed this, not least by transforming the authorial process. A sense of technology as liberator is clear from the 'Background' to his individual and exciting *Vancouver. A Visual History* (Vancouver, 1992), one of the most successful urban historical atlases:

> persons can bring their visions to reality without having to compromise their original ideas. In the past a book such as this would probably have not been done at all; if it were, it would have involved a series of different people controlling each phase of the development of the book, each with a different vision and drive. Much of the research would have been done by one person; the writing by others, perhaps under an editor; the cartography would have been scaled down and done entirely by a professional cartographer; someone else would have designed the book and so on ... I feel exceptionally blessed to have been one of the first people able to work in consultation with a series of topnotch professionals while still retaining effective control over the entire project.[26]

Computer cartography was also used in teaching. *America Past and Present*, a student text that offered an extensive package of supplements, included, in 1991, William

Hamblin's *American Historical Geography: Computerized Atlas*. This computer program, which included map exercises, involving for example the War of American
Independence, the Civil War, transport systems and elections, was provided free
when schools adopted the textbook.

Digitization brought a greater flexibility that affected the editorial process,
ensuring that it is possible to plan for coherence and continuity in an atlas. To
achieve this may require changes to some of the maps produced at an early stage in
the production process, in the light of what comes in later. This was not possible
with the artwork- and peelcoat-based mapmaking of 1970s and 1980s atlases, for
example the *Times Atlas of World History*, but such coherence and editorial control
are easier with the computer-based historical atlases of the 1990s.

Major research-based atlases also came to rely on computers for their cartography.
The *Historical Atlas of Canada* switched to them in 1990. At that stage, production of
volume two, the last of the three volumes to appear, was in jeopardy owing to costs.
There had been two earlier investigations of the costs and benefits of such a switch,
but it had been concluded that it was not technically feasible to achieve high-
resolution, high-quality cartography with computers. Advances in software for desktop publishing changed the situation and 50 of the 58 plates in the volume were
drawn on computer. Aside from cost advantages, the use of computer systems gave
greater flexibility than had been permitted by the earlier method of scribing on
sheets of plastic in order to produce what could be photographed as a stage of the
printing plate. A GIS was used in the *Historical Atlas of State Power in Congress 1790–
1990* by K.C. Martis and G.A. Elmes (Washington, 1993). Apportionment statistics
were put into an automated format and digital versions of the apportionment maps
were produced. Original versions of all maps were generated on a colour electro-
static plotter, and data and cartography were reformulated for production into colour
negatives for the final printing process.[27]

Technology offers new possibilities of depiction, but it is not clear how far this is
leading to changes in content. An investigation of one of the first attempts at
developing a digital state atlas, the *Atlas of Arkansas* (1989), 'has shown that, despite
its innovative format, its content and organisation deviate little from the traditional
atlas'.[28]

In addition, the quality and 'mappability' of the sources remain major issues.
Technology has had an important impact in this sphere by increasing the quantity of
the available data. Human beings are now less dependent on their own faculties and
senses for the gathering and analysis of data than ever before. One major shift was
a consequence of the combination of photography and the use of aerial surveillance,
first by planes and subsequently by satellite.[29] Aerial survey and photography were of
particular value for archaeological investigation. They made it possible both to
survey terrain that was otherwise difficult[30] and to discover sites and information that
were not visible on the ground.[31] Aerial photography has thrown new light on a host
of issues, including, for example, the settlement patterns of Roman Britain and
Alsace, on the routes of Roman roads and on urbanization in Aztec Mexico.[32]

Yet information gained by aerial photography has to be used with care. The data
it yields depend on a number of criteria, including optimum climatic and flying
conditions, the suitability of the subsoils and crop rotations for yielding photographic
information, the absence of restricted flying zones and the degree of damage and
destruction owing to ploughing and construction. Droughts are especially valuable,

those in Britain in 1976, 1984 and 1988 leading to conditions that produced more information from aerial photography. These criteria mean, however, that it is dangerous to assume that individual aerial surveys can yield comprehensive information.[33] Nonetheless, aerial photography can be linked with maps to produce attractive atlases, as in David Buisseret's *Historic Illinois from the Air* (Chicago, 1990).

Modern technological advances have vastly expanded the possible range of data sources. New forms of evidence have been discovered. For example, radiocarbon dating is of value for topics such as the dating of grains,[34] while ship- and air-borne towed magnetometers and deep ocean borehole core sequences have produced a widespread coverage of magnetic anomaly data, and palaeomagnetic evidence has thrown great light on continental drift.[35]

Increased and improved information was also provided for historical cartography as a consequence of the use of the computer as an analytical tool. This made it far easier to scrutinize data for patterns and relationships. The computer made it possible to map material that had hitherto not been mappable without enormous effort. It was especially valuable for the analysis and mapping of social and economic material. This was bulkier in form than the standard topics of political mapping – frontiers and wars – and much of it required prior analysis if it was to be mappable. This was because many social and economic topics entailed quantification and maps expressed values rather than location: zones of high unemployment rather than the location of individual unemployed people.

Computer-analysis played a major role in the changing nature of social science research from the 1970s and made it possible for mapping to play an integral part, both as a form of analysis and as a means to display information. Computers were important in the modelling of phenomena and problems, and, though modelling did not require maps, it was often related to graphic display and to an interest in the spatial aspects of problems.

A sense of the excitement and feeling of wider possibilities generated by the use of computers can be gained from the map supplement on Oregon in 1850 published in the *Annals of the Association of American Geographers* in 1975. William Bowen recorded that the population data had been computerized

> and combined with a wide assortment of historical and genealogical material into a master data bank . . . the initial cost of this comprehensive approach to data collection and organization was considerable; but so were the returns. The accuracy and detail of the resulting maps permitted for the first time a definitive analysis of the complex interrelationships established between a frontier's population, economy, and natural environment . . . detailed landscape reconstruction on a massive scale . . . almost instantaneous manipulation of incomprehensible masses of data and effortless generation of maps.[36]

The previous year Donald Dodd had used computer programs for data arraying and circle size computation in his *Historical Atlas of Alabama* (Tuscaloosa, 1974). The map of 'progression of settlement' in the *Atlas of Michigan* (East Lansing, 1977) was based on a computer analysis of the founding dates of about 1400 settlements.[37]

The uses of computers and associated software and hardware in analysis and depiction extend more widely. Aside from speed of analysis and production, computers also make it possible to refocus both data and maps by varying class intervals for analysis or depiction. Analytical 'density' follows from spreadsheet computer programs that make it practicable to map using smaller units and thus provide a map that is more responsive to local variations. More generally, use of computers leads to a measure of standardization in the production of maps. This is partly a matter of the available hardware and software, which affect issues of symbolization, colour choice and cartographic potential.

New technology may make publication in book form less common. The atlas in hard copy is now subsequent to a computer atlas and is indeed a fixed and rigid form of the material in the computer. That material can be scanned on screen, and such a process is both interactive and far less costly than publication in book form. As a result, it is increasingly likely that a growing proportion of maps will not be produced in atlas form or that such a publication will not be seen as a crucial aspect of a data collection, analysis and depiction process. For example, the very expensive *Atlas of Early American History* (Princeton, 1976) was followed by a project, again sponsored by the Newberry Library, to map American county development. It was originally planned not to publish the material in atlas form, but instead to produce a computerized data file. This was indeed done for fourteen states and the data file was distributed by the Inter-University Consortium for Political and Social Research.[38] However, publication in atlas form followed, and this has certainly increased knowledge of the project and made the material more accessible to non-academics.

Millennium, a historical atlas of Europe and the Middle East from AD 1000 to the present, was not published in book form. Launched in 1993 by Clockwork Software of Chicago, it was a software package designed to be read on screen, costing $89. Publicity emphasized how its maps evolved 'dynamically'. The full-colour maps provided an essentially political account that showed territorial shifts on a monthly basis, eliminating the need to delineate past, present or future changes on one printed map. *Historica*, an electronic historical atlas launched in 1995 by Living History of Bristol, offers 'historical maps for all periods in history for any region of the world. The maps can be included in sequences, where they change dynamically through time.'

Computer-aided cartography now permits great flexibility and innovation in preparing maps. Using a common base map, all sorts of features can be plotted with relative ease. It is possible to digitize terrain base maps and use them as relief models that can be viewed from any perspective or height, creating an accurate basis for the visualization that is so important to successful mapping. In his *New Social Atlas of Britain* (Chichester, 1995), Daniel Dorling used population cartograms. The maps of all general elections since 1955 use a cartogram base which changes over time. Constituencies appear and disappear over time and alter size as the sizes of their electorates change: as the population in southern England has increased, so the south of England grows in the map.[39]

Maps imprisoned in heavy-weight publications are very difficult to use as a teaching medium; and the idea of carrying around big wall charts (and negotiating fast-closing fire doors) seems positively archaic. Lecture rooms increasingly have facilities to play CD-ROMs or Photo CD, and CD cases can transport a large number of images. CD-ROM systems make it easy to store maps and also make it possible to dispense with many of the difficult choices associated with producing an historical atlas, because of there being insufficient resources to produce a hard-copy atlas that affords the full range of map options. For example, CD-ROM is particularly appropriate for changing distribution patterns. It is possible to produce a series of maps showing site distributions year by year, then string them together as a series, morphing from one to the other. All of it could be packaged on a CD-ROM, which would allow the viewer to zoom in on a particular area, morph through the images at a faster or slower speed, select for additional associated information on a particular site, print out specific maps of interest and so forth.

Computer mapping makes it easier to speculate cartographically, not least because the preparation and production of maps have become much faster. Pre-computer mapping entailed the need for expensive full photolithographic processing in order to see colour proofs and, as changes required complete reprocessing, they were expensive. In contrast, digital mapping on screen is easier and cheaper to edit and final filming can be postponed until after final editing and shortly before publication. It is also easier and cheaper to co-ordinate maps with pictures, text and captions: the combination of digitization and specialized software programs facilitate sizing, positioning and editing: text, pictures and maps are all scanned and combined in the digital file.

Commercial and individual mapmakers can now have access to the same technology and can employ similar methods. It is possible to superimpose layers of data onto chosen base maps. In former days this could only be done by placing a tracing of one map on top of another, and then only if they were the same scale. The idea and purpose remain the same, but the technology has improved. New technology interacts with changes in cartography. It can be argued that the term 'cartographer' no longer reflects what a mapmaker does. In the past, cartographers gathered data and drew maps depicting their own data. Today, many cartographers are little more than specialized draughtsmen, of varying technical and aesthetic talent, who depend exclusively on projections, borders and drainage copied from existing maps, and on the information gathered – and even mapped – by the author of the atlas or map.

It is unclear how far computer-assisted cartography will lead to changes in methods of depicting data. It has been suggested that reducing the pressures of compilation will lead to greater interest in dot maps and that if data are available for a uniform area of land as opposed to counties, parishes, etc., isopleth will replace choropleth maps because of the boundary limitations of the latter.[40] Modern techniques increase the ability of cartographers to show fine gradations of change and reduce the necessary role of arbitrarily fixed categories.

Maps on screen and the use of interactive devices are part of a process by which traditional methods of understanding maps and mapping have been thrown into a state of flux. They direct attention to an interactive kind of map-appreciation in which the reader can change the form of the information presented. Maps become less a static presentation of information and more 'part of a thinking-knowledge construction process' in which they are 'an element in a larger process of spatial information access'.[41]

It is only with electronic mapping that it is possible to develop fully a zoom effect that permits a concentration on particular but varying aspects of a wider picture. If, for example, a census of manufacturers is incorporated into a data system, with all the establishments coded and located, it is possible to show the broad pattern nationally of, for example, brickmakers, and then pick out major clusters and highlight the characteristics of the individual factories.

A large database also makes it possible to show diffusion or change over time more convincingly. This is especially valuable for the intensification of rural settlement. The mapping of change, however, is by no means restricted to historians or geographers. Indeed, cartographic methodology is increasingly affected by developments in data analysis and display made by other specialists, for example meteorologists, medical researchers and physical scientists.[42]

Many of the data problems for the finer-scale work on historical spatial patterns can be overcome by the development of accurate digitized maps and associated databases. Vast quantities of often poorly organized or presented data can be fully utilized once the basic infrastructure of detailed digitized maps has been constructed. Without the new infrastructure, the original data are almost meaningless, but unless the data are 'spatially referenced' they cannot be used for GIS.[43] GIS and the crucial readily usable yet sophisticated software solve the problem of adding different levels of meaning to maps. They make it easier to rework them and thus to experiment with different methods of digital display. Once a publisher has got its digitized maps onto a GIS system, it will be possible to claim that it has not just a library of historical maps, but a genuine database of them. Then it will be possible to enter the co-ordinate for, say Italy, and retrieve all the relevant data on the database, thus helping to produce a completely new book entitled, in this instance, *Historical Atlas of Italy*. Re-use of maps, which is already important in making historical atlases cheaply, for example, in making young peoples' versions of 'adult' atlases, will be far easier and more flexible.

Another advance is the use of GIS mapping systems for predictive mapping. The use of GIS facilitates the study of patterns and it is then possible, for example, to predict where archaeological evidence should be or should have been. As more information is digitized, so the potential of GIS increases. Furthermore, the comparison of GIS information sets that include historical data expands the range of GIS potential in temporal mapping.

Three-dimensional computerized maps may become far more common,[44] though they highlight the issue of data availability. Such maps could show variation by degree, for example a topography based on economic scales or religious density, and use a correlation with an independent variable to construct maps similar to three-dimensional weather maps. Time is the obvious third dimension as maps try to conflate temporal and locational descriptions of phenomena.[45] This reflects both interest in diffusion models and in the interaction of space and time in systems of control and organization, for example economic or geopolitical systems. By focusing on human activity in space and time, they offer the possibility of throwing light on debates about structure versus agency.[46]

It would be wrong to assume that science and technology simply set the pace. Instead, other considerations affect the implementation of technological innovations. In 1993 Mark Monmonier suggested that 'the next revolution in cartography seems likely to be administrative and managerial, rather than scientific and technological'.[47] He should have set the entire question in the context of commercial factors.

Technological shifts have altered the relationships between compilers, editors, publishers and printers, or at least the potential relationships. It is now possible to create and correct images on screen and for discussion about maps to take place at a distance while both parties compare images on their screens. Equinox, a major producer of historical atlases, moved from using outside typesetters to keyboarding in-house in 1989–90 because it was both cheaper and gave the publisher more control: it became possible to make instant corrections on screen. This offered great flexibility and widened the range of editorial/publishing activity. Equinox itself had to alter the specified typeface of the series as their keyboarding machine didn't have it available.[48]

As with earlier developments, technological changes in the last quarter of the twentieth century created and continue to create problems as well as opportunities for publishers. New technology is expensive, and the values and potential of CD-ROM systems carry costs. This is true both of animated maps and of combinations of maps with music and videos. New technology, for example, offers more flexibility, including the possibility of updating, which is very expensive by conventional means. Yet offering such a facility itself entails commitments and costs. More generally, new technology discourages investment as it dates. Indeed, the caution about being at the forefront of new cartographic technology that certain map publishers have displayed in the early and mid-1990s reflected their concern about the likely rate of return on investment and, more specifically, the risks of investing in particular systems that might become obsolete. A fear that CD-ROM would rapidly become obsolescent threatened investment confidence. Instead, it was more appropriate for most publishers to limit costs (and make them more predictable), and maintain their rate of production, by producing atlases that were low-key in total technological terms but that nevertheless benefited from shifts in production technology, not least compiling maps on screen. Computers do not have the registration problems that affect mapping that uses overlays, and therefore can offer a 'perfect fit' of information. Because they offer faster production techniques, salary costs in mapmaking have fallen. Furthermore, computer maps are more mobile as a product, better for global mapmaking. Conventional artwork in contrast is more fragile as well as more expensive. Film cannot be used indefinitely.

Technology can only go so far. If one of the purposes of historical cartography is to pin down generalizations precisely in space, then it is still the case that historical research skills are often required to do so, before any mapping process can take place. Second, it is necessary to reconstruct and understand past geographies with reference to the attitudes of the period; the meanings of location, distance, proximity, space and territory explain the spatial context of a given subject and period and cannot be assumed in modern terms.

Technological developments cannot overcome some important problems with map compilation. For example, a major problem with wide-ranging map projects, especially if they are collective efforts, is that differing standards are frequently used to compile maps in different areas. The standard for inclusion of information is that it should be thought significant by the compiler. However, to take the example of the Roman empire when, for example, Attica is compared with Britain, some of the differences will be due to 'historical reality', but others will be because what is significant in Britain is not in Attica. This problem would become more pressing if the maps were computerized and it were possible to compare the maps at the press of a button.

Aesthetic considerations come into play in the contrast between screen and book, but there are also practical differences. Most screens lack the resolution, colour-quality and size of the printed page. The last is especially important. Screens are not generally big enough to see a double-spread at the intended size at once, and this has implications in terms of density and range of information and the scope of the area that can be effectively comprehended in a given map.

Data availability remains an important problem. Despite the degree of governmental activity and continuity, and of scholarly research in the USA, James Scott wrote in *Washington. A Centennial Atlas* (Bellingham, 1989), that the ability to produce 'computer maps' depended

> on the existence of adequate data sets. Such data sets – sets that span the whole century of Washington's statehood – are unavailable or are grossly inadequate. Consequently, virtually all the maps in this centennial atlas have been drafted using traditional cartographic techniques.[49]

Conclusion

Aside from issues of data availability and depiction, there are also questions about hidden bias in GIS and, more generally, about the limitations of positivist mapping. Both are now exciting increased concern. GIS and the process of data collection, analysis and depiction have been located within the dynamics of late twentieth-century scientific culture as a social construction and an aspect of a social technology that is not democratic or value-free, but that reflects a technocracy with its own values and methods.[50] In part, such an analysis reflects a suspicious response to the power latent in any method that has a potential for aiding analysis and planning; it is not specific to maps. However, there is also a concern about mapping that relates to present interest in the power of maps as means to approach and present situations, and the process by which cartography reflects power.[51] Historical cartography can contribute to the debate. It can do so simply by showing 'distortion' in past and present historical cartography, but, more subtly, it can also do so by drawing attention to the problems of historical cartography, so that the very notion of distortion is made problematic, and the difficulty of arriving at, let alone sustaining, an agreed historic cartography for particular subjects is stressed. Brian Harley criticised

> academic cartographers, who have hitherto offered little beyond the unreal iconography of a positivist human geography, and scant hope through computer 'enhancement' that they will ever help us to experience the human struggles of the past, or the sense of its lived-in places. The obvious alternative is a greater pluralism of cartographic expression.[52]

Historical cartography will continue to use and benefit from technological advances in data collection and analysis, editorial compilation and scholarly production. It will probably do so within a context that is more aware of the emphases and compromises involved in mapping the past, in maps and history.

Concluding Remarks

Historical cartography reflects shifts in geography, history and cartography. In the 1950s and 1960s, when geography was essentially positivist and seen as a law-finding and depicting science of spatial relations,[1] historical cartography could be seen by geographers as the historical counterpart of spatial modelling in modern geography. Historians were similarly positivist, though they tended to neglect maps. Developments in cartography appeared to enhance the potential of spatial analysis.

More recently, there has been a reaction to positivism and a move towards a humanistic geography.[2] The role of cultural inheritance and other factors that cannot be explained in terms of spatial models has attracted greater interest, both in geography and historical geography.[3] Geographers are more aware of knowledge as a form of power and more inclined to see their own subject in that light.[4] A re-examination of modern geography has been linked to a re-evaluation of past geographies, especially as a teleological Western positivist model of objective geography has been queried.[5] Relativism, or at least pluralism, has also come to play a major role in studies of historic cartography, not least with efforts to understand the cartography of peoples conquered by Europeans, and also with a major weight being placed on Asian cartography. This is readily apparent with the *History of Cartography* volumes edited by J.B. Harley and David Woodward and published by the University of Chicago Press.[6] In addition, the role of space, its production and utilization in human terms and for human purposes, is increasingly seen as worthy of study,[7] and as posing analytical problems.[8] However, much social science research devotes insufficient attention to space and geographical milieus.[9]

These shifts in geography, history and cartography have hitherto made little impact on historical atlases, with the important exception of the attempt to broaden the coverage of Asia, Africa and other non-European societies. Success in that field has not, however, been rapid.[10] Commercial pressures, costs of compilation, pedagogic demands and mass-market expectations all interact to encourage a considerable measure of continuity in subject and image. It is still the case that time is seen rather as a setting than a sequence, and that little attention has been devoted to decision-making units and processes rather than aggregate geographical patterns.[11]

Yet the range of historical mapping has also increased greatly in the last quarter of the twentieth century and historical atlases have become a subject worthy of study in their own right. It would be unhelpful to conclude by emphasizing difficulties and deficiencies. The very problems that historical cartography faces indicate both the extent to which any account of historical atlases involves methodological and historiographical questions, and second, the importance of these questions. Rather than treating mental maps as a constant and historical cartography as a largely inconsequential sideline, historical atlases offer an important tool in understanding both past scholarship and the scholarship of the past. They require detailed study in their own right and should be used as a significant teaching and research tool. If historians are spatially illiterate and geographically ignorant, this will seriously affect their knowledge and understanding of the past.

Notes

1 Development to 1800

1. J.B. Harley, 'Maps, Knowledge and Power', in D. Cosgrove and S.J. Daniels (eds), *The Iconography of Landscape* (Cambridge, 1987), pp. 277–312, 'Silences and Secrecy: The Hidden Agenda of Cartography in Early Modern Europe', *Imago Mundi*, 40 (1988), pp. 57–76 and *Maps and the Columbian Encounter* (Milwaukee, 1990), section 3.

2. *Atlas de la Nouvelle Calédonie et dépendances* (Paris, 1981), section 18.

3. N. Peterson, 'Totemism Yesterday: Sentiment and Local Organisation among the Australian Aborgines', *Man*, 7 (1972), pp. 12–32; Peterson and Langton (eds), *Aborigines, Land and Land Rights* (Canberra, 1983); N. Williams, *The Yolgnu and their Land* (Canberra, 1986); H. Watson, 'Aboriginal-Australian Maps', in D. Turnbull, *Maps Are Territories. Science Is an Atlas* (Chicago, 1993), pp. 28–36.

4. J.B. Harley and D. Woodward (eds), *The History of Cartography* (Chicago, 1987–), II ii, *Cartography in the Traditional East and Southeast Asian Societies* (1994), p. 35; J. Needham, *Science and Civilisation in China* (Cambridge, 1954–), III, *Mathematics and the Sciences of the Heavens and the Earth* (1959), pp. 538–41. I am grateful to Weimin Que for his advice on the earliest Chinese maps.

5. Needham, *Science and Civilisation* III, p. 349; Harley and Woodward, *History of Cartography*, II ii, pp. 57–59.

6. A. Waldron, *The Great Wall of China: From History to Myth* (Cambridge, 1990).

7. I have greatly benefited from the advice of Naomi Standen. Her thesis is 'Frontier Crossings from North China to Liao *c.* 900–1005' (unpublished PhD, Durham, 1994). Harley and Woodward, *History of Cartography*, II ii, pp. 87.

8. D. Twitchett, *The Writing of Official History under the T'ang* (Cambridge, 1992).

9. On *fangzhi*: A. Kai [G. Alitto], 'Zhongguo Fangzhi Yu Xifang Difangshi De Bijao' (A comparison of the Chinese local gazetteer and Western local histories), *Manxue Yanjiu*, 3 (1985), pp. 59–71.

10. On Hong: Needham, *Science and Civilisation in China*, III, p. 586; A.W. Hummel, *Eminent Chinese of the Ch'ing Period* (Washington, 1943–44, reprinted Taipei, 1964), I, 373–75; J.D. Spence, *The Search for Modern China* (New York, 1990), pp. 143–44.

11. P.-É. Will, *Chinese Local Gazetteers. An Historical and Practical Introduction* (Paris, 1992), pp. 10–11; Hummel, pp. 25, 449; Harley and Woodward, *History of Cartography*, II ii, p. 93; H.L. Boorman and R.C. Howard (eds), *Biographical Dictionary of Republican China* (4 vols, New York, 1967), IV, pp. 9–11.

12. J.B. Harley and D. Woodward (eds), *The History of Cartography* (Chicago, 1987–), II i, *Cartography in the Traditional Islamic and South Asian Societies*, pp. 3–205, esp. p. 7.

13. Ibid., pp. 295–509.

14. London, British Library (hereafter BL), King's Topographical Collection II/60.

15. K. Nebenzahl, *Maps of the Bible Lands. Images of Terra Sancta through Two Millennia* (New York, 1986), pp. 8, 18–19.

16. BL. Additional Manuscript 10049.

17. A.-D. von den Brincken, 'Mappa Mundi und Chronographia', *Deutsches Archiv für die Erforschung des Mittelalters*, 24 (1968), pp. 118–86; O. Pächt, *The Rise of Pictorial Narrative in Twelfth-Century England* (Oxford, 1962); Harley and Woodward, *The History of Cartography*, I, *Cartography in Prehistoric, Ancient, and Medieval Europe and the Mediterranean*, pp. 288–90.

18. F. Schmidt, 'Naissance d'une géographe juive', in A. Desrumeaux and Schmidt (eds), *Möise géographe. Recherches sur les représentations juives et chrétiennes de l'espace* (Paris, 1988), pp. 13–30.

19. Z. Vilnay, *The Holy Land in Old Prints and Maps* (Jerusalem, 1963); E. and G. Wajntraub, *Hebrew Maps of the Holy Land* (London, 1986); J. Oswald, 'Zur Geschichte biblischer Atlanten', in H. Wolff (ed.), *Vierhundert Jahre Mercator. Vierhundert Jahre Atlas* (Vienna, 1995), pp. 213–14; C. Delano Smith and M.I. Grubev, 'Rashi's Legacy: Maps of the Holy Land', *The Map Collector*, 59 (Summer 1992), pp. 30–35.

20. Smith and E.M. Ingram, *Maps in Bibles 1500–1600* (Geneva, 1991), p. xvi. See also Smith, 'Maps in Bibles in the Sixteenth Century', *The Map Collector*, 39 (1987), pp. 2–14, and 'Maps as Art and Science: Maps in Sixteenth-Century Bibles', *Imago Mundi*, 42 (1990), pp. 65–83; Ingram, 'Maps as Readers' Aids: Maps and Plans in Geneva Bibles', *Imago Mundi*, 45 (1993), pp. 29–44; Oswald, 'Biblischer Atlanten', in Wolff (ed.), *Vierhundert Jahre Mercator*, pp. 214–18.

21. Smith, 'Maps in Bibles in the Sixteenth Century', *The Map Collector*, 39 (1987), p. 11.

22. P.D.A. Harvey, *Maps in Tudor England* (London, 1993), p. 8.

23. F. Plaut, 'Where is Paradise? The Mapping of a Myth', *The Map Collector*, 29 (1984), pp. 2–3; H.J. Haag, 'Die vermutlich älteste bekannte hebraische Holzschnittkarte des Heiligen Landes (um 1560)', *Cartographica Helvetica*, 4 (1991), pp. 23–26.

24. S. Tyacke (ed.), *English Map-Making 1500–1650* (London, 1983), p. 16.

25. R.A. Skelton, *Maps: A Historical Survey of their Study and Collecting* (Chicago, 1972), p. 66; Harley and D. Woodward, *History of Cartography*, I, 7.

26. Harley and Woodward, *History of Cartography* II i, 228–55.

27. F. Hellwig, 'Tyberiade und Augenschein. Zur forensischen Kartographie im 16. Jahrhundert', in J.F. Baur, P.C. Müller-Graff and M. Zuleeg (eds), *Europarecht. Energierecht. Wirtschaftsrecht* (Cologne, 1992), pp. 805–34; D.H. Fletcher, *The Emergence of Estate Maps. Christ Church, Oxford c. 1600–1840* (Oxford, 1995).

28. P. Burke, *The Renaissance Sense of the Past* (London, 1969).

29. F. Lestringant, *Mapping the Renaissance World. The Geographical Imagination in the Age of Discovery* (Oxford, 1994).

30. A.H. Robinson, *Early Thematic Mapping in the History of Cartography* (Chicago, 1982).

31. R. Flower, *Lawrence Nowell and the Discovery of England in Tudor Times* (London, 1935), p. 19; S. Mendyk, *Speculum Britanniae: Regional Study, Antiquarianism and Science in Britain to 1700* (Toronto, 1989); P.D.A. Harvey, *Maps in Tudor England* (London, 1993).

32. S.J. Fockema Andreae, *Geschiedenis der Kartografie van Nederland* (The Hague, 1947), p. 12; J.H. Hingman, *Inventaris der verzameling Kaarten berustende in het Rijks-Archief* (2 vols, The Hague, 1867–71) II, 299; C. de Waard, *Inventaris van Kaarten en Teekeningen* (Middelburg, 1916), pp. 1–6; W.S. Unger, *Catalogus van der historisch-topografischen atlas van het Zeeuwsch Genootschap Wetenschappen* I (1931), pp. 2, 5–7, 9–11, 101. I am particularly grateful to Paul Harvey for his assistance on this point.

33. S. Alpers, *The Art of Describing: Dutch Art in the Seventeenth Century* (London, 1983). One of her chapters is entitled 'The Mapping Impulse in Dutch Art'.

34. J. Hessels (ed.), *Abrahami Ortelii et virorum eruditorum ad eundem et ad Jacobum Colium Ortelianum epistolae* (Cambridge, 1887); E. Brandmair, *Bibliographische Untersuchungen über Entstehung und Entwicklung des Ortelianischen Kartenwerkes* (Munich, 1914), reprinted Amsterdam, 1954); C. Koeman, 'The History of Abraham Ortelius and his "Theatrum Orbis Terrarum"', introduction to facsimile of the first edition of the *Theatrum* (Lausanne, 1964), and *Atlantes Neerlandici* III (Amsterdam, 1969), pp. 69–70; P.H. Meurer, *Fontes Cartographici Orteliani. Das 'Theatrum Orbis Terrarum' von Abraham Ortelius und seine Kartenquellen* (Weinheim, 1991); J. Dörflinger, 'Geschichtsatlanten vom 16. bis zum Beginn 20. Jahrhunderts', in Wolff

(ed.), *Vierhundert Jahre Mercator*, p. 179; H.A.M. van der Heijden, *The Oldest Map of the Netherlands* (Utrecht, 1987), p. 162. There is a facsimile of the *Parergon* in Ortelius, *The Theatre of the Whole World, London 1606*, edited by R.A. Skelton (Amsterdam, 1968).

35. C. Koeman, *Geschiedenis van de Kartografie van Nederland* (Alphen aan den Rijn, 1983), p. 252; A. Löbbecke, *Untersuchungen zur Geschichtskartographie des 16. und 17. Jahrhunderts* (Vienna, 1992); Dörflinger, 'Geschichtsatlanten', p. 180; F. de Dainville, *La Géographie des humanistes* (Paris, 1940).

36. M. Pastoureau, *Les Atlas Français XVIe–XVIIe siècle* (Paris, 1984); C. Jullian, preface to L. Mirot, *Manuel de géographie historique de la France* (1929, 2nd edn, Paris, 1947), xlii.

37. BL. 865 (1), (2).

38. Heijden, *Oldest Map*, p. 17; W.E. Washburn, 'The Form of Islands in Fifteenth, Sixteenth and Seventeenth-Century Cartography', in M. Pelletier (ed.), *Géographie du monde au Moyen Âge et à la Renaissance* (Paris, 1989), p. 201.

39. F. Fernández-Armesto, *Edward Gibbon's Atlas of the World* (London, 1991), p. 91.

40. M. Bruchet, *Notice sur l'ancien cadastre de Savoie* (Annecy, 1896); G. Quazza, *Le riforme in Piemonte nella prima metà del '700* (Modena, 1957); D.M. Klang, *Tax Reform in Eighteenth-Century Lombardy* (Columbia, 1977); J. Andrews, *Plantation Acres* (Belfast, 1985); S. Helmfrid, 'Five Centuries of Sweden on Maps', in U. Sporrong and H.F. Wennstrom (eds), *Maps and Mapping* (Stockholm, 1990), pp. 39–42.

41. Y. O'Donaghue, *William Roy, 1726–1790: Pioneer of the Ordnance Survey* (London, 1977); J. Pallière, 'Un Grand Méconnu du XVIIIᵉ siècle: Pierre Bourcet (1700–1780)', *Revue historique des armées* (1979), pp. 51–66, 'Le Maître savoyard de la cartographie, Antoine Durieu, 1703–1777', *Actes du 109ᵉ Congrès National des Sociétés Savantes. Section de géographie* (Paris, 1985), pp. 59–67, 'Les cartes de 1760–1764 et la frontière franco-sarde', *Actes du 110ᵉ Congrès National des Sociétés Savantes* (Paris, 1985), pp. 39–45; J. Dörflinger, *Die Landesaufnahmen des Österreichischen Generalquartiermeisterstabes 1749–1854* (Karlsruhe, 1989); P.G.M. Dickson, 'Joseph II's Hungarian Land Survey', *English Historical Review*, 106 (1991), p. 617.

42. This map is displayed at the Musée de la Compagnie des Indes at Port-Louis in Brittany.

43. L. Gallois, 'L'Académie des sciences et les origines de la carte de Cassini', *Annales de Géographie*, 18 (1909), pp. 193–204; E.G. Forbes, *The Birth of Scientific Navigation: The Solving in the Eighteenth Century of the Problem of Finding Longitude at Sea* (Greenwich, 1974); D. Howse, *Greenwich Time and the Discovery of the Longitude* (New York, 1980), and (ed.), *Background to Discovery. Pacific Exploration from Dampier to Cook* (Berkeley, 1990).

44. *Atlas Geographus* (London, 1740 edition), p. 979.

45. Fernández-Armesto, *Gibbon's Atlas of the World*, pp. 7–8, 45.

46. G.R. Crone, 'John Green: Notes on a Neglected Eighteenth-Century Geographer and Cartographer', *Imago Mundi*, 6 (1949), pp. 85–91.

47. L.R. Shelby, *John Rogers. Tudor Military Engineer* (Oxford, 1967), pp. 94–101; P. Barber, 'Henry VIII and Mapmaking', in D. Starkey (ed.), *Henry VIII. A European Court in England* (London, 1991), pp. 145–51; D. Buisseret (ed.), *Monarchs, Ministers and Maps. The Emergence of Cartography as a Tool of Government in Early Modern Europe* (Chicago, 1992); J. Akerman, 'The Structuring of Political Territory in Early Printed Atlases,' *Imago Mundi*, 107 (1995), pp. 138–54; Torcy to Henry St John, 28 July 1712, London, Public Record Office, State Papers 78/154.

48. D. Chambers and B. Pullan (eds), *Venice. A Documentary History 1450–1630* (Oxford, 1992), pp. 405–6; *Daily Universal Register*, 11 August 1786.

49. Black, 'Fresh Light on Ministerial Patronage of Eighteenth-Century Pamphlets', *Publishing History*, 19 (1986), pp. 53–58.

50. Third Earl of Malmesbury (ed.), *Diaries and Correspondence of James Harris, First Earl of Malmesbury* (4 vols, London, 1844), II, 304–6; Lord Grenville, Foreign Secretary, to George III, 25 Sept., George III to Grenville, 26 Sept. 1792, BL. Add. 58857 ff. 37–39; Canning to John Hookham Frere, 20 June 1800, BL. Add. 38833 f. 2.

51. P. King, *Charlemagne. Translated Sources* (Kendal, 1987), p. 252.

52. P. Sahlins, *Boundaries: The Making of France and Spain in the Pyrenees* (Berkeley,

1989).

53. Oswald in Wolff (ed.), *Vierhundert Jahre Mercator*, pp. 220–23.

54. *Geographia Classica* (London, 1712), pp. ii–iv.

55. R.A. Butlin, 'Ideological Contexts and the Reconstruction of Biblical Landscapes in the Seventeenth and Eighteenth Centuries: Dr Edward Wells and the Historical Geography of the Holy Land', in A.R.H. Baker and G. Bigger (eds), *Ideology and Landscape in Historical Perspective* (Cambridge, 1992), pp. 31–62.

56. G. Hornius, *Compleat Body of Ancient Geography* (The Hague, 1741), p. 1.

57. W. Seymour (ed.), *A History of the Ordnance Survey* (Folkestone, 1980), pp. 62–63.

58. W. Bonacker, 'Johann Matthias Haas (1684–1742), sein Leben, seine Schriften und Karten', *Historische Verein für Schwaben, Zeitschrift*, 59–60 (1967), pp. 271–309; Dörflinger, 'Geschichtsatlanten', pp. 184, 191.

59. M. Pedley, *Bel et Utile. The Work of the Robert de Vaugondy Family of Mapmakers* (Tring, 1992), p. 233.

60. W.A. Goffart, 'Breaking the Ortelian Pattern: Historical Atlases with a New Program, 1747–1830', in J. Winearls (ed.), *Editing Early and Historical Atlases* (Toronto, 1995), p. 57.

61. Goffart, 'Breaking the Ortelian Pattern', p. 57.

62. Ibid., 59–60.

63. BL. Add. 33126 f. 383, 35378 f. 20.

64. Goffart, 'Breaking the Ortelian Pattern', p. 51.

65. A. Blessich, 'Un geografo italiano del secolo XVIII. Giovanni Antonio Rizzi Zannoni (1736–1814)', *Societa Geografica Italiana, Bolletino*, ser. 3, 11 (1898), pp. 12–23, 56–69, 183–203, 453–66, 523–37; J. Konvitz, *Cartography in France, 1660–1848: Science, Engineering, and Statecraft* (Chicago, 1987), p. 36.

66. Pedley, *Bel et Utile*, p. 16.

67. J. Black, 'Boundaries and Conflict. International Relations in *Ancien Régime* Europe', in C. Grundy-Warr (ed.), *World Boundaries II. Eurasia* (London, 1994), pp. 35–36.

68. M.V. Ozouf-Marignier, *La Formation des départements; La représentation du territoire français à la fin du XVIIIe siècle* (Paris, 1989); S. Woolf, *Napoleon's Integration of Europe* (London, 1991), pp. 87–90.

69. Seymour (ed.), *Ordnance Survey*, pp. 21–31; W. Ravenhill, 'The South West in the Eighteenth-Century Re-mapping of England', in K. Barker and R.J.P. Kain (eds), *Maps and History in South-West England* (Exeter, 1991), pp. 20–21.

70. H.-J. Kahlfuss, *Landesaufnahme und Flurvermessung in den Herzogtümern Schleswig Holstein und Lauenberg vor 1864* (Neumünster, 1969), pp. 22–59.

2 The Nineteenth Century

1. W. Hughes, *The Illuminated Atlas of Scripture Geography* (London, 1840), p. 4. On Hughes, see J.E. Vaughan, 'William Hughes, 1818–1876', in T.W. Freeman (ed.), *Geographers' Bibliographical Studies* (London, 1985) IX, 49–60.

2. C. Pearson, *Historical Maps of England* (London, 1869,) p. v.

3. W. Murphy, *A Comprehensive Classical Atlas* (Edinburgh, 1832), p. xvi; M.M. Austin, 'Hellenistic Kings, War and the Economy', *Classical Quarterly*, 36 (1986), p. 455.

4. W. Smith, *Dr. William Smith's Ancient Atlas* (London, 1874), p. 11.

5. R.J.A. Talbert, 'Mapping the Classical World: Major Atlases and Map Series 1872–1990', *Journal of Roman Archaeology*, 5 (1992), pp. 5–38.

6. Oswald in Wolff (ed.), *Vierhundert Jahre Mercator*, pp. 223–27.

7. H.G. May (ed.), *Oxford Bible Atlas* (Oxford, 1962), p. 97.

8. Ibid.

9. G.A. Smith, *Atlas of the Historical Geography of the Holy Land* (London, 1915), pp. vii–viii, xvii–xviii; R.A. Butlin, 'George Adam Smith and the Historical Geography of the Holy Land: Contents, Contexts and Connections', *Journal of Historical Geography*, 14 (1988), pp. 381–404; Y. Ben-Arieh, 'Nineteenth-Century Historical Geographies of the Holy Land', *Journal of Historical Geography*, 15 (1989), pp. 69–79.

10. W. Goffart, 'The Map of the Barbarian Invasions: A Preliminary Report', *Nottingham Medieval Studies*, 32 (1988), pp. 49–64, and 'The Map of the Barbarian Invasions: A Longer Look', in *The Culture of Christendom. Essays in Medieval History in Memory of Denis L.T. Behtell* (London, 1995), pp. 1–27.

11. P. Lapié and A.E. Lapié, *Atlas universel de géographie ancienne et moderne* (Paris, 1829),

p. 43.

12. A.H. Dufour and Th. Duvotenay, *La Terre* (Paris, 1840), p. ii.

13. H.-D. Schultz, 'Deutschlands natürliche Grenzen. "Mittellage" und "Mitteleuropa" in der Diskussion der Geographen seit dem Beginn des 19. Jahrhunderts', *Geschichte und Gesellschaft*, 15 (1989), pp. 248–81.

14. R.L. Poole, *Historical Atlas of Modern Europe* (Oxford, 1902).

15. T.C. Sargent, 'Thomas Livingston Mitchell and Wyld's Atlas of the Peninsular War, 1808–1814', *Cartography*, 13 (1984), pp. 257–58.

16. D. Bosse, *Civil War Newspapers Maps* (Baltimore, 1993).

17. L.W. Towner, 'The Mapping of the American Revolutionary War in the Nineteenth Century', in *Mapping the American Revolutionary War* (Chicago, 1978), pp. 116–19.

18. J. Ormeling, 'Justus Perthes: Europa's oudste kartografische uitgeverij', *Kartografisch Tijdschrift*, 18, 4 (1992), pp. 35–39.

19. D. Woodward (ed.), *Five Centuries of Map Printing* (Chicago, 1975), pp. 16, 94–96, 100–1, 111.

20. W. Hughes, *The Illuminated Atlas of Scripture Geography*, p. 6.

21. L. Gardiner, *Bartholomew 150 Years* (Edinburgh, 1976), p. 25.

22. A. Wolf, 'What Can the History of Historical Atlases Teach? Some Lessons from a Century of Putzger's *Historischer Schul-Atlas*', *Cartographica*, 28 (1991), p. 22.

3 *Nationalism and Eurocentrism in Nineteenth-century Historical Atlases*

1. N. Broc, 'L'Établissement de la géographie en France: diffusion, institutions, projects (1870–1909)', *Annales de géographie*, 83 (1974), pp. 545–68.

2. Drioux and Leroy, *Atlas d'histoire et de géographie*, p. iii.

3. Broc, 'Histoire de la géographie et nationalisme en France sous la Troisième République, 1871–1914', *L'Information historique*, 32 (1970), pp. 20–26; M. Heffernan, 'The Spoils of War: The Société de Géographie de Paris and the French Empire, 1914–1919', in M. Bell, R. Butlin and M. Heffernan (eds), *Geography and Imperialism* (Manchester, 1995), pp. 223–25.

4. A. Wolf, '100 Jahre Putzger–100 Jahre Geschichtsbild in Deutschland (1877–1977)', *Geschichte in Wissenschaft und Unterricht*, 29 (1978), pp. 702–18.

5. See also, for example, George Butler, *The Public Schools Atlas of Ancient Geography* (London, 1877; 1905 edition), p. v.

6. W. Hughes, *A Popular Atlas of Comparative Geography* (London, 1870), p. iii.

7. Clausolles and Abadie, *Atlas historique et géographique de la France*, pp. 5–6.

8. Sanis and Bailliencourt, *Géographie historique de la France*, p. 60, map 29.

9. M.-N. Bouillet, *Atlas universel d'histoire et de géographie*, p. i.

10. Ibid., p. 933.

11. *Atlas Melin*, pp. 4, 37.

12. For the relationship between imperialism and nineteenth-century geography, see B. Hudson, 'The New Geography and the New Imperialism, 1870–1918', *Antipode*, 9 (1977), pp. 12–19; F. Driver, 'Geography's Empire: Histories of Geographical Knowledge', *Environment and Planning. D: Society and Space*, 10 (1992), pp. 23–40; A. Godlewska and N. Smith (eds), *Geography and Empire: Critical Studies in the History of Geography* (Oxford, 1993).

13. E. Quin, *Historical Atlas*, pp. 1–2, 33, 41, 47, 59, 93.

14. E. Gover, *Atlas of Universal Historical Geography*, p. 17.

15. W.H. McNeill, M.R. Buske and A.W. Roehm, *The World. Its History in Maps* (Chicago, 1963), pp. 8–9.

16. W. Murphy, *Comprehensive Classical Atlas*, p. i.

17. Wyld, *Notes to Accompany Mr Wyld's Model of the Earth, Leicester Square* (London, 1851), pp. iii, xv–xvi, xviii–xix.

18. Introduction to M. Bell, R. Butlin and M. Heffernan (eds), *Geography and Imperialism 1820–1940* (Manchester, 1995), p. 5; D. Cosgrove, 'Contested Global Visions: One-World, Whole-Earth, and the Apollo Space Photographs', *Annals of the Association of American Geographers*, 84 (1994), p. 280.

19. Pearson, *Historical Maps of England*, p. vi.

20. E. McClure, *Historical Church Atlas*, pp. 39, 36.

21. E.L. Oxenham, *Historical Atlas of the Chinese Empire*, pp. i, iii.

22. R. Muir, *New School Atlas of Modern History* (London, 1911), p. xxiv.

23. Ibid., p. xix.

24. Gerster, *Atlas historique de la Suisse*, p. 47.

25. Bouillet, *Atlas universel d'histoire et de*

géographie, p. 931.

26. B. Konopska, *Polskie Atlasy Historyczne* (Warsaw, 1994), pp. 15–59.

27. B. Koen, 'Balgarskite atlasi v. perioda 1865–1944', *Godishnik na Nacionalniya politehnicheski muzey*, 16 (1988), pp. 113–30.

28. A. Papp-Váry and P. Hrenkó, *Magyarország régi térképeken* (Budapest, 1990), pp. 98–99, 120–21. I have benefited greatly from the advice of László Gróf.

29. G. Balla, 'Historical School Wall-Maps in Hungary', in *Making and Use of Historical Maps*, International Cartographical Exhibitions and Conferences XI, Budapest 1972, pp. 1–4.

30. E.H. Willard, *History of the United States* (New York, 1828), pp. ii–iii, 5. On Willard, see A. Lutz, *Emma Willard, Pioneer Educator of American Women* (Boston, 1964).

31. *Description and Illustration of Worcester's Historical Atlas*, p. 5.

32. F. Mood, 'The Rise of Official Statistical Cartography in Austria, Prussia, and the United States, 1855–1872', *Agricultural History*, 20 (1946), pp. 216–20.

33. G. Engelmann, 'Der Physikalische Atlas des Heinrich Berghaus und Alexander Keith Johnstons Physical Atlas', *Petermann's Geographische Mitteilungen*, 18 (1964), pp. 133–49; J.R. Camerini, 'The Physical Atlas of Heinrich Berghaus: Distribution Maps as Scientific Knowledge', in R.G. Mazzolini (ed.), *Non-Verbal Communication in Science Prior to 1900* (Florence, 1993), pp. 479–512.

4   Environmentalism and Nationalism

1. C. Pearson, *Historical Maps of England during the First Thirteen Centuries* (London, 1869), p. viii; E. Reich, *A New Student's Atlas of English History* (London, 1903), p. iii.

2. M.J.S. Rudwick, 'The Emergence of a Visual Language for Geological Science, 1760–1840', *History of Science*, 14 (1976), pp. 149–95.

3. J.R. Camerini, 'The Physical Atlas of Heinrich Berghaus: Distribution Maps as Scientific Knowledge', in R.G. Mazzolini (ed.), *Non-Verbal Communication in Science Prior to 1900* (Florence, 1993), pp. 481–82.

4. M. Bassin, 'Imperialism and the Nation State in Friedrich Ratzel's Political Geography', *Progress in Human Geography*, 2 (1987), pp. 473–95; H. Wanklin, *Friedrich Ratzel: A Biographical Memoir and Bibliography* (Cambridge, 1961); D. Livingstone, *The Geographical Tradition* (Oxford, 1992), pp. 196–202.

5. J.B. Harley, B.B. Petchenik and L.W. Towner, *Mapping the American Revolutionary War* (Chicago, 1978), p. 116.

6. P. Foncin, *Géographie historique* (Paris, 1888), p. 2.

7. W. Hughes, *The Illuminated Atlas of Scripture Geography* (London, 1840), p. 3.

8. C. Pearson, *Historical Maps of England* (London, 1869), pp. v–vii.

9. R.D. Mitchell and P.A. Groves, *North America. The Historical Geography of a Changing Continent* (1987), p. 4; D.W. Meinig, *The Shaping of America. II. Continental America 1800–1867* (New Haven, 1993), p. 200.

10. R. Peet, 'The Social Origins of Environmental Determinism', *Annals of the Association of American Geographers*, 75 (1985), pp. 309–33.

11. H. Vast and G. Malleterre, *Atlas historique. Formation des états européens* (Paris, 1900), pp. 26, 28–29, 35–36, 41–46, 40.

12. H.B. George, *The Relations of Geography and History* (5th edn, Oxford, 1924), p. 295. On George, see R.A. Butlin, 'Historical Geographies of the British Empire, c. 1887–1925', in Bell, Butlin and Heffernan (eds), *Geography and Imperialism*, pp. 169–72.

13. E. Reich, *A New Student's Atlas of English History* (London, 1903), p. iii. Reich's *Atlas Antiquus* (London, 1908) also contained much of military interest. Reich's obituary appeared in *Geographen-kalender Gotha*, 9 (1911), pp. 271–72. Poole's obituary was reprinted in F.M. Powicke, *Modern Historians and the Study of History: Essays and Papers* (London, 1955), pp. 154–55.

14. C.G. Robertson and J.G. Bartholomew, *Historical and Modern Atlas of the British Empire* (London, 1905), pp. v–vi, 10, 42.

15. C. Joppen, *Historical Atlas of India* (London, 1907), pp. 15–16.

16. Joppen, *Historical Atlas of India* (3rd edn, London, 1914), p. 5.

17. R. Muir, *A New School Atlas of Modern History* (London, 1911), pp. xix, xvii, xxii.

18. Ibid., p. xix.

19. A. Ward (ed.), *The Cambridge Modern History Atlas* (Cambridge, 1912), map 99, p. v.

5   *War, Environment and Ideology, 1914–45*

1. S.H. Isaacs, *The True Boundaries of the Holy Land* (Chicago, 1917), pp. 7, 16–19, 93.

2. J. Cvijic, *La Péninsule balkanique, géographie humaine* (Paris, 1918).

3. H.R. Wilkinson, *Maps and Politics. A Review of the Ethnographic Cartography of Macedonia* (Liverpool, 1951); B. Cozic, *Roots of Serbian Aggression. Debates Documents, Cartographic Reviews* (Zagreb, 1993).

4. C. Smogorzewski, *La Poméranie polonaise* (Paris, 1932); H. Kot, *Historia Nowożytnej Kartografii Śląska 1800–1939* (Katowice, 1970), p. 195; D. Le-Brun, 'Allemagne et Pologne, ou la carte comme arme de propagande', *Mappe monde*, 90–91 (1990), pp. 14–16.

5. F.W. *Putzgers Historischer Schul-Atlas* (Bielefeld and Leipzig, 1923), pp. 45, 104, 116–19.

6. Ibid., pp. 137–41.

7. Ibid., p. 137.

8. P. Schmet, *Atlas d'histoire de la Belgique*, published in the same book as *Atlas d'histoire universelle* (Namur, 1939), p. 108.

9. *Philips' New School Atlas of Universal History* (London, 1928), p. 9 referring to plate 7.

10. Ibid., pp. 21–22 referring to figure 23.

11. A. Wolf, 'What Can the History of Historical Atlases Teach? Some Lessons from a Century of Putzger's *Historischer Schul-Atlas*', *Cartographica*, 28 (1991), p. 23.

12. K.S. Kini and U.B. Shanker, *Oxford Pictorial Atlas of Indian History* (4th edn, Oxford, 1942), pp. 1, 66.

13. C. Fox, *The Archaeology of the Cambridge Region* (Cambridge, 1923), pp. 316, 320.

14. Fox, *The Personality of Britain* (4th edn, Cardiff, 1943), pp. 11, 14, 87–89; Fox's influence was discussed and reflected in I.L.L. Foster and L. Alcock (eds), *Culture and Environment: Essays in Honour of Sir Cyril Fox* (1963).

15. G. East, *The Geography behind History* (London, 1938), p. 21.

16. C. Paullin, *Atlas of the Historical Geography of the United States* (Washington, 1932), p. xi.

17. East, *Geography behind History*, p. 17.

18. P. Vidal de la Blache, *La France. Tableau géographique* (Paris, 1908); I. Lefort, *La Lettre et l'esprit. Géographie scholaire et géographie savante en France 1870–1970* (Paris, 1992); A.-L. Sanguin, *Vidal de La Blache 1845–1918: un génie de la géographie* (Paris, 1993); X. de Planhol, *An Historical Geography of France* (Cambridge, 1994), pp. xxi, 325–26; V. Berdoulay, *La Formation de L'Ecole Française de Géographie (1870–1914)* (2nd edn, Paris, 1995).

19. H. Jäger, 'Historical Geography in Germany, Austria and Switzerland', in A.R.H. Baker (ed.), *Progress in Historical Geography* (Newton Abbot, 1972), p. 62.

20. L. Febvre, *A Geographical Introduction to History* (London, 1932), pp. xx, 122, 360–61.

21. R.A. Butlin, 'Historical Geographies of the British Empire, *c.* 1887–1925', in Bell, Butlin and Heffernan (eds), *Geography and Imperialism*, pp. 169–72. New editions of Hereford George's *Relations of Geography and History* were published in 1903, 1907, 1910 and 1924, and the last was reprinted in 1930.

22. A.R.H. Baker, 'Reflections on the Relations of Historical Geography and the Annales School of History', in Baker and D. Gregory (eds), *Explorations in Historical Geography* (Cambridge, 1984), pp. 1–27; D. Livingstone, *The Geographical Tradition* (Oxford, 1992), p. 354.

23. Livingstone, *Geographical Tradition*, pp. 290–91, 296.

24. C. Koeman, 'The Application of Photography', in D. Woodward (ed.), *Five Centuries of Map Printing* (Chicago, 1975), pp. 152–53.

25. S.R. Gardiner (ed.), *A School Atlas of English History* (2nd edn, London, 1936), p. 6; map 66b.

26. *Atlas historique* (3 vols, Paris 1936–37), I, pp. 5–6.

27. A. Rébillon, *Les Temps modernes* (Paris, 1937), p. 10.

28. W.A. Seymour (ed.), *A History of the Ordnance Survey* (Folkestone, 1980), p. 239.

29. B. Konopska, *Polskie Atlasy Historyczne* (Warsaw, 1994), pp. 61–111.

30. E. Channing and A.B. Hart, *Guide to the Study of American History* (Boston, 1896), pp. 48, 45.

31. Hart, *American History Atlas* (5th edn, Chicago, 1942), pp. xx.

32. D.R. Fox, *Harper's Atlas of American History* (New York, 1920), pp. 107–9, 104,

109; W.R. Shepherd, *Historical Atlas* (3rd edn, New York, 1923), pp. 190–91, 198–99.

33. *Putnam's Historical Atlas Medieval and Modern* (New York, 1927), p. xxxii.

34. Paullin, *Atlas of the Historical Geography of the United States*, pp. ix, xi, xv.

35. Ibid., p. xi.

36. 'Report of the Conference on the Relation of Geography and History', in American Historical Association, *Annual Report for 1907*, I, 45–48; J.K. Wright, 'Miss Semple's "Influences of Geographic Environment": Notes towards a Bibliography', *Geographical Review*, 52 (1962), pp. 346–61.

37. R.A. Billington, *The Genesis of the Frontier Thesis* (San Marino, California, 1971), and *Frederick Jackson Turner: Historian, Scholar, Teacher* (New Haven, 1973).

38. Paullin, *Atlas*, p. xi.

39. Ibid., p. xiii.

40. Ibid.

41. Ibid.

42. Ibid., p. xii.

43. Ibid., p. xiii.

44. R.L. Poole, *Historical Atlas of Modern Europe* (Oxford, 1902), plate 89.

45. H. Kot, *Historia Nowożytnej Kartografii Śląska 1800–1939* (Katowice, 1970), p. 195. I should like to thank David Murphy for sending a copy of his unpublished paper '"The Suggestive Map": Geopolitics and Cartography'. See also G. Herb, 'Persuasive Cartography in Geopolitik and National Socialism', *Political Geography Quarterly*, 8 (1989), pp. 289–303.

46. G. Shaw and T. Coles, 'Directories as Elements of Town Life: The Case of National Socialist Germany', *Geographical Journal*, 161 (1995), pp. 296–306.

47. K. Kost, *Die Einflüsse der Geopolitik auf Forschung und Theorie der Politischen Geographie von ihren Anfängen bis 1945* (Bonn, 1988); M. Burleigh, *Germany Turns Eastwards: A Study of Ostforschung in the Third Reich* (Cambridge, 1988); M. Korinman, *Quand l'Allemagne pensait le monde: grandeur et décadence d'une géopolitique* (Paris, 1990); H. Frei, 'Japan and Australia in Karl Haushofer's Geopolitics of the Pacific Ocean', *Journal of International Studies*, 22 (Jan. 1989), p. 84; J. Loughlin and H. van der Wusten, 'Political Geography of Panregions', *Geographical Review*, 80 (1990), pp. 2–9.

48. M. Bassin, 'Race contra Space: The Conflict between German *Geopolitik* and National Socialism', *Political Geography Quarterly*, 6 (1987), pp. 115–34.

49. A. Pudelko and A.H. Ziegfeld, *Kleiner deutscher Geschichtsatlas* (Berlin, 1937), p. 25.

50. F. Eberhardt (ed.), *Neuer Deutscher Geschichts-und Kulturatlas* (Leipzig, 1937), pp. 6, 19, 32–35, 49, 52, 70, 85, 88, 90.

51. J.F. Horrabin, *An Atlas of Empire* (London, 1937), p. 6; A. Bithell, 'The Maps and Diagrams of J.F. Horrabin', *Bulletin of the Society of University Cartographers*, 18 (1984), pp. 85–91.

52. B. Kumsteller, *Werden und Wachsen* (Braunschweig, 1938), pp. 1–2, 14, 21, 24, 34–35, 32, 39, 50–51, 53, 57, 49, 57–59.

53. O. Subtelney, *Ukraine: A History* (Toronto, 1994), pp. 457–58, 470, 472.

54. W. Kubijowytsch, *Historischer Atlas der Ukraine. Ein deutsches Dokument aus dem Jahr 1941* (Munich/Paris, 1993).

55. Ibid., p. viii.

56. Lukinich, *Documenta Historiam Valachorum* (Budapest, 1941), pp. vii, liii.

57. D. Atkinson, 'Geopolitics, Cartography and Geographical Knowledge: Envisioning Africa from Fascist Italy', in Bell, Butlin and Heffernan (eds), *Geography and Imperialism*, pp. 265–97.

58. Ibid., p. 273.

59. G. de Agostini and A. Monti, *Dal' Risorgimento all' Impero* (Milan, 1938), pp. 37, 39, 44–45.

60. Goodall (ed.), *The War in Maps*, pp. 10–11, 14, 6.

61. Oxford, Bodleian Library, C 22:21 (29).

62. G. Balla, 'Historical / School Wall-Maps in Hungary', in *Making and Use of Historical Maps*, Budapest International Cartographical Exhibitions and Conferences XI (Budapest, 1972), p. 1.

63. E. Jutikkala (ed.), *Suomen Historian Kartasto* (2nd edn, Helsinki, 1959), p. 5. The first edition was published in 1949.

64. J.T. Adams and R.V. Coleman (eds), *Atlas of American History* (New York, 1943), p. vii.

65. A less charitable interpretation is offered by L.J. Cappon, 'The Historical Map in American Atlases', *Annals of the Association of American Geographers*, 69 (1979), p. 633.

6   Commercial Context 1945–

1. K. Nebenzahl and D. Higginbotham, *Atlas of the American Revolution* (Chicago,

1974), p. 9.

2. Conversation with Thomas Cussans of Times Books, 23 Feb. 1994.

3. Ex. inf. Donald Matthew; Banks, *World Atlas of Military History* (London, 1973), p. ix.

4. P.D.A. Harvey, 'The Medievalist's Atlas', *Nottingham Medieval Studies*, 30 (1986), p. 117.

5. L.J. Cappon, 'The Case for a New Historical Atlas of Early America', *William and Mary Quarterly*, 28 (1971), p. 122.

6. J.R. Cram and J. McQuilton (eds), *Australians: A Historical Atlas* (Broadway, New South Wales, 1987), pp. xi, xiii.

7. T.W. Moody *et al* (eds), *A New History of Ireland* IX (Oxford, 1984), p. 7.

8. J.E. Schwartzberg (ed.), *Historical Atlas of South Asia* (New York, 1992), p. xxii.

9. B.B. Petchenik, 'Cartography and the Making of a Historical Atlas: A Memoir', *The American Cartographer*, 4 (1977), p. 17; G. Martin, 'Cartography, Teleology and an Antipodean Contrast: The Historical Atlas of Canada', *British Journal of Canadian Studies*, 3 (1988), p. 86.

10. H.C. Darby and H. Fullard (eds), *The New Cambridge Modern History. XIV. Atlas* (Cambridge, 1970), p. xvii.

11. C. McEvedy, *The Penguin Atlas of Medieval History* (London, 1961), *The Penguin Atlas of Ancient History* (London, 1967), *The Penguin Atlas of Modern History* (London, 1972), *The Penguin Atlas of African History* (London, 1980), *The Penguin Atlas of North American History* (London, 1988), *The Penguin Atlas of Medieval History* (London, 1992).

12. F.W. Jessup, *Kent History Illustrated* (Maidstone, 1966, 2nd edn, 1973), p. 2.

13. J. McQuilton, 'Mapping the Past: Producing an Australian Historical Atlas', *Cartography*, 16 (1987), p. 44.

14. K.M. Davies, 'The Irish Historic Towns Atlas', *SUC Bulletin*, 21 (1988), p. 61.

15. J. Langton and R.J. Morris (eds), *The Atlas of Industrialising Britain 1780–1914* (London, 1986), p. xxi.

16. *New Zealand Historical Atlas Newsletter*, 1–5 (1991–94); 'The Historical Atlas of New Zealand: An Introduction', unpublished talk by Malcolm McKinnon, editor of the atlas, to the Massey University History and Geography Departments.

17. J. Schwartzberg (ed.), *Historical Atlas of South Asia* (2nd edn, New York, 1992), p. xxv.

18. I.C. Taylor, 'Thematic Atlases of

19. Canada', unpublished paper.

19. Davies, 'Irish Historic Towns Atlas', p. 65.

7   *Politics and Post-war Atlases*

1. *Povijesni Atlas* (Zagreb, 1971), pp. 4–5, 23, 25, 28–29, 33, 35, 47, 55, 58.

2. *Atlas i Historise se Kohes se Mesme* (Tirana, 1963), pp. 16, 24, 28–30, 36; *Povijesni Atlas*, p. 42.

3. *Atlas Istoric* (Bucharest, 1971), maps 85a, 104, 113–14.

4. *Atlas Historyczny Polski* (Warsaw, 1973), p. 49.

5. *Making and Use of Historical Maps*, Budapest International Cartographical Exhibitions and Conferences XI (Budapest, 1972), pp. 15, 8.

6. *Historický Atlas Revolučního Hnutí* (Prague, 1956), pp. 104, 114, 124, 141.

7. Ibid., pp. 113–14, 116, 123.

8. Ibid., pp. 129–32.

9. *Atlas Historik. Koha e re dhe e sotme* (Tirana, 1974), pp. 21, 20.

10. *Povijesni Atlas*, pp. 67–70.

11. *Atlas des Saale-und mittleren Elbegebietes* (Leipzig, 1959–61), sheet 56.

12. *Atlas zur Geschichte* (2 vols, 2nd edn, Gotha/Leipzig, 1976), I, pp. 15, 29, 36–37.

13. Ibid., I, pp. 15, 38, 46.

14. Ibid., p. 45.

15. Ibid., p. 47.

16. Ibid., pp. 48, 54.

17. Ibid., pp. 58, 60, 64, 71, 75, 79.

18. Ibid., p. 65.

19. Ibid., pp. 79, 83–85, 88–89, 92–93, 95. See also e.g. *Povijesni Atlas*, p. 45.

20. *Atlas zur Geschichte* I, pp. 90–91, 94.

21. Ibid., pp. 96, 107–9, 116–17; *Povijesni Atlas*, p. 47.

22. *Atlas zur Geschichte* I, pp. 101, 103, 105–6.

23. Ibid., p. 104.

24. Ibid., p. 98.

25. F.J. Ormeling, 'Cartographic Consequences of a Planned Economy – 50 Years of Soviet Cartography', *The American Cartographer*, 1 (1974), pp. 44–45.

26. Ibid., p. 39.

27. Ibid., p. 43. A positive re-evaluation of Soviet historical studies in this period has recently been offered: A. Kan, 'Soviet Historiography of the West under Stalin's Prewar Dictatorship', *Storia della Storiografia*, 21 (1992), pp. 45–63.

28. *Atlas Istorii SSSR dlia srednei shkoly* (3

vols, Moscow, 1949–54), I, p. 17; II, pp. 3, 11, 13, 15; III, p. 38.

29. Ibid., II, p. 12; III, pp. 19–20.

30. Ibid., III, pp. 33–36.

31. *Atlas Istorii Srednyth Vekov* (Moscow, 1952), pp. 17–18.

32. Ibid., pp. 36, 42, 44, 46, 55.

33. *Atlas Istorii Geograficheskikh Otkrytiy i Issledovanii* (Moscow, 1959), pp. 39–40, 71.

34. Ibid., pp. 25, 57.

35. *Atlas Istorii SSSR dlia srednei shkoly* (Moscow, 1959), pp. 31–32.

36. *Atlas Istorii SSSR dlia srednei shkoly* (3 vols, Moscow, 1960–63), I, p. 13; II, p. 7.

37. Ibid., III, p. 5.

38. Ibid., p. 7.

39. Ibid., p. 14.

40. *Atlas Istorii SSSR, 7-oi klass* (Moscow, 1982), p. 7.

41. Ibid., pp. 8, 13.

42. *Atlas Istorii SSSR, 8-oi klass* (Moscow, 1982), p. 11.

43. *Atlas Istorii SSSR, 9-yi–10yi klass* (Moscow, 1982), p. 13.

44. *Atlas Istorii SSSR* (Moscow, 1990), pp. 2, 3.

45. Ibid., pp. 4, 5, 6, 7, 12–13.

46. *Nasza Ojczyzna* (Wroclaw, 1981–82), pp. 19, 21–22.

47. *Dějepisný Atlas 6* (Prague, 1982), pp. 11, 17, 23.

48. *Dějepisný Atlas 7* (Prague, 1982), pp. 17, 16, 10.

49. N. Myers (ed.), *The Gaia Atlas of Planet Management* (London, 1985); J. Mackay, *The State of Health Atlas* (New York, 1993); M. Kidron and R. Segal, *The State of the World Atlas* (London, 1995). See also J. Crush, 'Towards a People's Historical Geography for South Africa', *Journal of Historical Geography*, 12 (1986), p. 3.

50. M. Kidron and D. Smith, *The New State of War and Peace* (London, 1991), pp. 54–55.

51. I. Pogonowski, *Poland. A Historical Atlas* (2nd edn, New York, 1988), pp. 11–14.

52. Ibid., pp. 48–49.

53. Ibid., pp. 129, 89. On Germany e.g. p. 98.

54. Ibid., p. 85.

55. Ibid., p. 100.

56. Ibid., p. 144.

57. Ibid., pp. 176–91.

58. Ibid., p. 177. See also pp. 182, 185.

59. Ibid., p. 202.

60. Ibid., p. 216.

61. E. Copeaux, 'Quelques Réflexions sur les représentations arméniennes de l'histoire', *Hérodote*, 74–75 (1994), p. 262.

62. P.R. Magocsi, *Ukraine: A Historical Atlas* (Toronto, 1985), p. i.

63. Ibid., p. iii.

64. Ibid., spread 7.

65. Ibid., spread 8.

66. *Grosser Historischer Weltatlas. III* (Munich, 1957), p. 197.

67. *Atlas de Portugal* (2nd edn, Coimbra, 1959), preface, no pagination.

68. See p. 128.

69. The dates of the other editions are 1946, 1949; 4th and subsequent editions *Atlas de Historia de España*, 1953, 1956, 1965, 1970, 1973 and 1977.

70. *Atlas historique* (Paris, 1987), pp. 210–11.

71. P. Ashdown, *Caribbean History in Maps* (London, 1979), p. 38.

72. *Times Atlas of World History* (London, 1978), p. 69.

73. *The Hamlyn Historical Atlas* (London, 1981), p. 8.

74. J.B. Garver, 'Mapping the Southwest: A Twentieth-Century Historical Geographic Perspective', in D.P. Koepp (ed.), *Exploration and Mapping of the American West. Selected Essays* (Chicago, 1986), p. 179. See also prefaces to *Atlas of Massachusetts* and *Historical Atlas of Texas*.

75. C. Sherlock, 'The Times Atlas of World History', *Bulletin of the Society of University Cartographers*, 16 (1983), p. 48.

76. J.M. Lambin and J.L. Villette, *Atlas des collèges* (Paris, 1993), p. 84.

77. A. Wolf, 'Das Bild der europäischen Geschichte in Geschichtsatlanten verschiedener Länder', *Internationales Jahrbuch für Geschichts-und Geographieunterricht*, 13 (1970–71), pp. 64–101.

78. J.E. Schwartzberg, 'Four Geographical Cross-Sections through Indian Economic History', *21st International Geographical Congress. IV: Regional Geography and Cartography* (Calcutta, 1972), p. 353.

79. R.R. Palmer (ed.), *Rand McNally Atlas of World History* (New York, 1965), p. 5.

8   Remembered Histories

1. Harley, 'Silences and Secrecy: The Hidden Agenda of Cartography in Early Modern Europe', *Imago Mundi*, 40 (1988), p. 70, and 'Victims of a Map: New England Cartography and the Native Americans', unpublished paper quoted in D. Wood, *The Power of Maps* (New York,

1992), p. 46; H.H. Tanner, *Atlas of Great Lakes Indian History* (Norman, 1987), p. xii.

2. *Place Names of the Ancestors* (Wellington, 1990), p. xiii.

3. D. and R. Whitehouse, *Archaeological Atlas of the World* (London, 1975), pp. 228–29, 224–25.

4. W.M. Mathes, 'Early Geographic Knowledge of Mesoamerica: A Century of Cartographic Evolution', *Journal of the International Map Collectors' Society*, 63 (1995), p. 8.

5. T. Zuidema, 'Hierarchy and Space in Incaic Social Organization', *Ethnohistory*, 30 (1983), pp. 49–75.

6. G. Urton, *The History of a Myth: Pacariqtambo and the Origin of the Inkas* (Austin, 1990).

7. J.H. Rowe, 'Inca Culture at the Time of the Spanish Conquest', in J. Steward (ed.), *Handbook of South American Indians. II* (Washington, 1946), pp. 183–330.

8. M. Pärssinen, *Tawantinsuyu: The Inca State and its Political Organization* (Helsinki, 1982).

9. Important recent work includes J. Hyslop, *The Inka Road System* (New York, 1984), and *Inka Settlement Planning* (Austin, 1990), and T. Dillehay and P. Netherly (eds), *La Frontera del estado inca* (Oxford, 1988). I have benefited from the advice of Terence D'Altroy.

10. R.H. Barlow, 'The Extent of the Empire of Culhua Mexico', *Ibero-Americana*, 28 (1949).

11. I have benefited from the advice of Ross Hassig on the Aztecs.

12. L.Y. Luciuk and B.S. Kordan, *Creating a Landscape. A Geography of Ukrainians in Canada* (Toronto, 1989), spreads 4, 3.

13. M.K. Asante and M.K. Mattson, *Historical and Cultural Atlas of African Americans* (New York, 1991), pp. vi, 11.

14. M.B. Newton, *Atlas of Louisiana* (Baton Rouge, 1972), pp. 49, 63.

15. W.G. Loy (ed.), *Atlas of Oregon* (Eugene, 1976), pp. 4, 6.

16. Ibid., p. 6.

17. Ibid.; M.D. Rafferty, R.L. Gerlach and D.J. Hrebec, *Atlas of Missouri*, (Springfield, 1970) p. 6.

18. C. Calloway, *The American Revolution in Indian Country: Crisis and Diversity in Native American Communities* (Cambridge, 1995), p. 159.

19. *Atlas of Utah* (Provo, 1981), p. 77.

20. Ibid., pp. 100–1, 104–5.

21. J.D. Forbes, *Atlas of Native History* (Davis, 1981). Introduction, no pagination.

22. J.M. Goodman, *The Navajo Atlas* (Norman, 1982), p. 54.

23. J.J. Ferguson and E.R. Hart, *A Zuni Atlas* (Norman, 1985), pp. 86–87.

24. E.A. Erickson and A.W. Smith, *Atlas of Colorado*, p. 32.

25. *Zuni Atlas*, pp. 24–25.

26. Ibid., pp. 56–57.

27. Ibid., pp. 58–59, 90.

28. C. Waldman, *Atlas of the North American Indian* (Oxford, 1985), p. x.

29. H.H. Tanner, *Atlas of Great Lakes Indian History* (Norman, 1987), p. 66.

30. Ibid., p. 160.

31. C.R. Goins and J.M. Caldwell, *Historical Atlas of Louisiana* (Norman, 1995), map 18; D.G. Anderson, 'Examining Prehistoric Settlement Distribution in Eastern North America', *Archaeology of Eastern North America*, 19 (1991), pp. 1–22.

32. C.E. Heidenreich, 'Maps Relating to the First Half of the Seventeenth Century and their Use in Determining the Location of Jesuit Missions in Huronia', *Cartographer*, 3 (1966), pp. 103–26, *Huronia: A History and Geography of the Huron Indians, 1600–1650* (Toronto, 1971), and 'Mapping the Location of Native Groups, 1600–1760', *Mapping History*, 2 (1981), pp. 6–13.

33. B.G. Trigger, *The Children of Aatentsic: A History of the Huron People to 1660* (Montreal, 1976), and *Natives and Newcomers: Canada's 'Heroic Age' Reconsidered* (Montreal, 1985).

34. R.C. Harris, 'Maps as a Morality Play: Volume I of the *Historical Atlas of Canada*', in J. Winearls (ed.), *Editing Early and Historical Atlases* (Toronto, 1975), p. 168; *Historical Atlas of Canada* (3 vols, Toronto, 1987–93), I, p. xiii.

35. Ibid., I, plate 47.

36. Harris, 'Morality Play', p. 177; *Historical Atlas of Canada*, I, plate 69, p. 173.

37. Ibid., II, plate 34.

38. Ibid., III, plate 2, p. 69.

39. J.R. Cram and J. McQuilton (eds), *Australians: A Historical Atlas* (Broadway, 1987), pp. 136–39.

40. Ibid., pp. 38–39.

41. Ibid., pp. 36–37.

42. D. Wadley (ed.), *Reef, Range and Red Dust. The Adventure Atlas of Queensland* (Brisbane, 1993), pp. 1, 15.

43. S. Davis and J.R.V. Prescott, *Aboriginal Frontiers and Boundaries in Australia* (Man-

chester, 1992); Davis, *Australia's Extant and Imputed Traditional Aboriginal Territories* (Carlton, 1993).

44. A. C. Wilgus, *Historical Atlas of Latin America* (2nd edn, New York, 1967), p. 21.

45. F. Fernandez-Arnesto, *Millennium* (London, 1995).

46. W.F. Miles, *Hausaland Divided: Colonialism and Independence in Nigeria and Niger* (Ithaca, 1994).

47. E. Leach, 'The Frontiers of Burma', *Comparative Studies in Society and History*, 3 (1960), pp. 49–68; A.T. Embree, 'Frontiers into Boundaries: From the Traditional to the Modern State', in R.G. Fox (ed.), *Realm and Region in Traditional India* (Durham, North Carolina, 1977), pp. 255–80; J.E. Schwartzberg (ed.), *A Historical Atlas of South Asia* (Chicago, 1978), pp. xxix–xxx, xxxiii–xxxv; N. Tarling (ed.), *The Cambridge History of Southeast Asia* (Cambridge, 1992), II, p. 8; M. Stuart-Fox, 'On the Writing of Lao History: Continuities and Discontinuities', *Journal of Southeast Asian Studies*, 24 (1993), pp. 106–21; T. Winichakul, *Siam Mapped: A History of the Geo-Body of a Nation* (Honolulu, 1994).

48. R.A. Kea, *Settlements, Trade, and Politics in the Seventeenth-Century Gold Coast* (Baltimore, 1982), pp. 23–32.

49. G.S.P. Freeman-Grenville, *The New Atlas of African History* (New York, 1991), pp. 48–49, 60, 74, 78.

50. J. Devisse, 'Trade and Trade Routes in West Africa', in I. Hrbek (ed.), *General History of Africa. III. Africa from the Seventh to the Eleventh Century* (Paris, 1992), pp. 191–211.

51. J.L. Newman, *The Peopling of Africa. A Geographic Interpretation* (New Haven, 1995).

52. J.D. Fage, *An Atlas of African History* (London, 1958), p. 17.

53. J. Thornton, *Africa and Africans in the Making of the Atlantic World, 1400–1680* (Cambridge, 1992), pp. xx, xxvi–xxvii, xxix–xxxii.

54. B. Catchpole and I.A. Akinjogbin, *A History of West Africa in Maps and Diagrams* (London, 1986), pp. viii, 132.

55. *Atlas of Uganda* (Entebbe, 1962), p. 70.

56. *Atlas de Burundi* (Gradignan, 1979), plate 11.

57. Ibid., plate 12; G. Lasserre (ed.), *Atlas d'Haïti* (Bordeaux, 1985), plate 3.

58. K.M. Barbour *et al* (eds), *Nigeria in Maps* (London, 1982), p. vii.

59. Ibid., pp. 36–37.

60. Ibid., p. 36; J.F. Horrabin, *An Atlas of Africa* (London, 1960), p. 59.

61. Ibid, pp. 38–39.

62. *Atlas of Ethiopia* (Addis Ababa, 1981), pp. 68, 74–76.

63. Y. Peron, *Atlas de la Haute-Volta* (Paris, 1975), pp. 20–21.

64. P. Pélissier, *Atlas du Sénégal* (Paris, 1980), pp. 22–25; E. Bernus and S.A. Hamidou, *Atlas du Niger* (Paris, 1980), pp. 24–27.

65. *Atlas de Côte d'Ivoire* (Abidjan, 1975), sections D 1a, b.

66. *Atlas de Cuba* (Havana, 1978), pp. 102–4.

67. *Zhongguo Renmin Geming Zhanzheng Dituxuan, 1927–1949* (Atlas of the people's revolutionary war in China, 1927–1949) (Beijing, 1981) and *War History Atlas of the People's Liberation Army* (Beijing, 1990).

68. Wu Zhong-Xing and Liao Ke, 'The Development of Cartography over the Past Thirty Years in the People's Republic of China', *International Yearbook of Cartography*, 20 (1980), pp. 42–43.

69. Z. Hai-Peng, *Zhongguo Jindai Shigao Dituji* (Atlas of modern China's history) (Beijing, 1984).

70. *Information China I* (Beijing/Oxford, 1989), maps I.8, 9. The maps are unpaginated.

71. Ibid, Maps I.11–17.

72. A. Herrmann, *Historical Atlas of China* (Taipei, 1964), p. 10.

73. C. Blunden and M. Elvin, *Cultural Atlas of China* (Oxford, 1983), pp. 14–15.

74. Ibid., pp. 20–21, 26.

75. Ibid., pp. 21–25.

76. Ibid., p. 30.

77. Ibid., pp. 36, 40–41.

78. P. Vidal-Naquet (ed.), *Atlas historique* (Paris, 1987), p. v.

79. G. Parker (ed.), *The Times Atlas of World History* (4th edn, London, 1993), p. 124.

80. A. Reynaud, *Le Polycentrisme dans la Chine des printemps et des automnes (741–472 avant J.C.)* (Rheims, 1985) and 'Cartographie et histoire: la différentiation de l'espace dans la Chine des printemps et des automnes (721–472 av. J.C.)', *Mappe monde 86*, 3 1986 pp. 17–21.

81. G. Chaliand and J.-P. Rageau, *Atlas politique du XXᵉ siècle* (Paris, 1988), pp. 139.

82. G. Scott, 'The Formation of the Turkestan Frontier between Russia and China in the Eighteenth Century' (unpublished D. Phil., Oxford, 1971).

83. T.J. Barfield, *The Perilous Frontier: No-madic Empires and China* (Oxford, 1989); S. Jagchild and V.J. Symons, *Peace, War, and Trade along the Great Wall: Nomadic-Chinese Interaction through Two Millennia* (Bloomington, Indiana, 1989).

84. I am most grateful for the assistance of Stewart Lone in the section on Japanese historical atlases. On Japanese archaeology, See M. Collcutt, M. Jansen and I. Kumakura, *Cultural Atlas of Japan* (Oxford, 1988), pp. 32–33.

85. I. Habib, *Atlas of the Mughal Empire* (Delhi, 1982), pp. xiv–xvii. For a critical review, See J.E. Schwartzberg, *Journal of Asian Studies*, 43 (1984), pp. 567–70.

86. L. Sternstein, 'An Historical Atlas of Thailand', *Journal of the Siam Society*, 52 (1964), pp. 7–20.

87. N. Tarling (ed.), *The Cambridge History of Southeast Asia* (Cambridge, 1992), I, pp. 402–9 (quote p. 405).

88. Harley and Woodward (eds), *Cartography in the Traditional Islamic and South Asian Societies* II, i, pp. 329–30.

89. D. Lombard, *Le Carrefour javanais. Essai d'histoire globale* (Paris, 1990).

90. J.L. Westcoat review of Schwartzberg, *Annals of the Association of American Geographers*, 83 (1983), p. 744.

91. J.A.S. Grenville, *National Prejudice and International History* (Leeds, 1968), p. 9; K. Hodgkinson, 'Eurocentric World Views – the Hidden Curriculum of Humanities Maps and Atlases', *Multicultural Teaching*, 5 (1987), p. 31, and 'Standing the World on its Head: A Review of Eurocentrism in Humanities Maps and Atlases', *Teaching History*, 62 (1991), pp. 21–23.

92. G. Barraclough (ed.), *The Times Atlas of World History* (London, 1978), p. 13.

93. Ibid., p. 13.

94. Ibid., pp. 94–95, 146–47, 170–71.

95. Ibid., pp. 128–29.

96. *Philip's Atlas of World History* (London, 1992), pp. 62–63, 22–23, 38–41, 45, 52–55.

97. J. Keegan (ed.), *The Times Atlas of the Second World War* (London, 1989), p. 206.

98. M. Benvenisti and S. Khayat, *The West Bank and Gaza Atlas* (Jerusalem, 1988), pp. 27, iii.

99. A. Simms and F. Opll, *Historic Towns Atlases* (Brussels, 1995), p. 7. On the different abilities of Illinois and Indiana to fund a state historical atlas, R. Burnette, 'Towards a Historical Atlas of Illinois: A Project Proposal. A Historian's Perspective', *Fifteenth Annual Illinois History Symposium*, 2 Dec. 1994. I would like to thank Professor Burnette for sending a copy of his unpublished paper.

9   A New Agenda: Post-1945 Historical Atlases and the 'Non-political'

1. N. Ohler, 'Atlanten und Karten zur Kirchengeschichte', *Zeitschrift für Kirchengeschichte* (1980), pp. 312–49.

2. F.H. Littell, foreword to *The Macmillan Atlas History of Christianity* (New York, 1976).

3. Langton and Morris, *Atlas of Industrialising Britain*, p. xxv.

4. G. Johnson, *Cultural Atlas of India* (Oxford, 1995), p. 56.

5. Schwartzberg, *Atlas of South Asia*, p. 193.

6. Ibid., p. 177.

7. Ibid., p. 200.

8. *Historical Atlas of Canada* II, p. 53.

9. *Atlas of Portsmouth* (Portsmouth, 1975), section 3:5.

10. R. Chevallier (ed.), *Tabula Imperii Romani Lutetia* (Paris, 1979), p. 9.

11. J. Bertin et al, *Atlas of Food Crops* (Paris, 1971), p. 12.

12. H. Carter (ed.), *National Atlas of Wales* (1989), section 4:4.

13. *Deutscher Planungsatlas. Atlas von Berlin* (Berlin, 1956), sheet 75.

14. W.C. Brice (ed.), *An Historical Atlas of Islam* (Leiden, 1981), pp. vi, 27.

15. H.H. Kagan (ed.), *The American Heritage Pictorial Atlas of United States History* (New York, 1966), pp. 284–85. On transport, see more generally J.E. Vance, Jr, *Capturing the Horizon: The Historical Geography of Transportation since the Transportation Revolution of the Sixteenth Century* (New York, 1986).

16. I.S. Black, 'Geography, Political Economy and the Circulation of Finance Capital in Early Industrial England', and 'Money, Information and Space: Banking in Early-Nineteenth-Century England and Wales', *Journal of Historical Geography*, 15 (1989), pp. 366–84, and 21 (1995), pp. 398–412.

17. D.J. Bell, 'Insignificant Others: Lesbian and Gay Geographies', *Area*, 23 (1991), pp. 323–29; S. Adler and J. Brenner, 'Gender and Space: Lesbians and Gay Men in the City', *International Journal of Urban and Regional Research*, 16 (1992),

pp. 24–34; G.M. Valentine, '(Hetero)-sexing Space: Lesbian Perceptions and Experiences of Everyday Spaces', *Environment and Planning. D: Society and Space*, 11 (1993), pp. 395–413, 'Desperately Seeking Susan: A Geography of Lesbian Friendships', *Area*, 25 (1993), pp. 109–16, and 'Out and About: Geographies of Lesbian Landscapes', *International Journal of Urban and Regional Research*, 19 (1995), pp. 96–111; D. Bell and G. Valentine (eds), *Mapping Desire. Geographies of Sexualities* (London, 1995).

18. *Philips' Junior Historical Atlas* (5th edn, London, 1929), p. vii.

19. D. Turnbull, *Maps Are Territories. Science Is an Atlas* (Chicago, 1993), p. 61.

20. *Philips' Atlas of World History*, p. 91; *Historical Atlas of Canada*, II, plate 44, III, p. 9.

21. J. Flouriot *et al*, *Atlas de Kinshasa* (1975), plate 10.

22. J. Doutier, P. Boutry and S. Bonin, *Atlas de la Révolution française. VI. Les sociétés politiques* (Paris, 1992), p. 15.

23. J. Bertin, *Semiologie graphique. Les diagrammes, les réseaux, les cartes* (Paris, 1967), pp. 408–11.

24. J. Letarte, *Atlas d'histoire économique et sociale du Québec 1850–1901* (Montreal, 1971), pp. 11–12.

25. R.H. Bautier, *Atlas historique Agenais* (Paris, 1979), p. 9.

26. D. Dymond and E. Martin, *An Historical Atlas of Suffolk* (Ipswich, 1988), p. 7.

27. M. Kowaleski, *Local Markets and Regional Trade in Medieval Exeter* (Cambridge, 1995), p. 10.

28. E. Kerridge, *The Common Fields of England* (Manchester, 1992), p. viii; C. Phythian-Adams (ed.), *Societies, Cultures and Kinship, 1580–1850. Cultural Provinces and English Local History* (Leicester, 1993), pp. xvii–xx, 9–18.

29. B. Frenzel *et al* (ed.), *Atlas of Paleoclimates and Paleoenvironments of the Northern Hemisphere* (Stuttgart, 1992), pp. 63, 131.

30. W. Schier, *Atlas zur Allgemeinen und Österreichischen Geschichte* (Vienna, 1982), p. 47.

31. M. McGranaghan, 'A Cartographic View of Spatial Data Quality', *Cartographica*, 30 (1993), p. 18.

32. E. Le Roy Ladurie, *Le Grand Atlas de l'histoire mondiale* (Paris, 1979), p. 5.

33. D. Gregory, 'Areal Differentiation and Post-Modern Human Geography', in Gregory and R. Walford (eds), *Horizons in Human Geography* (London, 1989), pp. 67–96.

34. G.M. Lewis, 'Changing National Perspectives and the Mapping of the Great Lakes between 1755 and 1795', *Cartographica*, 17 (1980), p. 6.

35. Isma'il Raji al Fārūqi, *Historical Atlas of the Regions of the World* (New York, 1974), p. vi.

36. *Atlas Historyczny Swiata* (Warsaw, 1992), p. 77.

37. A. Wheatcroft, *The World Atlas of Revolutions* (London, 1983), p. 8.

38. M. Freeman, *Atlas of Nazi Germany* (London, 1987), pp. 2, 4.

39. F. Braudel, *The Mediterranean and the Mediterranean World in the Age of Philip II* (2 vols, London, 1972), I, p. 169.

40. *Historical Atlas of Canada* I, p. 19.

41. *Times Atlas of World History* (London, 1978), pp. 182, 184–85.

42. Ibid., pp. 178–79.

43. *Atlas Historyczyny Swiata* (Warsaw, 1992), p. 67.

44. E.M. Ruiz, A.G. Castillo and E.D. Lobón, *Atlas Histórico. Edad Moderna* (Madrid, 1986), p. 90.

45. A. Banks, *A World Atlas of Military History* I (London, 1973), p. ix; A.J. Toynbee and E.D. Myers, *Historical Atlas and Gazetteer* (Oxford, 1959), p. vi.

46. D. Wood, 'Pleasure in the Idea. The Atlas as Narrative Form', *Cartographica*, 24 (1987), pp. 32–35.

47. C. Harris, 'Reality, Bias and the Making of an Atlas', *Mapping History*, 1 (1980), p. 14; P.D.A. Harvey, 'The Documents of Landscape History: Snares and Delusions', *Landscape History*, 13 (1991), p. 50. Mark Monmonier's *How to Lie with Maps* (Chicago, 1991) and Denis Wood's *The Power of Maps* (New York, 1992) are both relevant, though neither considers historical atlases.

48. D. Gregory, *Geographical Imaginations* (Oxford, 1994); A. Buttimer, *Geography and the Human Spirit* (Baltimore, 1994).

49. J. Riley-Smith, *Atlas of the Crusades* (London, 1991), p. 7.

50. R. Bartlett and A. Mackay, *Medieval Frontier Societies* (Oxford, 1990).

51. M. Hendy, *Studies in the Byzantine Monetary Economy* (Cambridge, 1985), pp. 109–23.

52. H. Inalcik, 'Ottoman Methods of Conquest', *Studia Islamica*, 2 (1954), pp. 103–29.

53. P.R. Magocsi, *Ukraine: A Historical Atlas*

(Toronto, 1985), map 10.

54. C. Nicolet, *Space, Geography and Politics in the Early Roman Empire* (Ann Arbor, 1991); J.S. Romm, *The Edges of the Earth in Ancient Thought: Geography, Exploration and Fiction* (Princeton, 1992). For Egypt the best introductions are R.K. Holz, 'The Cartography of Mendes', in Holz *et al*, *Mendes I* (Cairo, 1980), pp. 3–14, and J. Baines and J. Malek, *Atlas of Ancient Egypt* (Oxford, 1980).

55. C.R. Whittaker, *Les Frontières de l'empire romain* (Besançon, 1989), p. 32; B. Isaac, *The Limits of Empire. The Roman Army in the East* (2nd edn, Oxford, 1992), pp. 3, 417, 419, 426.

56. F. Miller, 'Emperors, Frontiers and Foreign Relations, 31 BC to AD 378', *Britannia*, 13 (1982), pp. 15–18; Whittaker, *Les Frontières*, pp. 11–19; R.J.A. Talbert, 'Rome's Empire and Beyond: The Spatial Aspect', in *Gouvernants et gouvernés dans l'Imperium Romanum, Cahiers des études anciennes*, 26 (1990), p. 217.

57. I have benefited greatly from discussing Harappan culture with Jim Shaffer. Schwartzberg's *Historical Atlas of South Asia* is cautious about drawing boundary lines, and in *Peoples and Places of the Past. The National Geographic Illustrated Atlas of the Ancient World* (Washington D.C., 1983), p. 204 the map indicates areas of concentrated Harappan sites and does not show a frontier. On the Lapita, P.V. Kirch, 'La Colonisation du Pacifique', *La Recherche*, 21 (1990), pp. 1226–35.

58. B.P. Hindle, 'The Road Network of Medieval England', *Journal of Historical Geography*, 2 (1976).

59. P.P. Karan and C. Mather (eds), *Atlas of Kentucky* (Lexington, Kentucky, 1977), pp. 13–15.

60. P. Taylor, *The Atlas of Australian History* (Frenchs Forest, New South Wales, 1990), p. 7.

61. *Historical Atlas of Canada*, I, plate 14.

62. *Historical Atlas of Canada*, III, plate 66.

63. For a listing of some relevant works, N. Ohler, 'Atlanten und Karten zur Wirtschafts- und Sozialgeschichte des Mittelalters und der Neuzeit', *Vierteljahrschrift für Sozial- und Wirtschaftsgeschichte*, 67 (1980), pp. 228–50.

64. M. Kowaleski, *Local Markets and Regional Trade in Medieval Exeter* (Cambridge, 1995), p. 10.

65. H.M. Jewell, *The North-South Divide: The Origins of Northern Consciousness* (Manchester, 1994).

66. R.D. Gastil, *Culture Regions of the United States* (Seattle, 1975); S. Arbingast, *Atlas of Texas* (5th edn, Texas, 1976); W. Zelinsky, 'North America's Vernacular Regions', *Annals of the Association of American Geographers*, 70 (1980), pp. 1–16; *This Remarkable Continent: An Atlas of United States and Canadian Society and Culture* (College Station, Texas, 1982), pp. 3, 11; J.B. Garver, 'Mapping the Southwest: A Twentieth Century Historical Geographic Perspective', in D.P. Koepp (ed.), *Exploration and Mapping of the American West. Selected Essays* (Chicago, 1986), pp. 171–72; J.D. Lowry, 'The Vernacular Southwest', *Bulletin of Special Libraries Association. Geography and Map Division*, 176 (June, 1994), pp. 2–11; M. O'Brien, 'Finding the Outfield: Subregionalism and the American South', *Historical Journal*, 38 (1995), pp. 1047–56.

67. Schwartzberg, *Historical Atlas of South Asia*, p. xxviii.

68. E. Homberger, *Penguin Historical Atlas of North America* (London, 1995), p. 5.

69. J.D. Hamshere, 'Data Sources in Historical Geography', in M. Pacione (ed.), *Historical Geography: Progress and Prospect* (London, 1987), pp. 46–69.

70. D.W. Holdsworth, 'The Politics of Editing a National Historical Atlas: A Commentary', in J. Winearls (ed.), *Editing Early and Historical Atlases* (Toronto, 1995), p. 192.

10   Technology and the Spaces of the Future

1. C. Koeman, 'The Application of Photography to Map Printing and the Transition to Offset Lithography', in D. Woodward (ed.), *Five Centuries of Map Printing* (Chicago, 1975), p. 153.

2. Ibid., p. 155.

3. J.B. Garver, Jr, 'Mapping the Southwest: A Twentieth-Century Historical Geographic Perspective', in D.P. Koepp (ed.), *Exploration and Mapping of the American West. Selected Essays* (Chicago, 1986), p. 180.

4. *Historical Atlas of Canada*, III, plate 66.

5. W. Horn, 'Die Geschichte der Isarithmenkarten', *Petermanns Geographische Mitteilungen*, 103 (1959), pp. 225–32; L.J. Cappon (ed.), *Atlas of Early American*

History (Princeton, 1976), p. 69.

6. G. Galton, 'On the Construction of Isochronic Passage-charts', *Proceedings of the Royal Geographical Society*, 3 (1881) pp. 657–58; F.C. Spooner, *Risk at Sea. Amsterdam Insurance and Maritime Europe, 1766–1780* (Cambridge, 1983), pp. 201–35.

7. U. Sporrong and H.-F. Wennström, *Maps and Mapping* (Stockholm, 1990), pp. 18, 23; R. Cromley, *Digital Cartography* (Englewood Cliffs, New Jersey, 1992), pp. 6, 9.

8. Sporrong and Wennström, *Maps and Mapping*, p. 98.

9. B. Petchenik, 'The Natural History of the Atlas: Evolution and Extinction', *Cartographica*, 22 (1985), pp. 56–57.

10. C.O. Paullin, *Atlas of the Historical Geography of the United States* (Washington D.C., 1932).

11. C.L. and E.H. Lord, *Historical Atlas of the United States* (2nd edn, New York, 1953), p. iii.

12. A. Breznay, 'Projects for Making Comparable the Historical Maps of Different Ages and Matters', in *Making and Use of Historical Maps* (Budapest, 1972), p. 12.

13. S.S. Hall, *Mapping the Next Millennium. The Discovery of New Geographies* (New York, 1992), p. 12; B. Rystedt, 'Current Trends, in Electronic Atlas Production, *Cartographic Perspectives*, 20 (Winter 1995), p. 5.

14. C.D. Tomlin, *Geographic Information Systems and Cartographic Modelling* (Englewood Cliffs, New Jersey, 1990); D. Martin, *Geographic Information Systems and their Socioeconomic Applications* (London, 1991); M. Monmonier, *Mapping it Out. Expository Cartography for the Humanities and Social Sciences* (Chicago, 1993); A.H. Robinson *et al*, *Elements of Cartography* (6th edn, New York, 1995), pp. 292–311. The journal *Cartography and Geographic Information Systems* contains much of relevance.

15. *Mapline*, 71 (Autumn, 1993), p. 5.

16. S. Schulten, '"Disturber of the Peace": Richard Edes Harrison 1901–1994', *Mapline*, 78–79 (1995), pp. 17–19.

17. I have benefited from discussing the *Times* historical atlases with Thomas Cussans and Barry Winkleman of Times Books.

18. G. Barraclough, *Times Atlas of World History* (London, 1978), p. 14.

19. Ibid., pp. 138–39, 170–71, 187.

20. J.P. Cole, *Geography of World Affairs* (London, 1966), p. 19.

21. G. Parker (ed.), *Times Atlas of World History* (London, 1993), p. 183.

22. Ex inf. Thomas Cussans.

23. J. Macdonald, *Great Battlefields of the World* (London, 1985).

24. A. Cliff and P. Haggett, *Atlas of Disease Distributions* (Oxford, 1988), p. 263.

25. *1987 Census of Agriculture. I. Agricultural Atlas of the United States* (Washington, 1990), pp. ix–x.

26. B. Macdonald, *Vancouver. A Visual History* (Vancouver, 1992), p. ix.

27. *Historical Atlas of Canada* II, p. xvii; A.B. Piternick, 'The Historical Atlas of Canada. The Project behind the Project', *Cartographica*, 30 (1993), p. 25; W.G. Dean, 'Atlas Structures and their Influence on Editorial Decisions: Two Recent Case Histories', in J. Winearls (ed.), *Editing Early and Historical Atlases* (Toronto, 1995), pp. 149–52; K.C. Martis and G.A. Elmes, *The Historical Atlas of State Power in Congress 1790–1990* (Washington, 1993), p. xv.

28. D. Hocking, C.P. Keller and C. Peterson, 'Thematic Content of Canadian Provincial Atlases', *Cartographica*, 28 (1991), p. 46.

29. T.J. Blachut and R. Buckhardt, *Historical Development of Photogrammetric Methods and Instruments* (Falls Church, Virginia, 1989).

30. R.R. Goodchild, 'Roman Tripolitania: Reconnaissance in the Desert Frontier Zone', *Geographical Journal*, 115 (1950), p. 170.

31. *An Historical Atlas of County Durham* (Durham, 1992), p. 13; R.W. Brown, 'Obtaining Aerial Photo Coverage for Historical Research of California', *Western Association of Map Libraries. Information Bulletin*, 25 (1994), pp. 123–27.

32. B. Jones and D. Mattingly, *An Atlas of Roman Britain* (Oxford, 1990), pp. 63, 177; R. Millon (ed.), *Urbanization at Teotihuacan, Mexico* (Austin, 1973), p. 9.

33. Jones and Mattingly, *Roman Britain*, pp. 250–51, 255.

34. J. Bertin *et al*, *Atlas des Cultures Vivrières/Atlas of Food Crops* (Paris, 1971), map 8.

35. H.G. Owen, *Atlas of Continental Displacement* (Cambridge, 1983), p. 5.

36. W.A. Bowen, 'Mapping an American Frontier: Oregon in 1850', *Annals of the Association of American Geographers*, 65 (1975), map supplement no. 18.

37. D.B. Dodd, *Historical Atlas of Alabama*

(Tuscaloosa, 1974), p. xii; L.M. Somers (ed.), *Atlas of Michigan* (East Lansing, 1977), p. 113.

38. J.H. Long (ed.), *New York. Atlas of Historical County Boundaries* (New York, 1993), p. x.

39. D. Dorling, *A New Social Atlas of Britain* (Chichester, 1995), p. 229.

40. A. Horner, '150 Years of Mapping Ireland's Population Distribution', *Bulletin of the Society of University Cartographers*, 22 (1988), p. 8.

41. A.M. MacEachren, *How Maps Work* (New York, 1995), pp. 460–61; K. Clarke, *Analytical and Computer Cartography* (Englewood Cliffs, New Jersey, 1990), p. 259.

42. C.R. Weber and B. Buttenfield, 'Cartographic Animation of Average Yearly Surface Temperatures for the 48 Contiguous United States: 1897–1986', *Cartography and Geographic Information Systems*, 120 (1993), p. 141.

43. D. Martin, *Geographic Information Systems and their Socioeconomic Applications* (London, 1991), p. 164.

44. J. Raper, *Three Dimensional Applications in Geographic Information Systems* (London, 1989).

45. T. Hägerstrand, *Innovation Diffusion as a Spatial Process* (Chicago, 1968); H.C. Prince, 'Time and Historical Geography', in C. Carlstein, D. Parkes and N. Thrift (eds), *Making Sense of Time* (London, 1978), pp. 17–37; A. Pred, 'Production, Family, and Free-time Projects: A Time-Geographic Perspective on the Individual and Societal Change in Nineteenth-Century United States Cities', *Journal of Historical Geography*, 7 (1981), pp. 1–36; D.J. Peuquet, 'It's about Time: A Conceptual Framework for the Representation of Temporal Dynamics in Geographic Information Systems', *Annals of the Association of American Geographers*, 84 (1994), pp. 441–61. I would like to thank Don Parkes for discussing the subject with me.

46. R.P. Miller, 'Beyond Method, beyond Ethics: Integrating Social Theory into GIS and GIS into Social Theory', *Cartography and Geographic Information Systems*, 22 (1995), p. 103.

47. M. Monmonier, review of D. Buisseret (ed.), *From Sea Charts to Satellite Images: Interpreting North American History through Maps* (Chicago, 1990), in *Annals of the Association of American Geographers*, 83 (1993), p. 721.

48. Discussion with Graham Speake, 30 Aug. 1994.

49. J.W. Scott, *Washington. A Centennial Atlas* (Bellingham, Washington, 1989), p. 34.

50. See, for example, *Cartography and Geographic Information Systems*, 22, (1995), including E. Sheppard, 'GIS and Society: Towards a Research Agenda', pp. 5–16; S.C. Aitken and S.M. Mitchel, 'Who Contrives the "Real" in GIS? Geographic Information, Planning and Critical Theory', pp. 17–29, and N.J. Obermeyer, 'The Hidden GIS Technocracy', pp. 78–83.

51. D. Wood, *The Power of Maps* (New York, 1992).

52. J.B. Harley, 'Historical Geography and the Cartographic Illusion', *Journal of Historical Geography*, 15 (1989), p. 87.

11 Concluding Remarks

1. C. Harris, 'Power, Modernity, and Historical Geography', *Annals of the Association of American Geographers*, 81 (1991), p. 671.

2. S. Daniels, 'Arguments for a Humanistic Geography', in R.J. Johnston (ed.), *The Future of Geography* (London, 1985), pp. 143–58.

3. See, for example, A. Clark, *Acadia. The Geography of Early Nova Scotia to 1760* (Madison, Wisconsin, 1968), p. 391.

4. Harris, 'Power, Modernity', pp. 671–83.

5. D.N. Livingstone, 'Science, Magic and Religion: A Contextual Reassessment of Geography in the Sixteenth and Seventeenth Centuries', *History of Science* 26 (1988), pp. 269–94; S. Toulmin, *Cosmopolis: The Hidden Agenda of Modernity* (New York, 1990).

6. For example, C.D.K. Yee, 'Reinterpreting Traditional Chinese Geographical Maps', in J.B. Harley and D. Woodward, *The History of Cartography II. 2. Cartography in the Traditional East and Southeast Asian Societies* (Chicago, 1994), p. 67; Woodward, Yee and J. Schwartzberg, 'Concluding Remarks', ibid., pp. 846–47, 849.

7. D.W. Meinig, *The Shaping of America. A Geographical Perspective on Five Hundred Years of America. II. Continental America 1800–1867* (New Haven, 1993), p. xiv; D. Hayden, *The Power of Place. Urban Landscapes as Public History* (Cambridge, Mass., 1995), p. 21; L. Knopp, 'Sexuality and

Urban Space', in D. Bell and G. Valentine (eds), *Mapping Desire. Geographies of Sexualities* (London, 1995), p. 159.

8. H. Carter, 'The Map in Urban History', *Urban History Yearbook* (1979), pp. 13, 21, 27; J. Aitchison and H. Carter, *The Welsh Language 1961–1981. An Interpretative Atlas* (Cardiff, 1985), p. 40; O.F.G. Sitwell, review of R.L. Gentilcore and C.G. Head's *Ontario's History in Maps* (Toronto, 1984), in *Journal of Historical Geography*, 12 (1986), p. 97.

9. J.A. Agnew, *Place and Politics: The Geographical Mediation of State and Society* (Boston, 1987), and 'The Devaluation of Space in Social Science', in Agnew and J.S. Duncan (eds), *The Power of Place: Bringing Together the Geographical and Sociological Imaginations* (Boston, 1989), pp. 9–29.

10. K. Hodgkinson, 'Eurocentric World Views – the Hidden Curriculum of Humanities Maps and Atlases', *Multicultural Teaching*, 5 (1987), p. 31, and 'Standing the World on its Head: A Review of Eurocentrism in Humanities Maps and Atlases', *Teaching History*, 52 (1991), pp. 21–23.

11. A.R.H. Baker, 'Rethinking Historical Geography', in Baker (ed.), *Progress in Historical Geography* (Newton Abbot, 1972), pp. 15, 26–27.

Map Acknowledgments

By permission of the British Library: 1 (K 9 Tab 8 (2) xxxii), 4 (K 208 h 8), 5 (38 e 6 f.17), 6 (144 c 1 f.12), 7 (38 e 10 pl.11), 8 (Ref. B 7 (2) pl. 40), 9 (Ref. B 7 (3) pl. 56), 10 (4 d 25 pl. VIII), 11 (3 b 11 pl.4-5), 12 (48 e 22 no 5), 13 (48 a 27 pl.33), 14 (61 d 5 p.41), 15 (18 b 25 f.22), 16 (30 a 14), 17 (10 d 30 no 4), 18 (32 a 30 no2), 19 (4 d 35 p.24-5), 20 (29 b 33 p.28-9), 21 (Ref D 6 (Eur) pl.78), 22 (29 b 40 no3), 23 (Ref. B 7 (4) no1), 24 (49 c 59 p.137), 25 (49 b 87 p.9 detail), 26 (Ref. D 6 (Eur 1) pl.89), 27 (C 18 a 26 p.24) © Westermann Schulbuchverlag GmbH, 35 (60 b 104 Map 7) reprinted by permission of University of Toronto Press Incorporated © University of Toronto Press 1985, 36 (Ref. G 5 N II) published by the Instituto de Estudos Geográficos, Coimbra, 37 (219 a 16) © Jack D. Forbes, 38 (58 e 37) copyright © by the University of Oklahoma Press, Norman, Publishing Division of the University, 39 (64 a 38 p.119) reprinted by permission of McGill-Queen's University Press, 40 (62 b 8 pl.69) reprinted by permission of University of Toronto Press © University of Toronto Press Toronto Buffalo London, 41 (62 e 44 (3) pl.2) reprinted by permission of University of Toronto Press © University of Toronto Press 1990 Toronto Buffalo London, 45 (215 a 46 (2) pl.58) reprinted by permission of University of Toronto Press © University of Toronto Press Incorporated 1993 Toronto Buffalo London, 49 (62 b 8 (1) p.14 reprinted by permission of Toronto University Press © University of Toronto Press Toronto Buffalo London; Reproduced by permission of the Trustees of the National Library of Scotland: 2; The Bodleian Library, University of Oxford: 3 (2027 b 33); © Sutton Publishing: 28, 29, 30; Published by Hippocrene Books, Inc., New York: 33, 34; © 1978 Times Books Ltd Reproduced with permission of HarperCollins. MM-0297-119: 42, 43, 44, 51; reprinted by permission of Routledge: 46, 47; Reproduced by permission from Swanston Publishing Ltd, Derby, England: 48, 50.

Index